MW00790274

*This
book belongs to*

_____

*...a wife after
God's own heart.*

A Wife After God's Own Heart

Elizabeth George

HARVEST HOUSE PUBLISHERS

EUGENE, OREGON

Cover by Garborg Design Works, Minneapolis, Minnesota

Cover photo © Denis Boissavy/Getty Images

A WIFE AFTER GOD'S OWN HEART
Copyright © 2004 by Elizabeth George
Published by Harvest House Publishers
Eugene, Oregon 97402
www.harvesthousepublishers.com

Library of Congress Cataloging-in-Publication Data

George, Elizabeth, 1944-
  A wife after God's own heart / Elizabeth George.
      p. cm.
Includes bibliographical references.
  ISBN-13: 978-0-7369-1167-2 (pbk.)
  ISBN-10: 0-7369-1167-7 (pbk.)
  Product # 6911677
  1. Wives—Religious life. 2. Christian women—Religious life. 3. Marriage—Religious aspects—Christianity. I. Title.
  BV4528.15.G46 2004
  248.8'435—dc22   2003018696

Printed in the United States of America

06 07 08 09 10 11 12 /BP-KB/ 10 9 8 7 6

For Jim—
Thank you for being
a husband after God's own heart
so that I could grow into
a wife after God's own heart!

Acknowledgments

As always, thank you to my dear husband, Jim George, M.Div., Th.M., for your able assistance, guidance, suggestions, and loving encouragement on this project.

About the Author

Elizabeth George is a bestselling author and speaker whose passion is to teach the Bible in a way that changes women's lives. For information about Elizabeth's books or speaking ministry, to sign up for her mailings, or to share how God has used this book in your life, please write to Elizabeth at:

Jim and Elizabeth George Ministries
P.O. Box 2879
Belfair, WA 98528

Toll-free fax/phone: 1-800-542-4611
www.ElizabethGeorge.com
www.JimGeorge.com

∾

Contents

Becoming...

A Wife After God's Own Heart

A wife after God's own heart. What wife wouldn't want to be this? And what wife doesn't yearn for a happy marriage that is satisfying and exciting? If you are like most women (and like me!), you can always use a little help, motivation, and wisdom for improving and refreshing your relationship with your husband. To help make your desires for your marriage a reality, I've written this honest and helpful book—after 38 years of marriage—to share what I've learned along the way about building a better marriage, a marriage after God's own heart! This instructive and encouraging book...

> ...covers *12 areas of your life as a wife*—What the Bible says about the areas that really matter to the health and vibrancy of your marriage.

> ...includes *a list of "little things" that make a big difference in your marriage* at the end of each chapter. These "little things" are designed to stimulate and guide you to work out the many "little" ways you can practically fulfill your role as a wife.

I've also written a companion volume—*A Wife After God's Own Heart Growth and Study Guide*—just for you. This companion volume will further embed God's desires for you as a wife into your heart and daily life. As you work through the practical insights, scriptures, and helpful hints included in this wonderful growth guide, you'll find your heart—and your marriage!—being miraculously transformed. Don't miss out on taking this additional step to becoming a wife after God's own heart! You'll be glad you did...and so will your husband!

Join me now on a journey down the path of comprehending and implementing God's desires for us as His wives. And to make this journey even more enjoyable, ask your husband to join you by reading the companion book, *A Husband After God's Own Heart,* by Jim George.

Dear friend, no matter what your age or what state your marriage is in today, and regardless of what season of marriage you and your husband have entered, *A Wife After God's Own Heart* is for you. It presents God's timeless guidelines for you as a wife. As you'll hear me say throughout the book and in each of the 12 areas of your marriage, *God's Word works!*

So read on! Explore with me what God, the Creator of marriage, has to say about your relationship with your husband. And share your journey with others. With this book in hand, you can...

...read it before you marry

...read it alone to enhance your marriage

...read it together with your husband

...read it along with a friend or small reading group

...read it in a women's or couples' Bible study

...read it in your women's Sunday school class

...read it in your couples' Sunday school class

May God richly bless you as you continue growing in Him, growing in your faith in Him, and growing in your understanding of His plan for you as a wife after His own heart!

1

Growing in the Lord

*Seek first the kingdom of God and His righteousness,
and all these things shall be added to you.*
MATTHEW 6:33

Whenever I think about the first 30 years of my life, I automatically think, *That's when I did everything wrong!*

Why would I say this?

Because, my new reading friend, that's when there was no rhyme or reason for my life. That's when there were no guidelines for my life, no instructions for how to live my life. That's when I wanted what I wanted and did things my way. In short, that's when I did not have a relationship with God…which is why I am choosing to begin our book here, with God as the Number One way to make a difference in your life and in your marriage.

And what was it that I wanted for those three difficult decades? I wanted a lot of things, and most of them were things that every person wants. My personal "I Want" list included happiness, fulfillment, a life of meaning and contribution. I don't remember wanting fame or fortune, or to climb any corporate ladders or shatter any glass ceilings. No, I wanted what I'm sure you also want—a life that matters and counts. I dreamed of a life of joy and graciousness. And thrown into my dreams was, of course, a happy marriage that was satisfying and exciting.

I did marry at age 20, as I was beginning my senior year of college. Jim was 22 and entering his senior and fifth year in pharmacy school. There was the usual stir and flutter and frenzy of emotions that accompanies every new budding love relationship. Ours was truly love at first sight as we passed and smiled at each other regularly on our way to and from classes. Then came the "blind date" in November...with a proposal for marriage on Valentine's Day...and the wedding on June 1. Wow, what a whirlwind of excitement!

Things went well for a while. And then... Well, both Jim and I would tell you that after eight years, things became awfully empty and got pretty rocky, even after two children were added to the makeup of the George family.

Then a "miracle" occurred, and we became a *Christian* family. By God's grace, our hearts were opened to the truth of Christ...and by God's grace, we responded to that truth. And, beloved, that has made all the difference in the world! Things have never been the same. Before becoming Christians, we were like a couple with a great car...only we had no key. We couldn't get the car started. We couldn't make it work. We couldn't use it. We couldn't go anywhere.

My friend, a relationship with God *is* the key, the key to all of life, including your marriage. And that's what this chapter is all about—growing in the Lord. And that means learning what God, the Creator of all things *and* of marriage, has to say. You see, God and God alone possesses the instruction book for your marriage, and He's made it available to you. He knows what makes a marriage work. And He's written His divine guidelines right in the Bible. We'll look at what God has to say to you and me as wives in the chapters to come, but for now, let's see why it's important for you as a wife to grow in the Lord.

First Things First

I've chosen as our theme verse for this chapter a beloved favorite of many Christians. They are the words—and the heart!—of Jesus. They were spoken to His disciples and His followers. And they address the concerns of daily life. After telling His listeners not to worry, Jesus said they should instead "seek first the kingdom of God and His righteousness, and all these things shall be added to you" (Matthew 6:33).

Now, how does Jesus' teaching apply to you and me as wives? Well, married or single, *every* Christian is to put first things first. *Every* Christian is to seek the Lord first and foremost. God expects *every* Christian to grow. For instance...

🌶   The apostle Peter wrote that we are to "grow in the grace and knowledge of our Lord and Savior Jesus Christ" (2 Peter 3:18).

🕊   He also urged you and me to, "as newborn babes, desire the pure milk of the word, that you may *grow* thereby" (1 Peter 2:2).

🕊   And the writer of Hebrews, in Chapter 5, chastised his readers with this scathing rebuke: "By this time you ought to be teachers, [but] you need someone to teach you again the first principles of the oracles of God; and you have come to need milk and not solid food. For everyone who partakes only of milk...is a babe" (verses 12-13). In other words, these people had not grown.

So how do we grow in the Lord? Answer: By putting God first. That's how spiritual growth occurs. And the most tried-and-true way to put God first is to read His Word, the Bible, and obey it. I like to think of spiritual growth as a three-step process. Keep in mind as you note them that all three steps are absolutely necessary to grow in the Lord. There are no shortcuts to spiritual growth.

Step #1—*Discover* through reading the Bible what God says about your life and how He wants you to live it. How is this done? By listening to God's heart through His Word. By reading and paying attention to the teachings in the Bible. By learning more about Him and His standards for righteousness.

Step #2—*Discern* through studying the Bible the meaning and implications of what you are reading. This is the point where you pray and seek to understand what God has said in the Bible.

Step #3—*Do* through heartfelt obedience what you have read and learned, discovered and discerned. This is the step where you do something about what you now know to be the will of God. This is where you put your knowledge into action in your life.

How's Your Heart?

Now, here's a question for you: How's your heart? Is your heart strong in faith...or weak? Is it a hot heart...or perhaps one that's losing its fire? A woman—and a wife— after God's own heart is someone who follows hard after Him and close behind Him (see Psalm 63:8). Therefore prayer and awareness of weak—or sinful—areas in your walk with God can be the beginning of even greater growth. God desires that we develop spiritual muscle so we are strong enough to

> *God desires that we develop spiritual muscle so we are strong enough to be His kind of wife.*

stand against the powers of this world and to resist its pressures. God asks that you and I "do not conform any longer to the pattern of this world, but be transformed by the renewing of your mind" (Romans 12:2).

Here's another question for you: Are you satisfied with your current condition, spiritual maturity, and rate of growth? If so, you will grow no more. However, if there is a holy desire to grow in the Lord, to know God in a deeper, more intimate way, to be a woman after *His* heart, to strive toward His standards, to please Him, to be more Christlike, to identify, attack, and triumph over ungodly conduct and practices...then yours is the soft, responsive-to-God heart that will grow in the Lord.

Deciding to Grow

I'm sure you are as busy as I am. Honestly, every morning when I wake up, I wonder if I am going to make it through the day in front of me—if I'm going to get everything done, if I'll have the time and energy it will require to take care of my responsibilities at home and to others. Then one day it hit me that *I* sit in the driver's seat concerning most of the structure of my every day, including growing in the Lord. *I* decide whether the things of the Lord are really that important to me...or not. *I* decide whether I will make the effort to grow...or not. *I* decide whether I will schedule in the time it takes to grow, to meet with God regularly, to stop, look, and listen to Him by reading my Bible...or not.

> *The most important thing you must decide to do each and every day as a wife is to put the Lord first.*

So, dear one, as you can see, you and I are our own best ally...or our worst enemy, depending upon our choices concerning spiritual growth. I remember the day some months after becoming a Christian that I wrote an impassioned letter to God about the issues in my life at that time. It was sort of my covenant with Him to seek to grow—my commitment to grow in Him. It expressed the desires of my heart to mature as a Christian, along with my dreams of honoring and serving Him. I included the issues and areas in my life as a wife and mother that definitely fell under the "Needs Improvement" column. And I included the practices in my life that I labeled "Sin Areas," purposing to be done with them. I prayed on paper that God, through His great grace, would come to my aid and sustain my deepest desires to grow.

I saved the spiral stenographer's pad where I wrote my "Letter of Commitment" to God those many years ago. It has aged (about 30 years worth!), and how I thank God it was written in ink and not pencil! And now I want to ask two things of *you*. First, realize that this is the *commitment* section of this chapter. A section like this will occur throughout the book that asks you (and me!) to determine to grow, to determine to move out, to determine to take action, to determine to do the "putting off and putting on" of the practices and attitudes God calls us to, to determine to pay the price to follow after God—to put Him first, whatever that cost may be and however high it may soar, no matter what. I know my heart is racing right this minute as I'm writing about the most important thing you and I must decide to do each and every day of our lives—to put first things first and make the choices that can help us grow in the Lord.

Second, I want you to write out in your own way, in your own words, and from your own heart, your personal commitment to God. Make a commitment—a decision—

and determine to grow into the woman—and wife—you yearn to be—a woman after God's own heart, one who will do all *His* will (Acts 13:22). You'll be glad you did! And by the way, save it in a special place and read it often.

Tending Your Growth

Just as any skill or talent requires careful attention, so does your precious, priceless spiritual growth. What will it require?

> *Spiritual growth results from discipline.* Winning a race requires purpose and discipline. Paul uses this illustration to explain that the Christian life takes hard work, self-denial, and grueling preparation. As Christians, we are running toward our heavenly reward. The essential disciplines of prayer, Bible study, and worship equip us to run with vigor and stamina. Don't merely observe from the grandstand; don't just turn out to jog a couple of laps each morning. Train diligently—your spiritual progress depends upon it.

> *Spiritual growth results from self-denial.* At times we must give up something good in order to do what God wants. Each person's special duties determine the discipline and denial that he or she must accept. Without a goal, discipline is nothing but self-punishment. With the goal of pleasing God, our denial seems like nothing compared to the eternal, imperishable reward that will be ours.[1]

My dear friend, your "special duties" as a wife definitely require discipline and denial. And your *reward* for
faithfully tending your growth? How about a gentle and
quiet spirit that is precious in God's sight (1 Peter 3:4)?
How about bringing honor to God as you live out His Word
and His will for wives (see Titus 2:5)?

Reaping God's Blessings

Oops! I almost got ahead of myself. This is the *blessings*
section, but I just had to mention those two spiritual growth
truths. But let's go on and count—and consider—a few
more blessings you will reap as you grow in the Lord. As
you tend to your growth you'll find...

Your behavior changes. How? You will take on more of
the character of Christ. You'll become more Christlike as
God's Word and your walk of obedience work together to
conform you to His image (Romans 8:29). In short, your
life will be changed.

Your relationship with your husband changes. (And,
by the way, this goes for your relationships with *all*
people!) As your behavior changes (for the better, of
course), and as you put more and more godly practices
into place and heed more and more of God's commands,
and as you grow in the Lord, you'll be a better wife. You'll
manifest more of God's love, peace, patience, kindness,
and goodness. You'll display more of a spirit of meekness
and gentleness, not to mention greater self-control (Galatians 5:22-23). Now I ask you, why wouldn't these spiritual changes make a difference and bless you and others,

beginning with your closest, most intimate relationship—
your husband? They do...and they will!

And think of the difference such glorious changes will
make in your dear husband's life. He'll be more relaxed...
instead of waiting for the next blow-up or attack. He'll be
more comfortable with you, knowing the two of you can
communicate peacefully. He'll be more appreciative of you
as a wife as he senses your heartfelt concern and support
of his endeavors. He might even talk to you more often and
about deeper subjects (like the issues and challenges on
his job), knowing he has a tender, sensitive, sympathetic,
and wise listener to share them with, knowing he has a
wife who will pray for him.

You are blessed. Growth is definitely rewarding. You'll
experience unspeakable rewards as you surprise yourself
by the way you handle life's challenges and difficulties, as
you marvel at your peace of mind, as you (miracle of miracles!) hear yourself speaking with wisdom and expressing
comfort and encouragement to your dear husband. Oh,
you will most definitely be blessed! And when the rewards
and blessings tumble in, there is only one response to
make and one person to thank—and that is the response of
thanksgiving and gratitude to *God* for His marvelous grace!

Heart Response

On one very special evening, Jim and I had the opportunity to dine with the founder of Harvest House Publishers.

As we asked questions of this legendary man and he shared openly, he made a statement I'll never forget. He said, "Three words will sell a book—*simple, love,* and *home.*"

My precious reading friend, I'm not selling anything, but here's how I'm thinking after reading what I've shared in this opening chapter. Growing in the Lord is *simple!* There is nothing new or earth-shattering here. Life-changing, yes, but you probably already know these simple (there's that word again!), foundational guidelines to spiritual growth. Like the cookbooks I received at my bridal shower, they were simple, basic, fundamental—the first-steps and the how-tos of cooking. As simple as simple can be. Aren't you thankful that God keeps it simple when it comes to such a mystical, mysterious element as spiritual growth? We only need to know what God says is the basic recipe for being a woman and a wife after His own heart...and to faithfully follow His recipe. That's what "great creations" are made up of. And I'm praying that you and I will become just such creations as we faithfully follow these very few-but-simple steps for growing in the Lord!

Little Things That Make a Big Difference

1. Read your Bible every day.

Keep in mind that something is better than nothing, so aim for at least five minutes a day of Bible reading. That's about how long it takes to read one chapter in your Bible. Because of the subject matter of this book, and especially that of the next chapter, I suggest this schedule for your first five days:

> Day 1 . . . . . . Genesis 1
> Day 2 . . . . . . Genesis 2
> Day 3 . . . . . . Genesis 3
> Day 4 . . . . . . Ephesians 5
> Day 5 . . . . . . Colossians 3

Then go back and begin at Genesis 4 and finish the book of Genesis one day at a time, one chapter at a time.

2. Pray for your husband three times every day.

Pray before he wakes up, at noon, and right before he comes home from work. Of course it will be easy to repeat this exercise every day for a week. Then, of course, you'll want to do it for life!

3. Plan to go to church this week.

Whether you are a little rusty on your church attendance, haven't been going at all, or don't know where to go, planning to attend this week will set your personal church wheels in motion. Place this all-important "date" on your calendar. Then make any necessary phone calls to neighborhood churches or friends to find out where to go, the exact times of the weekly services, and any other information you might need regarding a couples' class or a program for your children. Then begin the night before to get your act together—lay out your Bible, organize for a no-hassle breakfast, and get to bed a little early.

It's important that you talk to your husband about your desire to go to church. Ask him if he would like to go along with you and see what it's like. Tell him you value his opinions. Also share the information you've gathered and ask for his input. If he doesn't want to go to church with you, that's okay. Your assignment is to be friendly, excited, and to make a move in the direction of attending church yourself. God's job is to work on your husband's heart. And, of course, you'll be praying for him!

4. Sign up for a Bible class or Bible study.

I know you're busy, but you should never be too busy to take care of your spiritual growth. This "little" exercise may require making a few phone calls, but it will be worth it when you experience the exhilarating joy of growing in the Lord, which

is the most important way to make a big difference
in your life and your marriage!

5. Purchase or borrow a Christian book on any topic.

Ask your friends and other Christians for their
favorite Christian book titles. You can't buy every
book, but you can create a list to remind you which
ones to purchase in the future. And don't forget to
make good use of your church library. It's been said
that "by spending 15 minutes a day you can read
25 books in a year."[2] Now, can't you scrape up 15
minutes today...and every day? As you learn from
authors and teachers and scholars who share their
knowledge and their passion for God and His Son,
you, too, will grow in knowledge!

6. Write a letter of commitment to God.

On paper, pour out your desire to grow spiritually.
It will only take you about five minutes...but those
few minutes could set in motion the direction for
the rest of your life!

2

*W*orking *a*s a *T*eam

Two are better than one,
because they have a good reward for their labor.
ECCLESIASTES 4:9

s I shared in the previous chapter, I lived....no, I *survived* 30 years of life without any guidelines. Then, as a new Christian who had failed miserably as a wife for eight years, I wanted to know exactly what it was that God wanted me to know, be, and do. I was a new creature in Christ, and I wanted to find out the "new" way—God's way—of being a wife. So I dug into my Bible (which was also new!) to find out what it said about my role as a wife. Briefly, here's what I found regarding the roles for both husband and wife, which together make up God's winning combination. As you read, I think you'll notice that God's plan is quite simple.

God's Winning Combination

As you read through these guidelines from the Bible, please invite God to open your heart to His instructions and His plan for your life as a wife. And by all means, hang in there. These are God's foundational laws for your marriage, and they never have changed...and they never will. Here we go!

A husband is to lead in his marriage and family. In the most basic terms, when God created the first husband–wife team, the man and woman were told as a couple to "be fruitful and multiply; fill the earth and subdue it" (Genesis 1:28). However, after their fall into sin, things changed. God then said to the woman in Genesis 3:16, "Your desire shall be for your husband, and he shall rule over you" (or "be your master"—TLB).

Later, in the New Testament, God repeated this guideline: "Wives, submit to your own husbands, as to the Lord. For the husband is head of the wife....Therefore, just as the church is subject to Christ, so let the wives be to their own husbands in everything" (Ephesians 5:22-24). Also, "wives, submit to your own husbands, as is fitting in the Lord" (Colossians 3:18). This means that in the same way you and I submit to the Lord, we are to also willingly follow our husband's leadership.

(*A thought:* Don't you think it's interesting to note that God did not tell husbands to *lead?* No, His communication was with us as wives, letting us know that we should *follow* our husband's leadership.)

A husband is to work and to provide for his wife. Things began well in the Garden of Eden, with man and woman as the inhabitants of a perfect environment. But, my friend, they certainly did not end well! After God's first couple disobeyed Him, He said to the man, "In toil you shall eat of [the ground] all the days of your life....In the sweat of your face you shall eat bread" (Genesis 3:17,19). As a result of the curse God placed upon the soil after Adam and Eve rebelled against Him, men would struggle to extract a living from the soil. In other words, all their lives men would have to work and labor and "sweat" so they and their families could eat and live.

A husband is to love his wife. This guideline is seen in several different scriptures. "Husbands, love your wives, just as Christ also loved the church and gave Himself for her" (Ephesians 5:25). "So husbands ought to love their own wives as their own bodies; he who loves his wife loves himself" (verse 28). "Husbands, love your wives and do not be bitter toward them" (Colossians 3:19). "Husbands... dwell with them with understanding, giving honor to the wife, as to the weaker vessel" (1 Peter 3:7).

These teachings mean that a Christian husband is to show the same kind of love toward his wife as Christ showed to the church when He died for her. A husband is also to treat his wife with tender loving care, caring for her in the same meticulous way he cares for his own body. In addition, a husband is to be kind to his wife, being thoughtful and considerate of her needs as "the weaker sex," and watching out for bitterness and harshness.

A wife is to help her husband. In fact, we might say this is why God created a wife for Adam, the first man.

When God surveyed His remarkable handiwork on Day Six of Creation, one more thing was needed. As the Bible reports, "Adam gave names to all cattle, to the birds of the air, and to every beast of the field. But for Adam there was not found a helper comparable to him" (Genesis 2:20). "And the LORD God said, 'It is not good that man should be alone; I will make him a helper comparable to him'" (verse 18). In other words, man needed someone "who could share man's responsibilities, respond to his nature with understanding and love, and whole-heartedly cooperate with him in working out the plan of God."[1] The result was Eve, the first woman and the first wife. *She* was the helper God created for Adam. *She* was God's solution to man's need for a helper and a companion. *Together* they were perfectly complete.

A wife is to submit to her husband. This makes sense after learning that the husband is to lead in the marriage. If someone (God says the husband) is to lead, then someone (God says the wife) must follow. To repeat a bit, here's how God expresses it: "Wives, submit to your own husbands, as to the Lord...as is fitting in the Lord....Be submissive to your own husbands."[2] This means wives must adapt themselves to their husbands' leadership and their way of leading.

A wife is to respect her husband. God instructs, "Let the wife see that she respects her husband" (Ephesians 5:33). A Christian wife is to "reverence" and respect, praise, and honor her husband. And finally...

A wife is to love her husband. Here's where the fun begins! Married women are "to love their husbands" (Titus 2:4). In other words, we are to be affectionate and treat our husbands in a loving manner—to cherish and enjoy our husbands as a best friend!

What a winning combination! The husband leads, loves, and works hard to provide, while the wife follows, loves, helps, and appreciates his efforts.

Following God's Plan

Do you know how some wives follow God's plan? They become husband-watchers. You see, they know what God says their husbands are supposed to do and be. They know how their husbands are supposed to treat them. And instead of taking care of their own faithfulness to their God-given assignment as wives, they take on the self-appointed role of playing "Holy Spirit" in their husbands' lives, pointing out their faults and shortcomings. These wives may even assume a "when...then" attitude. In their hearts (and maybe even verbally), they say, "*When* he does this or that, *then* I'll do this or that." They postpone obedience to their roles as wives and make it conditional to that of their husbands'.

But I am sharing both the husband's and the wife's roles in this chapter for two reasons. First, you and I should know what the Bible teaches about marriage. And second, if we are aware of our husbands' roles and responsibilities, we can be more understanding of the pressures on them and become better "helpers." I in no way mean for you to keep records concerning your spouse's behavior or to "grade" him as a husband. (That wouldn't be very "respectful," would it?) And I certainly don't intend for any woman to postpone obedience to God's clear communication to her as a wife while waiting on her husband to change...or grow...or move out in action...or become a contender for the "Husband of the Year" award. No, God is clear about what you and I are to do.

So, we must once again search our hearts. Instead of rating our husbands, let's check our own score in the Wife Department. How do you fare when it comes to following God's plan for a wife? Are there any pitfalls in your marriage that may be directly attributed to neglecting to do things God's way? Is there any tension caused by a failure to adhere to God's recipe for a happy marriage, a recipe made up of four basic ingredients: *help, submit, respect,* and *love?*

To help us apply God's teaching, I've put these four biblical elements into an easy-to-remember formula using the word W-I-F-E.

W arm up his life with your love

I mprove his life as a helper

F ollow his leadership with a willing heart

E steem him highly with utmost respect

But What If...?

I have to stop right here and address two situations many wives (perhaps you, dear one?) find themselves in. I can almost hear you wondering...

"But what if I'm married to a man who is not a Christian?" Very briefly, God's Word and your roles still stand in such a marriage. Your job from God is not to change your husband or to save him. Both of these results occur by a divine, supernatural work that only God can accomplish in a husband's heart. Your assignment from God is to love, follow, assist, and minister to your non-Christian husband while living in a Christlike manner before his eyes. Also, you cannot expect a husband who is not a Christian to act like a man who is. Remember, too, that God can help you do anything...including love an unbeliever.

> *Your assignment from God is not to change your husband, but to love, follow, assist, and minister to him.*

"But what if I'm married to a 'passive' Christian?" This is a husband who is a Christian, but who will not provide leadership. Whatever you ask, the answer you receive is "It's up to you," "Whatever you want," or "It doesn't matter to me." Again, your roles still stand in such a marriage—you are to help, follow, respect, and love your mate. You will definitely want to learn better ways of asking for direction and for discussing the issues in your marriage and family. You will also want to guard your heart against frustration and bitterness and guard your mouth against criticism, put-downs, and blow-ups. Two wrongs do not make a right. Your mate's failure to lead does not give you the right to sin.[3]

I regret that space is so limited in this book to discuss this vital area of marriage. Indeed, entire books have been written on living out the roles of a wife in a variety of marriage situations. But help for any Christian woman's marriage comes first from these few simple basics. So check again: As a wife, how are you measuring up in the four key areas (help, follow, respect, and love)? A wife after God's own heart desires to follow God's perfect plan...with all her heart.

Back to the Basics

If you're like me, no matter how long you've been married or how wonderful your husband is, you've probably pinpointed a weak area or two on your side of your marriage. After all, no wife is perfect: There is always room for improvement, and there are always items to be placed on the "Needs Improvement" list. I know in my life the four key areas seem to go in cycles. Just when I get one under control, a red flag starts waving in another. And then I have to stop, pray, revisit God's blueprint, and refresh my commitment to follow His plan for my part of my marriage. Back to the basics I go!

And here's something else I've discovered. As I am writing this chapter, Jim and I have been married 38 years. I've found that, like other areas of my life, our marriage has its "seasons." For instance, we experienced the season of child-raising and its wear-and-tear demands on us as a couple. Sometimes I didn't approve of Jim's way of disciplining our children. At other times I thought he should spend more time with them. And then we had to agree on how, when, and where we would take vacations (not to mention how we would pay for them!). At each season and step along the way—through the preschool years, the grade school, junior high, and high school years—evaluations and adjustments had to be made. You see, even though I was going through these stages and phases as a *mother*, I was also going through them as a *wife*. And Jim and I, as a couple, had to go through them together. We had to work as a team in order to meet the challenges and make it through.

Then we moved into our girls' college years—years when our daughters came and went. One day it was just the two of us...and the next day they would show up with a gang of friends. These were the days, too, when young men began to show up, adding new elements to the mix...and new tests to our marriage and family. Again, Jim and I went through these days as parents, but we also had to go through them as a couple. This meant we were constantly fine-tuning, re-tuning, and re-turning to our basic roles of leading and following. (This is also why the next chapter on communication is so important—it takes a great deal of communicating to work as a team!)

In God's timing, we next entered the period of being the parents of newlyweds—a whole new remarkable-but-different season as we had to figure out our new roles in our daughters' lives and welcome two wonderful sons-in-law into our family. Again the adjustments had to be made... together.

Then came Jim's transition from being a full-time professor at a theological seminary to being a full-time, stay-at-home writer. How does a wife go from 35 years of getting her husband off to work to suddenly working alongside him every minute of every day? (And you would not believe the number of women who have asked me to write a book on this "season"!) What *did* I do? Once again, back to the drawing board I went—God's drawing board! And, sure enough, nothing had changed. I was still to help, follow, respect, and love my husband as we entered this surprisingly joyous season of marriage.

Jim and I have endured—and enjoyed!—a few other seasons, too, such as the deaths of all our parents and the addition of grandbabies to our family mix. And I know there are more seasons (Lord willing!) awaiting us as we continue to grow in our marriage. But I also know that God's rules, God's guidelines, God's precepts for me as a wife will never change. They make up His unchanging plan for me as a wife, as well as for you as a wife.

> *Your commitment to follow God's plan makes a difference in the atmosphere in your home and improves the climate of your marriage.*

Making a Difference

So now I ask you to please stop, pray, and revisit God's blueprint. Refresh your commitment to actively follow His plan for your roles in your marriage. And remember, the goal is to work together as a team, today and every day throughout life and its seasons.

Your commitment to follow God's plan for a wife makes a tremendous difference. How? It will make a difference in the atmosphere in your home, in your communication as a couple, in your heart as love for your husband blossoms and abounds, and in the way you treat him with greater respect. It will also improve the climate of your marriage, paving the way for the two of you to dwell together in harmony. And the children? They will be the blessed inhabitants of a pleasant and peaceful home-sweet-home!

Dear fellow wife, when you and I are faithful to follow God's plan for us, the possibilities are spectacular. The Bible refers to the following possible by-His-grace changes that can occur in your husband and family as you, the wife, faithfully follow God's plan.

- ❦ *Sanctification of the unbeliever*—The unbelieving partner and the children of a mixed marriage (one believer and one unbeliever) are "sanctified." In other words, "one Christian in a marriage brings grace that spills over on the spouse."[4] This means your husband—and children—are privileged to participate in the protection of God and the opportunity of being in close contact with you as a believer, as a member of God's family (1 Corinthians 7:14).

- ❦ *Salvation of the unbeliever*—The condition described above (being a partaker of the blessings God bestows on a believing wife) can ease the path to conversion for the unbelieving spouse and children.[5] Your unsaved husband may become "saved" (by God's grace!) as he partakes of God's blessing in your life and witnesses Spirit-filled behavior (1 Corinthians 7:14,16).

🌸 *Spiritual life*—An unbelieving husband might (again, by God's great grace!) be "won over" to Christ, or a nominal, lackluster Christian mate (like the passive husband referred to in this chapter) might be stirred to spiritual growth as a result of your godly conduct (1 Peter 3:1-2).

I repeat, the possibilities are spectacular...and the blessings unending and eternal! Why would we *not* take action to become wives after God's own heart today?

"Two Are Better Than One"

I hope and pray you are beginning to taste and embrace the magnitude—and the beauty—of being a wife after God's own heart. And, oh, the blessings! I love the scripture verse at the beginning of this chapter about working as a team. Actually, there are two verses that go together:

Two are better than one,
because they have a good reward for their labor.
For if they fall, one will lift up his companion.
But woe to him who is alone when he falls,
for he has no one to help him up.
ECCLESIASTES 4:9-10

These verses paint a picture of some of the blessings of marriage. It's obvious that a "team" of two people who work together well will get more done. Also the work is done more quickly and efficiently. Plus the quality of teamwork can be superior to the efforts of one person. And in a twosome there's someone to help you through the difficult times, as well as someone to share your joys. There is no substitute for the help, compassion, companionship, care, and strength that bless a couple when they work as a team. Truly, two— you and your dear husband—are better than one!

If you are like most women, you capture your precious memories on camera and then place them in a photo album...and pore over them later by the hour. I know I never go anywhere without my camera in my pocket or purse. No, I don't want to miss a single once-in-a-lifetime photo opportunity!

Well, my friend, we have just been allowed to peek into God's photo album of His prize-winning couple. Indeed, they are a winning combination and stand forever as a model for us to learn from and emulate. The husband leads, loves, and works hard to provide, while the wife follows, loves, helps, and appreciates his efforts. Why not purpose to follow after God's plan with all your heart, soul, mind, and strength (and that's what it's going to take!), to become a wife after God's own heart?

Little Things That Make a Big Difference

1. Thank your husband for living out his roles.

Specifically remark on a decision your husband has made regarding the direction the two of you will take. Thank him that he works hard on his job. Instead of complaining because he gets home late or puts in extra hours or goes the extra mile at work, praise him for his diligence, his desire to do things excellently, and his efforts in providing for you and your family. Let him know, too, that you notice the many ways he helps you, "the weaker vessel," out. These are ways that your husband expresses his love for you, so thank him! And don't worry if he doesn't do these things. Just keep your eyes and ears—and your heart!—open so they catch the ways that he does express his love. Then, of course, thank him!

2. Ask your husband how you can help.

Every day ask your husband two questions: "What can I do for you today?" and "What can I do to help you make better use of your time today?" Stand by with a notepad and pen in hand, a prayer in your heart, and a willingness to help your husband in the ways he believes he can best be helped.

3. Show greater respect for your husband.

God wants you to *show* your respect for your husband. So think of one way you can do just that.
Then, of course, follow through. Let your admiration shine forth for all to see, especially him! Do
you look at him when he's talking? Do you refrain
from interrupting? Do you ask him to do things
instead of telling him? Do you practice sweet
speech in your conversations? Do you need to stop
putting him down when you talk to others? It
wouldn't hurt to keep a list of ways to show respect
as a reminder...in case you slip up. It happens!

4. Think of a way the two of you can have fun this week.

Later we'll enjoy an entire chapter on this fun
aspect that really matters in a happy marriage (see
Chapter 10). For now, though, your marriage was
founded on friendship, and you need to nurture
that friendship "love" spoken of in Titus 2:4. So be
creative! Your fun time together doesn't have to
cost any money—only the price of your time to
think of an activity, set it up, and make it happen.
Let the fun begin!

5. Pray to follow God's plan for a wife.

Consider God's four guidelines for you as a wife
(see Genesis 2:18; Ephesians 5:22; Ephesians 5:33;
and Titus 2:4) and pray over them. Take your time

and express your heart to God. Make your commitments, purpose in your heart to pursue God's plan for you in each area, and then move ahead through your day seeking to comply with God's blueprint for a wife. To stay on your wifely toes, pray every day to be a wife after God's own heart!

6. Seek out another woman as a mentor.

Look around for a woman who is doing a good job at being a Christian wife—one who can help you become a better teammate to your husband. Phone her and ask to meet with her one time. Then go to your get-together with a list of questions in hand. No price can be put on the wisdom, guidance, and support a more spiritually mature woman can give you as you grow into God's kind of wife!

3

*L*earning to *C*ommunicate

Sweetness of the lips increases learning.
The heart of the wise teaches his mouth,
and adds learning to his lips.
PROVERBS 16:21,23

*M*ost every bride returns home from her honeymoon with stars in her eyes and dreams in her heart about the romantic road that stretches endlessly ahead of her and her beloved. I know I did. Jim's and my honeymoon was brief—only two days long—because we had to be at work on the Tuesday that followed our Memorial Day weekend wedding. *Never mind,* I thought, *we have the rest of our lives to be together!* Truly, it seemed like we were standing on the threshold of a lifetime of joy, love, excitement, and passion.

But on that day when Jim returned to work and I went to my job on the university campus, real life set in. I walked to my nine-to-five job, while Jim commuted an hour in heavy traffic to Oklahoma City to his job at the

43

pharmacy inside a large Costco-type warehouse. Jim worked until nine o'clock at night, only to face another one-hour drive back home. When he staggered through the door that first night, dead tired, I conceded, *Well, there goes our first amorous dinner and our first love-filled night in our first-ever "home"* (albeit a one-bedroom apartment). This scene was repeated for the remainder of our first should-have-been-blissful week, until Saturday arrived ...and Jim staggered out the door at four o'clock in the morning to travel to his monthly two-day weekend U.S. Army Reserve meeting. When he arrived home in the dark Sunday night and fell into bed so he could get up the next day and begin his daily commute to work for yet another week, we both realized we had some adjustments to make.

Every couple has their bouts with reality checks and fine-tuning. And every couple has to learn how to communicate so the needed adjustments can be made more smoothly. All couples have to do the communicating and the adjusting over...and over...and over again as the issues and challenges of life change, not only daily, but also within each day.

Thank goodness God's Word gives us guidelines not only for our marriages but for our communication. The Bible tells couples like you and your husband the best way to share and receive information as you work your way through emotions, disappointments, and confusions to reach solutions to the barrage of challenges you encounter. So pay attention! The section that follows is a life-saver...and a marriage-saver!

"Like Apples of Gold..."

In poetic language the writer of Proverbs 25:11 paints this word picture of good communication:

A word fitly spoken is like
apples of gold in settings of silver.

Dear wife, this kind of beauty should be the goal for all of your communication, but especially with the person most important and closest to you—your husband. So here are several of God's keys to godly speech. Your words are to be...

...soft. "A soft answer turns away wrath, but a harsh word stirs up anger" (Proverbs 15:1). The words we choose to use have an effect on the hearer. Harsh, loud, caustic speech leads to arguments and quarrels, while soft, gentle words bring about peace. And here's another fact: "A soft tongue can break hard bones" (Proverbs 25:15 TLB)!

...sweet. "Sweetness of the lips increases learning" or influence (Proverbs 16:21). Do you want to get your point across? Then realize that "pleasant words promote instruction" and understanding (16:21 NIV).

...suitable. "Pleasant words are like a honeycomb, sweetness to the soul and health to the bones" (Proverbs 16:24). Kind, sweet words have a medicinal effect on both body and soul.

...*scant.* "In the multitude of words sin is not lacking, but he who restrains his lips is wise" (Proverbs 10:19). The more you talk, the more you are sure to sin! Another Bible translation is very vivid and down-to-earth in its language: "Don't talk so much. You keep putting your foot in your mouth. Be sensible and turn off the flow!"[1] As someone put it, "Sometimes the most skillful use of the tongue is keeping it still."[2]

...*slow.* "Be swift to hear, slow to speak, slow to wrath" (James 1:19). In even fewer words, make it your aim to "listen much, speak little, and not become angry" (TLB)! Why? Because "the wrath of man does not produce the righteousness of God" (verse 20 NKJV). No good ever comes from sinful anger.

Do you want your speech to be like apples of gold in settings of silver? Like 14-carat gold fruit in a sterling silver basket? Priceless? Indescribable? Admirable? Exquisite? Desirable? Then learn to speak with godly wisdom when you communicate with your husband. Choose words that are soft, sweet, suitable, and, by all means, scant.

"Like a Constant Dripping"

What happens when you and I don't communicate God's way? What results from a failure to pay attention to God's wise guidelines for our speech? Proverbs has more word pictures for us, detailed in these verses:

"The contentions of a wife are a continual dripping" (Proverbs 19:13).

"Better to dwell in a corner of a housetop, than in a house shared with a contentious woman" (Proverbs 21:9).

"Better to dwell in the wilderness, than with a contentious and angry woman" (Proverbs 21:19).

"A continual dripping on a very rainy day and a contentious woman are alike" (Proverbs 27:15).

I'm sure you get the picture! The message is that a crabby, cranky, nagging, quarrelsome, complaining, ill-tempered wife annoys her husband in the same way a constant drip gets on our nerves and "drives us crazy." In fact, as these proverbs report, it not only drives a husband crazy, but it can also drive him away. To escape the constant drip, drip, drip of a wife's sour, negative words, a husband will choose to live in the attic, on the porch, on the rooftop, or even in the wilds. He would rather risk the elements, do without the shelter and comfort of home, even take his chances against the threat of wild animals than stay one more second in the presence of a belligerent wife.

> *Make it your goal to employ the sweet speech that marks you as a wife after God's own heart.*

So I urge you to evaluate your speech patterns. Ask God to reveal if you are falling into the "contentious" category...or if you are articulating the sweet speech that marks you as a wife after God's own heart. Are you majoring on yourself or are you majoring on your husband—on helping, following, respecting, and loving him? Are you a listener or a whimperer? Do your words minister a calming influence or do they resemble a raging torrent of destruction?

Performing Radical Surgery

If you don't like your evaluation of your communication tactics and topics or the results of such tactics and topics (and, believe me, every wife falters and fails in this area!), then something has got to change. Radical surgery must be performed on your heart and your tongue. I'm sure you desire to utter words that are fitting of a wife after God's own heart—words that are pleasing to the Lord and that portray you as a wise and sympathetic wife. I'm sure you wish for your speech to minister to your husband and edify your relationship with him.

So I'm suggesting that, in order to turn the corner on your communication, you must...

Take it to the Lord in prayer—Pour out your struggles, disappointments, complaints, bitterness, fears, and failures to God. That's what dear Hannah did. Hannah was a woman and wife after God's own heart. There's no doubt that she had an extremely difficult marriage and family situation. To begin her list of woes, she was married to a man who had two wives. And to top that off, "Hannah had no children" (1 Samuel 1:2). The other wife, however, did. But Hannah's heartaches didn't stop there. Adding insult to injury, the other wife "provoked her severely, to make her miserable, because the LORD had closed her womb" (verse 6).

What was Hannah's solution? As we discuss the answer, note this too—Hannah is one of the few women in the Bible about whom nothing negative is reported. To our knowledge, gained by what is—and isn't—reported in the Bible, Hannah didn't lash out at her husband or at his other wife. What did she do instead? When Hannah "was in bitterness of soul...[she] prayed to the LORD" (verse 10). In His presence she wept in anguish and silently prayed in her heart before the Lord, pleading with Him and vowing to Him about the issues in her miserable home life (verses 10-13).

Do you perhaps have an unbearable, seemingly impossible situation at home? What under your roof tries and tests your soul? Name it—and then take it to the Lord in prayer. In His presence you may express all that you feel and fear. You can divulge your personal bitterness of soul. Precious reader, thank God that you and I "do not have a High Priest who cannot sympathize with our weaknesses, but was in all points tempted as we are, yet without sin. Let us therefore come boldly to the throne of grace, that we may obtain mercy and find grace to help in time of need"

(Hebrews 4:15-16). Let us *boldly* take our problems to the Lord in prayer.

Make a decision to "cut it out"—While you are pouring out your heart to God admitting your faults in the Communications Department, confess your failures in the Sweet Speech Department. Then ask God to help you do "radical surgery" on your speech. Seek His help in cutting out and eliminating the practices, words, decibel levels, and emotions that go against His communication principles, that fail to honor Him, and that fail to accomplish His will for your mouth.

This principle of drastic action comes from a lesson taught by Jesus when He told offenders of God's law how to deal with the eye or hand that sins. He said of the eye to "pluck it out," and of the hand to "cut it off" (Matthew 5:29-30). As you can see, Jesus called for radical surgery!

Beloved, you and I, as women after God's own heart who desire to be wives after God's own heart, must treat our sinful speech patterns in a drastic way. They are wrong, unproductive, even counterproductive. They do not accomplish the will or purposes of God (James 1:20). Therefore, we must be done with such speech. In short, we must "cut it out"!

So please, partner with God. Ask for His help in curbing wild, rampant, destructive, and ungodly speech. Yet another proverb tells us, "There is one who speaks like the piercings of a sword, but the tongue of the wise promotes health" (Proverbs 12:18). Your communication with your husband (or anyone!) will improve a thousand percent when you cease wielding the sword of rash, venomous words.

If you want to be wise, then remember that "in the multitude of words sin is not lacking, but he who restrains his lips is wise" (Proverbs 10:19). A sure way to be wise—and to cut it out—is to restrain your lips. Just say nothing. Try it for a day. It will be difficult, but it will be the best day of your life...and of your husband's, too! It will be a day marked by wisdom.

> *Wise, godly speech and increased persuasiveness is all about how you say what you say.*

And it will be a day of glorious victory, peace, and self-control you'll want to mark on your calendar. It will be a day lived as a wife after God's own heart.

Proceeding Ahead

In a previous chapter we learned that companionship is one of the benefits and blessings of marriage. As Solomon observed, "Two are better than one." Of course you and I as wives should be able to share our concerns with our husbands. But wise, godly speech like "apples of gold in settings of silver" and increased persuasiveness is all about *how* we say what we say. It's when we fail in these laws of sweet speech that we have to...

- come to a halt (say nothing),

- take a break (from our old and unsuccessful ways of communicating),

🐦 take a step backward (pray and search our hearts),

🐦 regroup (make a decision to do it God's way), and then

🐦 proceed ahead.

That's what I had to do, over...and over...and over again. I remember it all too well. At the time when our daughters were preschoolers, my Jim had four (yes, four!) jobs. Jim had resigned from his pharmaceutical sales job to answer his "call" to ministry and go back to school for theological training. And, bless his heart, this dear man did not want me to go to work with two little ones in the home. This was a time when not only did I wish Jim could spend more time with our girls, but I wished he could spend more time with *me!*

At first I handled our new situation in the wrong way. I whined. When that didn't work, I cried. When that didn't work, I screamed. When that didn't work, I stomped and sulked, making good use of "the cold shoulder." What a brat I was!

God's Better Way

But then I began growing in my knowledge of the Bible. Soon I understood more about Jim's roles as a Christian husband (one role was to *provide* for his family). I also understood more about my roles as a Christian wife (one being to *help* Jim). And I also discovered God's good-better-and-best methods of communication—the ones we are discussing in this chapter. I knew in my Spirit-convicted heart that something had to give. Something had to change. So, my friend, here is what I did in my efforts to learn to communicate God's way. I began...

...learning to pray. At the first hint of frustration or self-pity, I prayed.

...learning to say nothing. Whenever my emotions approached the danger point, I again prayed, and then did whatever was required to stop the flow by saying nothing.

...learning to wait. I knew Jim was tired and almost stretched to the limit (and so was I!). By God's grace, I learned to wait for the right time to communicate. For us that became once a week during our 89-cent Coke date at the fast-food restaurant across the street while an angelic neighbor watched Katherine and Courtney.

...learning to make a list. While I waited, I faithfully and carefully—and prayerfully—wrote down everything I felt Jim and I needed to talk through. This list included issues like methods of disciplining our daughters, decisions that needed to be made, and financial concerns. (The chapter on finances is coming up soon!)

...learning to make an appointment. If our Coke date wasn't going to work out, I would approach Jim and schedule another time for us to talk about pressing matters. By doing this, Jim could pick the time that was best and most convenient for him. From that moment on, we both anticipated the exact time for our talk.

...learning to write it out. Many times I would, with much prayer, write out the exact words I wanted to say—how I wanted to "present my case" and any options or solutions I had thought of. I learned this from Proverbs 15:28—"The heart of the righteous *studies* how to answer, but the mouth of the wicked pours forth evil."

...learning "to take the blame." This is my own phrase for communicating about serious issues with "a meek and quiet spirit" (1 Peter 3:4 KJV). My principle drawn from these guiding words for women was (and still is), "Meekness takes the blame." Let me explain. With this motto in mind, I would say to my husband, "I'm having a problem understanding this...or seeing how this can work...or accepting this change. Can you help me out...or help me with my thinking?" Without this motto in mind, my mouth would automatically blurt out something hostile and accusing like, "Why do you always..." or "Your idea is stupid" or "How come you don't..." Did you note the difference? You and I can begin our sentences with "I" or with "you." The choice is ours.

And I've found that when I begin with "I" (as in "*I'm* having a problem understanding this" instead of "Your idea is stupid"), our communication as a couple goes much more smoothly.

Now, how's that for "learning" to communicate? Needless to say, these seven disciplines (and there are more) put me—and my marriage—on the path to improved communication and increased blessings. And they can do the same for you!

Heart Response

I love music, orchestras, and concerts. Perhaps that's because I played the violin in my junior high school orchestra. I like to think that I did my part and made a positive contribution to the group and those in our audiences.

But what do you think would have happened if, on Day One of my violin undertaking, I grabbed my new school-issued violin, ran onto the concert stage, plopped down in a chair, and began playing with the other members of the group? What a racket you would have heard! What squeaks, screeches, squawks, and scratches you would have been forced to endure!

But, no. Both you and I know what it requires to play in harmony in any setting, whether in an orchestra, in a choir, in a drama troupe, on a sports team...or in a marriage. It requires learning the proper techniques. And it demands time as you practice, practice, practice!

If I could say one thing to you after reading through this important chapter on this oh-so-vital skill of communicating with your husband, I would say this: Don't just run in to talk to your husband, plop down, grab at anything your sometimes-empty brain finds handy, and blurt out thoughtless or insensitive words. Instead take the time to prepare your heart and your words. Pray about timing, tone, and topics. Ask God for help with godly discipline over the thoughts of your heart and the words of your mouth (see Psalm 19:14). Make it your aim to convey information, to bless your precious husband, and to create harmony. Seek to do an excellent job of verbalizing your heart to your husband in a godly way and with godly wisdom. By all means, make an effort and take the time to learn—and apply—God's rules for communication. You'll be glad you did. And I guarantee your husband will, too!

Little Things That Make a Big Difference

1. Follow God's guidelines for good communication.

Are your words soft, sweet, suitable, scant, and slow? Begin reminding yourself each day to "put away" speech patterns that don't match up to God's standards and to put these five elements of wholesome communication in their place instead. Ask God to guide you when you are communicating with your husband.

2. Identify any speech patterns that must go.

Read Jesus' words about "radical surgery" in Matthew 5:29-30. As you consider your speech, what must go—at any cost!—and when? (And remember, delayed obedience is disobedience.) By making a decision to "cut it out," praying faithfully, sprinkling a few well-placed sticky-note reminders around the house, and, of course, by the mighty grace of God, you can give it up.

I still remember going through such an exercise (and exorcise-ing!) when I became convicted about screaming at my two little preschoolers. I knew it was wrong and destructive. And yet I did it...until I reached the radical surgery stage. Sure, there were slip-ups. And sure, change took a l-o-n-g time! But progress was made day-by-day, decision-by-decision, word-by-word. God enabled me to grow and to change in a way that bettered our home life and blessed my family. Again, what must go—at any cost!—and when?

3. Make it a goal to encourage your husband.

Have you ever been wounded by the "wieldings" of someone else's sharp tongue (see Proverbs 12:18)? And worse yet, have you ever done damage to another person in the same way, with your words (like I did when I screamed at my little girls)? Your goal as a wife after God's own heart is to help, heal, and minister to your husband with your words—not to slash and slice him to pieces. Your rash words can resemble the thrusts of a sword or they can disperse refreshment that promotes health, edifies, encourages, and delivers grace to your husband (Ephesians 4:29).

Words

A careless word may kindle strife.

A cruel word may wreck a life.

A brutal word may smite and kill.

A gracious word may smooth the way.

A joyous word may light the day.

A timely word may lessen stress.

A loving word may heal and bless.

4. Be quick to say you're sorry.

The sooner you can say you are sorry for temper, for negative responses, for hurtful words, or for sinful attitudes, the better! This is the quickest and best way to defuse a situation that could get worse or clear up any disturbance in your relationship with your husband so the two of you can go on with a God-pleasing life.

I've found out a few things about this "little thing." One is that whenever there is a disagreement or argument between Jim and me, everything else gets put on hold until we get things settled. No progress is made...nor is there any energy to make any progress! So we've both learned to be quick to say we're sorry. I've also learned that if I am faithfully and regularly acknowledging my sin to God, it's much easier to apologize to my husband because I'm already in the habit of saying "I'm sorry" to God.

5. "Say what you mean, but don't say it meanly!"

I like this advice from a book I purchased in an airport.[4] Enough said!

6. Seek to please God with your words.

King David of the Old Testament prayed, "Let the words of my mouth...be acceptable in Your sight, O Lord" (Psalm 19:14)! God is the first person you must please with your words. And that is the desire of every woman after God's own heart.

4

Enjoying Intimacy

Now that you are growing in the Lord, working as a team with your husband, and on the road to better communication, we finally reach the hot topic of intimacy in marriage. And believe me, you and I better be strong in the Lord, committed to our marriage, and able to communicate, because success in the Sex and Affection Department will require all three!

Created for Intimacy

I know we've already looked at the story of God's creation of mankind, but let's revisit it. That's when God created the first-ever couple, Adam and Eve. That's also when everything was perfect. All was well. In the beginning,

Adam and Eve enjoyed *perfect* intimacy because sin had not yet entered God's perfect creation.

What did the perfect marriage look like? What made up that flawless union? First of all, the environment was perfect (Genesis 1:31). It was the Garden of Eden. Also both partners—the man and the woman—were perfect. God Himself formed the man from the dust of the ground, breathing into him the breath of life (Genesis 2:7). Then God brought forth a companion, a mate, a helper, a wife, for the man from his own rib. The woman was created "from man" and "for the man" (1 Corinthians 11:8-9).

What bliss! When Adam first saw Eve, he exclaimed, "This is now bone of my bones and flesh of my flesh; she shall be called Woman, because she was taken out of Man" (Genesis 2:23). In the delightful, everyday language of another translation, Adam is reported as excitedly shouting, "This is it!...She is part of my own bone and flesh!"[1] Imagine his joy!

In the perfect environment, this perfect couple enjoyed a perfect existence...and perfect intimacy. "They found their complete gratification in the joy of their one union and their service to God."[2] As the Bible reports it, "They were both naked, the man and his wife, and were not ashamed" (Genesis 2:25).

In the Bible's account of the creation of the first marriage, God's Word lays down a principle for all married couples: "Therefore a man shall leave his father and mother and be joined to his wife, and they shall become one flesh" (verse 24). In other words, the man would "cleave" or "glue himself to" his wife.[3] The couple would begin a new and separate unit founded on intimacy.

But...What Happened?

But then something happened to the perfect place, the perfect people, their perfect marriage, and their perfect relationship with God. In a word, sin happened. The serpent tempted Eve...who listened to him instead of God (Genesis 3:1-6), Eve tempted Adam...who listened to her instead of God (Genesis 3:6)...and all was no longer perfect.

And the results? They are innumerable, my friend. And their ramifications continue around the globe to this day. But to list a few,

- sin entered God's perfect environment,

- the blissful couple who was naked and not ashamed (Genesis 2:25) was suddenly embarrassed as "they knew that they were naked" (Genesis 3:7),

- clothes were introduced for the first time as "they sewed fig leaves together and made themselves coverings" (verse 7),

- both the man and his wife were severely chastened by God (verses 16-19), and

- Adam and Eve lost their home as God drove them out and sent them away from the Garden of Eden (verses 23-24).

Beloved, there has never been such a disruption as this. And the entrance of sin spelled disruption for Adam and Eve's marital intimacy…as well as for yours and mine. Intimacy has been a struggle for all couples since the day Adam and Eve chose to listen to others instead of to God and God alone.

Rekindling Intimacy

Here's where the truth of an earlier statement comes to our rescue. I mentioned at the beginning of this chapter that the Bible contains God's forever-principles on every topic, including marriage. In His Word we learn how to rekindle, rebuild, and rediscover intimacy. From God we can learn how to overcome the sin and tension that is now a factor in every human relationship—even that between a married couple—as a result of "the Fall."

What exactly does God say a wife can do to pursue and enjoy intimacy with her husband? My answer comes from the marriage ceremony I heard performed many times at my former church by the pastor to our singles' ministry as he shared passages regarding marriage from the Scriptures with each eager bride and groom. Even without notes, I can still remember them. And the best thing is, they come from the Bible, which means they work. Hear now these why's and how's regarding sexual intimacy in marriage.

> *Proclaimed*—God proclaimed that you and your husband are to leave your parents and be joined together as "one flesh" (Genesis 2:24-25). God intends the

two of you to come together in marriage and sexual intimacy and become a new whole, complete in each other.

Procreation—God desires that the oneness created between a husband and wife in sexual intimacy result in another generation of offspring who will continue to multiply and fill the earth (Genesis 1:27-28).

Pleasure—Sexual intimacy was also designed by God to provide pleasure for both partners (Proverbs 5:15-19). This pleasure thrives as each spouse chooses to serve the other and determines not to deprive one another (1 Corinthians 7:5).

Purity—Sex within marriage is pure (Hebrews 13:4) and provides power against sexual temptation, contributing positively to the purity of both husband and wife (1 Corinthians 7:2).

Partnership—Each marriage partner has a God-given assignment to satisfy the other's physical needs and to see that his or her own needs are satisfied (1 Corinthians 7:3-4).

Protective—Sex in marriage is a safeguard against lust, temptation, and Satan's alluring, worldly tactics (1 Corinthians 7:5).

Dear reading wife, God has spoken! This is His perfect plan for sexual intimacy between you and your husband. Now, our role as wives after His own heart is to think about and perceive sex in the way He does and to fulfill His Word and His plan with our actions.

Giving Your All

As you can see, sexual pleasure in marriage is God's will, God's plan, and God's gift to both partners. Therefore you must now determine to give intimacy your all. It won't

> *Your greatest progress and victory in intimacy will be made as you choose to view, perceive, and think about sex as God does.*

be easy because what was natural and perfect at creation now requires effort. However, blessings abound as you follow after God's own heart, look to Him for help, and make the effort. What follows are a few of my personal do's and don'ts for enjoying intimacy. They have been gained from God's Word, from "giving my all," and from applying them through the

many seasons of my marriage to Jim. As you'll quickly see, three out of the four are mental assignments. Our greatest progress and victory will be made as we choose to view, perceive, and think about sex as God does. (Remember, that's where things turned bad for Adam and Eve—they failed to listen to God and listened to others instead.)

☞ *Do* battle against shyness and embarrassment when it comes to sex with your husband. Instead of thinking about your *self* (about what your body looks like or doesn't look like, about how you wish it looked or how you think it should look), think instead about God's perfect plan—"They were both naked...and were not ashamed" and the two became "one flesh" (Genesis 2:24-25). Think also about your husband and the pleasure your body brings to his eye (see Proverbs 5:19). After all, yours is the only body he is supposed to look at! So don't withhold it. Pray...and dive in! Give your all! Give yourself, your love, and your body to your husband in this God-ordained, God-sanctioned way.

🎀 *Do* remember that "marriage is honorable among all, and the bed undefiled" (Hebrews 13:4). In other words, sex in marriage is pure. Sex is not dirty and sex is not immoral when enjoyed with your husband. Again, pray! Ask God to dispel any thoughts that oppose His teachings regarding the right, privilege, and enjoyment He intended sex to bring to both you and your husband.

🎀 *Do* give yourself permission to delight in giving and receiving sexual pleasure during lovemaking. Enjoying intimacy is not only okay—it's God's will. Sex—and sexual pleasure—is God's perfect plan for both husband and wife. The husband in Proverbs 5:15-19 was saturated, satiated, satisfied, literally intoxicated and drunk with the sexual refreshment and affection received from his wife. And clearly, Isaac and Rebekah were enjoying some level of the excitement of sexual love as a couple when the pagan King Abimelech "looked through a window, and saw, and there was Isaac, showing endearment to Rebekah his wife. Then Abimelech called Isaac and said, 'Quite obviously she is your wife'" (Genesis 26:8-9). In other words, the king witnessed caresses that indicated marital intimacy.

🦋 *Do not* withhold sex from your husband. As the Bible puts it, "Let the husband render [fulfill] to his wife the affection due her, and likewise also the wife to her husband. The wife does not have authority [or full rights] over her own body, but the husband does. And likewise the husband does not have authority [or full rights] over his own body, but the wife does. Do not deprive one another except with consent for a time, that you may give yourselves to fasting and prayer; and come together again so that Satan does not tempt you because of your lack of self-control" (1 Corinthians 7:3-5). In plain language, both husband and wife are to fulfill their marital duty to meet their spouse's normal and natural sexual needs. And marriage partners are commanded not to withhold sexually from their mate unless it is...

...by agreement,
...for a time,

...for a purpose, and

...with a prompt reunion planned.

Turning a Corner

By now I trust you are sensing from the Scriptures how highly God regards sexual intimacy in marriage and how important He intended it to be. And I pray that the verses shared have impacted your life, your heart, and your marriage. As a married woman, you are to give your all when it comes to the sexual side of your marriage. And you are to give it freely, unashamedly, joyfully, heartily, regularly, purposing not to withhold this most precious gift—and right!—from your husband.

Do you need a change of heart and attitude? If yes, how can you begin to turn a corner? How can you alter your thinking and your attitude, enhance your sex life, and improve your marriage? I'll have a good number of "little things" for you at the end of this chapter. But for now, do these two "big things."

> *When it comes to the sexual side of your marriage, you are to give your all...freely, unashamedly joyfully, heartily, regularly.*

The first, of course, is pray. Talk over this vital, foundational area of your marriage with God. He has revealed His plan, and you and I as wives must thank Him for it. If it comes from the heart and mind of God, then it is good, perfect, and acceptable. In prayer agree with God that sex with your husband is okay, that it has His stamp

of approval, that it is one of your husband's rights and priv-
ileges in marriage, and that it is according to God's will.
And while you are praying, confess your inhibitions as selfishness to God. With all other men you are to be cool and
reserved physically, but not with your husband. End your
prayer time by purposing to believe what the Bible says—
to cling to it, to remember it, and to follow it. You and I, as
wives after God's own heart, are *not* going to listen to the
world. No, we are going to listen to God.

And here's the second "big thing"—Talk to your husband about your sex life. Pray about what you will say. Pray
about how you will say it (remember God's rules for good
communication!). Pray about the best time to say it. And
pray for your husband's receptivity. Your goal is to communicate to your precious mate that you want to do a
better job of being his sexual partner, that you want to
make an effort to improve. (And remember, God will help
you find the words.) If your husband is a Christian, ask
him to pray for you and with you, to encourage you, to talk
openly with you. And if he is not a Christian, go ahead and
ask him to encourage you and talk openly with you.

Trusting God

Dear wife, only God knows how...and in how many
ways...He will choose to bless you for your whole-hearted
obedience in this crucial, foundational component of your
marriage. You will have to trust Him for that. But you *will*
be blessed. Count on it! As you turn a corner and move out
in response to God and to His Word, you will be trusting

Him. For many women (perhaps you?) this is a giant step of faith. But God loves—and requires—obedience in His children. I repeat, *you will be blessed!* Don't you think one blessing to your heart will be knowing your husband is blessed? You and your husband are "heirs together of the grace of life" (1 Peter 3:7). The two of you "are partners in receiving God's blessings" (TLB). This partnership has little to do with Christianity, but much to do with marriage, for marriage is "the best relationship earthly life has to offer."[4]

Heart Response

How I wish I could see you and talk to you in person. How I would love to know exactly where you need encouragement. But I can't, so I'll just have to speak my heart to you based on the mail I receive and on the concerns of the many women I have talked with. And why were they contacting me? The three most recent women were motivated to seek help and advice because they were fortunate enough to have husbands who spoke up honestly and shared their bouts with sexual temptation, suffering, irritableness, and sexual frustration. The bottom line in each case was the husband's desire for sexual intimacy more often. And as I listened and empathized, prayed and searched for words to comfort, exhort, and encourage these dear sisters-in-Christ, it was the scriptures we have shared together in this chapter that came to my mind and out of my mouth.

I know there are different and even difficult scenarios in each woman's unique marital situation. I recognize that there are problems...and there are problem-husbands. And I thank God there are pastors, counselors, and wise older women to help us with the application of God's principles in our individual circumstances. Perhaps you are a wife who needs to share your situation with one of these wise people. If so, I encourage you to do so. Also there are many books written that address a variety of conditions. I recommend that you read these books. But in the meantime—and always—you have God's Word to guide you. When in doubt, check it out! "What does God have to say about sexual intimacy, and how can I make giant strides in applying His guidelines to my marriage?" You will be helped and blessed each and every time you implement His truth and follow His instructions! As I said before, they work!

Little Things That Make a Big Difference

1. Take your calendar in hand and schedule sex!

How does that sound to you? Cold? Sterile? Unemotional? Lacking in romance? But talking openly with your husband and planning ahead as a couple can revolutionize your sex life. Intimacy doesn't just happen, you know. So to ensure that it does for you and your hubby, schedule it. Talking with your husband with calendar in hand also gives him an opportunity to express the frequency he'd like to see in the Intimacy Department of your marriage. After all, according to the records kept by one marriage counselor, when asked to create their Top-Five List of "most basic needs," time and time again husbands expressed that "#1" was "sexual fulfillment."[5] And note this too—When wives were asked for the same information, sex did not appear at all on the Top-Five List!

2. Talk about sex with your husband.

We just spent one chapter on communication, and here is a primary place to put the principles to work for you...and start talking! If the two of you can communicate joyfully, seriously, lovingly, tenderly, and specifically, then the two of you can steadily move toward greater enjoyment of intimacy.

After all, you'll want to be enjoying sex for a l-o-n-g time! Two counselors reported these encouraging findings: "In our national survey on long-term marriage, we discovered that sexual satisfaction actually goes up, not down, for those married thirty-plus years."[6]

3. Take time to prepare for sex.

Just like a gourmet meal takes time in preparation, so do your intimate times together. Think about it...enjoying a full-blown meal requires creating a menu, searching for the right recipes, making a list of ingredients, taking a trip to the store to gather the necessary items, putting out the money for the goods, spending time cooking in the kitchen, time setting the table, time making the atmosphere just so, and then time to serve, time to partake, and time to savor. The same applies to your times of lovemaking with your husband. You need to schedule and allow time...to think, to pray, to prepare, to run to the store to purchase something special, to set the scene and the mood, to enjoy, to linger. Wow, what a "feast" that will be! Lucky husband! Lucky you!

4. Try to go to bed at the same time.

Is this "little thing" ever important in the Good Sex Department! Sure, there may be times and careers that require that the husband go to bed before his

wife, but in many marriages this is not the case.
The wife simply chooses to stay up later than her
husband. So here's a question for you: How can you
cuddle, be available sexually, and not to mention
get a good night's sleep yourself if you and your
husband don't go to bed together?

5. Tackle the excuse of "I'm too tired!"

And what woman isn't? (I'm chuckling as I write
about tiredness!) But you're a smart woman. You
know how to run a home, raise children, perhaps
homeschool your children, or excel on your job. So
you also know how to figure out what has to be cut
back or cut out of your life so that you're not too
tired for this most-important part of your life—your
sex life. Your assignment is to find the culprits that
are robbing you of sleeptime and change them so
you are not too tired to enjoy sex with your husband, not to mention improving your health and
well-being! (P.S. It wouldn't hurt to have your
sweetie's input on your analysis.)

6. Take care of yourself.

There are many little ways you can make yourself
more attractive for your husband. Good grooming
costs only a few minutes. So why not clean up, fix
up, dress up, makeup...a little? Also a little exercise goes a long way! A 20-minute walk, five days a
week, will cause you to tone your body and lose 12

pounds in a year without ever changing what you eat. Plus losing a little weight never hurts in the Lovemaking Department. Every woman puts on a few pounds while fulfilling her role as chief cook, while bearing children, and while centering her life at home. If this is your case, losing those pounds will give you energy *and* breathe fresh life into your sex life.

7. Take a short trip together.

A good, old-fashioned getaway can also refresh your marriage and buy you time for prolonged intimacy, conversations, dreaming, planning, and plain ol' fun! Children are a blessing, but once they begin arriving, time alone together must be planned. With planning, prayer, and preparation, you can take a nice 24-hour getaway for a very small amount of money.

5

Managing Your Money

My husband, Jim, recently gave me a startling statistic that revealed the importance of wise money management in marriage. He said he had read that almost 90 percent of all marital arguments can be traced back to the issue of money.

And not too long after Jim shared this information with me, I viewed a television commercial that humorously backed it up. The scene was the delivery room in a hospital where a woman was in the throes of giving birth. As the soon-to-be-mother's labor progressed, more procedures and medications were being provided to assist the birth.

The nervous husband stood by, wringing his hands. To the doctor he said words equivalent to, "Can I assist you? Do you really need so many nurses?" To the anesthesiologist he questioned, "Are you sure she requires an epidural?" To his wife he said, "Honey, it's been 36 hours. Can't you hurry this up?"

Then the narrated pitch came, and I discovered that the ad was for medical insurance...and the issue was money. And there you have it—a glimpse at the way money matters can eat its dismal way into every phase of a married couple's life, including the joy of welcoming a baby into their happy union!

Money Matters to God

As we step into this all-important chapter, I want to explain that I am moving us through the issues and aspects of a married couple's life in a particular order. First, as a wife after God's own heart, we noted that every part and parcel of your life begins with a strong relationship and commitment to God. Then we addressed knowing and living out the roles that God's Word lays down for us as wives so that we contribute our part to the husband–wife team. I placed communication next because everything in a couple's life must be discussed so decisions can be made and principles established. Then came intimacy as a key to a happy marriage.

And now I believe we must address finances. Why? Because before you have a roof over your head and before children are added to your family unit, money matters must be dealt with. Even before the wedding, money is a heavy concern as a couple wrestles through questions such as "Can we make it financially?" and "How will we pay for the wedding?"

Not only is money important to an engaged couple, a married couple, and a full-blown family (right up to and through retirement and the sunset years), but it matters to God. Let's hear from Him through His Word about this minute-by-minute concern in every marriage.

Money is to be earned. And that requires hard work. Remember the role of the husband as established by Genesis 3:17-19? God told Adam that he would have to eat and provide "in toil" and "in the sweat of [his] face." I realize that in many marriages the wife also contributes to the family income. But my point here is that God intends that income be earned by intense, earnest work and effort, rather than by being stolen or gained by lying, cheating, begging, or fraud.

> *"Wealth gained by dishonesty will be diminished, but he who gathers by labor will increase."*

Note the work ethic in these proverbs. Regarding money gained in sinful ways, Proverbs 10:2 states, "Treasures of wickedness profit nothing." Regarding laziness, begging, and mooching, Proverbs 10:4 teaches, "He who has a slack hand becomes poor, but the hand of the diligent makes rich." Putting these principles together, Proverbs 13:11 reports,

"Wealth gained by dishonesty will be diminished, but he who gathers by labor will increase." And Proverbs 28:19 adds, "He who tills his land will have plenty of bread, but he who follows frivolity will have poverty enough!"

Money is to be given. After money is earned, this next principle from God must be put into immediate application. Your money comes from God (Deuteronomy 8:18) and is to be used for Him, His purposes, and His people. Therefore, Christians are to give of their money regularly and purposefully, sacrificially, generously, and cheerfully.[1] Certainly others benefit from your giving as burdens are eased and ministries are funded. So follow in the faithful footsteps of the wise home-manager in Proverbs 31: "She extends her hand to the poor, yes, she reaches out her hands to the needy" (verse 20).

And here's an added bonus! Not only do others benefit, but you do, too. As our Lord Jesus taught, instead of laying up "treasures on earth," you are to "lay up for yourselves treasures in heaven...for where your treasure is, there your heart will be also" (Matthew 6:19-21). A woman—and a wife—after God's own heart tends to her heart by tending to her giving.

Money is to be managed and saved. Next comes the stewardship of God's money. Character is needed and bred as you learn thrift, diligence, carefulness, self-control, the virtue of waiting, and the skills of saving, stretching, record-keeping, and wise decision-making. By keen oversight of the finances, yours can be a house (and marriage!)

of peace and plenty. As Proverbs promises, "Through wisdom a house is built, and by understanding it is established; by knowledge the rooms are filled with all precious and pleasant riches" (Proverbs 24:3-4). Your family unit, your character, and your enterprises will be blessed as you respond to God's assignment to you as a wife and home-manager to studiously and painstakingly manage and save money for the good of your loved ones.

Money is not to be desired. As Christians we are to beware of greed and the love of money. We are to "be rich in good works, ready to give, willing to share" (1 Timothy 6:18). As a few more proverbs put it, "Better is a little with righteousness, than vast revenues without justice" and "better is a little with the fear of the LORD, than great treasure with trouble" (Proverbs 16:8 and 15:16). As the apostle Paul exhorted, rather than greediness, desiring to be rich, and loving and chasing after money, we are to "flee these things and pursue righteousness, godliness, faith, love, patience, gentleness" (1 Timothy 6:11). Dear one, your riches will one day be gone (verse 7). Therefore realize that "godliness with contentment is great gain" (verse 6).

Money Matters in Marriage

Knowing a little more of what God says about money, and knowing that it is His money and that we as wives are, in our own sphere and in our own way, stewards of His money, it is time to make some decisions. Will we or won't we follow God's perfect plan? Will we or won't we heed His desires and instruction? Exactly what will we do with the money He entrusts to us for faithful management? And exactly what is it that we desire to do with money?

I've written extensively on the money management of the woman portrayed as God's ideal wife in Proverbs 31:10-31.[2] And I can still remember the complete makeover of my heart, my head, my home, and my marriage as I witnessed this incredible woman's making and management of finances for her dear family. Threaded throughout the 22 verses that make up her portrait is the theme of money and money management. Her character qualities shine as she "girds" herself physically to do the work (verse 17), uses her mind to budget and increase the family funds, and creates goods to barter and sell to further benefit her beloved family. As a result, God was honored (verse 30), the poor were served (verse 20), her husband was elevated (verse 23), and she was known by all as "a virtuous wife" (verse 10). "*Her* worth" to her husband, children, and community was "far above rubies" (verse 10).

That's what I want for you (and me), my friend! I want you to represent the Lord and His will well (Titus 2:5). And I want you to be a blessing, first and foremost to your dear sweet husband. I want you to grow in character, be content with what you have, support your husband's efforts, and be a diligent homemaker and financial warrior as you "build your home" (see Proverbs 14:1). I want you to be a woman filled with every good virtue and God's fruit of the Spirit (Galatians 5:22-23). And your faithful watch care of your joint assets and the place where you live will accomplish all this and more as you look to our dear Lord for His gracious enablement.

Money Should Matter to You

By agreeing with God about the importance of doing your best to manage your part of the family finances, and by making a commitment to Him to do a better job with *His* resources, money, and the wise management of it will begin to matter to you. Therefore you'll want to be sure you are...

🐚 *Praying*—because managing God's money is not only a spiritual issue requiring spiritual disciplines and character qualities, but it is a matter of obedience.

🐚 *Giving*—because God asks you to.

🐚 *Saving*—because it will better your family. Save for your children's and grandchildren's educational funds. Save for a home or home furnishings. Save for retirement. Save for a special trip, vacation, or missions trip. Save, too, to fund someone's ministry.

🐚 *Budgeting*—because a budget maps out the path for your lifestyle.

🐚 *Doing without*—because a host of spiritual disciplines are birthed and enhanced as you do so.

🐚 *Bewaring*—of greed, lust, bitterness, and envy.

🐚 *Growing*—in contentment.

Mastering Your Money

Now that you understand more about God's guidelines and plan for your money, how can you begin to put them to work in your marriage? How can you begin to master your money...and your heart? Here's an initial list of "Things to Do."

☞ Present to God the firstfruits of all your income. That's the advice of Proverbs 3:9-10—"Honor the LORD with your possessions, and with the first-fruits of all your increase; so your barns will be filled with plenty, and your vats will overflow with new wine." Giving back to God paves the way for even greater blessing. Oh, please, don't give God your leftovers. Give Him the first...and the best.

☞ Put those communication skills to work! Talk over this area of your marriage with your husband. Take this book to your hubby and show him what you're learning about money management. Let him know you'd like to talk about it sometime. And by all means, be sweet, be patient, be wise. Rather than begin preaching and lecturing, ask what he thinks about what you've shared.

☞ Put some personal goals into motion. Whether or not your husband agrees to talk about, change, or take charge of the way you approach money man-agement as a couple, you can personally make some changes. For instance, you can determine to

shop less, to spend less, to work on a heart of contentment, to become a more skillful home manager, to live a simpler life, to be more prayerful
and creative about taking care of your family's
needs at home.

🐝 Purchase a book about the financial in's and out's
of home management. Let such a book teach you
how to become a tightwad (in a good sense, that
is)—how to save, how to cut spending, and how
to manage your part of the household budget.
This can only help your finances, and in no way
takes away from your husband's leadership of the
family.

Doing Your Part

I hope and pray the scriptures included in this chapter
have helped to open your eyes—and heart!—to at least two
primary ways you as a wife
after God's own heart can put
these biblical principles to
work in your marriage and
contribute on the "earning"
end of the finances. First, you
contribute much to your
husband by the wise, thrifty,
diligent management and
oversight of your part of
the household budget. And
second, you contribute even

> *You contribute much to your marriage by the wise, thrifty, diligent management and oversight of your part of the household budget.*

more by heartily supporting your husband (versus nagging, whining, and complaining because he's always at work or always tired from the demands on his job) as he puts forth the effort—and the hours—to do his part in providing for your family.

Here's how I saw my daughter Courtney put this attitude to work in her marriage. On one particular visit Jim and I took to her home, Paul was in U.S. Navy submarine school from 6 A.M. (before the children woke up) to 10 P.M. (after the children were in bed) almost every day for a year. However, he did have a one-hour break for lunch. Subtracting time for Paul's trip home and back to his school meant Paul and Courtney and their two babies had 40 precious, golden minutes together every day at lunchtime.

Now, here's how Courtney handled this. First and most important, there was no nagging, whining, or complaining. Instead, Courtney blocked off every morning to cook a full-out meal, to carefully and beautifully set the table, to make sure the children were napped and rested, dressed, and as cheerful as possible, to bake homemade cookies, and see that a thermos full of strong coffee was set by the door. At 12:10 their squealing little family was standing at the front door to welcome "Daddy" home. Quickly the kids were hoisted into high chairs, prayers were offered to God, and everyone was treated to a gourmet meal at a gala table. When their 40 minutes were up, all lined up again at the door to kiss Daddy goodbye as Courtney handed Paul the thermos and a sackful of fresh cookies to help him make it through until ten o'clock.

Dear wife, this is the way it is (or is supposed to be!). You and I are to support our husbands as they support us. We grease the skids, so to speak, by making his life easier with our joy, support, encouragement, effort, creative planning, and wise scheduling. That's our job-assignment from God. Like the wise wife in Proverbs 31:12, we are to do our husbands "good and not evil all the days of [our] life." Then, in time, we reap a multitude of rewards. As I shared earlier, there was a period of time in my marriage when Jim worked practically all day and all night at four different jobs to provide for our family. In fact, for the 30-plus years he was in the Army Reserves, he had two jobs (and sometimes more). Our family reaped the benefits of Jim's hard work then, and we are reaping them now as our home mortgage is paid off and we are enjoying full medical benefits and some monthly income from his three decades of exertion on all of his many jobs. My thoughts go something like this, *Surely, if my husband is to provide, I can do my part by helping to make life easier for him in as many ways as I can.*

Now, don't you agree?

Heart Response

May I add one final principle here in our Heart Response section? Beloved wife after God's own heart, you and I must realize that in God's economy, *many things are more important than money.*

For instance, your *character* is more important than money—"Those who are of a perverse heart are an abomination to the LORD, but the blameless in their ways are His delight" (Proverbs 11:20). Your *reputation*, too, is better than money—"A good name is to be chosen rather than great riches" (Proverbs 22:1). *Wisdom* is also more important than money—"The crown of the wise is their riches" (Proverbs 14:24); "how much better to get wisdom than gold! And to get understanding is to be chosen rather than silver" (Proverbs 16:16). And *humility* is better than money—"By humility and the fear of the LORD are riches and honor and life" (Proverbs 22:4).

And here's another twist—*you,* as a godly wife, are better than money to your husband! "Houses and riches are an inheritance from fathers, but *a prudent wife* is from the LORD" (Proverbs 19:14). In fact, according to the Bible, *you,* as a godly wife, are your husband's greatest asset. With a godly wife of character, humility, wisdom, and faithfulness beside him, the Bible says your husband "will have no lack of gain" (Proverbs 31:11). Why? Because as "a virtuous wife" *your* "worth is far above rubies" (verse 10).

Little Things That Make a Big Difference

1. Honor your husband's direction.

Every husband handles finances differently. Your job is to learn how your husband wants the money managed. Would he rather you make purchases with cash, check, debit card, or credit card? Find out and then honor his desire. Also get into the habit of checking with him before you make purchases or order repairs. Your shopping, spending, and home improvements shouldn't be a secret mission, a covert operation, or a surprise. Ask him, show him, and inform him about your plans. Discuss Christmas and birthday gifts and spending allowances in advance. Go over any repairs or improvements you think are necessary. Always seek to know his wishes...and then honor them.

2. Create a budget.

Of course, the best scenario would be for you and your husband to create a budget together. But if he's not interested or too busy to think it through, make—and keep—one for the areas of the family finances where you are involved (food, household items, clothing, gifts). Follow these three steps in keeping a budget and become an expert at the financial management of those items in your daily sphere:

✿   *Determine*...a reasonable amount for each category

✿   *Record*...what you spend

✿   *Wait*...until the funds are available

3. Help out with managing the finances.

See how many ways you can help out with bill paying, recordkeeping, filing, and organizing. Ask your husband the best way you can assist him or lighten his burden in the family's Accounting Department. Is it keeping stamps on hand? Is it taking the bills to the post office? Is it learning how to use a computer program to keep track of expenses? Two sure ways to help out are to keep your checkbook up to date and to check your bank balance daily.

4. Set up a financial center.

Do you want to improve the money management around your home? Then organize all financial functions in one location by setting up a financial center. It doesn't have to be large or elaborate. Just a little table in the corner will do. Simply make sure everything you need is there: pens, pencils, a good lamp, stapler, stamps, envelopes, notepads, accordion folders for filing bills and receipts, maybe a two-drawer file cabinet with a box of file folders in one drawer...and, of course, a copy of your household budget. If you are really limited in space, you can keep everything in a portable plastic file box with a handle on it and move it from place to place.

5. Give to God's purposes.

In a feature article for couples entitled "What Draws Us Closer to God?" tithing and giving to the poor and needy were noted as two acts that not only draw a couple closer to one another but also to God.[3] Together you and your husband can decide where you want to focus your giving. Obviously, your church should be first. Then where? Realize that giving to your church and sharing with others breeds many wonderful qualities in you, your husband, and your family, and it blesses the lives of countless others.

6. Keep a list of things you want or need.

Every time something comes up that you want or need, jot it down on an ongoing list. Then, as with all lists, prioritize what you see according to desire or urgency. Also jot down an estimate of the cost or price of the items. As we noted in Little Thing #1, you'll want to share your list with your husband. Then use your "wish-and-want list" as a prayer list.

7. Set up a savings plan.

Again, the ideal would be for you and your husband to do this together. But if that doesn't work out, then see what you can do in the Savings Department.

Just having a savings plan will motivate you to cut corners, cut spending, and cut out coupons—whatever it takes to tuck some money away for emergencies or for family fun. And speaking of fun, consider keeping a piggy bank or money jar that you and your husband put all your change into every day for some fun purchase or trip. You'll be surprised how quickly savings will amass (and how much fun you'll have)!

6

$\mathscr{K}$eeping $\mathscr{U}$p the $\mathscr{H}$ome

Through wisdom a house is built,
and by understanding it is established;
by knowledge the rooms are filled
with all precious and pleasant riches.
PROVERBS 24:3-4

$\mathscr{H}$ow is your home-sweet-home? And how's the atmosphere under your roof? As you and I both know, keeping up the home can be another source of tension in a marriage.

One day a young married friend phoned me at home and asked what she should do. She explained that she and her husband had purchased their first-ever home...which provided them with their first-ever lawn...and a new problem. She asked, "Mrs. George, what should I do? My husband works very hard, and when he gets home, he just doesn't seem to have the desire or the energy to mow the lawn. And he wants to relax on the weekends. Meanwhile our grass is getting higher and higher. I asked him if I could mow it for him, and he said no, that it was his job. Several weeks later I asked him if we could hire a gardener or a teenager from the neighborhood to cut it, and again, the answer was no, he would do it. And guess what? It's still not done. I want to be submissive, but what can I do?"

My hat went off to this lovely young wife. And my heart went out to her. She wanted to honor her husband, she wanted to follow his wishes, she wanted to help him, and she loved him. But an issue centered at and around the home was becoming a real problem. What can a wife after God's own heart do about keeping up the home where she and her husband live?

God's Perspective on a Home

During the years that I've been reading through my Bible, I've looked for scriptures relating to certain topics that apply to my roles as a Christian woman, wife, mother, and homemaker. Two of those topics are "time management" and "home." One day I hit the jackpot—a verse that addressed both! It's a haunting verse concerning King Hezekiah, the fifteenth king of Judah. As this man lay sick and dying, God sent His prophet Isaiah with these words of instruction: "Set your house in order, for you shall die, and not live" (2 Kings 20:1). Given the historical time line of this announcement in Israel's history, God was possibly letting King Hezekiah know that he needed to not only tend to his domestic and private affairs, but also to those of the state of his kingdom.

But for me, the advice arrowed its way straight into my heart as a homemaker. *I* needed to set my house in order, to see to the affairs in *my* home.

Did you know that your home is important, not only to you and your husband and children, but to God? In fact, God has a great deal to say about your home, homemaking, and home management.

You are to "build" your home. That's what the wise wife does. "The wise woman builds her house" (Proverbs 14:1). One sourcebook points out that the unique combination of the words "woman" and "house" and the reference to "wisdom" place this verse with four other scriptures that translate "mother's house," a term for the family household. Such a term "reflects a woman's perspective and also expresses female agency in managing an agrarian household in ancient Israel." The scholars add, "The link here with wisdom adds the dimension of female technological expertise and sagacity to the managerial aspects of senior women in family life."[1] In short, a woman of wisdom views taking care of her house as an important role and priority in her life. And she manages her home, property, and household with wisdom, expertise, and intelligence.

> *A dedicated homemaker keeps a keen eye over all that goes on in her home.*

Now let me share the second half of Proverbs 14:1. While the wise woman is busy building her house, "the foolish pulls it down with her hands." This means that while the wise wife is painstakingly pouring her efforts into building her house and increasing its wealth, the foolish wife is lessening its value by mismanagement.[2]

Are you, dear homemaker, building up your home...or are you breaking it down?

You are to watch over your home. That's what the ideal wife we looked at earlier did. "She watches over the ways of her household, and does not eat the bread of idleness" (Proverbs 31:27). Therefore as wives after God's own heart, you and I should follow heartily in her footsteps. After all, she's God's ideal wife. Here is a diligent, careful, energetic, and dedicated homemaker who keeps a keen eye over all that goes on in her home, both with the people and the place. *How,* we wonder, *did she do it?* God gives us the answer: She "does not eat the bread of idleness." In other words, she is "not content to go through life eating and sleeping...and is never lazy."[3] Shallow, unproductive activities have no place in her life. Why, she's on assignment from God to keep watch over the affairs of her household!

How's your eye? Is its gaze fixed at home?

And how are your efforts? Are they focused on the place where you live?

And how's your energy level? Where do you register when it comes to the Eating and Sleeping Department versus the Never-Lazy Department? Are you giving your all—your every minute—to building your home-sweet-home?

You are to manage your home. There's some history behind this management aspect of your homemaking. You see, the apostle Paul did not want the young widows in the early church to "be idle, wandering about from house to house, and not only idle but also gossips and busybodies, saying things which they ought not." Instead he desired that they "marry, bear children, *manage the house*" (1 Timothy 5:13-14). There are several principles here we can draw out for all wives. First, it is a good thing to have a home to manage. Paul definitely saw managing a home as better than being lazy, a gad-about, a gossip, and a busybody. But second, a wife is to "manage" her house. Taking care of and guiding the work that goes into making a house a home is a good thing.

You are to keep your home. This principle for all married women who desire to follow after God comes from Titus 2:5. Here considerable emphasis is placed on the foundation of the home, and the older women in the church are instructed to spend their time teaching the younger women to, among other things, be homemakers. The message to you and me today, as well as to the women of Titus' day, is that we are to spend our time in our own homes being the "guardians of the house."[4] And how is this done? The oldest manuscripts convey the answer in their translations: We are to be "workers at home," "active in household duties."[5] In other words, we are to be doing the work it takes to make a house a home.

As a bonus in our understanding, three other scriptures teach the same principle. Two of them will sound familiar. And be on guard—two of them are taught from the negative, pointing to the woman who does *not* take care of her home.

    ❦   Proverbs 7:11-12—These verses describe, of all things, an adulteress. She is doing the opposite of the wise homemaker who tends to her house and housework. She is "out there," walking the streets, instead of being at home. "Her feet would not stay at home. At times she was outside, at times in the open square, lurking at every corner."

    ❦   Proverbs 14:1—One scholar translates this now-familiar verse as "wisdom builds the house of life: frivolity pulls it down."[6] Spending her precious time on frivolous things, the home of the foolish woman is not only *not* "built," but it is actually destroyed.

    ❦   1 Timothy 5:13-14—Once again, this verse calls us to analyze what we are doing and where we are spending our time and effort when we are not at home taking care of our business there.

I don't know about you, but I love to know what God says and what God wants from me. Knowing helps me to understand why something is important because I can then whole-heartedly roll up my sleeves, look to God for His divine enablement, dive in, and do it. With these few

principles for homemaking to guide us as wives and homemakers after God's own heart, we can certainly better
understand our role in the vital area of marriage of keeping
up the home.

Problems and Solutions

However, here's what I found to be true. Once I determined to dive in, I immediately encountered a few problems. Do you relate to any of them? Are you plagued by
any on this list?

I'm so tired! (And what woman isn't?) Tiredness is a
fact of life. Therefore, I approach my every day and my
whole life as a quest for energy. I am doggedly trying to
discover how to gain energy, how to sustain it, how to
ensure it, and how to boost it. I study my energy levels,
down to what kind of response the food I eat has on my
body and mind. I chart my peak energy times and note the
not-so-peak ones.

And here's something else I've learned. When I am the
most tired is when I need to do whatever it takes to get
myself moving. My son-in-law is a physics teacher, and he
shared the following Law of Physics with me: A body at
rest tends to remain at rest, and a body in motion tends to
remain in motion.

Solutions—Try your hand at paying attention to and
recording your energy levels. And while you're at it, try to
put your finger on what may have contributed to a burst of
energy or to a drop in your momentum. Also pick one

activity you will willfully participate in when you feel like you simply cannot continue on or keep moving. This is usually when I turn on the *Headline News* and begin rinsing out dishes, loading or unloading the dishwasher, and wiping off counters. Sometimes I peel carrots or potatoes, or measure and rinse rice and get it into the rice cooker. I willfully make the effort on some no-brainer activity. Amazingly, such a small exertion gets me going again...or keeps me going. As one of my life mottos says, "Something is always better than nothing" no matter how small that "something" is.

And here's a big "something"—Do whatever you have to do to get your rest. I know it sounds impossible, but you must work on it. For me, I try to head for the bedroom around seven o'clock. I don't go to bed then, but I can start on my bedtime rituals, take another look at my planner, go through the junk mail, turn through magazines, and take care of a plethora of other little odd jobs...and all from my wonderful bed! This practice helps me get to bed one to two hours earlier than I would if I kept puttering or lazing around downstairs and translates into one to two hours of additional sleep per night. So what can you do to get to bed earlier so that you get more rest? Eliminate some evening television? Cut your caffeine intake? Get the children into bed earlier?

I have so many children! I can't help but think of "the old woman who lived in a shoe," who had so many children she didn't know what to do! But, truthfully, I meet many women who have between six and ten children. And, truthfully, *any* number of children presents a new set of demands on *any* woman and couple.

Solutions—Here's another principle that guides my life in every area every day. It's my version of a Law of Economics: "When something goes up, something else must go down." For instance, when the two of you—you and your husband—get your life into a groove, and then a baby is added, something has to give, has to be eliminated or set aside, has to go down. Then, as additional children are added, more and more things have to go. Why? Because something more important (to you and to God—see Genesis 1:28 and Psalm 127:3-5)—precious children—has come to take the place of lesser things, even frivolous things. For me, with two little ones only 13 months apart, night classes had to go. Also my little "running around" capers had to be pared down to one morning per week. And suddenly my telephone time had to be cut way down because it seemed like my washing machine was "calling" me as it worked overtime taking care of the mountains of little pieces of laundry that had to also be folded and put away.

Determining what you trim out of your life to make time for caring for your God-given children will be something you and your husband decide together. You'll want to be in agreement so you are operating from a solid base and the same set of principles. So, once again, sharpen up those communication skills and put them to work for you as the two of you seek God's will and what is best for your family.

I don't know what to do! Which translates, I lack time management skills. Perhaps in your heart you are crying out, "Yes, I want to do it. I want to keep up my home." But at the same time you are wondering, "But how am I supposed to manage my time and my tasks? What do I do first, how does one plan, and how in the world does one attack a project?"

Solution—Good news! Management skills can be learned. I am a living, breathing, walking testimony to this truth. If you desire it, you can learn it. How? By asking your husband. By asking others. By taking classes. By reading books. By using good planning tools and calendars. But I warn you, it will take time—time each day as well as a lifetime. Thirty years ago I discovered this adage to be true: "Life is what happens to you while you're failing to plan it." And I woke up one day with a husband and two babies and didn't know what to do. *Life* had happened.

So I started asking for help, taking the classes, reading the books, using a planner—all in a quest to learn how to manage my time and my good housekeeping projects. And, lest you think I've arrived, I'm still learning. I've grown a lot, but I'm still asking productive people for better ways of getting things done. I'm still reading (although I already own ten feet of time management books on my bookshelves). I'm still listening when others give a seminar or have a tape or CD available. I'm still on the lookout for a better planner and organizational system. And I hope you are doing the same.

I don't know how! Now that you've ordered your projects, put your plans on paper, know where to start and what to do, your next dilemma is *how* to do it. This is a clear case of lacking homemaking skills.

Solution—Good news again! Expertise in taking care of your home can also be learned. And once again I am a living, breathing, walking testimony to this fact. Here's where godly, older women come in. According to Titus 2:3-5, these ladies are to be available and actively teaching the in's and out's of being a wife after God's own heart to their younger sisters-in-Christ. And the curriculum includes the area of homemaking skills (verse 5). So see if you can latch on to one of these dear saints! Pray, ask for help, and then try doing what you are being taught.

Again, this will require time—time meeting with another woman, time each day as you keep up your home, and time for a lifetime as you obtain your skills, perfect them, improve them, and use them. But, oh, will it be worth it! What better place or way could you be spending the precious time God gives you than by working out His will right under your own roof, than by blessing your husband and family by your loving efforts at home?

I don't care! Oh dear! I hope this isn't true of you because this is the worst of all the "problems"…and the one that no one can fix or help unless the owner of such an attitude has a change of heart. And it's the most scary of all the scenarios because it is a *spiritual* problem. You see, you and I can know that we should take care of and keep up our homes, and we can know that we need to do it. We can know that our husbands would appreciate it and desire our assistance in this area. We can even know that God wants us to do it—but still we just plain ole don't care to do it.

Solution—This "problem" falls into a completely different category than the others. This is not a problem of ignorance, busyness, or physical tiredness. No, in the case of an I-don't-care-attitude, we are facing a sin issue. A rebellious spirit. A cold-hearted decision to say, think, and act with the attitude of *So what?* and *I don't care!*

Someone has written that "the honor of the Word of God is the supreme sanction for right conduct."[7] And, as Titus 2:5 states, after instructing us to be "homemakers," you and I are to do so in order "that the word of God may not be blasphemed." In other words, we are to follow God's instructions so that our behavior in no way dishonors, defames, maligns, discredits, scandalizes, or causes suffering to the Word of God and the gospel of Jesus Christ.

As you can see, a defiant attitude toward God's will and God's Word is most serious. I love a line of poetry that suggests, "Little one, search that heart of thine."[8] And now I'm asking you to do just that—to search your heart and, as David prayed, "see if there is any wicked way in me" (Psalm 139:24). If there is, I beg you to confess it, forsake it, and, with God's help, change your mind-set regarding your home. God wants you, as one of His women, to become a better steward of your home. Don't miss out on the blessing of a happy home!

I have a job! More and more women enter the work-force each year. And if you fall into the category of women who must tend to a job on top of tending to their home-front, it will help to follow a few guiding principles. I've devoted Chapter 9 to this subject, and it's filled with solu-tions to this real-life issue. But for now, look at the chapter titles on the Contents page. They represent "things that really make a difference in your marriage." Every one of these areas of a wife's life must be nursed. Each is a stewardship handed to us from the heart and mind of God. Each is according to His wisdom and His will. This list provides us with

> *We are called to set aside "self" and do the work of building a home where love reigns and order prevails.*

God-assigned duties and responsibilities. And, as the Bible says, it is required of a steward that he or she be found faithful (1 Corinthians 4:2).

Heart Response

As I pause to survey the past 30 years of seeking to be a wife according to God's plan, how I thank Him for His desire for me to be a homemaker! And how I thank Him for what He has graciously worked into me as I've pursued His desire—the skills, the character qualities, the confidence of being in His will, doing His will, and, hopefully and prayerfully, doing it well. And how I am humbled that keeping up my home is a way that I can bring honor and glory to Him. And how I praise Him that, in some small ways, I have grown in Christlikeness as I have learned to serve my husband and children under our roof, to set aside "self" and do the work (although it is a labor of love) of building a home where love reigns and order prevails. Of course, there have been the failures, the squabbles, the bloops and blunders. But through it all, there is no blessing like that of a happy home. Now, dear fellow homemaker, take the challenging words that follow to heart. And as you focus your energies on keeping up your home, may yours be a happy one enjoying the blessing of God.

> Six things are requisite to create a "happy home."
> *Integrity* must be the architect, and
> *Tidiness* the upholsterer. It must be warmed by
> *Affection,* lighted up with
> *Cheerfulness;* and
> *Industry* must be the ventilator, renewing the atmo-
> sphere and bringing in fresh [vitality] day by day;
> while over all, as a protecting canopy and glory,
> nothing will suffice except
>
> *The blessing of God.*[9]

Little Things That Make a Big Difference

1. Make the beds daily.

This is truly the definition of a little thing! After all, what does it take to make a bed, maybe two minutes? Even if there is clutter in other places in a bedroom, a smooth, wrinkle-free bed gives the appearance of order and serenity. Of course, you'll want to get to that clutter one of these days. But make bed-making a daily habit. And if you have children, have them do the same.

2. Make a daily to-do list.

Start keeping up your home in this small, simple, time-tested way. Make a to-do list. Write down what you hope or need to get done each day that will enhance your home and family life. Go a step further and star or circle the most important one. Then, of course, do it! As you begin to master this little thing, you'll want to begin working on a master plan for caring for your home that includes...

...a weekly plan,   ...a semi-annual plan,

...a monthly plan,   ...an annual plan.[10]

...a quarterly plan,

3. Make a weekly meal menu.

For the smooth running of any household, a menu ensures that you and your loved ones eat (...and, as the old adage promises, the way to a man's heart is through his stomach!). So begin by making your menu for one week at a time. This allows you to have some special meals, some fast meals, and some made with leftovers. A menu also means you only go to the grocery store once a week. And here's another little thing—prepare as much of the evening meal as you can first thing in the morning. Our days certainly have a way of slipping away from us, don't they? And when yours does, you still have a meal to put on the table...all because you started early.

4. Do one thing you've been putting off.

What is the one thing you've been putting off around your house that, if you did it, would give you tremendous relief and great joy? Is it organizing the master bedroom closet? Is it cleaning out the refrigerator? Is it washing the windows? Is it sorting through the junk in the garage? Even if you only work on your project 15 minutes a day, your rewards will be large!

5. Keep a daily log of time spent on your housework.

This is very simple. Several times a day, jot down an estimate of the total number of minutes you've invested in any and all household chores. Your time log doesn't have to be exact or to the minute. What you are looking for is a record that will give you an idea of how much time you are actually devoting to your home-sweet-home. And one picture is worth a thousand words! If the truth reveals that your actual time is low, then you can make plans to put in a little more time and effort each day.

6. Work on your attitude.

Long before the seven dwarfs were whistling while they worked, God addressed the importance of a good attitude toward work. *How* do we work? "Heartily, as to the Lord and not to men" (Colossians 3:23) and "willingly" (Proverbs 31:13). Therefore, a wife after God's own heart does her best in her work at home. She works with a positive attitude. She works to the glory of God (Martin Luther said a dairy maid could milk cows to the glory of God!). She works to better the lives of her loved ones. And she works with all her heart! How's your attitude?

7. Work on growing.

Once you get into keeping up your home, you'll be so blessed by the wonderful results that you'll begin taking pride in the place where you and your husband live. Then you'll want to learn new skills, new organizational methods, and new time management principles. So read, read, read! Ask your organized friends for recommendations of their favorite books on keeping up their home. Look for ways to constantly improve your work. You'll be glad you did...and so will your husband!

7

$\mathcal{R}$aising $\mathcal{Y}$our $\mathcal{C}$hildren

*And these words which I command you
today shall be in your heart.
You shall teach them diligently to your children.*
DEUTERONOMY 6:6-7

$\mathcal{I}$ have been asked again and again to write a book on child-raising. In fact, I've even been asked to write such a book with my two daughters, who are now raising their own children. But honestly, I in no way feel like the great parenting expert. As I look back down that rocky path, I shudder. So many mistakes. So many failures. And, praise be to God, also so much of His great and overwhelming grace!

Nothing, in my opinion and experience, is more humbling than being a mother. When I think of a marriage, I think of two adults. With your husband, you can at least work on your communication skills and learn and adjust your methods and means of transmitting and receiving information. But with children? Well, all is different. You are dealing with a baby...who becomes a child, a youth, an adolescent, a young adult, an adult. And the rules for living with and communicating with offspring at their varying ages and stages are...well...different. And here's where a great challenge comes in.

Parenting 101

I don't know where you are on the Parenting Scale. Perhaps you have no children...and, then again, perhaps you have a handful. Maybe yours are all little toddlers who are crawling on the floor, clamoring, and pulling on your legs all at the same time. Or possibly yours are in school—even high school. Or perhaps, like me, God has sent you into Round 2 and yours are your grandchildren. Whatever the case or age level, God is giving you an assignment like no other. While specific techniques for child-raising will come, go, and change, there are certain core values and fundamental practices that won't. As we go through some guidelines I am calling "Parenting 101," keep in mind that I am moving us in a natural progression from no children to grandchildren.

1. *Desire them*—It helps a wife to know *and believe* each and every day of her married life that children are a good thing. This teaching on the value of children and their place in God's perfect plan for a couple comes from Genesis 1:28. Here God commanded the two members of the first-ever marriage to "be fruitful and multiply," to "fill the earth." God also said "children are a heritage from the

LORD" and "the fruit of the womb is a reward." He con-
cludes, "Happy is the man who has his quiver full of them"
(Psalm 127:3,5).

Hannah in the Old Testament hoped desperately for
children. Sarah, too, longed for them. So did Rebekah,
Rachel, Manoah's wife, Elizabeth…and the list of women in
the Bible who desired children stretches on.

I know children come to us in many ways and means,
some initially more pleasant and joyful than others. But
the assignment God gives to you as a woman and mother
after His own heart is to pray fervently and seek to have
His heart-attitude and mind-set toward the children who
will or do make up your family.

2. *Pray to have them*—Hannah desired children so
fiercely that she prayed to have them. In fact, her desire
was so intense that she took her prayers to another level
and made a vow to God (1 Samuel 1:10-11). The godly
mother of Proverbs 31 appears to have also prayed and
possibly made a vow. She referred to her son as not only
the son of her womb, but as the "son of my vows" (verse 2).

So, dear friend, is the category "children" somewhere
near the top of your prayer list? Whether you have children or not, that is their rightful place as you talk each day
over with God through prayer.

Even to this day, on my own prayer list my children
and grandchildren appear as third, right behind my walk
with God and my relationship with Jim. They are "tops" in
my heart and in my prayers!

3. *Welcome them*—When any and all babies arrive, realize that they are not the *end* of your life. Oh, no! They are the *beginning!* In fact, *they*—the next generation—are life itself. I love Sarah's attitude. First, when she heard that she just might (at age 90!) finally become a mother for the first time, she marveled, "After I have grown old, shall I have *pleasure…?*" (Genesis 18:12). In other words, Sarah was *thrilled* that she might have a child! Then, when she welcomed her little Isaac, she as much as sang in complete wonder, "God has made me laugh, and all who hear will laugh with me" (Genesis 21:6).

4. *Take them to church*—Once you hold your little newborns in your arms, begin their religious training in and for the Lord. On Day One of their little lives, start pointing them toward God. And on each baby's first Sunday as a member of your family, begin taking him or her regularly to church. Also, if your church has some kind of baby dedication ceremony, participate whole-heartedly. Mary took baby Jesus to the Temple at eight days old to fulfill a ritual required by God's Old Testament law (Luke 2:21) and again at 40 days old (verse 22). So follow suit, dear mom. Begin early to impress upon your heart and your infant's heart the importance of the Lord and the Lord's Day. Your tiny ones should never *not* know about God and His Son—your Savior—Jesus Christ. Beloved, devoted mom, it's

> *It's never too early to begin pointing your little ones' souls heavenward.*

never too early to begin pointing your little ones' souls heavenward...but it can subtly become too late. Please, don't wait!

5. *Love them*—Of course you love your family. But you must also pray each day for a heart of love. Why? Because as mothers we get tired. And many days we get so tired that we seem stretched to the limit. And the more children we have, the more tired we become. It's a given. What mother couldn't use a good night's sleep—regardless of how old her children are? But we are to love our children (rather than resent them, complain about them, grow impatient with them, desire to get away from them).

And we are to go a step further and express that love to God, to our children, and to others. I have to tell you that I cried when my daughter Katherine told me she fell apart and bawled her heart out when she left her little firstborn, Taylor Jane, for the first time to attend a women's retreat. (And Taylor was already 18 months old!) I cried because I cherish and share the heart of love that Katherine's tears indicated. And I cried, too, because I've been the speaker at many such women's retreats where the moms in attendance openly expressed how they couldn't wait to get away from their children. Actually, they called their God-given children "the brat-pack," "rug rats," and "the little monster." They wanted some "me" time, some "down" time, some space.

Please don't get me wrong. I understand the tensions, strains, wear-and-tear, and the toll the constancy of child-raising can have on a mom. After all, I've been one. But I do also believe our actions—and our mouths—betray our hearts more than we think. So, how high is your love quotient? Exactly what is your heart-attitude toward your role of mother and toward your children? Pray to love them, to love being with them, and to love being a mother—that's the whole point of the Bible's teaching and calling to wives and mothers "to *love* their children" (Titus 2:4).

6. *Teach them*—Look now at the scriptures at the beginning of this chapter. They are from God's law in Deuteronomy 6:6-7, and they tell you, as a parent after God's own heart, exactly what you are supposed to do every day of your life. You are to...

...teach your children

...teach God's Word

...teach diligently

...teach daily

These instructions from the heart of God show us that you and I are to teach our children, no matter what their ages. We are to teach them God's Word formally and purposefully. We are to teach them about God informally by talking about Him all day long, at every opportunity throughout the day, from the child's waking moment until he or she drops off to sleep. We are to impart information from the Bible itself, and we are to teach our children about God and godly living through everyday life experiences.

Can you tell that teaching your children requires that *you* love God and His Word and that you love your children? And can you tell that teaching your children requires time? Time every day? Time for a lifetime?

7. *Train them*—You and your husband (who is hopefully involved) are God's first choice for training your children. Yes, the church helps. So, perhaps, does a Christian school or preschool. And so do grandparents and other relatives. But God clearly assigns the training of children to those children's parents. Proverbs 1:8 specifically states, "My son, hear *the instruction of your father,* and do not forsake *the law of your mother.*" Your job, dear mother after God's own heart, is to teach your children godly character qualities and godly ways. It is your assignment from your heavenly Father to teach and train your sons and daughters to respect others, to share, to be kind, to handle money properly, to work at a job, to be honest, to stay pure (see the parental training and instruction of Proverbs 5 and 7), and so on. Obviously, as their ages go up, the intensity of the subject matter goes up. But each and every step along the way matters. Don't skip, pass over, avoid, downplay, or take for granted any teaching that relates to your children's whole life experience.

Let's purpose to follow in the faithful, dedicated footsteps of the God-honoring mother of Proverbs 31:1-9. This woman's wise, grown son wrote, "The words of King Lemuel, the utterance which his mother taught him" (verse 1). Mom, this man had preserved the wise counsel that his *mother* taught him! And what, pray tell, was the essence of the teaching he shared in verses 1-9? First, his mother warned her son to avoid a life of dissipation and sensual lust. Second, she pleaded with him to refrain from the excessive use of wine and strong drink. Not bad advice, is it? And is it ever practical! As she prepared, groomed, and launched her son into manhood, this devoted mother spoke up from her heart. She poured out her love in the form of impassioned teaching in an effort to save her beloved son from future problems, harm, and ruin.

Now, I just had two thoughts of application. First, to participate in and accomplish all of this training, you, dear mom, must *be there*, as in be at home. And second, you must *be aware* of each child's development, tendencies, shortcomings, and strengths, not to mention how he or she spends time...and with whom. "Even a child is known by his deeds, whether what he does is pure and right" (Proverbs 20:11). How are you doing on these two requirements?

8. *Guide them*—Once your children are older and more "on their own" (off to college, out of the house, or working away from home on a summer job), you can still guide them by staying in touch and talking about the concerns of their lives and the decisions they are having to make. Samson discussed his desire to marry with his parents (Judges 14:1-4). Plus, there is much indication that the wise son, King Lemuel, who recorded his mother's advice in Proverbs 31:1-9, also followed her advice for selecting a wife (verses 31:10-31). As a godly parent, you are now— and always will be—a God-given asset to your children,

whatever their ages. So don't be afraid to offer your wisdom and advice.

9. *Befriend them*—Once your little ones have run the gamut and graduated to adulthood, you want to move quickly and naturally into the friendship category. Yes, you are still a most capable teacher, trainer, coach, cheerleader, confidante, counselor, and guide. But you now have the privilege and crowning joy of becoming your son's or daughter's adult friend. And what do we women do in the case of our friends? We stay in touch. We call, we talk, we send cards, emails, and little gifts. Our home is always open. And our hearts (of loving care), shoulders (to cry on or lean on), and arms (to hold) are always available.

If you are a mother of adult children, I beg you, don't hold back. Let them know they are important to you in as many ways as you can. Let them know, too, that they are even more important to you than your best friends. I well remember calling my parents when I was a college student to let them know I was homesick and wanted to come see them for a weekend visit. Can you imagine the blow of being told that it wasn't a good weekend because they were scheduled to play bridge with their friends? I got the message, loud and clear, that playing cards with another couple was more important to them than I was. What message are you sending to your adult children? Is it one of cherished best-friendship?

10. *Mates? Welcome them!*—We'll deal with expanding and extended family in the next chapter. But for now, just

file this away—It is vitally important that you welcome your son's and daughter's mates into your heart when they marry. You must bond and meld, for you see, once they are married, you are "family"! In the case of our two daughters, Jim and I approached their courtships and engagements with a cool reserve, knowing that anything can happen to a couple right up to the second they walk down the aisle, even to and through the exchange of wedding vows. But I have to tell you that once Katherine and Courtney walked back up the aisle on the arm of their new (and for real) husbands, those men were mine. Both Pauls (yes, each daughter married a Paul!) instantly became, in my heart, not merely sons-in-law, but sons—*my* sons. They are the sons I never had...the sons God gave to me through marriage. I would gladly die for either one of them.

And what happens after the activity and frenzy of the wedding ceremony? Your adult married children must leave you and their childhood home (Genesis 2:24) and cleave to their mates. But they need to know of your utter joy and delight. And they need your understanding, support, love, prayers, and encouragement.

Jim and I got to express this support in an unusual way. One evening we hosted one of our newlywed couples for a dinner at our home. During conversation, my daughter casually stated while we were eating, "Oh, I would never move away from you, Mom and Dad!" Now, how did we encourage her? Selfishly, these words were music to our ears. But we soon talked to her privately and reminded her of the leaving and cleaving aspect in marriage, that her role was to follow her husband as he provided for her. Jim and I want what's best for our girls and their Pauls, and God's best requires that we let go and give our young families freedom to pursue God's best for them, and, of course, to love and pray for them and to visit as often as we can....

11. *Grandchildren? Welcome them!*—Surely you can see that the cycle of family life continues on and on and on. Some things never change, and one of those things is the heart of a mother. I have a confession to make. I am the grandmother of five little tykes, all four and under, and I can hardly wait until they marry and have their own babies and place them into my arms. I can't wait to welcome a third generation and begin this cycle of praying, loving, teaching, training, and befriending all over again, Lord willing. Oh, what joy that will be! What fulfillment! What answers to a lifetime of prayers! What praise to God! And what a new responsibility!

12. *Pray for them*—And now we start the sequence all over again! What is a mother? She is a woman who prays for her children, their mates, and their children. Perhaps being a prayer is her first and finest role in life. She is the one who is always praying... and her children know it. And now, just as you prayed before your children were conceived, prayed when they were conceived, prayed when

> *What is a mother? She is a woman who prays for her children. Perhaps that is her first and finest role in life.*

they were born, when they were preschoolers, grade schoolers, junior high schoolers, high schoolers, and college students or in the workforce, you continue to pray for them now...and forever. Such a life of prayer and dedicated prayer effort on behalf of our precious children is "the very highest energy of which the mind is capable."[1]

Heart Response

When it comes to what God's Word tells us about being wise and godly mothers, I have to first tell you that I have written my heart out on this subject in almost every book I've written. Why? Because any Christian woman who has children, stepchildren, or grandchildren, has an important duty and responsibility before God concerning those children *He* has placed in her life. And now, in yet another book, I'm humbly addressing the topic of godly parenting and the awesome role of being a mother again. And I have to report to you that my heart is pounding as I am freshly reminded through the Scriptures of what an overwhelming, life-consuming, life-long priority raising children is for a woman after God's own heart. I'm back on my knees, feeling inadequate (which I most definitely am without God's gracious assistance!). And, once again, I'm looking to our all-powerful, all-wise, all-caring God who promises that "with Him all things are possible" (see Matthew 19:26)— even the impossible task of godly parenting.

So do as I'm doing...

Acknowledge the role God has given you.

Commit afresh to live out that role...by His grace.

Make every effort to follow through.

Pray even more fervently, frequently, and faithfully!

Little Things That Make a Big Difference

1. Have a schedule.

Notice I didn't say *follow* a schedule! That's next to impossible for the mom in a busy household. But at the same time, every wise mother has a daily schedule and routine. If you want your day to run more flawlessly, begin with a plan in mind. Schedule meal times, nap times, play times, errand time, bath time, and bed time. As much as is possible, stick to your schedule. Be strong and say *no* to deviations. Your goal is to get your children into a groove so they expect to do certain things, in a specific order, and at certain times. Also plan in time for your housework. And plan in a breather for yourself. Of course there will be the odd day out (errands, Bible study), but your children will pick up on and welcome the general pattern you set for their days. Even if you have a job, you can still schedule and create a morning and evening routine that gives your family a sense of structure, normalcy, and home.

2. Get up before the children do.

Speaking of schedules, this one's for you, dear mom—You must beat the children up! By this I mean you must get up before the rest of the family does. Getting up after they do is a form of suicide.

You start your day behind, and guess what? You never catch up! So what happens when you get up a little earlier? You have time to officially wake up, sit quietly alone, read from the Bible, make your to-do list for the day, and pray for your day and your dear family. You'll be a better mom for it.

3. Set up a recreational area.

When your children have an exciting, inviting place to play or be creative, it centers them at home. Boredom dwindles because there are so many things to do and a place to do them. This is a "little thing," but it makes for happier, more active children. Plus, as an added bonus, it streamlines everyone's task of picking up (which you've scheduled in three times a day—before lunch, before Daddy comes home, and before bedtime, right?). Everything is in one room or one place. You can have cubbyholes or lockers or boxes or baskets for each child to put his or her things into. You can have a general storage area (cubbyhole, locker, box, basket, or closet shelf) for general art supplies, craft items, musical instruments, or audio/video/computer equipment. Sounds like a fun place to me!

4. Have a daily instruction time.

While you are making a schedule and creating a routine for your family, plan in a daily instruction time. This is a time when *every* child who is still at home during the day can sit around your breakfast, dining, or Ping-Pong table and receive some hands-on instruction from Mom. You can set up a craft. You can have the children work a lesson in a workbook or sticker-book designed to help them with their alphabet, shapes, and numbers. You can work with flash cards. You can play a teaching or story tape for their age level. Just be sure each child sits in a chair (or high chair!) and has something structured to work on that's age-appropriate. Make it a little bit formal, a whole lot of fun, and be sure you pray when you begin. We all need God's help when it comes to learning!

5. Have a daily Bible time with Mom.

While you are making a schedule and creating a routine for your family, plan in a daily Bible time. This is not an instructional time, but an enjoyable time, as reading the Bible should always be. This is when you pause for a snack, pile on the couch with Mom in the middle, and have cookies and milk while Mom (or an older child) reads from the Bible, a rhyming Bible, or a Bible storybook. Make it fun, warm, and cozy—something *very* special that all of you get to do together. Afterward, have everyone pray a sentence prayer relating to the Bible story. Then, of course, when Daddy gets home, have the children tell him what they read about in their Bible time. Start with the wonderful stories of Jesus, the action heroes-of-faith from the Old Testament, and the tales and adventures of the apostle Paul. Be sure the Bible is a part of your children's everyday life—no matter what their ages!

8

Extending Love to Family

> *If it is possible, as much as depends on you,*
> *live peaceably with all men.*
> ROMANS 12:18

The penalty for bigamy is two mothers-in-law.

The wife isn't always boss in the American home. Sometimes it's her mother.

To the average husband, the "blessed event" is when his mother-in-law goes home.

"Double trouble" is a mother-in-law with a twin sister.

These one-liners make gentle fun of mothers-in-law, but the good news is that these quips don't reflect everyone's experience. And, dear reader, as a Christian woman—a woman after God's own heart—they *shouldn't* reflect your relationship with your mother-in-law...or with any of your extended family.

What bliss it was for Jim and me as an engaged couple to finally get married. After all of the courting, planning, preparing, and the wedding, off we went on our honeymoon with stars in our eyes and an abundance of love and joy in our hearts.

But after the wedding, real life arrived. It was then Jim and I realized that as a couple we were a new unit, and that each of us came with a full-blown family attached. We now had new issues to deal with. For instance, which set of parents were we going to spend time with first? How often should we get together with our parents? Should we use our hard-earned money (of which there was never enough!) to travel far distances to visit out-of-state parents and in-laws? What about those brothers and sisters who had been our best friends since childhood? And how should we deal with the strain we sometimes feel in these relationships?

God's Perfect Plan

Well, thank the Lord that for every problem He has a solution—a *divine* solution. And in the case of family problems, God has help for His couples. We've already looked at God's plan for newlyweds to "leave" their parents and "cleave" to their spouses (Genesis 2:24). Once a "child" is raised and married, God means for that offspring and his or her mate to form a new union separate and apart from their parents. God also plans for the marriage to be indissoluble—to be Super Glued together ("glue" being the literal meaning of the word "cleave")—until death parts the partners.

God's perfect plan of leaving and cleaving places a two-fold responsibility on all members of the husband's and wife's families. First, the parents on both sides are to voluntarily step out of their "child's" life and release their hold on their adult child. They are to bless the new couple's union through marriage, support them, encourage them, and above all, pray for them. The first years of a marriage are rocky enough without adding the tension of in-law problems. And the second responsibility is that of the newly formed couple to step away and out of their family home and circle. You see, each family must divide before it can multiply.

It's like a dance. The young couple has to step away, and the family units need to let them do so. And yet, once the new twosome has stepped out, they are to step back in. They are still family, but the flavor of the family takes on a new mix. Each family unit has changed in that the married adult child now has a partner—a soul-mate, a one-flesh relationship and friendship with someone else. And it is the two-become-one that returns to each former family unit to strengthen and better that unit as a family is extended, multiplied, and promoted by a new generation. In the end, God has made each family become two—two units that are friends and dedicated to one another, two units that love and cherish one another and gladly invite the other into their hearts.

And God has other plans for His couples. Read on!

The First Law with a Promise

Everyone loves a promise, especially if that promise promotes quality of life. And God has a promise for you and me *if* we follow the law that He laid down with it. I'm referring to one of God's laws as handed down in the Ten Commandments. Commandment #5 states, "Honor your father and your mother, that your days may be long upon the land which the LORD your God is giving you" (Exodus 20:12). An adult is obligated to honor his parents as he does God and to assume responsibility for them.

> *God asks for obedience to His command to honor parents, and He promises a spiritually blessed life to the one who obeys.*

This "law" is also repeated in the New Testament. In the book of Ephesians we read, "'Honor your father and mother,' which is the first commandment with promise: 'that it may be well with you and you may live long on the earth'" (Ephesians 6:2-3). In other words, God asks for obedience to His command to honor parents, and He promises a spiritually blessed life on the way to the higher blessing of eternal life.

Love Lived Out

In the daughter-in-law/mother-in-law combination of Ruth and Naomi, we see God's Law of Honor and Blessing and Love lived out. These two wives after God's own heart

make up the Bible's classic study of a God-honoring in-law
relationship.

What happened to bring them together? A *marriage*
happened. Ruth married Naomi's son, and the two women
became family. As we join them now, both of their husbands have died. They are two lone widows, each of whom
has no one else for support or sustenance. Let's see what
you as a wife can learn from their relationship that can be
applied to yours with your in-laws. And as you read, keep in
mind that the same principles apply to your relationship
with your own parents. So seek to apply them all around—
to your ties with mother and mother-in-law and with father
and father-in-law. God is showing you how to honor your
parents, whether they be parents or parents-in-law.

Ruth respected her mother-in-law—The words of
Ruth's impassioned pledge of loyalty shout her respect for
her mother-in-law and express unlimited love:

> Entreat me not to leave you, or to turn back from
> following after you; for wherever you go, I will
> go; and wherever you lodge, I will lodge; your
> people shall be my people, and your God, my
> God. Where you die, I will die, and there will I be
> buried (Ruth 1:16-17).

In fact, Ruth regarded Naomi so highly that she re-
nounced her homeland and voluntarily chose to go to Judah
and begin an entirely new life with her mother-in-law. Ruth

also admired, respected, and desired the bond her mother-in-law, Naomi, had with the God of Israel.

How high is your respect level for your mother-in-law? A good exercise is to sit down with your spiral notebook or journal and write out "Ten Things I Appreciate About My Mother-in-Law" (or mother...or father...or father-in-law). Believe me, as you focus and dwell on the positive strengths of your husband's mother, you can continually thank God for her qualities and verbalize them to her...and to your husband. This will sweeten your friendship with both!

Ruth was loyal to her mother-in-law—Ruth, as her husband's wife, and Naomi, as Ruth's husband's mother, were family. And, as her fervent declaration reveals, Ruth chose to cleave to Naomi and leave her own pagan homeland. She further pledged undying devotion. To seal her loyalty, Ruth uttered an oath, "The LORD do so to me, and more also, if anything but death parts you and me" (Ruth 1:17).

> *You are on a mission to love, cherish, honor, and respect your family members.*

How can you express your loyalty to your mother-in-law? I would say the Number One way is to say nothing negative about her. Determine that you will not gossip about her. It's easy to fall in line with the "girls" when they start exchanging mother-in-law stories. But, oh no, not you! Why? Because you are a woman and a wife and a daughter-in-law after God's own heart. You are on a mission to love, cherish, honor, and respect your family members. That's God's assignment—and commandment!—to you.

So when you are tempted to let loose, bite your tongue instead, pray in your heart, and then say nothing. Or you could open your mouth and begin reciting the ten things you most appreciate about your mother-in-law and give testimony to how blessed you are by her. But whatever it takes, please don't get involved in mother-in-law bashing. It poisons your heart, fails to embrace God's perfect plan for your life, hurts her reputation, and leads to no good.

And here's another practice to perfect. Don't put your husband's mother down to him either. Surely the two of you have better, more constructive, more worthy things to talk about than sinking into the shallowness of defaming family members. Instead, burn these instructions from the heart of God into the tablet of yours: "Let no corrupt word proceed out of your mouth, but what is good for necessary edification, that it may impart grace to the hearers." "Let all...evil speaking be put away from you, with all malice" (Ephesians 4:29,31). "Speak evil of no one" (Titus 3:2)... and that includes your in-laws.

Ruth wanted to be with her mother-in-law. Naomi thought first of her two daughters-in-law when she encouraged them to stay in their familiar homeland. She appealed to each of them, "Go, return to your mother's house. Turn back and go your way" (Ruth 1:8,12). Yet the ever-loyal Ruth followed Naomi down the long road to Bethlehem. Words are one thing, but actions are quite another. Yes,

Ruth pledged her loyalty, and she proceeded to act on her words. Off to Bethlehem she went, walking beside her mother-in-law. Ruth would be a stranger in a strange land, but she wanted to be with Naomi.

I don't know your age, but if you're on the younger end of marriage, express to your mother and mother-in-law your desire to be with them by doing something as simple as extending an invitation to a family dinner at your house or apartment or for a lunch for just the two of you. And if you work, call and say, "Mom (whether she's your mother or mother-in-law), would you like to meet me on my lunch hour? I found this really cute restaurant I think you'd like. I'd love to treat you." Or, "Mom, I'm running out to the mall. Want to go with me? Want to meet me there? I thought we'd have some fun!"

If you're a little older, that means your dear mom or mom-in-law is a little older too. Yes, some things will change...but not your heart. Show your desire to be together by swinging by and picking her up and taking her to the mall or to lunch (or the cafeteria, depending on her age). You can spend time with her by driving her to her hair appointment or doctor's appointment and sitting with her while she waits. And if she's a widow, maybe you can drive her to church or to her family reunion. Or you can send her an airline ticket to come visit you and your bustling family. You can even fix up a room for her...so she can stay as long as she likes.

And how about the far-end of the days of your relationship with parents? I have personally spent parts of about eight years of my life in hospitals and nursing homes because I wanted to be with my parents and parents-in-law as they declined physically and mentally. Being with them meant the expense of airline tickets, being away from my home and immediate family for days at a time, watching their homes while they were being tended to in a care facility.

But here's one scene I'll never forget. As I was walking down the hall in my mother's nursing home on the way to her room, I passed the room of another resident. (By this time, I knew them all.) And there on the bed lay four women—the grandmother who was in her eighties, her daughter in her fifties, and two teenage granddaughters. Honestly, they looked like four girls at a slumber party! They were all laughing and giggling together at something on TV and loving on each other as their arms entwined. The two younger generations of family wanted to be with their senior matriarch. You and I can be sure they—a daughter in the fast-lane of life and two teenagers with all their things to do, people to see, and places to go—gave up something to be in their beloved mother's and grand-mother's dismal room that so needed their cheer. But they did it. And I'm glad they did—and I'm sure they are too, because the next time I walked down that hallway the room was empty. That well-loved mother and grandmother (who was also a mother-in-law to her daughter's husband) had died.

Can't you give up something and spend more time with your parents on both sides soon...before it's too late?

Ruth served her mother-in-law. How? By helping, providing, assisting, and working hard. Life was tough for the
two women in the hilly, desert country of Judah. Ruth volunteered to obtain food for Naomi and asked, "Please let
me go to the field, and glean heads of grain" (Ruth 2:2).
And off she went to literally gather their daily bread...only
the barley she reaped was in raw form, which required
even more labor from the lovely, servant-hearted Ruth
before it could be eaten.

And you? How can you serve the parents in your two
families? As surely as the ends of the teeter-totter on a
playground exchange positions, so the roles in life reverse.
No matter what your parents' ages, health, and stamina are
today, one day you will exchange positions just as this
poem pictures it.

> As once you stroked my thin and silver hair
> So I stroke yours now at the set of sun.
> I watch your tottering mind, its day's work
>   done,
> As once you watched with forward-looking
>   care
> My tottering feet. I love you as I should.
> Stay with me; lean on me; I'll make no sign.
> I was your child, and now time makes you
>   mine.
> Stay with me yet a while at home, and do me
>   good.[1]

Dear one, ours is a life of service to anybody and everybody. That's what a woman after God's own heart does. And a wife after God's own heart serves her husband first...and then extends that circle of love to include her parents and her in-laws (and even the out-laws!).

Ruth took her mother-in-law's advice. In Ruth we are allowed to behold a truly humble and teachable daughter-in-law. In a very unusual situation, Ruth was counseled by her mother-in-law in the customs of the day in her new land (Ruth 3). And how did Ruth handle being instructed by her mother-in-law? She followed Naomi's counsel to the T...and God worked everything out for Ruth's—and Naomi's—good.

I see just such a heart in my daughter Katherine. Katherine is a member of the MOPS organization (Mothers of Preschoolers), and her mother-in-law, who lives 3,000 miles away, is a mentor in her local MOPS group. I love it when Katherine shares with me the wise advice her mother-in-law has given her regarding parenting and training up her two little ones. Katherine, who is deep into the throes of child-raising, is a sponge. You see, she is not only a woman and a wife after God's own heart, but a mother after His heart as well. And she welcomes every crumb of advice and is a ready listener who takes advice—even from her mother-in-law. As I said, I love this quality in Katherine, and I hope and pray you too, no matter what stage of life you're in, are a wife who seeks, listens to, and follows any godly, practical advice your elders pass on to you. As a proverb warns, "The way of a fool is right in his own eyes, but he who heeds counsel is wise" (Proverbs 12:15).

Ruth blessed her mother-in-law. What a dark and difficult life these two brave and faithful women endured! But, all joy! Ruth married a kinsman...and then a baby was born. And what did Ruth do? She placed her infant son into Naomi's arms. Ruth shared her happiness and her new life as a new family unit with the elderly woman she respected, followed, served, and listened to. And then Ruth went one more step in blessing Naomi...

Ruth let her mother-in-law help her. The Bible paints this tender picture: "Then Naomi took the child and laid him on her bosom, and became a nurse to him" (Ruth 4:16). I wonder if Ruth and Boaz were ever able to pry that baby out of Naomi's arms! But what a sweet scene. A baby *is* new life, but a baby also *brings* new life. And our Naomi enjoyed that blessing of fresh life because a loving, loyal, kind, and giving daughter-in-law let her lend a helping hand. Ruth entrusted her most precious treasure to her mother-in-law. What a daughter-in-law!

Oh my, the lessons are piling up, aren't they? Do you share your little ones with their eager grandparents on both sides? Do you work at finding ways and means of making sure your children are linked to their grandparents? Do you welcome a helping hand, no matter how rusty and out of practice it is?

And then there's the flip side. If you are the grandmother, do you volunteer to help out? Are you communicating your desire to babysit and assist to the busy young mothers in your family? Are you following in dear Naomi's footsteps as she served and eased the load for the younger woman in her life? It saddens me every time a young mom comes up to me at a speaking event and says something like, "I love the way you are involved in your daughters' lives and want to help out with their children. How can I encourage my parents and in-laws to be more involved in our family?"

Dear older reader, your family needs your help, plus I believe it is God's plan. I know distance can be a serious hindrance. But I also believe we grandmothers must pay the price, make the sacrifices, and go the many extra miles—and sometimes hours—required to help out. There are many ways to communicate our heart and our interest. I know I regularly remind my daughters that I want to be their Number One pick for a babysitter at all times. Even if Katherine or Courtney need to go for a haircut, a doctor or dental appointment, a heavy-duty grocery shopping venture, or have a date night, I want to assist them. Plus I want time and input into the hearts and lives of the little ones who make up our next generation.

What can you do today to convey a heart that cares?

"Love Lived Out." I entitled this section with these words for a reason. First, Ruth and Naomi were an "odd couple," but they weren't so oddly matched that love couldn't—and didn't—conquer all. Each woman made the effort, sacrificed, served, honored, respected, and wanted the best for the other. Theirs became a bond that was forever and eternally forged and could not be broken. Each woman lived out God's instructions to "as much as depends on you, live peaceably with all men" (Romans 12:18).

And my second reason for the title "Love Lived Out" is because this noble twosome who traveled together from the mountaintop experiences of bliss into and through a deep and dark valley of sorrow, emerged triumphantly together on the other side. And how did this happen? Each had one person who deeply and genuinely cared for her, albeit an in-law! These ladies put the long line of in-law jokes to rest forever because love lived out formed the strongest bond of all—the bond of family.

Heart Response

Believe me, I have much more I would like to say on this subject of extending love to your family. After all, we didn't even touch upon sibling relationships—both yours and your husband's siblings—and their mates...and the list goes on!

But here's the final challenge to our hearts. If you and your mother or mother-in-law or daughter or daughter-in-law haven't gotten along all that great up to this moment, it's now time for that to change—at least as much as you can make it possible. For now, file away the fact that as a Christian adult married woman—*and* a woman and wife after God's own heart!—you are bigger than the pettiness of bad relationships with your family and in-laws. Indeed, you have all of the resources of a mighty and powerful God at hand to help you. You have the weapon of prayer, and the arsenal of the truths of Scripture, not to mention the sweet strength of God's fruit of the Spirit (Galatians 5:22-23). This means you and I, my beloved reading friend, have no excuses for not bettering our family relationships.

So let's agree to "put away childish things" and ways and "grow up in all things into Him who is the head—Christ" (1 Corinthians 13:11; Ephesians 4:15). That's what a wife after God's own heart does. Now, the question is, Will you? Believe me, doing so will *really* make a difference in your marriage!

Little Things That Make a Big Difference

1. Say *yes* as often as you can.

When it comes to getting together, babysitting for one another, car-pooling, housesitting, or helping out extended family members, say *yes* as often as you can. You are a *family,* for goodness' sake! Therefore you should also be a *team.* Each good deed done is a link in the chain that will draw you closer to one another until your hearts are knit together.

2. Budget for family get-togethers.

I'm sure you've heard people explain that they can't go to their family reunion because they don't have the money...yet they continue to drive through fast-food restaurants, eat out, purchase large-screen TVs, subscribe to cable and internet lines, and on and on their list of optional monetary outlay goes. If something is important to us, we always seem to make a way for it. And family should be important—important enough to make some sacrifices, both financially and time-wise. So budget (see Chapter 5) in a way that "buys" you time to be with your extended family. The Law of Good Relationships says, "The more time you spend together, the better friends you become."

3. Visit your parents.

Certainly there is some leaving and cleaving that must take place when you marry (see Chapter 2), but you are also to honor your parents. A key way to show your love and appreciation is to visit them and to invite them to visit you. Yes, it requires some planning, work, time, and expense on your part. But the dividends will begin to build and build until you have a wonderful relationship. So take calendar in hand and call and invite each set of parents for a visit. When is the best time for them to come? For you to go visit them? Will the dates work out for everyone? Stay at it until you have a working plan. And don't rule out meeting halfway for a weekend together. Whatever it takes in time and money, give it your best effort. You'll be glad you did as the years roll by and the good memories pile up!

4. Stay in touch.

You're a master planner when it comes to your home, husband, and children. So put that brain of yours to work on figuring out as many ways as you can for staying in touch with both sets of parents and all siblings, nieces, and nephews. After all, they are *yours,* given to you by God. Therefore you have a God-ordained role in their lives, and they in yours as well. So use that cell phone with so many monthly minutes and call your family often. Put that internet cable you are paying for to work on your family and email away. Send pictures, photographs, updates, round-robin newsletters. Share funny stories, ball scores, prayer requests...whatever it takes to stay in touch.

5. Take lots of pictures.

I'm sorry, but I can't resist this one. It seems obvious, and yet it's so easy to let family times together just happen without a record of them. So carry a small camera with you or pick up a disposable one, especially when you know you are going to be with family. Ask a stranger to snap a quick picture of you with your relatives. Get a shot of your parents hugging and smiling. The same with you and your siblings. Line up the nieces and nephews and fire away! Don't let a single get-together slip by unrecorded.

6. Pray for your family.

You cannot neglect the person you are praying for, and you cannot hate the person you are praying for. So as a wife after God's own heart, make it your heart's goal to pray faithfully for *all* family members—both the in-laws and the out-laws! Create a prayer page for each person. Then begin noting birthdates, anniversaries, favorite foods and colors, hobbies and collections. Companies and corporations go to great lengths to find out and update all kinds of information about their customers and account holders. Surely you can do the same for family!

9

Tending Your Career

Women must likewise be...faithful in all things.
1 TIMOTHY 3:11 NASB

What is a woman after God's own heart? She is a woman who, like King David of old, seeks with all her heart to fulfill God's will (Acts 13:22). And that, my friend and fellow seeker of God's heart, is what we are pursuing in this book about our "career" as a wife after God's own heart—to *learn* what God's will is so that we can *do* God's will, for as someone noted, "To know God's will is man's greatest treasure; to do His will is life's greatest privilege."[1]

Doing God's Will

Before we tackle the topic of tending to a job, I want to remind you that throughout this book we've been discovering what God's will is for a woman and a wife. Here's what we've established to be our God-given priorities so far.

145

Love God—A wife after God's own heart is first and foremost a woman whose heart belongs to God. God is not only her first priority, He is her ultimate priority and her consuming passion. As a Christian she makes and takes the time to nurture her relationship with God. She has no greater love than her love for God and His Son, Jesus Christ. She delights in keeping God's "first and great commandment"—"You shall love the LORD your God with all your heart, with all your soul, and with all your mind" (Matthew 22:37-38). This passionate and passionately tended love-relationship with the Lord creates a rich, deep reservoir she can draw from in order to whole-heartedly tend to her other God-given roles and relationships.

Love her husband—As a wife, a married woman practices God's priorities by loving her husband (Titus 2:4). After God, she gives her all to her mate-for-life. She makes and takes the time to achieve a best-friend relationship with him. After her time with God, she pours out the best portions of her time, energy, love, and devotion to build and better her marriage. She focuses her efforts on her marriage and on her marriage partner—on improving his life, on serving him, and on striving to live together in harmony. She seeks, with God's help, to live out her God-given roles as a wife—to help, follow, respect, and love her husband.

Love her children—As a mother and as someone who desires to do God's will, God's woman will next make and take the time required to cultivate relationships with her children, no matter what their ages (Titus 2:4). Hers is a lifelong commitment to be an involved, hands-on, fiercely loving and caring mother. She is going to raise her children and give them their primary input. That's her role...and another one of her passions. Why, she's a mother after God's own heart!

Love her home—To a wife after God's own heart, home is next (Titus 2:5). She directs her energies toward building, watching over, and establishing a place where the successful nurturing of her marriage and family can take place. She loves her home (and her family!), takes joy in being there, improves it with her efforts, and is "the queen of fuss" when it comes to her home-sweet-home! She lovingly fusses over the people...and the place.

Commenting on the woman who concentrates on living out these first four God-given priorities, one has noted, "The woman who creates and sustains a home, and under whose hands children grow up to be strong and pure men and women is a creator second only to God."[2]

Love and serve God's people—A woman who aspires to wear the label "a woman after God's own heart" and to possess such a heart has a vital relationship with Jesus Christ. And that relationship thrusts her into the family of God, the body of Christ—the church. As a Christian she is spiritually gifted by God "for the profit of all" (1 Corinthians 12:7), to benefit the church universal and, in particular, the church where she attends. This service to God and His people is a duty and a responsibility every Christian is given, and it is also a privilege that cannot be bought. This service is not optional.

But oh, the blessings that belong to the woman who follows God's plan for serving others! We'll spend an entire chapter on these blessings later, but for now, mark it well—our service to God's people in the church is highly important. It is assigned by God and therefore comes *before* and ranks *higher* in priority than a job, career, or profession.

Now, with our God-given priorities in mind, we can ask and answer a few questions.

Asking...and Answering a Few Questions

I know that many women work. In fact, I think the latest statistic is that more than 50 percent of married women are in the workforce. I'm a realist, and I'm in touch with thousands of women on a regular basis. I receive a lot of mail and email, talk personally with busy working women at conferences, and repeatedly participate in question-and-answer sessions. From personal experience I know about the hearts and lives of God's women, and I want to give you some food for thought, some prompts for heart-evaluation, and some checkpoints to pray about.

Two letters in particular seemed to go straight to the heart of the matter. In one a precious woman asked, "How does a woman with a 9 A.M. to 5 P.M. job keep her priorities in order?" Another sister-in-Christ wrote, "What advice do you have for someone who has to go to a job, then come home and do cleaning, cooking, discipline the children, etc.?"

Obviously these are complicated questions, and each woman asked hers from a different set of circumstances, painstakingly taking pages to lay out the details of the conditions of her life. How did I answer these letters? And how can you apply these truths to your own situation? Please take the time to answer this set of questions. Doing so will help you to understand and evaluate your own situation.

1. *Why am I working?* Asking yourself this question is like taking a good look in the mirror. There are women whose husbands want them to work, and there are those who are working because they want to. I've even talked to women whose husbands don't want them to work, yet they continue to keep their jobs. Your answer to this question will help clarify your motives and reasons for having a job.

2. *Have I explained my desires and concerns to my husband?* If you fall into the category of working because your husband insists or wants you to work, then you need to pray diligently and ask God for wisdom in approaching your husband (see #9). You need to sweetly and intelligently (versus emotionally) present your case and sound reasons for staying at home to your husband. Use all of your good communication skills (see Chapter 3). Put them to work for you as you discuss priorities. And be sure you follow Esther's example in Esther 5—*wait* until the right time to present your case!

3. *Have I properly researched my options?* Is there a way I can stay at home and still bring in an income? Could I manage a business from home? Could I make boutique items to sell? Is there a small internet business I could initiate? Perhaps I can get a newspaper route? (I know at least a dozen women who throw papers in the early morning while listening to Bible teachings on tape, memorizing Scripture, and praying for their families.) Or will my employer allow me to do my work at home? (So many of my readers are discovering this is an option that is getting *yes* as an answer!)

What about saving more and spending less? How much money could I save by cooking instead of eating out? Can I join a food co-op to save money? Do I really need the new clothes? Do the kids have to have the latest toys? Can we make do with the tools we have on hand?

I have treated this subject of options to a full-time job at great length in my book *Beautiful in God's Eyes—The Treasures of the Proverbs 31 Woman.*[3] That book centers around the context of the life of the remarkable woman portrayed in Proverbs, Chapter 31. "The Proverbs 31 woman," as she is referred to, crafted a life of skillfully managed priorities, industry, and productivity. Drawing from her daily life, I worked hard to give biblical and practical advice to women like you, whether you are a woman who wants to stay at home or a woman who works outside the home. I do not hesitate to direct you to this book for a fuller picture of this most excellent model for every woman and wife after God's own heart.

4. *Do I have goals that will allow me to quit working?* Goals such as paying off debts, stepping down from full-time work to part-time work, selling items not needed, a strict (or stricter!) budget, downsizing expenses? Rather than thinking that staying at home is not an option, you and your husband can make quitting your job a goal. Once it's a goal, you can take the intermediary steps that will one day make your dream a reality.

5. *What can (or must) be eliminated from my life?* If your husband insists that you work, streamlining your life is mandatory. You'll have to carefully curb your outings, commitments, participation, and involvements (even in worthy purposes and pursuits) that can cut into managing your home life and nurturing fulfilling relationships there.

> *As a working woman you will have to truly believe and live like every minute counts—and it does!*

6. *How can I do a better job of managing my time?* This is a question each woman should ask every day. But for the working woman, it is a must! To make the machinery of a quality life run smoothly, you'll need to master and become an expert at time management. Read every book you can on the subject. Take every shortcut you can. Learn the tricks of doing more in less time...and of working smarter instead of harder. As a working woman you will have to truly believe and live like every minute counts—and it does!

7. *Am I neglecting my relationship with the Lord?*
Again, if you work, your time with the Lord will energize all
that you must do. So make sure you spend quality time
with Him in prayer and study. It will make you sweeter,
more patient, and boost your love for the family you are to
serve each day when you return home.

8. *Is my perspective right?* If you work, your attitude
should be that your job is "simply something else I do." It
is not your life. Yes, it takes a lot of time, but no, it is not
your priority mission in life. Your real, God-given assignments are waiting for you at home. True fulfillment comes
from the strong and lasting relationships you are building
right under your own roof. Family lasts a lifetime—a job
does not.

9. *Am I diligently and fervently praying for God to
work in my husband's heart?* Do you believe that God
hears and answers prayer, my friend? Ask *Him* to move in
your husband's heart. Also ask God to reveal solutions and
ideas that will provide the means for you to stay at home.
And ask Him for His grace to sustain your many responsibilities.

10. *Am I faithfully endeavoring to follow God's priorities for my life?* Every woman and wife after God's own
heart must acknowledge that no job and no set of circumstances can ever negate God's Word to us as married
women to love Him, love our husbands, love our children,
love our homes, and love and serve His people. It is imper-
ative that we follow God's guidelines in these vital areas.

A Word of Testimony

I grew up in a wonderful, busy, bustling family where every one of the children began working at an early age. That meant that I began my working "career" by tending to our neighbors' houses and pets while they were on vacation. Next came babysitting in the neighborhood. Then at age 16 I got my first after-school job at a local hardware store helping the bookkeeper post the day's sales receipts. And at Christmastime I always had an additional gift-wrapping job. My summers were also filled with jobs as my parents and I were saving for my college fund. On and on my little résumé of part-time and odd jobs went. Even when I finally went off to college, I worked after school, on weekends, and during the summers.

Then I met Jim. And guess what? Jim had grown up in exactly the same way. Jim had begun his long list of work experiences at age 14 by pitching watermelons off a truck at his local grocery store. So the two of us workhorses married and kept right on working while we completed our college educations. And we did it! We finished college, graduating on the same day. I wish you could see the one-and-only picture we have of that day. We are standing together, diplomas in hand, with black circles under our eyes, haggard looking...wearing the two biggest smiles you ever saw. Yes, we did it!

By then Jim and I had been married one whole year. Wow, what a year! And then we set off on the trail of wherever Jim's career as a pharmacist and a pharmaceutical salesman took us. Wherever that was, I continued to work.

For a few months, I logged well production for an oil company. Then I taught in a rural school for nine months. During this time Jim and I were able to use our earnings and savings to purchase our first little home. Then another transfer came...and I worked in an insurance company keeping track of group insurance payments. Then another transfer came...and I ended up being the executive secretary to an educator who ran an intellectual retreat center.

But I have to tell you this. Throughout all of the going to college, the working here and there, and the transfers and moves, I knew that the day our first baby arrived my working would be over. And sure enough, the day baby Katherine arrived, I was done being a "career" woman. And 13 months later, Katherine was joined by her sister, Courtney.

Have I held down a job since then? I have to say *yes*. Exactly twice, to be exact. The first was when both of my daughters were in grade school. I taught in the preschool, two mornings a week, for nine months, in exchange for half-tuition for Katherine and Courtney. And the second time was many years later when our daughters entered high school, were in braces, driving....Well, you know the scene—and the expenses! During this short stint I did bookkeeping two nights a week in my home. After the girls were in bed, I pulled out our card table, set up the tub

> *Your home—the people and the place—is always to be the priority over any profession.*

of records that had been dropped off, turned on some music, put in a few hours' work, and then set the tub by the door, ready to be picked up the next day.

So, yes, I worked for those two periods of time that were carefully arranged around our family schedule. But the goal was that no one (husband, children, home, or ministry) would suffer and (hopefully!) everyone would benefit.

I have to say that I am a homebody. Why? Because that's where my husband is, where my children were in days gone by, where my home is, and where the preparations required to teach God's Word to the women in my church (a part of my service to God's people) took place for so many years. Because that's where my heart is, was, and ever will be. Therefore I try to do everything at home and from home. Now, for instance, I write at home. And if I travel to speak, Jim and I go together. And if he travels to speak, I accompany him, if at all possible.

But I don't write or teach at the expense of my marriage, family, and home. No, I seek daily to fuel my relationship with God, with Jim, with my married children and grandchildren, to love, care for, and fuss over our home, and to serve the body of Christ through my writing and speaking ministry. I do laundry, make meals, keep house, run errands...and *then* write. My eye is on my home, my heart is at home, and my deepest desire is to live out the priorities God has set down for me as a married woman (...which also means that my deepest fear is that I will fail to do so).

So I ask you, as I ask myself regularly, Where is your heart? Is it at home—at your home-sweet-home? Every woman, and perhaps especially the woman who tends a career, must ask and answer that question every day. You see, being a woman and a wife after God's own heart is all about the heart—your heart.

Heart Response

I know every married woman's situation is different. Many work outside the home, and many don't. But every married woman is called to practice her priorities, which as a woman after God's own heart are God's priorities. Therefore you and I must ever and always remember this—No price can be put on doing God's will. No paycheck or dollar amount of income and benefits from a job can ever substitute for living your life according to God's will. Your job from God is to help your husband, to nurture your relationship with him, to love and care for your children, and to be about the business of building your house. You may have a job, but your home—the people and the place—is always to be the priority over any profession.

Beloved, we've been considering a woman's priorities in this chapter and in this book. We've been searching for help with what God wants for us as wives. The priorities we've uncovered to this point are revealed in the Bible and are unchanging. They come to us from and as "the word of God which lives and abides forever" (1 Peter 1:23). "The counsel of the LORD stands forever, the plans of His heart to all generations" (Psalm 33:11). That means that no matter what we want, or what society tells us to want, or what anyone else wants for us, we as women after God's own heart are to want what God wants. We may tend a career, but we must first and foremost desire to fulfill God's will when it comes to the priorities He wisely and sovereignly sets down for our lives.

Where is your heart?

(And P.S., if you are having trouble accepting, desiring, and owning God's will for your life as a married woman, then "ask God to make you willing to be willing"![4])

Little Things That Make a Big Difference

1. Review your priorities every day.

As a Christian, everything you do is to be done excellently...and that includes your job. Part of what this means is that you must constantly check your priorities. Reviewing them first thing every morning helps you keep your marriage, family, home, and job in perspective. It helps you remember that your marriage, family, and home are more important in God's big picture than your job. It helps you remember that as a Christian wife it is the time you spend with your husband at home *before* and *after* work that is your greatest and grandest work for the day!

Be careful not to view your job as more important than the work you do at home—building lasting relationships and creating a home that blesses you and your family. Those at home will never be impressed by the work they never see you do on a job, but they will carry forever in their hearts the memories of a loving, attentive mom and the knowledge that they were Number One!

2. Aim for an organized morning.

If the time you spend at home with your husband is priority time, then aim for an organized morning that allows you and your sweetie time to talk, touch base, have some breakfast, and a word of prayer. If you have time to clean up the kitchen too, you'll be extremely glad later. If you're also trying to get children off to school, then they also need time to talk, touch base, have breakfast, and share a word of prayer. So put the skills you use at work to work for you at home. Do some micro-managing—do some detailed planning.

What can and must you do the night before so everyone isn't yelling at each other the next morning, when they're running late and frustrated because they can't find what they need? Can you set the breakfast table the night before? Can you set out the cereal boxes, vitamins, and sugar? And don't forget the devotional book and Bible! Put school books, backpacks, and briefcases by the front door. Lay out car keys, cell phones, purses, and wallets. If anyone takes a lunch, fix as much as you can after dinner and set it out on the kitchen counter. Run the dishwasher, take out the trash, and, of course, get a good night's sleep. *Whew!* Know in your heart that everything you do the night before pays huge dividends the next morning!

3. Use your lunch hour wisely.

If you work an eight-hour day, those eight hours belong to your employer. However, your lunch hour belongs to you. And if you treat it well and use it wisely, it can become one of your greatest opportunities for staying on top of things or even getting ahead at home.

What can you do on a lunch hour? Pay the bills. Run some errands. Pick up food items and dry cleaning. Make important personal phone calls. Get your hair cut. Work on a continuing education certificate. Write letters. Do your Bible-study homework. Have a doctor or dental appointment. Some women even fit in a workout on their lunch hour. See how many things you can do in the five lunch hours that are yours during the week so your evenings and weekends can be memorable family times.

4. Be all there when you are at home.

Ah, home-sweet-home! At last your day at work is over. And now your "job" is to be sure it's over. Leave work at work! Leave the disputes, emotions, confusion, and any hurt feelings or disappointments you may have experienced on the job at the job. Your husband deserves your attention when he gets home. *He* is the most important person in your life. He deserves a listening ear, a nice meal, and a pleasant evening.

So train yourself to be all there when you are at home. Pray on the way home. Thank God that your day at work is O-V-E-R! Purpose not to rehash your day and the latest office gossip. You are a wife (and a mom and a homemaker) first...and then a worker. So, once again, when you finally make it home, be all there! Give your all. Enjoy your family to the max. Soak up every pleasure home and family bring to your heart. Ah, home-sweet-home!

10

Making Time for Fun

Rise up, my love, my fair one,
and come away!
SONG OF SOLOMON 2:13

As you now know from the previous chapter, both Jim and I are workhorses. And that's a good thing! Being hard workers means that we each strive to be conscientious, faithful, and disciplined. But there's a downside to such dedication. Can you guess what it is? Well, let me fill in the blank for you. It's failing to stop and make time for fun as a couple. If Jim and I aren't careful, we can give ourselves to all work and no play! So, just as we learned to persevere at our work and in the upkeep of our home, we have learned (and are still learning!) to remember to have some fun along the way.

How Did It All Begin?

When I met my dear Jim, the nickname given to him by his friends in college was "Smilin' Jim George." He had

161

bright eyes, a huge smile, a quick laugh, and a light-hearted, adventuresome attitude toward life. What fun we had as we began spending time together! Sure, much of our time was filled with studying in the library and typing our papers and reports. But we also enjoyed seeing the "Boomer Sooners" play live at the University of Oklahoma (our alma mater) on Saturday afternoons, being with Jim's or my friends, going bowling or on frequent Coke dates, and then talking on the phone for hours afterward. There was never a dull moment, and fun was at the center of all we did. We made everything fun—even poring over our studies and being responsible employees.

After "Smilin' Jim" and I married, the fun escalated. Marriage meant we could take off on weekend adventures to go water skiing, to play at the Six Flags amusement park, to stay a night in Oklahoma City when Jim went to his Army Reserve meetings. As a couple we tried snow skiing, sailing, and tennis. We took night classes together at the local community college where we learned the basics of photography and how to play chess. We learned how to strip and refinish old furniture to furnish our little apartment, even completing a class project on designing and building bookcases...and the list goes on. Again, there was never a dull moment.

This is how our wonderful friendship and marriage all began. And it's been a refreshing exercise for me to go back and revisit the "fun" memories of the good times we had. And now I want to ask you to do the same thing. Just take a few minutes to remember—to really remember!—how it all began for you and your husband. I guarantee that recalling the memories of the playful pleasures you once enjoyed will be the spark that ignites more fun in your day today! Your bond with your husband probably began the same way mine did with Jim—with the craziness and fun shared by two people hopelessly and helplessly in love. The two of you, too, probably talked your heads and ears off. And you, too, were probably both deliriously happy.

But...What Happened to the Fun?

If you're like most couples, real life set in all too soon. After your honeymoon was over, reality began to nibble away at the fun that was unique to the two of you. On the heels of all of the thrills came such challenges as job pressures, monthly income and bill paying, learning to communicate (with a few disagreements thrown in along the way!), dealing with family...well, you know the scene! Here are a few of the culprits that showed up on Jim's and my doorstep. See if you can relate.

Responsibility—There's no doubt that the seriousness of life can cut its way into your fun as a couple. It's a fact that the older we get the more serious life becomes. And it's sobering to have to "grow up," to mature, to put away childish things (1 Corinthians 13:11), to shoulder greater and greater responsibility. As Christians we have a purpose for our life and work to do for Christ (2 Timothy 1:9). We are also to be diligent and faithful in all things (1 Timothy 3:11). Properly honoring and representing Christ calls for us to put away procrastination, sloppiness, and negligence (Titus 2:5). We are also to do all things "heartily, as to the Lord" (Colossians 3:23) and to "serve the Lord Christ" in all we do (verse 24). These real responsibilities of daily life are definitely serious...and challenging.

Money matters—Every couple has to not only make money but also make ends meet. On top of taking care of your relationship with God and your husband and your workmanship at home, you now have the added pressure of money. Almost 100 percent of newlyweds have more month than money! And that spells *pressure!* When things are stressed in the Money Department, things can be stressed in the Marriage Department, which can also affect the Fun Department. We can soon wonder, "What happened to the fun? Is this all there is to married life?"

Children—No parent would argue against the biblical truth that babies are a blessing. "Behold, children are a heritage from the LORD" and "happy is the man who has his quiver full of them" (Psalm 127:3,5). A blessing, yes! But children can stretch you to the limit. They arrive with a long list of added responsibilities on the parents' parts, which means there is more growing up to do, more maturing that must take place as you begin to care for a completely helpless human being. Which soon leads to...

Exhaustion—If you and your honey are like Jim and me, you get up early and stay up late. You're just trying to take care of the business and responsibilities of life, not to mention the number of children being added to your two-some! And soon both husband and wife are exhausted (which means "to be used up and completely expended, drained of power and tired out")...and *that's* no fun!

And now another fact must be faced: No matter what your age or how long you've been married, there is a lot for a wife, mother, and homemaker after God's own heart to do! And honestly, I haven't seen the number or the intensity of my list of obligations go down as my age has gone up. No, it's quite the opposite. As soon as our child-raising years were over and our daughters married, Jim and I were faced with the decline and deaths of all our parents. While responsibilities diminished on the parental end of our life, they boomed, exploded, and multiplied on the other end with the addition of two sons-in-law and five new babies for our family! Oh no, things have *not ever* slowed down for us! No wonder on some days we both wonder, "But what happened to the wonderful fun things we used to do?"

Discouragement—Every day has its joy (Psalm 118:24). And each new sunrise is a vision of hope (Psalm 30:5). But each day also comes with its trials (James 1:2). When you add up responsibility, children, exhaustion, and mix in a few failures along the way in any or all of these departments, it's easy to become discouraged. If a woman and wife isn't careful how she handles such discouragement, she can become depressed. Whenever I speak on my book *Loving God with All Your Mind*[1] (which contains the story of my difficulties with depression and the truths from

Scripture that continue to give me daily victory), I share these startling statistics:

🐦 Some form of depression affects over 17.5 million Americans each year.

🐦 The highest overall age for depression is between 25 and 44.

🐦 Depression can affect anyone, regardless of background, though major depression strikes women twice as often as men.[2]

And what are a handful of the culprits that can lead to depression? "Unhappily married people have the highest rates" of depression. Plus "loss of jobs and major financial reverses" many times contribute to depression. (Are you noticing the many topics already covered in this book about nurturing a marriage after God's own heart?) And every woman knows that "down-type feelings" and "feelings of sadness"[3] can easily lead to depressed moods that sap her and her marriage of not only fun, but of God-given joy.

Recapturing the Fun

So what can you (and I!) as a wife do to curb such joy-robbers? What can you do to help recapture the fun in your marriage? What can you do to weave the laughter, the impish gaiety, the sparkle back into the climate in your home and your heart?

First of all, realize that joy must begin in *your heart*. The Bible explains that "a merry heart makes a cheerful countenance" (Proverbs 15:13). In other words, your thoughts and attitudes—not your circumstances—make all the difference. So what are you thinking? Are you fueling memories of past events that are creating a cesspool of bitterness or disappointment? Are you kindling a critical spirit? A sad spirit? As one

> *If you belong to God through His Son Jesus Christ, yours is the deepest, purist, fullest joy that any person can possess.*

scholar comments regarding this verse, "Sad thoughts crush the spirit,"[4] So you and I must cultivate such a merry heart...and that begins with a head full of happy thoughts and a heart full of happy attitudes. As the same writer put it, "Gay heart, gay looks."

Next, realize that the ultimate source of all joy is *the Lord!* "The *joy* of the LORD is your strength" (Nehemiah 8:10). Everyone (including you) who trusts in the Lord and takes refuge in Him can and should *rejoice* (Psalm 5:11)! And "the fruit of the Spirit is...*joy*" (Galatians 5:22). Dear wife, if you belong to God through His Son Jesus Christ, yours is the deepest, purest, fullest joy that any person can possess. So...

> Purposefully rejoice each day—The psalmist exulted, "This is the day the LORD has made; we *will* rejoice and be glad in it" (Psalm 118:24). Before your feet hit the floor each morning (and before you speak to your husband), remind your

heart and soul of this truth. And remind yourself again every time you hit a speed bump during your God-designed day. Purposefully rejoice.

🎵 Purposefully play music—I play music practically all day every day. After years of discouragement and depression, I *learned* to get the music going early each day...which gets the music going in my heart! King David, "the sweet psalmist of Israel" (2 Samuel 23:1), knew well that music lifts the soul and turns a person's thoughts and emotions toward God when he organized music as a part of the temple worship services (1 Chronicles 25). Music will set your spirit free from this disheartening world to soar and sing. "Psalms and hymns and spiritual songs" will cause *you* to sing and make melody in *your* heart to the Lord (Ephesians 5:19).

🎵 Purposefully put on a smile—Go ahead, do it! Then share it. Give it away! Let the joy within your heart rejoice the hearts of others ...beginning with the one closest to you, the one who would benefit the most— your precious husband. The Bible explains that "a merry heart makes a cheerful countenance" and "the light of

> *Let the joy within your heart rejoice the hearts of others...beginning with the one closest to you... your precious husband!*

the eyes rejoices the heart" (Proverbs 15:13,30). Your cheerful countenance and smile will have a heartwarming effect on those in your presence. It's contagious! It gladdens the heart of everyone you meet. What a gift!

Please realize that *your creativity* is a key to opening the door of the Fun Department. Many wives wait for their husbands to initiate the fun. A wife may dream of a husband who sits around "dreaming up" creative and romantic events and outings (as if he isn't busy enough providing for the family, taking care of the finances and the upkeep of the home and car, being a good dad after he gets home from work...and on and on his list goes!). I had my wake-up call in this area when I was a seminary wife...who was sitting around waiting for my poor Jim, a full-time student with four part-time jobs, to "dream up" a little fun for the two of us. A guest speaker encouraged all of us wives to become "the planner of fun" for our marriage. He said, "You plan and prepare the picnic or whatever. I guarantee, your husband will show up and he will enjoy it. But don't wait for him to think of it!" So be creative! What will you plan first?

Where Do I Start?

I'll share a lot of "Little Things That Make a Big Difference" in the Fun Department in your marriage in a few pages, but for now here are a few "little things" some of our couple-friends do for fun.

Cook together—One thing my daughter Katherine and her Paul enjoy doing for fun is to pick a dish they would like to eat. It has to be something new and different. Then they go on-line together and find a recipe on the internet, print it out, make their grocery list of ingredients, shop for the items together, divide up the labor—the washing, chopping, measuring, mixing, stirring—get in the kitchen together, and *voila!* a mouth-watering and fun memory! Not only do they have fun, but, as you well know, they have to develop some pretty good communication skills to both work in the kitchen on a mutual project. And now Paul and Katherine extend their gift to others. Every time they come visit Jim and me, they find or bring a recipe, go to our local grocery store, take over the kitchen, and treat us to a special, fun meal!

Play a game together—This sounds trite and is probably on everyone's list of ways to have fun, but few couples will actually give up their TV time to do it. The specific couple I'm thinking of was staying in a hotel in Hawaii where Jim and I were speaking. We continually saw this laughing twosome sitting on their lanai, playing games like chess and cribbage. They had clearly turned their backs on their in-room television viewing and movies to play games and have some fun. Both Jim and I commented on the two of them and the fun they were obviously having. And both Jim and I said, "Why don't more couples do that?! Why spend money going out when something this much fun is free?"

Tour a museum together—Jim and I have best friends who, for 20 years, have toured a museum exhibit once a month. Together they watch the newspapers for listings of exhibits in nearby museums. Then they get their calendars out and "make a date." Like two little children, they anticipate their outing. Then the day finally arrives...and the fun begins! They plan to have fun, make time for fun, have fun, and have a string of fun memories. And can you imagine the fun Jim and I have had over the years listening to them talk about what they've seen and learned on their exploits? Why, they've even included the two of us on a few of their museum outings. What fun...and for little or no money!

Go downtown together—My pastor and his wife know how to have fun on their day off. They take a ferry ride from the Olympic Peninsula side of Puget Sound here in Washington and spend a part of the day in downtown Seattle. They go everywhere on foot, even in the rain. Nothing stops them! They know every little coffee shop, sandwich bar, farmers market, tourist attraction, trolley route, side street, and back alley. And they stay physically fit from pounding the pavement on Seattle's steep hills. It's their "thing," the little inexpensive, adventuresome thing they do that is just theirs to enjoy. I'm sure that looking forward to their thing and their day is something they savor all week long. Now, where is "downtown" for you? And how long has it been since you've been there?

Go to a park together—Let me point again to our Paul and Katherine. Paul never goes anywhere without a ball or a frisbee. And that includes going to his present job on Madison Avenue in New York City. On many of Paul's lunch breaks or after work, Katherine will bundle up the babies and either walk, take a train, or a taxi to meet him. And off they go to The Park—as in Central Park—to talk as they push the stroller so their toddlers can run and play, to toss a frisbee or a ball, and to stay late and catch fireflies. Every city park is special...and free! Now, when can you and your honey go there together?

For years I've approached my daily planner every morning with what I call "The Three F's" in mind. These "F's" represent major areas of my life that I need to tend to each day in addition to a few of the obvious ones—my spiritual life and my relationship with Jim. They are Family, Fitness, and Finishing Fully (as in finishing my writing, my speech-writing, my projects, whatever it is that needs to be done—and finished!—each particular day).

Well, one morning my darling Jim took his pen in hand and reached over and wrote in a fourth "F" that he wanted me to add to my daily aims—*Fun!* I hadn't realized it, but the culprits to fun had eaten their way into that important element upon which Jim's and my relationship had begun!

And so now, after 38 years of marriage, I am paying more attention to fun.

I opened this chapter with one of my favorite "couple" verses in the Bible. The words are those remembered by a bride, the Shulamite. They are the prose "voiced" (Song of Solomon 2:8) by her bridegroom to and for her, his "beloved." In her dream or her reflections, her husband cries out to her to "rise up, my love, my fair one, and come away!" (verse 13).

Is it possible that you, dear wife, need to lighten up? To have some fun? To be more playful? To get out there and do something enjoyable with your husband? The married couple described in Song of Solomon were madly and passionately in love. And it was of her husband, the person she walked and visited and played with and had fun with, that this wife said, "This is my beloved, and this is my friend" (Song of Solomon 5:16).

How's your friendship with your beloved? Are you purposefully, willfully, and decisively making time for fun?

Little Things That Make a Big Difference

1. Plan one fun activity a week.

Someone needs to be in charge of the Fun Department, and maybe that someone can be you! Begin your stint as the chief organizer of your fun-as-a-couple time by planning one activity per week. It doesn't have to cost a lot—or even cost anything. All you have to do is be creative.

Can you get into the kitchen and cook a meal together? How about setting up the fondue pot and cooking while you eat? Can you go bike riding for a few hours with a picnic in your backpacks? Or what about getting up before daylight on a Saturday for a walk on the beach and gathering seashells while the sun is rising? Could you have a "backward" meal—begin with dessert and end with salad—or have your husband draw numbers that you've assigned to items on your dinner menu, and eat them in the order he picks?

See how many things you can come up with for fun that costs little or nothing. Keep a list going so you never lose a great idea for fun. And sure, once in a while do something fun that costs a little—something you've saved up for. What a bountiful treasure of wonderful memories you will be creating!

2. Recreate an old date from the past.

Think of something you and your husband both enjoyed in the past and then try to recreate it. How about attending a college football game? Or visiting a favorite restaurant from the past—whether it's a fancy place, a dive, or a greasy spoon? Whatever it is, it's a part of your past. So revisit it and keep the memory alive. Did you spend time together in days gone by bowling? Playing miniature golf? Roller skating? Camping? Then do it again. Let the good old days roll again!

3. Recreate your honeymoon.

Maybe you will and maybe you won't be able to actually recreate your honeymoon. Many couples do. But you can definitely pull out your wedding photos or pop in your wedding video. You can purchase the smallest of small bakery cakes and concoct some kind of punch and serve it with a handful of mixed nuts and butter mints. Just have fun!

4. Make each anniversary unique.

Each anniversary is a milestone. That's one more year of being together that you and your hubby can celebrate! Don't wait for your busy husband to come up with a plan for this unique day. Make this a special and fun day. Give the children an early dinner and an early bedtime, and then have a special meal for just the two of you. And then plan for a special time of intimacy.

And here's another factor. Very few couples can actually celebrate their anniversary on the actual date. Decide that that's okay. It's not the date that's important—it's the celebration of another year of marriage that is. So work around commitments and responsibilities and family obligations. Just be sure you celebrate somehow and in some way.

5. Choose a couple hobby.

I'm sure you can think of a multitude of potential couple hobbies—golf, tennis, biking, camping, kayaking, chess, refinishing furniture, and photography are some examples. You name it! Your "little thing" assignment is to experiment and choose what you would like to be yours as a couple. Find a hobby that you both can participate in and enjoy with a minimal amount of training. Remember, some hobbies become more enjoyable as you get better at them or take a few classes together. But also remember, these are "little things," so find something that only takes a little something to get you started. Then be sure you schedule it into your lives.

6. Make a list of things you've always wanted to do.

What have either of you always wanted to do that can be done together? Pick one. Was it your idea?

Then you are in charge of making it happen. Visit that old, musty, used bookstore downtown that has always intrigued you. Then enjoy a cup of coffee or hot cocoa next door at the coffee shop. Take a picnic to a city park. (Now, why is it you haven't ever been there before?) These are little things... and there should be a ton of little things on your list. But you can also put some big things on it too, such as having someone take a picture of the two of you at the top of the Eiffel Tower, touring Israel, walking on the Great Wall of China, going on a photo safari in Africa. Wow, what fun the two of you will have making your list—a list that spans the globe and unites your hearts...even if you never actually do most of the things on it!

11

Serving the Lord

For you serve the Lord Christ.
COLOSSIANS 3:24

Some acts are life-changing. We don't know their impact at the time, but afterward our days are never the same. This is exactly what happened to me one quiet Sunday afternoon. Our two little preschoolers were napping. Church had been thrilling that morning. And Jim and I sat down to go through an exercise together—and it set off a bomb in our lives as Christians and established the direction we have followed for the past 30 years. The two of us—as a couple—asked our hearts one question, which we tried to answer on paper: "What are your lifetime goals?"

How did my list turn out? Well, believe me, I still have the original papers! With a heart filled with passion for God and thanksgiving to my Savior, I targeted these three desires:

1. To be a growing woman of God.

2. To be a supportive and encouraging wife and mother.

3. To teach the Bible so that women's lives are changed.

So far in our book about being a wife after God's own heart, we have focused on growing in the Lord and being a supportive and encouraging wife and mother. Now it's time to address our responsibility and duty as Christian women to serve the Lord.

Serving as a Christian

Every Christian, married or not, is to serve the Lord and the church, the body of Christ. Like the old-time saying reminds us, "We are saved to serve, not to be served." Several factors help us to live a life of service.

We serve out of motivation—Here's a truth about every believer: Before we become Christians, we are selfish and self-serving. We don't know any other way to live. As I shared in the beginning pages of this book, that was how I lived my life before I became a Christian. I wanted what *I* wanted. I wanted to do what *I* wanted to do. I thought of only one person—*me!* And I served only one person—*me.*

But then the day I became a Christian through faith in Jesus Christ, I was overwhelmed (and still am to this day) that Jesus died for me. His death wiped away my sins and gave me new life—eternal life!—and a fresh start. I was "born again" (John 3:3)! I was "a new creation" (2 Corinthians 5:17) who had been given *new* life and a *new* heart.

And God's transforming grace and power was at work in me. I realized instantly that I owed a debt I could not pay— but I could, out of pure gratitude, serve my Lord to my dying breath. Oh, how I wanted to do just that! Gratitude is truly a great motivator for serving the Lord!

We serve like Jesus, our model—In our Savior, our Lord Jesus Christ, we have a perfect model of a life of service. How did Jesus live His life? In His own words, "I do not seek My own will but the will of the Father who sent Me" (John 5:30), and "My food is to do the will of Him who sent Me, and to finish His work" (4:34). And that will and "work," dear reader, was the work that accomplished our salvation from sin—the work of dying on the cross. Jesus explained His work and His mission with these words: "The Son of Man did not come to be served, but to *serve*, and to give His life a ransom for many" (Matthew 20:28). Thus, "Jesus...went about doing good" (Acts 10:38). And we as Christians are to "follow His steps" (1 Peter 2:21). Therefore...

> Go, labour on; spend and be spent—
> Thy joy to do the Father's will;
> It is the way the Master went;
> Should not the servant tread it still?[1]

We serve out our mandate—The Bible is very clear that every Christian, including you and me, is to serve the Lord. In fact, we are "spiritually gifted" to serve and expected to use those gifts in service. We are instructed that "the manifestation of the Spirit is given to each one for the profit of all" (1 Corinthians 12:7). "Through love" we are to "serve one another" (Galatians 5:13). Therefore, in obedience, we serve. It's our mandate!

And what is waiting for us on the other side of such obedience? The blessing of knowing we are serving God. The blessing of becoming more Christlike. The blessing of living out the highest form of leadership—that of humble service. And the blessing of demonstrating Christlikeness in the world: "The world cannot always understand one's profession of faith, but it can understand service."[2]

We serve as our ministry to others—The Bible informs us that the spiritual gifts that each Christian possesses are "for the profit of all" (1 Corinthians 12:7). Christians who are on the receiving end of the ministry of these gifts are benefited. Although Christians have been given a variety of spiritual gifts (verse 4), every one of them ministers to the members of the church, the body of Christ. When you discover, develop, and use your spiritual gift, others are edified, built up, encouraged, strengthened, comforted, helped, and matured in Christ.

There are many ways women serve others in the church—as many ways as there are gifts. My own personal goal is "to *teach* the Bible so that women's lives are changed." The reason I stated my personal desire in these words is because other women in my church were ministering their gift of teaching and my life had been marvelously changed as I drank in what they shared. I knew nothing about being a Christian or about spiritual gifts...or about teaching the Bible, for that matter. But I did know that somehow and in some way, the time and care and effort these women took to share with others was having a positive and powerful impact on my life as a new Christian woman, wife, and mother. And I thought and prayed, *Oh Lord, if I could do that for one more woman, if I could just pass on what I've learned, if I could just change one life the way these ladies have changed mine...how worthwhile that would be!*

And God has truly answered my prayer! I'll go into more specifics later, but for now, remember that your faithful service and the faithful use of your spiritual giftedness ministers to others more than you'll ever know. God planned it that way!

> *We serve the Lord. This truth attaches great dignity to our service, however seemingly small or menial.*

We serve our Master—It always helps me to know *why* I should do something, which is what we've been considering so far regarding our service in the body of Christ. But I also like to know *who* it is I am doing anything for. And in the case of spiritual service and ministry, the Bible tells us *Who* we are serving: "for you serve the Lord Christ" (Colossians 3:24). This truth attaches great dignity to our service, no matter how small or menial it may seem.

Serving as a Couple

As the subtitle of this books states, there are 12 things that really make a difference in your marriage that I've chosen to include in this book about being a wife after God's own heart. And serving the Lord as a couple is one of those "things." This may or may not be possible for you in your unique marital situation, but let's look at two couples after God's own heart who ministered together in serving others.

Meet Sarah and Abraham—Together Sarah and Abraham make up one of God's dynamic couples of faith. Each had a heart after God. Each loved God. Each followed God. Each trusted God. And each has been eternally honored by God for the faith exhibited in Him in situation after situation for year after year and decade after decade (Hebrews 11:8-19). How did this husband and wife serve the Lord as a couple?

Sarah and Abraham worked together as a team. One day when Abraham was resting in the door of his tent in the desert, he spied three men coming his way. He jumped up, ran to meet them, bowed before the men, invited them in, and offered a little water and a place to rest along with the promise of food...

...which is where Sarah came in! Abraham rushed into their tent, spouted out orders to Sarah to Quick! Make some bread cakes! He even gave her the recipe! Then off Abraham scurried, disappearing to take care of the meat for the meal they were jointly preparing for their guests. Together they pulled it off, and their mutual ministry of hospitality created a place of refuge and refreshment in a ruthless climate for their visitors (Genesis 18:1-8).

Just an afterword: The three "men" who stopped by Sarah and Abraham's tent for a little visit just happened to be "the Lord" and "two angels."[3] These heavenly visitors were on a two-fold mission. They had come to deliver a message to Sarah and Abraham that, after 25 years of waiting, they would finally have a child (Genesis 18:9-15). They had also come to deliver Abraham's nephew, Lot, out of the evil environment in Sodom and Gomorrah before the angels destroyed it (Genesis 19:1-29).

Pointing to the ministry of hospitality to others, instances like the kindness Sarah and Abraham served up to three desert travelers, the Bible says "do not forget to entertain strangers, for by so doing some have unwittingly entertained angels" (Hebrews 13:2)! When you minister to someone, you never know how far-reaching that service may be!

Meet Priscilla and Aquila—Here's an amazing couple who served the Lord together. In fact, throughout the New Testament there is a trail of shining examples of their team ministry. First, Priscilla and Aquila took in the apostle Paul and provided a home for him (Acts 18:1-3). Many scholars believe that Paul may have stayed with this fine couple for the entire year and a half he ministered in Corinth. Priscilla and Aquila also took aside the Jewish teacher Apollos and "explained to him the way of God more accurately," and then sent

> *"It is not the possession of extraordinary gifts that matter…but the dedication of what we have to the service of God."*

186 A Wife After God's Own Heart

him on his way to a greater ministry as "he vigorously refuted the Jews publicly, showing from the Scriptures that Jesus is the Christ" (Acts 18:24-28).

Adding to their résumé of ministries, Paul later wrote that Priscilla and Aquila had been his "fellow workers in Christ Jesus, who risked their own necks" for his life (Romans 16:3-4). Paul also sent greetings to the church at Corinth from Aquila and Priscilla and "the church that is in their house" (1 Corinthians 16:19). Then, when the political and religious climate cooled down, Priscilla and Aquila returned to their roots in Rome and hosted another "house church" (Romans 16:5). Everywhere they went this admirable couple served the Lord.

Together Priscilla and Aquila worked as tentmakers, knew and shared the teachings of God's Word, opened their home, and encountered life-threatening persecution. What a couple! They were constantly on the move. But their eyes and ears, not to mention their hearts, were open to those in need. They were ready, willing, and able (at least with the little they had!) to serve the Lord any where, in any way, at any time, and at any cost. Jim and I have picked Priscilla and Aquila as our model of not only a marriage after God's own heart, but of a couple who together served the Lord heartily. Maybe you and your husband can do the same.

Abraham and Sarah, Priscilla and Aquila. Two couples after God's own heart...in two different time periods...in two different lands...ministering to two different kinds of people—one to the Lord Himself and His angels, and the other to the Lord's church and His servants Paul and Apollos. Yet each couple had a heart for God, a marriage that withstood the rigors of trials and time, a "home" that they opened up, along with their hearts, to others. In marriage and in ministry, each couple operated as an effective team, bringing twice the love, twice the strength, and twice the service to those in need. These two noble couples gave freely of their means and possessions in their ministries to others. They lived out this truth about serving the Lord: "It is not the possession of extraordinary gifts that makes extraordinary usefulness, but the dedication of what we have to the service of God."[4]

Principles for a Wife's Ministry

There are as many service-scenarios in a marriage as there are couples, but several principles for a wife's ministry apply in all circumstances. This set of principles will help you in your particular husband/wife situation. In my situation, my Jim has been in ministry for almost 30 years (which is a service-scenario in itself!). So we know how to serve the Lord together. But I want to quickly say that it was not always like this!

No, I remember all too well our "start-up" days as a Christian couple—days when we were trying to get the 12 issues we are addressing in this book into place...and serving the Lord was one of them. In our case, Jim wanted to serve the Lord, but I didn't...or didn't know how to. I remember, too, our first efforts at mutual ministry—learning how to use my home for the good of others, how to make it...and my heart...available to God. I remember discovering, with God's help, how to be willing to serve others whenever Jim phoned home to say there was someone who needed assistance or money or a place to stay.

How does a wife assist her husband in serving the Lord? And how does a wife serve the Lord if her husband is lagging behind? And how does a wife serve the Lord if her husband is not a Christian?

1. *Serve those at home first*—For decades I've had a personal motto I use when it comes to my service to others and to my church: "Don't give away to others what you have not first given away at home." This saying reminds me of my God-given priorities every day. I am to serve my husband and children, to give my love to those at home *first*...and then move on to share with others—not the other way around. I know how easy it is to get the order backward, and so do other women just like you and me. For instance...

Recently I talked to a woman who had resigned as the director of women's ministries at her church. Why? She said she withdrew from her position because her priorities were out of order. She told me that she found it much easier and more rewarding to minister to the women at church than to take care of the needs of her two preschoolers and her husband at home.

Another woman who served as a music and worship leader and soloist at one of my conferences left that conference deeply convicted of her wrong priorities. (In fact, she was on her way to a pay phone to call her husband and ask his forgiveness!) She told me afterward that when she said goodbye to her husband as she left home that morning to attend the "A Woman After God's Own Heart" seminar, she really meant the "goodbye." She had announced to him that she wouldn't be coming back—ever. Beloved, she went *home* from that seminar a *wife* after God's own heart!

In both cases these women were giving away to others what they were definitely not giving away at home. But I say of these two women, *Bravo!* for recognizing their wrong priorities and *Praise God!* for wanting to do the right thing! As a wife, you are to serve your husband first before any and all others. What's important is not what those at church think of you, but what those at *home* think of you. What's important is not that those at church are taken care of, but that those at *home* are tended to. That's a wife's job, a wife's priority, and a wife's privilege!

Dear wife, when the people and the place at home are taken care of, loved, served, and fussed over, it is *then* that we go over to the church and take care of and tend to others. That's what a wife after God's own heart does.

2. *Serve with your husband's blessing and support*— If and when you do desire to sign up for a ministry or volunteer to help in some way at the church, please—oh please—ask your husband first. Your relationship with your husband, your submission to his desires for your marriage and his leadership of the two of you as a couple, and your service to him is to be "as to the Lord" (Ephesians 5:22) and to be done "heartily, as to the Lord and not to men" (Colossians 3:23).

I personally make it a policy to never commit to anything or to take on any project without asking for Jim's input, thoughts, ideas, and approval. It's not because I'm afraid of my husband or see Jim as a parental figure. No, it's because I value the relationship and friendship we have as a couple *more than* I desire to do what I want to do. After all, if my time is involved in the ministry, that's Jim's time too. If money is involved, that's Jim's money too. If stress is involved (like the stress I incurred the first time I signed up to teach a women's Bible class), then that stress is bound to come Jim's way too.

It's like this. I want to serve the Lord, but I also want God's blessing on that service. And I believe that a mega-measure of God's blessing comes with my obedience to God's standards for me as a wife to honor my husband by giving preference to him (Romans 12:10), to esteem him as better than myself (Philippians 2:3), and to, as much as depends on me, live peaceably with my husband (Romans 12:18). Therefore I ask for Jim's opinion and approval on all things, including ministry opportunities. I don't ever want to find myself in a position of functioning in ministry (of all things!) without my husband's backing. So I serve *only* with my husband's blessing and support. Then I can serve with a free heart. Why? Because I know Jim's on board—and praying for me. Together we've released and designated some of my precious time and energy for ministry, which means it's a joint ministry. Sure, we evaluate afterward, but many times I make it through a ministry commitment only because I know in my heart that I have Jim's support.

And what's a wife to do if her husband says *no* (and, believe me, Jim has said *no* many times!)? If you are that wife, I say you should thank God. Your husband is key to helping you keep your priorities straight because his input can sound the alarm when things are out of balance. His direction is a way God guides you. So when my Jim says *no*, I personally thank God for a husband who leads and who speaks up. And then I decline the ministry opportunity without a bitter bone in my body. Following God's will that I follow my husband's leadership keeps me—and my service—in the center of God's will. *No* in an area of service can be God's will and direction as much as a *yes* can be.

3. *Serve however you can*—When Jim and I began going to church as a Christian couple, we didn't know anything about how to serve the Lord or about the Bible or about spiritual gifts. But with grateful hearts for our Savior, we knew we wanted to do something. So we did any and everything we could do! We washed dishes after socials. We set up chairs, took down chairs, stacked chairs, moved chairs for meetings. We put hymnals in the pews and vacuumed the sanctuary. We washed pots and pans during conferences. We greeted people coming to church services. We hosted a Bible study in our home. We drove senior citizens to church. We worked concession stands for the children's fair. We painted. We gardened. We helped complete the office ceilings during the remodeling of our church. On and on the list of our multi-faceted serving ministry went. We didn't need to have any special skills to do these wonderful ministries. We only needed to show up with a heart to serve.

Later, as we grew in our knowledge of God's Word, our ministries evolved. We took a counselor training course and began ministering in the prayer room after church services. We took an evangelistic outreach class and joined the visitation ministry. We took a Sunday school teacher training course and began assisting in children's classes. We took a discipleship training class and began ministering to others one on one. We took several Bible courses and began sharing in small group settings. And during all of the ministries and the taking of the classes and the growing spiritually steps, we used our home. Anyone and everyone was welcome there, whether local or from across the world!

But what if your husband doesn't want you to serve in these ways? Consider what you can do in your situation. I can't tell you how many women I know who bake cookies for ministry...from home, who fix meals for others...from home, who make phone calls to organize some ministry or check up on those who are home-bound...from home, who write letters and notes of encouragement...from home, who type lists of church information...from home, and who, of course, pray for others at church and around the world... from home. The ways to help and minister from home are unlimited—if you have a heart for serving the Lord!

All of this to say, my reading friend after God's own heart, serve however you can!

> Three things the Master asks of us,
> And we who serve Him here below
> And long to see His kingdom come
> May pray or give or go.

He needs them all—the open hand,
The willing feet, the praying heart,
To work together and to weave
A threefold cord that shall not part.[5]

Heart Response

And there's one more principle that's at the heart of everything...

Develop a servant's heart—As a woman after God's own heart, we—and every Christian!—can and should embrace the fact that every day of our God-given life is to be a time of glorious service. We are to be God's servant to all. We are to willingly serve everyone God allows to cross our path every day, beginning with our precious husbands. We are to mimic the Savior, who came to serve instead of to be served, and who went about doing good.

So I urge you to *pray!* Pray for a servant's heart every day—preferably first thing in the morning. Praying will remind you who you are, who you belong to, why you are here, and how God wants you to live your life. So, no matter what your marriage situation is like, boldly ask God for His love to serve your husband. Ask Him for His love to serve friends and foes, the familiar (your husband and children)...and the stranger. Ask God for greater compassion and for ears that hear and eyes that see where you can help. Ask for His tender mercies...and a heart for serving Him and the people He places in your path.

194 A Wife After God's Own Heart

Little Things That Make a Big Difference

1. Pick one little thing to do at your church.

It can take a while to mature and prepare for some ministries. But there are a myriad of service and volunteer ministries you can do at your church that benefit multitudes. You can address and stuff envelopes, sanitize the nursery and its toys, vacuum the sanctuary, place items in the pews, bake a meal for a shut-in, greet visitors, assist a preschool teacher...and the list goes on and on. If you're not sure where to begin, ask someone in the church office. That someone will definitely know where the needs are! And sometimes those needs are "little things" that will make a big difference in your church being perceived as friendly and efficient.

2. Check your heart...and check your schedule.

This may sound strange since we are addressing our service to the Lord and His people. But it is easy for an eager Christian woman to overindulge in service...to the point of neglecting her marriage and family and home. Are your family members at home happy with the care and attention they are receiving? Is your husband fully (and I mean *fully!*) supportive of your involvement at church? Don't be like the woman who left home on a Saturday morning to lead the "worship" at an all-day seminar sponsored by her church—and who announced to her husband when she closed the door that she wasn't ever returning. Don't be like the wife and mother who found organizing and directing a full-blown ministry to the women at her church easier and more fulfilling than managing her home and caring for her husband and two little ones. Clearly these women had their priorities backward and were overindulging in ministry! So first do these two "little things"—check your calendar and check with your husband concerning your ministry involvement.

3. Agree with your husband on how to serve as a couple.

Few things are more rewarding for a Christian couple than serving the Lord *together!* Each of you brings so much to a couple's ministry. And you fill in each other's strengths and weaknesses when you team up to serve. For instance, perhaps your husband can lead or chair a ministry...and you can assist with the secretarial work for that ministry. Or if he needs to arrange an organizational meeting, you can volunteer to host the meeting in your home. If you both like people, you can sign up as greeters one Sunday a month. Do the two of you like to work with children? Then take on a class of little ones...together. How about helping with "the moving ministry"? You can cook a meal for an unsettled family while your husband helps move their furniture. Just be sure you both agree on how and how often you will serve. The list of ways the two of you can minister together is unending. It's as long as your hearts are big!

4. Serve in at least three ways.

A bit of information regarding serving others helped me get started down the road to ministry. Basically it points out three ministries that are not optional for a woman after God's own heart, but are commanded—serving, giving, and showing mercy. Here's how these ministries are explained:

> *Serving* (also sometimes called helps or ministering) is the basic ability to help other people, and there is no reason why every Christian cannot have and use this gift.

> *Showing mercy* is akin to the gift of ministering and involves succoring those who are sick or afflicted.

> *Giving* is the ability to distribute one's own money to others, and it is to be done with simplicity, which means with no thought of return or gain for oneself in any way.[6]

So what can...and will...you do this week to serve, show mercy, and give?

5. Pray for others.

Are you a stay-at-home woman? Do you have little ones at home? A job at home? Do you have a work schedule that doesn't allow you to be at church as much as you would like? Well, you can always pray. Ask your church for a list of weekly prayer requests. Also carry a special notebook to church to record the prayer requests shared by others. Then pray for those in your church and around the world. Remember, the effective fervent prayer of a praying *woman* accomplishes much (James 5:16)!

12

Reaching Out to Others

*You shall be witnesses to Me
in Jerusalem, and in all Judea and Samaria,
and to the end of the earth.*
ACTS 1:8

Throughout this book I have shared about becoming a Christian. For the first 28 years of my life I did not have a relationship with God through His Son, Jesus Christ. I was selfish, my life was hopeless, and I was clueless about being a wife, mother, and homemaker. My heart was definitely not filled with love, joy, peace, and patience! Instead I had a bleeding ulcer, chronic colitis, and exema up to my elbows! I was most miserable, and I'm sure Jim and my two daughters were, too.

But then something happened. In simple terms, someone reached out to me with the truth of the gospel of Jesus Christ. And because God had graciously prepared my heart, I received that truth, was born again, and God's grace and transforming power began working in my heart. From that very second, God put me on the path to becoming a woman after His own heart. And that direction affected my marriage to Jim as I also began growing into a wife after God's own heart.

But how did such a transformation happen? Again, the short answer is that someone reached out to me. In fact, God used a series of people to reach out to me—people who followed Jesus' words at the beginning of this chapter. Jesus told His followers then to "be witnesses to Me in Jerusalem, and in all Judea and Samaria, and to the end of the earth" (Acts 1:8), and His words still stand for you and me today. Only the locations have changed!

If you are a Christian, I'm sure you can recount the trail of people—of witnesses—God used to bring His truth to you. And now I want you to become a part of the trail of witnesses that God just might use in the lives of others to introduce them to the Savior. As we move through this chapter, keep in mind we are moving through *your* Jerusalem (those in your home), *your* Judea and Samaria (those in your neighborhood and your family), and on to the end of the earth (the world)!

Reaching Out to Your Husband

The person closest to any wife is her own dear husband. And many Christian wives are married to men who are not believers in Christ. What advice does God give to such a wife?

If this describes your marital situation, these words possess the pure wisdom of God: "Wives, likewise, be submissive to your own husbands, that even if some do not obey the word, they, without a word, may be won by the conduct of their wives, when they observe your chaste conduct" (1 Peter 3:1-2). Here the apostle Peter counsels all Christian wives to "be submissive to your own husbands."

But then Peter addresses the wife who is married to a husband who does "not obey the word." This is a husband who is a non-Christian. How do you reach out to such a husband? God is very clear: You are to, "without a word," live out your Christianity by your "conduct." This doesn't mean you can never speak or speak up. But it does mean you are not to preach, lecture, harass, goad, or nag. Instead God wants your *life* to send a loud message from Him to your husband's heart. And God chooses to—and is able to!—deliver that message through your reverent and respectful behavior as a wife. Living a loving life preaches a louder and lovelier message than your lips could ever proclaim!

> *Living a lovely life preaches a louder and lovelier message than your lips could ever proclaim.*

Just a personal note here... In the early days of my marriage to Jim, we were "unequally yoked"...only in our case, Jim was the believer and I was the unbeliever. I can well imagine the tightrope an unequally yoked woman walks because I dished out plenty of hostility, put-downs, and scorn to Jim about his beliefs in Jesus Christ. I lived out this truth in the Bible: "But the natural man does not receive the things of the Spirit of God, for they are foolishness to him; nor can he know them, because they are spiritually discerned" (1 Corinthians 2:14). But Jim was so very patient, kind, forgiving, and loving. It's hard to resist such Christlike behavior! Jim was a major link in the chain God forged to draw me to Himself. I pray that you will be just such a link in the life of your husband!

In addition to godly behavior, you can—and should!—pray. "The effective, fervent prayer of a righteous [wife] avails much" (James 5:16)! Who knows what your godly conduct and your faithful prayers can, by God's grace, accomplish in your husband's heart?

Reaching Out to Your Children

Following on the heels of your love for your dear husband are your precious children, if you have them. Your job assignment from God is to reach out to them with the life-saving message of Jesus Christ. These flesh-and-blood gifts from God are entrusted to you as a woman and a mother after God's own heart, and God expects you to teach, instruct, and train your children for Him and His purposes. And these roles are not optional. No, they are commanded by God:

> These words which I command you today shall
> be in your heart. You shall teach them diligently
> to your children (Deuteronomy 6:6-7).

Train up a child in the way he should go
(Proverbs 22:6).

Bring them up in the training and admonition of
the Lord (Ephesians 6:4).

Fellow mother, we are to give our all each and every
day to obey these commands and do our part to lead our
little (and big!) ones to the knowledge of God and His Son,
Jesus Christ. No price can be put on a soul, especially
those of our nearest and dearest—our children! As a mom,
I found that I needed to make a fresh commitment to God
daily as a personal reminder of the importance of reaching
out to my flock of children, no matter what age they were
at the time. If I didn't have this fresh, daily reminder, I
tended to let things slide, to take the easy road, to do as
little as possible, to lose sight of my mission as a *Christian*
mother. So as a dedicated Christian mother, you must see
to it that you not only discipline and train your children
but that you...

> ...read the Bible regularly to them,
>
> ...study the lives of God's great heroes of the faith
> with them,
>
> ...have daily devotions with them,
>
> ...help to hide God's Word in their hearts,
>
> ...take them to church, Sunday school, and church
> activities,
>
> ...speak of the Lord continually to them,

...point the events of their lives to biblical truth,

...pray for and with them at bedtime,

...teach them about Jesus, and

...freely and frequently share God's plan of salvation.

And, of course, as a passionate and devoted mother, you must pray for them. Remember James 5:16? "The effective, fervent prayer of a righteous [mother] avails much." Who knows what your godly conduct, your dedicated teaching, and your faithful prayers can, by God's grace, accomplish in your children's hearts, no matter how young or old they are?

Reaching Out to Your Neighbors

Next come your neighbors. They may not be as close to you emotionally as your family members are, but you live near them day-in, day-out. That means you probably see your neighbors more often than you see your own extended family. And, as a wise proverb reminds us, "Better is a neighbor nearby than a brother far away" (Proverbs 27:10). In other words, when you have a need or an emergency, your neighbor is there to turn to for help—not your relatives!

Jesus has something to say about neighbors. Quoting from the Old Testament Law of Moses, He said that as a woman after God's own heart, you are to "love the LORD your God with all your heart, with all your soul, and with all your mind" and "love your neighbor as yourself" (Matthew 22:37 and 39).

So, as a wise woman who wants to reach out to your neighbors, you must first have a heart full of love for them. And I've always found that prayer is how such a heart and such a love is cultivated. That's how Jim and I approached our neighbors and neighborhood. We picked one day each week to pray specifically for our neighbors. We listed each family on a special prayer page, along with their children's names. Then, as we spent time in the yard or passed one another getting in and out of the car, we would take a minute (no matter how busy or rushed we were!) to greet our neighbors by name, to be friendly, and to find out something else about their lives...which was noted on their personal prayer pages. Amazingly, as we prayed regularly for our neighbors, they came to have a place in our hearts...and in our lives! Prayer entwined our lives with theirs. Prayer turned strangers into loved ones!

Make it a project to pray and ask God to help you think of as many ways as you can to help your neighbors, to have them in to your home and over for dinner. As you live out your Christianity before their eyes, you can be sure religion will come up. As your neighbors see you leave

> *A heart filled with God's love will smooth the way for reaching out.*

for church each week, your interest in church is guaranteed to come up! And remember, it doesn't matter if they understand you and your Christianity. Just be a friend. Keep opening your door...and your heart. Keep serving, loving, helping, befriending. And by all means, keep asking if they would like to go to church with you or go to a choir concert or church picnic, your women's Bible study, an exercise group, or a quilting class at church. Ask if their children would like to go to your church's organized children's ministry.

In these ways—and more!—friendships are built. Then, as you already know, you can talk to a friend about anything...including Jesus Christ!

Reaching Out to Your Family

Reaching out with the gospel message of Jesus Christ to extended family members can definitely be a touchy area. But the good news is that it is nothing that God cannot enable you to handle graciously and in a Christlike manner. A heart filled with God's love will smooth the way for reaching out to family—both your relatives and those of your husband! (Please revisit Chapter 8, "Extending Love to Family"!) Hopefully you've already been working on your love for, acceptance of, and responsibility toward these God-given family members.

But your goal with family should always be, as the scripture verse for Chapter 8 states, to, "if it is possible, as much as depends on *you*, live peaceably with all men" (Romans 12:18). As a Christian, you have the living Christ living in you to help you to live out the part that depends on you (Colossians 1:27). You have God's fruit of the Spirit at work in you—His love, His joy, His peace, His patience, His self-control to aid you (Galatians 5:22-23). Therefore, from your end of family relationships, you *can* get along, reach out in love, and come to their aid with the help and service and understanding needed. So the issue and the hard question then becomes, Do you want to?

I know some family members can be a challenge. They may even want nothing to do with you. And when that's the case (as in any and all cases!), you pray! God is well able to soften hard hearts as you lift up your sincere prayers on their behalf. My prayer principles stand for difficult family members: *You cannot hate the person you are praying for* and *You cannot neglect the person you are praying for.* Try it! You'll find out firsthand that these are true. Not only does prayer change family members—prayer changes *you*!

So think through the family members God has given you. In fact, make a list in your prayer notebook. Then make it a point to find out birthdates for everyone on your list...and send something each year, no matter what! Find out anniversary dates too...and send something annually, no matter what! Collect email addresses...and send a regular update and inquiry, no matter what! Reach out, stay in touch, seek to shore up broken relationships and better those you enjoy. Again, members of your own family can become your best friends...and with a friend you can talk about anything—including Jesus Christ!

Reaching Out to the World

We've now covered the many people who make up your daily life—your husband, children, family, and your neighbors. (And space doesn't even allow us to address reaching out to those wonderful people at your workplace!) So who's left? Why, the whole world! But take cheer! You can be a

part of extending the truth about Christ and His love to
those in the world...beginning right at your own church.

I've already mentioned that my Jim served for some 25
years as a pastor and Bible teacher. In fact, Jim was Pastor
of Evangelism at our former church. That means we served
for many years in our church's outreach ministries. What
kind of ministries? We've both been involved in the
church's prayer room where people came for help, guidance...and in search of a relationship with God. We've put
in time at the church's information booth where visitors
came for information and directions to classrooms...as well
as to God! And the list goes on. Jim and I have both participated in the visitation ministry. We've both reached out
in jails, at missions for the homeless, and at shelters and
halfway houses. We've "manned" the hotline at church,
participated in college campus and street ministries. We've
gone on short-term missions trips together and even served
as missionaries in Singapore.

Reaching Out...Carefully!

Such opportunities for reaching out to others exist
through your church, too. But...*be careful!* As a wife after
God's own heart, you must always go right back to the
"Principles for a Wife's Ministry" shared in the previous
chapter. Those principles are:

#1. Serve those at home first.

#2. Serve with your husband's blessing and support.

#3. Serve however you can.

If your husband doesn't want to be involved, or if he wants you to be less involved, or if he objects to your involvement, go very slowly, very carefully, and very wisely. When it comes to your spiritual ministry and reaching out to others through your church, you want to, once again, serve with your husband's blessing and support (#2). You must also remember that you don't live at the church. No, you live in a home where you have a husband to serve (#1), love, care for, spoil, pamper, and reach out to if he's not a Christian.

Of course, the ideal scenario is to serve in an outreach ministry together with your husband. But the truth is that not many women get to live out this ideal. If this is your situation, and if your heart is willing to please your husband (1 Corinthians 7:34), then, believe me, there are still countless ways that you can reach out to others. So, rather than be bitter, put your trust in God and thank Him that He is in control of the circumstances of your marriage. Then pray and make it a personal project to see how many ways you can reach out from home (#3)...while you are honoring your husband's wishes. God will bless and honor you for that because honoring your husband is what a wife after God's own heart does (Ephesians 5:22 and 33)!

——————*Heart Response*——————

And now, dear friend and devoted-to-your-dear-husband wife, after traveling the road together through this book

about being God's kind of wife, I want to reach out to *you!*
It just occurred to me that I know nothing about your personal relationship with God. I've assumed a few things
about you along the way simply because you have chosen
to read this book with its lofty and hopeful title. I've
assumed that...

...perhaps you are reading this volume because you
were looking for help in your relationship with your husband or ways to better your marriage. If so, *bravo!* I hope
and pray that the truths presented from the Bible, my personal insights, and the little things that make a big difference have indeed made a b-i-g difference! Or,

...perhaps a friend reached out and invited you to a
Bible study and this is the book the women chose to use.
Again, *well done!* for going to the study...and for completing the book! Or,

...perhaps your couples' Sunday school class is using
this book (along with my husband's book for the men, *A
Husband After God's Own Heart*)[1] and you and your husband joined the group. I say to you, *you are blessed!* What
a blessing to go through these areas of your marriage
together! How I pray your marriage has been enriched!

There's no doubt that this is a practical book. But I'm
sure you also picked up on the more major theme threaded
throughout the book—that of being *God's* kind of wife, of
being a woman and a wife after *God's* own heart. You see,
this book is also a spiritual book. So, as our joint journey
ends and we part ways, I want to reach out to you. I believe

you probably fall into one of these categories of women and wives:

—You are a woman after God's own heart and have embraced Jesus Christ as Lord. If so, I trust that after reading the truths in this book your faith in God has been built up, your dedication to following God's rules for your marriage has been kicked up a notch, and your commitment to be God's kind of wife has been firmed up. To you I say, *Keep on keeping on!* Keep on following God's plan for you as a wife. And by all means, keep on growing in the Lord! Or,

—You desire to be a woman after God's own heart, but you are unsure of your relationship with God through Jesus Christ. You like what you've been reading and desire to follow after God with your whole heart, but you're not sure you are a child of God. To you I say, *Come to the cross!* For you I share this acrostic that presents the truths of Jesus Christ's death. It is a statement of who Jesus Christ is and what His death on the cross accomplished in the plan of God. I am also sharing a prayer that might guide your heart to the right words for receiving Jesus Christ into your heart and life by faith.

C-hrist, God-in-flesh, gave His life (Philippians 2:8) as a

R-ansom, a payment, for our sins (Matthew 20:28),

O-ffering up His life as a sinless sacrifice (Hebrews 10:14),

S-uffering unto death (Hebrews 12:2) to secure our

S-alvation from sin and death (Colossians 2:13-14).[2]

A Prayer from My Heart

Jesus, I want to accept You as my personal Savior. Please come into my life and help me obey You from this day forward. I know I am a sinner, but I want to repent of my sins and turn and follow You. I believe You died on the cross for my sins and rose again victorious over the power of sin and death. I thank You with all my heart! Amen.

So now, my beloved friend, I leave you with one question. Have you embraced the Christ of the cross as your Savior? If not, know that I am praying for you to do so. Becoming a child of God will truly make *all* the difference in the world in every part of your life—including your marriage! And if so, reach out to others with God's message of the cross as you travel the path of life as a woman and a wife after God's own heart!

Little Things That Make a Big Difference

1. Invite your friends and neighbors to a Bible study.

Are you unsure about how to witness to people? Are you uncomfortable sharing with others? You can always introduce your friends and neighbors to Christianity by taking them with you to a Bible study. Your women's study and your couples' study are great places to take the women you know and the couples on your block. Simply reach out and invite them! Each time you begin a new study, pick up extra flyers to give to your associates, neighbors, friends, and the other moms at school along with a fresh invitation to join you. Your friendliness and enthusiasm for your group study just might encourage people to come along and take a look for themselves. Then...who knows what might happen!

2. Participate in activities with your friends and neighbors.

When it comes to reaching out to others, establish a general policy of saying *yes* to your neighbors when they invite you to do something (...with your husband's approval, of course!). Make it a point to go to as many Tupperware, Pampered Chef, or Avon parties as possible that are hosted by your unbelieving neighbors, co-workers, and school acquaintances. If these wonderful people invite you to a backyard barbeque, go! If someone's child is having a birthday, move heaven and earth to participate. If someone's daughter is getting married, do everything in your power to attend the wedding. If your neighbor's husband is in a baseball playoff, throw on a pair of jeans and you and your husband try to be there. Attempt to join your neighbors and associates in their endeavors as often as you can. They need to know that you are vitally interested in them. Don't be so wrapped up in your church that you are perceived as distant or aloof—as people who could care less about neighbors' and friends' lives...and souls.

3. Open your home.

Never underestimate the power of a Christian home! As a believer, "you are the light of the world." Therefore your home is like "a city that is set on a hill" (Matthew 5:14). It is full of light, ablaze with the glory of God at work in you and in your home. Therefore, fling wide the doors of your wonderful home. Like the wise woman in Proverbs 9, call to those who need the truth, "Turn in here!...Come, eat of my bread" (verses 4-5). If a neighbor is going through a rough time, have her over for coffee. If a new family moves in, have them come for a chili supper. Consider an open house every year for you and/or your husband's co-workers. Have the school moms to your house for coffee cake and a gab session. Hospitality is a

marvelous gift you can give to others and a wonderful way to make friends. And with a friend, you
can talk about anything—including Jesus Christ.

4. Give a book or a Christian tract.

You may be unsure about how to witness or you
may be uncomfortable sharing with others, but you
can always introduce your friends and neighbors
to Christianity by giving them a book or a tract.
You do the giving, and then stand back and see how
God chooses to use it in the lives of others. If a particular Christian book has helped you improve your
marriage, share the good news! Give the book to
other wives. If a book on biblical child-raising
principles has given you greater confidence in your
parenting, share the good news! Give the book to
other mothers. And how about housework? Has a
book by a Christian homemaker shown you better
methods and quicker ways to take care of the place
where you live? Then share the good news! Give
the book to other struggling home managers. Have
a generous, thoughtful heart. Speak up when something helps you as a woman. Then put a book or a
tract into the hands of those who so need the help
the Bible and the Savior can give them!

5. Pray for your unbelieving friends and acquaintances.

The greatest way to "love your neighbors" is to
pray for them. This is also the greatest way to
develop a heart of compassion for your unbelieving

friends and neighbors. As you faithfully bring their need for the Savior and the difficulties of their lives before God through prayer, your heart becomes mightily involved. Your "care quotient" goes up as you invest your time and spiritual energy in praying for them. Keep a prayer list. Let others know you are praying for them. Check up regularly on the issues in their lives.

$\mathcal{N}$otes

Chapter 1: Growing in the Lord

1. Neil S. Wilson, ed., *The Handbook of Life Application* (Wheaton, IL: Tyndale House Publishers, 1992), pp. 270-71.
2. Mark Porter, *The Time of Your Life* (Wheaton, IL: Victor Books, 1983), p. 114.

Chapter 2: Working as a Team

1. Charles F. Pfeiffer and Everett F. Harrison, eds., *The Wycliffe Bible Commentary* (Chicago: Moody Press, 1973), p. 5.
2. Ephesians 5:22; Colossians 3:18; and 1 Peter 3:1.
3. For a more in-depth discussion of these and other problems in marriage, please see Elyse Fitzpatrick and Carol Cornish, gen. eds., *Women Helping Women* (Eugene, OR: Harvest House Publishers, 1997).
4. John MacArthur, *The MacArthur Study Bible* (Nashville: Word Publishing, 1997), p. 1738.
5. Pfeiffer and Harrison, eds., *Wycliffe Bible Commentary*, p. 5.

Chapter 3: Learning to Communicate

1. The Living Bible.
2. Sid Buzzell, gen. ed., *The Leadership Bible* (Grand Rapids, MI: Zondervan Publishing House, 1998), p. 742.
3. Walter quoted in Eleanor L. Doan, *The Speaker's Sourcebook* (Grand Rapids, MI: Zondervan Publishing House, 1977), p. 298.
4. Ellen Fein and Sherrie Schneider, *The Rules for Marriage* (New York: Warner Books, Inc., 2001), pp. 83-85.

Chapter 4: Enjoying Intimacy

1. The Living Bible.
2. MacArthur, *MacArthur Study Bible*, p. 19.
3. Pfeiffer and Harrison, eds., *Wycliffe Bible Commentary*, p. 6.
4. MacArthur, *MacArthur Study Bible*, p. 1944.
5. Willard Harley in Alice Gray, *Lists to Live By*, The First Collection (Sisters, OR: Multnomah Publishers, 1999), p. 122.
6. Claudia and David Arp in Alice Gray, *Lists to Live By*, p. 137.

Chapter 5: Managing Your Money
1. 1 Corinthians 16:1-2; 2 Corinthians 9:5-7.
2. Elizabeth George, *Beautiful in God's Eyes—The Treasures of the Proverbs 31 Woman* (Eugene, OR: Harvest House Publishers, 1998).
3. Alice Gray, *Lists to Live By for Every Married Couple* (Sisters, OR: Multnomah Publishers, 2001), pp. 30-31.

Chapter 6: Keeping Up the Home
1. Carol Meyers, Toni Craven, and Ross S. Kraemer, *Women in Scripture* (Grand Rapids, MI: William B. Eerdmans Publishing Company, 2001), p. 306. The four other references referred to are Genesis 24:28; Ruth 1:8; Song of Solomon 3:4; 8:2.
2. Robert Jamieson, A.R. Fausset, and David Brown, *Commentary on the Whole Bible* (Grand Rapids, MI: Zondervan Publishing House, 1973), p. 466.
3. Curtis Vaughan, *The Old Testament Books of Poetry from 26 Translations,* quoting translations by Ronald Knox and Kenneth Taylor (Grand Rapids, MI: Zondervan Bible Publishers, 1973), p. 632.
4. Jamieson, Fausset, and Brown, *Commentary on the Whole Bible,* p. 1387.
5. Ibid.
6. Vaughan, *Old Testament Books of Poetry,* quoting translation by James Moffatt, p. 530.
7. Pfeiffer and Harrison, eds., *Wycliffe Bible Commentary,* p. 1394.
8. "Where Shall I Work Today," cited in V. Raymond Edman, *Disciplines of Life* (Minneapolis: World Wide Publications, 1948), p. 209.
9. Frank S. Mead, *12,000 Religious Quotations,* quoting James Hamilton (Grand Rapids, MI: Baker Book House, 2000), p. 230.
10. For additional help in creating a master plan for your home, visit www.flylady.net.

Chapter 7: Raising Your Children
1. Mead, *12,000 Religious Quotations,* quoting Samuel Taylor Coleridge, p. 338.

Chapter 8: Extending Love to Family
1. Cited in Edith L.Doan, *The Speaker's Sourcebook,* (Grand Rapids, MI: Zondervan Publishing House, 1977), p. 169. The author of the poem is unknown.

Chapter 9: Tending Your Career
1. Author unknown, cited in Edith L. Doan, *The Speaker's Source-book,* p. 282.
2. Mead, *12,000 Religious Quotations,* quoting Helen Hunt Jackson, p. 230.
3. George, *Beautiful in God's Eyes.*
4. Roy B. Zuck quoting F.B. Meyer in *The Speaking Quote Book* (Grand Rapids, MI: Kregel Publications, 1997), p. 409.

Chapter 10: Making Time for Fun
1. Elizabeth George, *Loving God with All Your Mind* (Eugene, OR: Harvest House Publishers, 1994).
2. See www.coloradohealthnet.org/depression, 3/11/99.
3. Ibid.
4. Derek Kidner, *The Proverbs* (Downers Grove, IL: InterVarsity Press, 1973), p. 114.

Chapter 11: Serving the Lord
1. Horatius Bonar.
2. Mead, *12,000 Religious Quotations,* quoting Ian MacLaren, p. 404.
3. Genesis 18:13-14,22; 19:1.
4. Mead, *12,000 Religious Quotations,* quoting Frederick Willaim Robertson, p. 404.
5. Author unknown, cited in Edith L. Doan, *The Speaker's Source-book,* p. 223.
6. Charles Caldwell Ryrie, *Balancing the Christian Life* (Chicago: Moody Press, 1969), pp. 96-97.

Chapter 12: Reaching Out to Others
1. Jim George, *A Husband After God's Own Heart* (Eugene, OR: Harvest House Publishers, 2004).
2. Elizabeth George in Rob Holt, *What the Cross Means to Me* (Eugene, OR: Harvest House Publishers, 2002), p. 27.

If you've benefited from *A Wife After God's Own Heart,* you'll want the companion volume

A Wife After God's Own Heart
Growth and Study Guide

This guide offers thought-provoking questions, reflective studies, and personal applications that will enrich your life.

This growth and study guide is perfect for both personal and group use.

Double the benefits of *A Wife After God's Own Heart,* by giving your husband the companion volume

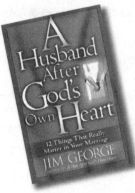

A Husband After God's Own Heart

This book by Jim George is rich with practical insights and guidance that will bring greater mutual love, friendship, romance, and happiness to your marriage.

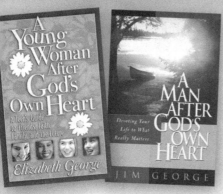

A Woman After God's Own Heart® Study Series

BIBLE STUDIES FOR BUSY WOMEN

"God wrote the Bible to change hearts and lives. Every study in this series is written with that in mind—and is specially focused on helping Christian women know how God desires for them to live."

—Elizabeth George

Sharing wisdom gleaned from more than 20 years as a women's Bible study teacher, Elizabeth has prepared insightful lessons that can be completed in 15 to 20 minutes per day. Each lesson includes thought-provoking questions and insights, Bible study tips, instructions for leading a discussion group, and a "heart response" section to make the Bible passage more personal.

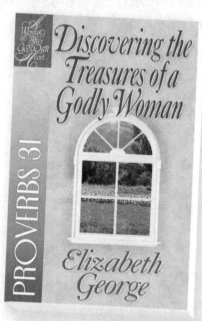

Proverbs 31 0-7369-0818-8

Philippians 0-7369-0289-9

1 Peter 0-7369-0290-2

1 Timothy 0-7369-0665-7

Judges/Ruth 0-7369-0498-0

Esther 0-7369-0489-1

James 0-7369-0490-5

Life of Mary 0-7369-0300-3

Life of Sarah 0-7369-0301-1

HARVEST HOUSE PUBLISHERS

www.harvesthousepublishers.com

Books by Elizabeth George

Beautiful in God's Eyes—
The Treasures of the Proverbs 31
Woman

God's Wisdom for a Woman's Life

Life Management for Busy Women

Loving God with All Your Mind

Powerful Promises for Every Woman

The Remarkable Women of the Bible

A Wife After God's Own Heart

A Woman After God's Own Heart®

A Woman After God's Own Heart®
Deluxe Edition

A Woman After God's Own Heart®
Prayer Journal

A Woman's Call to Prayer

A Woman's High Calling

A Woman's Walk with God

A Young Woman After God's
Own Heart

Children's Books

God's Wisdom for Little Girls—
Virtues & Fun from Proverbs 31

Growth & Study Guides

God's Wisdom for a Woman's Life
Growth & Study Guide

Life Management for Busy Women
Growth & Study Guide

Powerful Promises for Every Woman
Growth & Study Guide

The Remarkable Women of the Bible
Growth & Study Guide

A Wife After God's Own Heart
Growth & Study Guide

A Woman After God's Own Heart®
Growth & Study Guide

A Woman's Call to Prayer
Growth & Study Guide

A Woman's High Calling
Growth & Study Guide

A Woman's Walk with God
Growth & Study Guide

Books by Jim George

God's Man of Influence

A Husband After God's Own Heart

A Man After God's Own Heart

Books by Jim & Elizabeth George

God Loves His Precious Children

God's Wisdom for Little Boys—
Character-Building Fun from Proverbs

Powerful Promises for Every Couple

Powerful Promises for Every Couple Growth & Study Guide

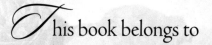

$\mathcal{T}$his book belongs to

_____

a mom after God's own heart.

Elizabeth George

HARVEST HOUSE PUBLISHERS

EUGENE, OREGON

Cover by Garborg Design Works, Minneapolis, Minnesota

Cover photo © Janie Airey/Digital Vision/Getty Images

A MOM AFTER GOD'S OWN HEART
Copyright © 2005 by Elizabeth George
Published by Harvest House Publishers
Eugene, Oregon 97402
www.harvesthousepublishers.com

Library of Congress Cataloging-in-Publication Data

George, Elizabeth, 1944–
A mom after God's own heart / Elizabeth George.
    p. cm.
Includes bibliographical references (p.).
ISBN-13: 978-0-7369-1572-4
ISBN-10: 0-7369-1572-9 (pbk.)
1. Mother and child—Religious aspects—Christianity. 2. Parenting—Religious aspects—Christianity. 3. Child rearing—Religious aspects—Christianity. 4. Christian education of children. 5. Mothers—Religious life. I. Title.
    BV4529.18.G46 2005
    248.8'431—dc22   2005004646

Printed in the United States of America

05 06 07 08 09 10 11 12 / BP-CF / 10 9 8 7 6 5 4 3 2

Contents

Acknowledgment

As always, thank you to my dear husband, Jim George, M.Div., Th.M., for your able assistance, guidance, suggestions, and loving encouragement on this project. And a special "thank you" for the contribution of your wisdom in the "From a Dad's Heart" sections in this book.

A Word of Welcome

♡

Dear Mom,

Without even meeting you, I can tell you are someone very special! Why? Because you're choosing to read this book. When you consider its title, it becomes pretty obvious that you desire to be a mom after God's own heart. This book is packed with information and how-to's that will show you how to fulfill the desires of your mother-heart—how to become a mom after God's own heart. As we begin our journey together, a few things will make it even sweeter.

Open your book... and enjoy it! Vital information is here. Encouragement is here. God's Word is here. I've even tried to make it easy to read for you as a busy woman and mom. In my mind I've pictured you reading this book in a quiet moment after the kids leave for school...or while the little ones are napping...or as you wait up for your teen to come home...or as you rock your baby to sleep...or maybe even as you recline against a tree while your kids enjoy a romp in the park. Enjoy your book! Carry it with you, and let God's Word instruct you and give you a power boost and a pat on the back all at the same time.

Open your heart... to the priorities and topics covered in this book. They are tailor-made just for you, mom. They'll give you God's wisdom and guide-lines for this major role in your life.

Open your heart... through prayer to the Holy Spirit. Ask Him to illuminate God's Word, to help you understand God's plan and priorities for your life, and to transform you, heart and soul.

Open your heart... to others. Look around. Are there other moms in your church or neighborhood who would benefit from learning what being a mom is all about? Invite them to get *A Mom After God's Own Heart* too, and go through it together. Then you'll be growing as moms and in the things of the Lord. And to really accelerate your understanding, go through the *A Mom After God's Own Heart Growth and Study Guide*. You'll love it!

Open your heart... and dream! Dream of becoming the mom you yearn to be—a mom after God's own heart.

And now let's put feet on those dreams! It is the prayer of my heart that the contents of this special book for moms like you will encourage you, excite you, instruct you, and inspire you to follow after God's own heart!

In His great and amazing love,
your friend and fellow mom in Christ,

Elizabeth George

FOCUSING ON THE HEART

*F*ocusing on the Heart

Keep your heart with all diligence,
for out of it spring the issues of life.

PROVERBS 4:23

*N*o matter what you do each day...or in life...doing things God's way is a matter of the heart. Whether it's deciding how to spend your money or your time, how you treat people, how you dress, or how you do your work, your choices reveal your heart. And the same is true when it comes to how you raise your children—no matter what their ages.

Why is the condition of the heart—both yours as a mom and the heart of your child—so critical? The Bible answers this all-important question.

At the Heart of All Things

As you already know from personal experience, the heart is the chief organ of physical life. It's obvious to everyone that the heart occupies the most important place in the human system. But the heart, as used in the Bible, also stands for our entire mental and moral activity, including the emotions, the ability to reason, and the will. The heart is also used figuratively for "the hidden springs of the personal life."[1] That's why God warns and instructs us to "keep [our] heart with all diligence, for out of it spring the issues of life" (Proverbs 4:23).

God begins molding a mother after His own heart on the inside— in the inner woman and her heart— and then works outward.

In other words, we are "to present our entire beings to God....[and] the heart is first. It speaks of the inner life, the mind, the thoughts, the motives, the desires. The mind is the fountain from which the actions flow. If the fountain is pure, the stream that flows from it will be pure. As a man thinks, so is he."[2]

So what does this have to do with being a mom? First, we need to know how important our child's heart is. W.E. Vine, giving insights into Matthew 15:19-20, wrote, "human depravity as in the 'heart,' because sin is a principle which has its seat in the center of man's inward life, and then 'defiles' the whole circuit of his action." That's the bad news. But, second (and here comes the good news),

Scripture regards the heart as "the sphere of Divine influence" (Romans 2:15; Acts 15:9).³

So here, my fellow mom, is our twofold challenge. To raise (and keep on raising!) a child after God's own heart, we must till the soil of each tender heart and sow the seed of the Word of God while praying fervently for "Divine influence." At the same time, we must devote ourselves to diligently training and to dealing with and disciplining the sin that is a part of every child's life.

But where does all of this mothering, committing, praying, dedicating, dealing with, and disciplining begin? It starts in *your* heart, dear mom!

As moms, our job assignment from God is to raise children after God's own heart—children who seek to follow God and hopefully experience salvation through Jesus Christ. And following-through on God's plan for us is all about our hearts. It's all about fulfilling God's instructions to us. He wants us to focus on giving our heart, soul, mind, strength, and time to influencing and shaping the hearts of our children toward God and His purposes.

Children with a Heart for God

You can probably think of men and women in the Bible who had hearts for God, who followed after Him. But there are also a number of children in the Bible who had hearts for God, ranging all the way from pre-schoolers to pre-teens to young adults. These children loved and served God in a variety of ways. And each one of their stories has lessons for us as moms after God's own heart, no matter what our children's ages.

Samuel—Everyone from toddlers to grandparents alike loves the story of the boy Samuel's response to God's call. (You can read about this part of Samuel's life in 1 Samuel 3:1-21.) It's what we dream of for our own growing children...that they never know what it's like to not love and follow God. That's how I see Samuel. He's the young guy whom most believe at around 12 or 13 years old heard God calling him...and answered.

What made Samuel a child after God's own heart? In 1 Samuel 3 we read that he—

> *heard* God's call...and
>
> *answered* Him. He
>
> *listened* to what God had to say, and he
>
> *responded* to the voice of the Lord, saying, "Here I am!...Speak, for Your servant hears" (verses 4 and 10).

From the heart-actions of the boy Samuel it's apparent that "children (even at a very young age) are able to make significant spiritual commitments and substantial contributions to the work of God."[4]

Where does such a heart come from? Certainly, first and foremost, it comes from God Himself. He is the Maker and Creator of all good things, including a heart that hears, listens, answers, and responds to Him. But on the heels of this right response we might also add "...and from Samuel's mother." Who was she? Her name was Hannah, and she was the woman who prayed to God and vowed,

O LORD of hosts, if You will...give Your maidservant a male child, then I will give him to the LORD all the days of his life (1 Samuel 1:11).

The answer to this prayer from Hannah's heart was Samuel...who was dedicated to the Lord before he was even conceived! And to fulfill her vow, Hannah took Samuel to the house of the Lord in Shiloh when he was weaned, at about age three. And there she handed her little tyke over to Eli, God's priest, to be raised under his direct superintendence and instruction in the shadow of the house of the Lord.

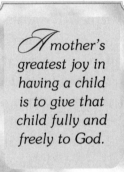

A mother's greatest joy in having a child is to give that child fully and freely to God.

By age three it appears little Samuel was well' on his way to becoming a child after God's own heart. From that tender age he "ministered to the LORD before Eli the priest" (1 Samuel 2:11). And where did such a heart begin to take shape? Again it all began in the plan of God. But another factor in God's plan was the faithfulness of a mother after God's own heart. Imagine...a mom who could pray the prayer Hannah prayed in 1 Samuel 2:1-10! (Be sure to read it for yourself.)

Imagine her fervent love for God, her knowledge of God through the Pentateuch (the first five books in the Bible) and from His dealings with His people throughout history. Imagine her intense instruction to her little one and her passionate prayers on his behalf as she prepared to deposit her preschooler in Shiloh.

I pray that such a burning dedication to God—and to teaching and training our children—is true of you...and me too.

David—David was the original man after God's own heart (1 Samuel 13:14). But he was also a boy after God's own heart. Scholars believe David was between 10 and 16 years old when Samuel, who grew up to be a prophet and priest, anointed David to be king over Judah.[5] David was brought up to be a shepherd. And there on the slopes of Judah's rolling hills, David, already a lover of the Lord, tended his father's sheep, wrote prayers to God, and sang them to the Lord while playing on his stringed instrument. When concluding a study of David's life, one scholar wrote in a homily entitled *God's Love for Little Boys,* "It is impossible to overestimate the great things which become possible when a young life is surrendered to Almighty God."[6]

And where did such a soft heart for God in a little boy come from? Of course, it began in the sovereign plan of God. But look also at David's spiritual family tree:

> Salmon [who married Rahab] begot Boaz, and
>
> Boaz [who married Ruth] begot Obed;
>
> Obed begot Jesse, and
>
> Jesse begot David (Ruth 4:21-22).

These men and women, husbands and wives, mothers and fathers, and grandmothers and grandfathers were filled with faith and used by God. The Bible doesn't tell us much about David's mother and father, but it does tell us about David's lineage and his love for God at a young age...and his knowledge of God had to come from some faithful, obedient sources.

God works through faithful parents who, in spite of dark and difficult days, walk obediently with Him.

Are you a mom after God's own heart, ready and desirous to be used by God in your children's lives? Then ask God to help you faithfully pass on your faith and trust in God from generation to generation so your little ones might be boys and girls and young men and women after God's own heart. Make it the regular prayer of your heart.

Daniel and his friends—Everyone also loves the incredible tales of Daniel and his three friends— Shadrach, Meshach, and Abed-nego (see Daniel 1–3). These young men—the best of the best—were carried away as captives to Babylon by King Nebuchadnezzar. There they were selected for careful training for the king's service. I say "the best of the best" because to be prepared for royal governmental service these youths had to be handsome, physically perfect, mentally sharp, and socially poised and polished (Daniel 1:4). But did you know that many scholars believe that when the book of Daniel opens, these four friends are teenagers, "children...about fourteen or fifteen years of age"[7] or between 14 and 17?[8]

And who were the parents of Daniel and his friends? No one knows for sure. But here's what we do know. This band of four captives was "of the children of Israel" (verse 3): They were descendants of the patriarch Jacob (also known as Israel). They were also "of the king's descendants" (verse 3). In other words, they were of the family of David. And they were "children of Judah" (verse 6), the most noble tribe of Israel. But whoever their parents were, the actions and choices these young men made shout out a loud testimony and build a strong case that their parental training was extremely strong and godly. In their teen years, when so many youths are tempted to question or turn away from their upbringing, these adolescents did the opposite. In fact, they were willing to make God-honoring decisions and stand up for their faith...even if it meant death.

> From a godly home life and upbringing, a child can learn how to live a godly life in a sinful world.

Now, imagine *your* child at age 14 to 17, being separated from you and having to make such hard choices. What do you think your teen would choose? Or if your child is younger, what do you hope and pray he or she would choose?

Are you getting it, dear mom? (I know I am!) As moms after God's own heart, we must teach, train, and counsel our children every chance we get. God's truth must be imparted. And we need to pray, pray, pray for God to write our faithful teaching of His Word on the tablet of our children's hearts (Proverbs 3:3). For who knows—like Daniel and Company—what hard times and choices will arise for our beloved children?

Timothy—Here's another young man after God's own heart. Most likely in his late teens or early twenties,[9] Timothy was referred to by the apostle Paul as "a true son in the faith" (1 Timothy 1:2). This young man, in time, became Paul's disciple and right-hand man.

How did this happen? And who was Timothy anyway? Here's what we know about his family.

♡ *Timothy's father* was a Gentile and "a Greek" (Acts 16:1) and not a believer in Jesus Christ.

♡ *Timothy's grandmother, Lois,* was a Jewess who knew and understood the Old Testament well enough to respond to the gospel of Christ when Paul and Barnabas came into her town (Acts 14:6-7,21-22).

♡ *Timothy's mother, Eunice,* was "a Jewish woman who believed" (Acts 16:1) and joined her mother Lois in embracing Christ as her Savior.

♡   *Of Eunice and Lois,* Paul wrote to Timothy, "I call to remembrance the genuine faith that is in you, which dwelt first in your grandmother Lois and your mother Eunice, and I am persuaded is in you also" (2 Timothy 1:5).

So how does a Timothy come about? From what furnace is such a godly young man forged? Certainly and foremost, from God. And, additionally, from the hearts and prayers of godly relatives. In Timothy's case, it was two godly female relatives—a devout mother and grandmother. Even though his father was not a believer in Christ, God provided the boy Timothy with a faithful female spiritual tag-team. And they provided the seed and cultivated the soil where his faith in Christ could take root and bloom and grow.

Do you need encouragement? Take these words to heart—"Despite division within the home, Timothy's mother instilled in him a character of faithfulness that carried into adulthood....Don't hide your light at home: Our families are fertile fields for receiving gospel seeds. It is the most difficult land to work, but it yields the greatest harvests. Let your [children]...know of your faith in Jesus."[10]

Mary—Here's a young woman after God's own heart. Mary, the mother of our Lord, was only about 14 years old when she "found favor with God" (Luke 1:30). She was chosen to be the human vessel for physically bringing the Son of Man into the world. Was she a woman of nobility, wealth, or education? No. Was she married to someone important? No. In fact, she wasn't married at all.

Well, what was she then? What qualified Mary to be so blessed and honored...and trusted...by God? It was the focus of her heart. You see, Mary was a woman—albeit a young one—after God's own heart. We hear Mary's heart for God in these two instances:

> *Mary's response to God*—When told the mysterious thing that was about to happen to her—about the details of Jesus' birth—Mary replied, "Behold the maidservant of the Lord! Let it be to me according to your word" (Luke 1:38).

> *Mary's response in praise*—Mary's son Jesus said, "Out of the abundance of the heart the mouth speaks" (Matthew 12:34). And that's exactly what we hear in "Mary's Magnificat" or canticle (Luke 1:46-55). Out of her tender young heart tumbled God's own Word. Drawing from the words of the prayers, the law, the psalms, and the prophets of the Bible, which Mary knew by heart, her lips leaked her heart's content. Her heart, soul, and mind were saturated with God's truth.

The role of godly parents is to make sure the hearts and minds of their children are saturated with the Word of God.

How could this be? How can such a thing happen to—and be true of—a mere teenage girl? We know it was God's doing…and God's choice. He, the Sovereign One, found favor in and graced the young Mary and blessed her among women (Luke 1:42).

And who were her parents? We don't know. But we do know culturally that as a female, Mary was taught, encouraged, instructed, and educated in the Scriptures mostly at home. *Someone* at home made sure Mary knew about God.

——— *Heart Response* ———

Are you inspired? Encouraged? Thirsty to live out God's plan for you as a mom? Doing things God's way is always a matter of the heart. That includes choosing to focus your heart on raising your children God's way and praying with each breath that they will develop hearts after God.

Dear mom, no matter what your situation at home is— whether your children believe in Jesus Christ or not, whether they are young or older, whether their dad is a Christian or not (whether there is a dad or not!), whether you are new in the faith or know a lot, whether years of ignorance or neglect of God's Word have gone by up to this point—do your best. From this second on, give your best efforts.

And since you want your children to love God and follow Him, set the focus of your heart on God and let them see you love Him and follow Him. Just be a mom after God's own heart. He'll help you take care of everything else that goes with parenting.

From a Dad's Heart

Hi, this is Jim George, Elizabeth's husband and the father of our two grown daughters, who are now in the throes of trying to raise their seven little ones to be children after God's own heart. Throughout this book I'll be picking up my pen to add my thoughts and advice about what it means to be a mom after God's own heart who is seeking to raise children with a heart for God. My goal is...

♡ to encourage you in your efforts. Christian parenting is hard work! But keep in mind that you are fulfilling one of God's highest callings upon your life—to raise your children to love and serve Jesus Christ.

♡ to provide a dad's and husband's perspective on this serious matter of training up children for God's purposes. Your husband may or may not be vitally involved in this day-in, day-out process. Or he may

be a man whose job takes him
away from home more than
either of you likes (as was the
case for Elizabeth and me). And
your husband is probably a very
busy man as he provides financially for you and the kids.

Each of these reality scenarios puts added
pressure on you. But hopefully I will be bringing you fresh insights on the importance of
your role and responsibilities as a mom. I'll also
be offering you some help along the lines of
communicating with your husband about family
matters. I'll present tips and principles that will
benefit you as a parent. And, if your husband is
interested in what you are doing and reading,
you can share this section—or any part of this
book, for that matter—with him.

As you know, parenting is a challenge. But
everything of value is that way, and no one and
no pursuit should be more important to you
than your family—except God. So remember
the apostle Paul's words to your heart...

Be steadfast, immovable, always
abounding in the work of the
Lord, knowing that your labor is
not in vain in the Lord (1 Corinthians 15:58).

Whatever effort, hardships, sacrifices, or inconveniences being a parent requires of you, your hard work is *never* in vain in the Lord.

Now prayerfully consider Elizabeth's "Little Choices that Reap Big Blessings"—choices that will help you be the mom after God's heart you desire to be.

_Little Choices That Reap Big Blessings

1. Develop a template for your weeks.

What does your average week look like? What patterns do your days fall into? And what do you want your week to look like? Or what must your week look like to accomplish (with God's help) the raising of children with a heart for God? A week is a fairly little increment of your life. But because it's repeated again and again, it's a mighty thing.

Fine-tune what's already going on in your home so you are truly putting first things first. Mastermind a schedule that allows time for both you and your children to have a daily Bible or Bible-story time (depending on their ages).

Also plan in time for getting ready to go to church (clothes, Bibles, any preparations) so no one is stressed out by the time you all get there. Then plan your church day. Fill it with loads of fun, and of course, like a good mom, plan lots of food!

2. Analyze your TV time.

(And this goes for your kids' TV time too.) Do you know exactly how much time you, "a mom after

God's own heart" (and your "children after God's own heart"), are watching TV? Chart or record it for a while if you like. Then think about how you could use that time to grow in your knowledge of God, to put better things into your heart and mind, to pray for your family to follow God.

How did the young woman Mary come to know the scriptures that became the heart of her prayer of praise? How did Hannah manage to pour life-changing religious teaching into her little boy before he was three years old? How did the young lad David find the time to meditate on God's nature, write his worshipful poetry, and offer it up to God in song? We know the obvious answers, don't we? (And it has nothing to do with TV—and everything to do with time!) These acts of devotion occurred because there was *time* for them to occur. There was also a passionate heart-desire to see them occur. These faithful believers were fiercely intent on knowing God.

Dear mom, with the TV off (or at least on less), these activities that shape both heart and soul—of both mother and child—are more likely to happen.

3. Choose a devotional book.

A mom after God's own heart feeds her soul, but she's also intent on feeding the souls of her children. Select a devotional book for yourself, and one that's age-appropriate for each child. Then set aside a special time each day for enjoying these books. They will soon become treasures. If your children can read, have them read their books to you. If your children are older, have them tell you what they're learning. And be sure you share how you're growing too. Lead the way to God's heart!

4. Memorize one verse.

Hannah knew God's Word. Mary knew God's Word. Daniel and his friends knew God's Word. Timothy's mother and grandmother (and Timothy too) knew God's Word. And David sang God's Word. (Are you noting the common denominator in these moms and children after God's own heart?) Choose a verse to memorize this week. Don't know where to begin? Then memorize Luke 10:27, Acts 13:22, or Colossians 3:2. Each one is a verse about the heart.

And pick verses for your children. Again, be sure they are age-appropriate. Even an 18-month-old can remember "God is love" (1 John 4:8) and "Be kind to one another" (Ephesians 4:32). Then see how creative you can be at celebrating each verse learned by heart. What fun!

5. Pray for your heart.

Being a mom after God's own heart and raising children after God's own heart is "a matter of the heart"—*your* heart. So pray, dear one, for your heart. Give it to God. And give it to Him each fresh new morning as it arrives with fresh new challenges. Open your heart up fully to Him. Dedicate it to God (Luke 10:27). Cleanse and purify it through prayer (James 4:8). Then pray from the heart for your dear precious offspring as only you, their mom, can.

TRAINING CHILDREN FOR GOD...
FOR GOD...
AND FOR LIFE

Ten Ways to Love Your Children

1

*T*ake Time to Nurture Your Heart

*And these words
which I command you today
shall be in your heart.*

DEUTERONOMY 6:6

God has blessed Jim and me with two wonderful daughters—Katherine and Courtney—who, to date, have been married 10 and 11 years respectively. And now they are seeking to be moms after God's own heart to the seven little ones they have between them. As they continually tell me, "Mom, it's payback time. For everything we dished out to you, we're getting it right back!"

When Courtney was expecting one of her children, our church in Washington hosted a baby shower for her, and our pastor's wife asked me to share a devotional during the party. It was then, when I sat down to prepare something for the shower talk, that I wrote out a brief bare-bones list I entitled "Ten Ways to Love Your Children." Believe me, it was a soul-searching exercise to go cover to cover through my Bible and look back at my own attempts at child-raising. And it was a lot of fun at the shower to pass my list on to the other mothers and grandmothers, who were at every age and stage in the parenting process.

Then several years later, my list of ten child-raising principles made its way into one of my books as I wrote about being a mom in a particular chapter.[1] And in time, as I began to speak and share these parenting practices and interact with more and more moms and grandmoms, God planted a desire in my heart to expand them into a book to (I hope and pray!) help moms like you.

So here they are—ten ways to be a mom after God's own heart, also known as "Ten Ways to Love Your Children." As we go along, I want to ask you to do three things. First, please pray. And second, please open your heart to the scriptures presented in this book. They are God's instruction for mothers—from His heart to ours. Third, if you want to know more about being a mom after God's own heart, the additional questions in the Growth and Study Guide book[2] will take you through even more of what God has to say on this vital subject.

> *Prayer is the only way of becoming the mom God wants you to be.*

Dear reader, the Holy Spirit will use and empower God's Word to teach you and transform you into a mom after God's own heart. After all, your heart is where raising a child after God's own heart begins. So obviously, the first way to love your children is to take time to nurture your heart.

It's All About Your Heart

Imagine this scene. God's people have at last arrived at the borders of the Promised Land, "a land flowing with milk and honey" (Deuteronomy 6:3). They are gathered together for a time of preparation and instruction before crossing the Jordan River to enter their new homeland. It was then and there that their faithful leader Moses gave them a second recitation and review of the law of God.

At the core of Moses' heart was a concern for the generations to come—generations who were not present when God initially gave His law to His people. Moses knew it was critical that those present pass on their knowledge of God's law and the history of His dealings with the Israelites to their children. Hear now Moses' words—and his heart—from Deuteronomy 6:4-12. They contain major instructions to us as parents today.

> 4 Hear, O Israel: The LORD our God, the LORD is one!
>
> 5 You shall love the LORD your God with all your heart, with all your soul, and with all your strength.

6 And these words which I command you today shall be in your heart.

7 You shall teach them diligently to your children, and shall talk of them when you sit in your house, when you walk by the way, when you lie down, and when you rise up.

8 You shall bind them as a sign on your hand, and they shall be as frontlets between your eyes.

9 You shall write them on the doorposts of your house and on your gates.

12 ...lest you forget the LORD.

Did you notice how many times God used the words "you" and "your" in these verses that make up a call from God to a total commitment to Him? Be sure and count them for yourself, but after several tries, I came up with 21 times. Twenty-one! These repeated personal pronouns make it obvious that God's message to your heart is that you are to center your life on the Lord. In other words, being a woman—and a mom—after God's own heart is all about *you* and *your heart*. (I hope this is sounding a little familiar!)

A quick walk-through of these verses reveals what God has in mind for His moms...and for you.

Verse 4—"Hear, O Israel: The LORD our God, the LORD is one!" These words began the *Shema,* the Jewish "confession of faith" in the one and only true God. "It is the heart principle of all the covenant stipulations."[3] Today—

as it was then—there are those who put their trust in different "gods." Exactly where is your trust? Your heart? Your commitment? I hope it's to the God of the Bible!

Verse 5—"You shall love the LORD your God." Here God calls you to love Him with an unreserved, whole-hearted commitment of love, a love that includes "*all* your heart...*all* your soul and...*all* your strength." This love is to be an entire, all-consuming "sacred fire"[4] that causes all of your life to reach toward God.

Verse 6—Why is it important that "these words" that make up a part of the law of God be in a mother's heart? Because God knows that when His Word and teachings reside in a person's heart, that person can then think upon them, meditate on them, understand them...and obey them, which is the end-result desired of every person (and mom!) after God's own heart.

Verse 7—Once God's Word and instructions are in your heart, you can then pass them on and "teach them diligently to your children." You can place God and His Scriptures at the heart of the conversations in your home and throughout each day as you "talk of them when you sit in your house, when you walk by the way, when you lie down, and when you rise up."

Verse 8—The instruction of this verse is saying that it's good to be actively meditating on the commandments of God at all times. You can never forget or get away from something that is as near to you as a "sign on your hand" and "between your eyes."

Verse 9—You are to do whatever it takes to make the Scriptures familiar to your heart and to your children... even if it means you "write them on the doorposts of your house and on your gates."

Verse 12—Why all of this attention to having your heart filled with God's instructions and purposefully passing it on to your children? God said through Moses it is "lest you forget the LORD." God forbid that we or our children—our "heritage from the LORD" and His "reward" (Psalm 127:3)—should forget the Lord! God's Word in your heart will keep you from forgetting God—from forgetting your dependence upon Him, from forgetting your need of Him, and from forgetting your obligations to Him and to your children.

Taking Care of Business

Dear mom, are you hearing God's message? Before we can even get to mothering and training our dear precious children, we need to take care of business with God. We need to take care of our own hearts. We need to take time to nurture our hearts. You see, *we* are to love the Lord. And *we* are to love and obey His Word. His Word is to reside in *our* hearts. It really is all about us as moms and our hearts.

And what will happen (by God's grace) if our hearts are dedicated to God? What will happen if our hearts are filled with love for the Lord and with His instruction? We will be godly mothers. And then...*then!*...we can more successfully teach God's Word to our children. Complete devotion to the Lord must first be in the heart of the mother—in your heart and my heart. And then our godly training of our children and our diligent teaching of God's Word will follow.

I like the way one scholar summed up Deuteronomy 6:4-9 for us: "We are to love God, think constantly about his commandments, teach his commandments to our children, and live each day by the guidelines in his Word."[5]

> *The prerequisite for teaching your children about God successfully is that you love God completely.*

Let the Transformation Begin!

My girls are 13 months apart, which means that during their at-home years, I often felt like I had twins! So I had to really be on my toes because there would be little-or-no catching of the mistakes I made on the first child so they weren't repeated on the second one. What I was—or wasn't—doing to love and raise my children was being done to both of them at the same time.

So early on I realized the importance of getting God's powerful Word into my heart each day. I tasted the powerful effect it had on my parenting and on the atmosphere in our home. And the same is true for you. What happens to us moms when we don't take time to nurture our hearts? Here's my list. I found myself...

...running on empty. And when we're spiritually running on empty, our hearts are hollow and numb. Without spiritual refueling, our parenting is empty and the evidences of our apathy creep into our children's lives. All becomes dull and devoid of spiritual energy, purpose, motivation, and accomplishment in both parent and child.

...heartless. If we are heartless, our parenting becomes heartless and rote. We unconsciously put ourselves and our child-raising on autopilot. We find ourselves giving in and giving up the fight for godly standards and behavior. We begin putting up with things the way they are. We fail to make the effort to see that we live out God's calling to be moms after Him. We fail to make sure our children's hearts are being continually molded heavenward.

...worldly. If we are preoccupied with the things of this world and enamored by earthly pursuits and rewards, our parenting will be worldly. We won't be following God's criteria and God's ways. We'll be walking and parenting in the ways of the world. We'll slip up on holding the line on conduct and choices and discipline. The things of this world will creep into our homes and into our children's hearts.

...carnal or unspiritual. If we are fulfilling the lust of the flesh instead of walking in the Spirit (Galatians 5:16), our parenting will show it. As Paul points out, "the works of the flesh are *evident*" (verse 19). There will be screaming, yelling, belittling, name-calling, maybe even the slapping or shaking or pushing of children around.

This is all serious stuff...all brought about because the goodness of God's Word is not regularly refreshing and reminding us of Christ's better ways. God's solution? Pick up the Bible and read it. When we do, God touches and transforms our hearts into those of moms after His heart.

Strength for Each Stretching Day

Recently my Courtney had Baby #4, our beautiful little Grace. Jim and I were there at Courtney's home in Connecticut on baby-watch duty when she and Paul left in the middle of the night for the hospital. We stayed about ten days afterward to help out and ease the usual adjustments of a busy household to a new baby.

I carry one very special memory with me... Each day at breakfast Courtney sat and ate with (and tended to) her five-, four-, and two-year-olds, and Jim and me. (In case it hasn't sunk in yet, that's six people for breakfast...not to mention a baby in a bassinet!) Beside her place mat was her beat-up, well-worn *One Year Bible*.[6] And later, after the dishes were cleared away, the kitchen cleaned up, faces and hands wiped, and the little ones sent on to their next activities, Courtney sat down again at the breakfast table, by herself, with a large glass of water...and read her Bible.

Now I ask you, how does a mom handle each stretching day? How does she manage, in a God-pleasing way, her marriage, her housework, the first baby, the second baby, the third baby, and the fourth baby...all of whom quickly become active toddlers and preschoolers? Answer: She looks to God's empowering—and peace-producing!—Word. And doing so makes a difference—a huge difference!

> *The degree of our spiritual strength will be in direct proportion to the time we spend in God's Word.*

I don't know how other mothers manage to fit in their daily Bible time, but this is how one mom does it as near to every day as she can. It's a powerful habit every mom can build into her life.

Heart Response

What does it take to read through the *One Year Bible*—or any Bible? It takes about 10 to 12 minutes a day. That's roughly the same time as a quick internet session. That's one-half of a good conversation on the phone with your sister, mom, or best friend. That's one-third of a sitcom on TV. That's one-sixth of a television talk show.

But with an earnest, hungry heart, you rise up from those dozen minutes in the Word filled. You are enthused (from *entheos,* meaning *inspired in* or *from God*) instead of heartless and apathetic. You have set aside worldliness and instead set your mind and heart on things above "where Christ is, sitting at the right hand of God...not on things on the earth" (Colossians 3:1-2). And God's spiritual "fruit of the Spirit"—His "love, joy, peace, longsuffering, kindness, goodness, faithfulness, gentleness, self-control" (Galatians 5:22-23)—is evident.

For top performance, refuel daily from God's Word.

Remember, God's Word makes all the difference in the world in your heart, in your day, and in your parenting. This handful of minutes is such a tiny investment to make in something that produces such massive daily—and eternal—dividends!

The excellent and godly mother in Proverbs 31:10-31 rose up each day to tend to the fire of the house (verse 15)...and to the "sacred fire" of her heart (verse 30). Won't you do the same? It's a little choice that will reap big benefits...both in your heart and in the hearts of your children. It will accelerate you down the path to being a more dedicated mother after God's own heart.

From a Dad's Heart

I think you can see the foundational importance of this chapter when it comes to being a mom after God's own heart. You cannot effectively impart to your children what you do not possess yourself. And what better possession is there to pass on to your children than your own heart and passion for God?

And you can make a difference even if your husband isn't a Christian! No matter how little support you receive from him, you can still mark your children for life and eternity. Why can I confidently say this? Because my mother did just that in my life. My father was not a Christian, nor was he interested in spiritual things. But my mother faithfully instilled God's principles into my life.

I can still picture my mom with her open Bible on the kitchen table. Each day she would sit down for a few minutes between her duties and read, study, and pray. And she always talked to me about what she was reading, even up until our last talk here on earth several years ago. She also read Bible stories to me when I was a little boy underfoot. It was during one of these casual talk-times that she introduced me to Jesus Christ as Savior. She took me to church several times a week. It wasn't easy, but she passed on to me what was most precious to her—a love for Jesus.

If you are reading this book and, like my mother, are having to do most, if not all, of the spiritual training of your children by yourself, don't be discouraged. And also don't use your difficult situation as an excuse. Raising your children is too important an assignment from God. Make sure you are growing spiritually yourself, so that you can be a spiritual model for your children.

Or, if you are reading along and your husband is involved in the spiritual training of your children, be sure you don't let or expect him to do it all. Your children need not only a dad after God's own heart, but they also need a mom after God's own heart. You can never give your kids too much spiritual input. Let them know how important God is to you.

My life is a living testimony to a mom who took the time to nurture her heart. And with an abundant love for Jesus overflowing from her heart, she nurtured my heart, so that today and any day I have an opportunity, I rise up and call her blessed (Proverbs 31:28).

Little Choices That Reap Big Blessings

1. Read your Bible every day.

When you do, you'll hear God's voice and His personal and direct instructions to you. The Bible is the ultimate book on parenting, and as you look to it for help, you'll find the words of Isaiah 30:21 to be true: "This is the way, walk in it." God's Word will guide you each step of the way through each day.

Is your husband gone a lot (or unreachable when a crisis occurs)? Or is he by choice uninvolved in the Child-Raising Department? Or too busy? Every mother experiences one—or all—of these scenarios at some time in her mothering career. But when they occur, God's sure, faithful, error-proof Word of instruction is always there to help you know exactly what to do. Just read it—even for ten minutes a day—and your knowledge will multiply so rapidly you'll surprise yourself by how quickly and thoroughly you learn to handle mothering God's way!

(To help you with this little choice that reaps the biggest of all blessings, I've included a "Quiet Times Calendar" in the back of your book for marking the days you read your Bible. You'll be

encouraged as you look it over and see all the
boxes you've marked.)

2. Learn from the parents in the Bible.

As you read your Bible, you'll find examples of
parents and parenting methods—both good (for
instance, Hannah and Mary and Joseph) and bad
(Eli and Isaac and Rebekah). Through them you
can learn what to do...and what not to do...as a
mom and a parent. Try to jot down what you are
learning in the form of a principle. (For example,
regarding Isaac and Rebekah, the principle could
be simply stated, "Never show favoritism.") These
biblical principles will guide you through the
years.

3. Start saying *no*.

God's Word empowers you when you read it and
gives you the strength you need to be a loving-
but-firm parent. It's tough to stand up to pressure
and say *no* to the world, to others, to your child.
It's also hard to say *no* to yourself and your flesh
and get up early, stay up late, and go into action
in the middle of the night when there's a need (all
of which are required of a mom!). That's when
strength is absolutely necessary—spiritual, mental,
emotional, and physical strength.

Dear faithful mom, God's strength comes to your
rescue at just such times to energize you to
follow-through on whatever you must do to
follow His will. All of your parenting will benefit

from the strength you draw from God to say *no* to what does not honor Him or benefit your children.

4. Cherish the good times.

Faithful parenting is challenging work. But it is truly a "labor of love" and certainly a choice that reaps the greatest blessings of all to a mom's heart.

And I admit, sometimes it seems like you'll never get a break, that you'll never make it, that you're going to lose it, that there is no hope and no end in sight, that things seem to be getting worse instead of better. That's why you need to take notice of those peaceful, idyllic pockets and moments of joy and goodness that happen along during your days. You know, those times when all things are well, when things are going the way you—and the Lord—want them to go, when the children are charming, delightful, cheerful, and loving.

Thank God profusely for these good times. Cherish them in your heart-of-hearts. Enjoy them to the hilt. And remember them forever by recording them in a special notebook, album, or memory book. Doing so will give you something to return to over and over again when you need to see some light and remember some good times. Remembering the good times will keep you going for days on end when you are tempted to wonder if being a mom is worth the struggle. Recalling them will turn your heart into a fountain of joy...which, in turn, will refresh your days and your commitment to God's job assignment to you to "train up" your children for Him.

5. Refuse to give up.

Burn this "little choice" into your heart, mind, and muscles! Even when there's no one else—no husband, mother or mother-in-law, sisters, support group, friends, or mentors—to help you or tell you that you are doing the right thing, that you are doing a good job, God shouts forth His "Well done, good and faithful mom" through His Word (Matthew 25:21). When you take time to nurture your heart in God's Word, you receive—directly from God!—the encouragement you need to keep on keeping on in your parenting.

2

Teach Your Children God's Word

And these words
which I command you today
shall be in your heart.
You shall teach them diligently
to your children.

DEUTERONOMY 6:6-7

Oh, the joy of having a baby! At last, someone to love, to sing lullabies to, to share nursery songs and rhymes with, someone to whom you want to teach everything you know. And what a thrill it is to one day hear a little voice singing, reciting, and reading to you!

I grew up with two brilliant and dedicated school-teachers as parents. My dad taught vocational education, and my mother was an English teacher. She was a great and enthusiastic mom, especially when it came to reading to her children. She read...and read...and read(!) to me and my three brothers. And throughout the day she was forever bursting forth with some part of a memorized poem or rhyme. So you can probably guess what I began doing when I became a mom of two little girls. I started reading Mother Goose to them and singing classic little children's songs to and with them.

The Starting Point for a Mom After God's Heart

Then, miracle of miracles, by God's great grace, I became a Christian! After 28 years of floundering in my personal life and trying everything that came down the pike (whether it was the fad-of-the-day, philosophy, psychology, Eastern religions, or self-realization), I heard the gospel of Jesus Christ...and God graciously opened my heart to believe in Him.

In the split-second it took me to think-pray-respond-and-say, "Hey, I believe this!" I was a new creature in Christ (2 Corinthians 5:17). I was born again (John 3:3)! God gave me a new heart and a new life, the kind only He can give! And that split-second of placing my trust— and heart and life—in Jesus was the beginning, the starting point, of every mom after God's own heart, including you, dear reading mom.

And my life changed as God began His transforming work...which meant things changed for my children too. First of all, I purchased a Bible. And I dove into it and devoured it! I was starving to death...and oh-so-thirsty! My life until then had been helpless, hopeless, and purposeless. And God came to my rescue and put me on sure footing. I felt like David must have when he wrote that God "brought me up out of a horrible pit, out of the miry clay, and set my feet upon a rock, and established my steps" (Psalm 40:2). So I read...and I read...and I read my new Bible—over and over and year after year. I marked in it. I memorized parts of it. And I studied through it.

A second thing that happened to me as a new "mom after God's heart" was I began to teach my little ones about God too. That's because of Deuteronomy 6:4-12. This passage marked my mothering for life! We spent the previous chapter on these verses, but for our purposes here, I want to point us specifically to verse seven:

> *The soul of a child is the loveliest flower that grows in the garden of God.*[1]

> You shall teach them diligently to your children, and shall talk of them when you sit in your house, when you walk by the way, when you lie down, and when you rise up.

Through this verse God spoke to my heart about my children's hearts. Through it He gave me my job assignment as a mom after His own heart—He wanted me to be a *teacher* after His heart too! And His message is to you as well. From Deuteronomy 6:7 we learn...

— *Who* is to teach? Every believing parent.

— *Who* are you to teach? Your children.

—*What* are you to teach? God's Word.

—*How* are you to teach? Diligently.

—*When* are you to teach? All day long, every day.

—*Where* are you to teach? At home and everywhere.

As we look at training your children for God and at the importance of teaching God's Word to your children, hopefully you are already centering your life on the Lord and focusing your time and energy on Him. As we agreed, you and I, dear mom, are to love the Lord and His Word. We are to be God's kind of *women,* which will make us God's kind of *moms.* God's instructions to parents begin "and these words which I command you today shall be in *your* heart" (Deuteronomy 6:6). When this is true of our hearts, we can successfully teach the Word of God to our children.

> *He who teaches the Bible is never a scholar; he is always a student.*

Christian Education 101

Do you think you need to have a teaching degree, credentials, or experience in order to do what God asks of His moms in the Bible? Well, good news! You don't! All you need is a heart eager to answer God's call to you in Deuteronomy 6:7. God does not require anything of you but a heart that desires to follow after Him and obey His directive to teach your kids. He expects His moms to perform this important role:

> My son...do not forsake *the law of your mother* (Proverbs 1:8 and 6:20).

> The words of King Lemuel, the utterance which *his mother taught him* (Proverbs 31:1).

In the Bible, teaching almost appears to be the Number One duty of a Christian parent. The Bible instructs, if you love your children, teach them...and the earlier the better. So dear mom, teach your growing young ones...no matter what. Moms tell me all the time, "But my children don't want to have devotions. They don't want to sit and listen to me read the Bible or Bible storybooks to them." And my answer is always the same—"Give your children what they need, not what they want." You're the adult. You know what's best and what wisdom will be needed in the future. You are also in charge as "God's agent." You have a "mandate to act"[2] and to teach. This doesn't mean you shouldn't try to make your teaching enjoyable and interesting. Consult other moms and Sunday school teachers for ideas. And check out books and games to make your teaching time with your children fruitful and fun.

Your faithful teaching of your children gives them a base of information (God's truth) from which they can live their lives God's way. Your instruction equips them to function throughout life with wisdom and helps them avoid many mistakes and heartbreaks. Therefore the wise mom daily makes sure that her children hear the

Who is best taught? He who first learned from his mother.

THE TALMUD

instruction of the law of God, the Word of God.

From the Cradle to the Grave

How early does a mom after God's own heart begin teaching her little one? While researching Deuteronomy 6:7, I found this guideline based on Jewish customs: "The life of a Jew is religious from the cradle to the grave. In the room occupied by the mother and her newborn infant the rabbi puts a paper containing Psalm 121 in Hebrew."[3] This particular psalm is one of powerful assurance that God is our helper, keeper, protector, and preserver throughout all of life.

Imagine the heart, faith, and emotion of the mom who holds her baby and prays Psalm 121 over her newborn—"The LORD is your keeper...your shade at your right hand. ...The LORD shall preserve you from all evil; He shall preserve your soul...your going out and your coming in from this time forth, and even forevermore....He will not allow your foot to be moved; He who keeps you will not slumber...nor sleep" (verses 5-8,3-4).

Here's a moving instance of a mom with a heart for teaching God's Word to her child "from the cradle." I heard about it when I attended a fund-raising luncheon for a crisis pregnancy center. At that gathering, the woman in charge moved us as an audience when she told us about a pregnant unmarried teen who became a Christian through the ministry of this particular center.

The expectant—and forgiven and grateful-to-God mom-to-be began memorizing Bible verses for her own soul...and then started to think about the baby on its way. So she began saying and reciting her verses to her tummy and the little unseen person there.

As her birth date approached, this teen girl (who was growing into a woman after God's own heart) asked for and received permission from the hospital where she would give birth to carry her memory verses into the delivery room. Why did she ask such a thing? Because she wanted the first sound her baby heard to be the Word of God. She wanted to hold the seconds-old infant in her arms and read—teach—aloud God's Word from Minute One, Day One, Word One of that little one's life.

Now, that's a mom after God's own heart! A mom can never begin too early to *teach* God's Word *diligently to her children.*

"Whetting" a Child's Heart

Exactly what does it mean to teach God's commands diligently to your children? Some say this instruction from Deuteronomy 6:7 could read, *"Thou shalt 'whet' them diligently upon thy children."* Spiritually speaking, to "whet" means to frequently repeat God's words to your children, to try any and every way of instilling the Scriptures into their minds and making them pierce into their hearts.

Here's the way it goes. We know that to whet a knife, it is turned first on this side, then on that, and stroked again and again, slowly and systematically, across the sharpening stone. In this same way faithful parents are to carefully and persistently teach the Bible to their children. Their aim is to sharpen them spiritually, to put a godly edge on them.⁴ The repeated efforts of faithful parents will stimulate their children's appetites for the "milk" and, eventually, the "solid food"—meat—of the Word of God (Hebrews 5:12-14 and 1 Peter 2:2).

Yes, but How?

God not only tells us to teach our children, but He is faithful to also tell us *how* and *what* to teach them.

Verbal instruction—First on God's list in Deuteronomy 6 is audible, verbal instruction—"you shall teach them diligently to your children" (verse 7). We'll cover informal verbal instruction in the next chapter when we address what it means to "talk" of God's Word. But for now, I want to focus on the formal and verbal teaching of the Bible to your child.

The curriculum moms are to teach is, first and foremost, the Bible. As the school among the Jews was called "the house of the book,"⁵ so your home must be "the home of the Book." And it helps to have a time that's set aside and scheduled for reading the Bible, a time when some part of the Bible is read out loud. It doesn't matter for how long it's read. Even a few minutes a day will make a powerful impression on your family. You can read from

*Pray, "Great Teacher— God, oh, make Thou me the teacher that I long to be!"*⁶

the books of Psalms or Proverbs, a Gospel (Matthew, Mark, Luke, John), or from any book in the Bible...or even share a portion of a chapter of the Bible. Just be sure you read.

And don't worry about what your children are or are not getting out of your Bible reading times. What they do get is the firsthand experience of seeing your love for the Bible and your wholehearted commitment to God and His Son. They'll realize God's Word is important to you...therefore it will become important to them. They also get to hear the scriptures. And, as the Bible teaches, "faith comes by hearing, and hearing by the word of God" (Romans 10:17). Your family members also receive a familiarity and respect for the Bible that will help them to love and live the Word of God as they age.

Visual instruction—God also points to the importance of visual teaching and reminders. Regarding His commandments, God instructed those in Moses' day to "bind them as a sign on your hand, and they shall be as frontlets between your eyes. You shall write them on the doorposts of your house and on your gates" (Deuteronomy 6:8-9). To obey these instructions, God's people actually wore literal one-inch square boxes on their hands and heads that contained portions of God's law. They also inscribed sentences from the Torah on the lintels and posts of their doors. These were meant to remind them of "the unseen Guest in the house Whose presence should control and hallow all that is said and done in it."[7]

Today we, as New Testament believers, don't need to literally follow these guidelines. That's because God's Word sinks deep into our hearts. It is "written not with ink but by the Spirit of the living God, not on tablets of stone but on tablets of flesh, that is, of the heart" made, not of stone, but of flesh (2 Corinthians 3:3). But still there is a place for visual reminders of God's Word. For instance...

> I've met teenagers who wear a "purity ring" on their wedding band finger to remind them to stay pure until they are married, to "abstain from sexual immorality," and to keep their bodies "in sanctification and honor, not in passion of lust, like [those] who do not know God" (1 Thessalonians 4:3-5).
>
> Other people I know (including adults, teens, and children) wear bracelets with the initials "WWJD" to remind them to always ask the question—in any and every situation—"What Would Jesus Do?"
>
> One mom of a household of teens tacked up a plaque on the doorframe to her kitchen that cited Joshua's declaration of devotion to God in Joshua 24:15: "As for me and my house, we will serve the LORD." She told me, "The members of my family probably pass through the kitchen doorway a hundred times every day. Seeing this verse gives us a

hundred good daily reminders of Whom it is we serve."

Adults and kids alike display plaques, posters, and framed art in their rooms at home, on their computers, and in their work places that feature Bible prayers and verses of Scripture. In our house, I hung a number of scriptures on our walls that I embroidered and framed.

I'm sure you can add to this list of visual instruction and reminders of our Great God, and please do! But what am I saying? Or rather, what is God saying to us as parents, as moms, in Deuteronomy 6:7? By now we know the answer. He is telling us to "teach" His Word and His commands "diligently" to our children—"to drill"[8] them into their hearts and minds.

Heart Response

As a mom, there is no one you love more on this earth than your children (and of course, their dad!). And teaching your children about God and His ways is not optional. God is assigning and authorizing you to teach His Word to your children steadily and purposefully, all day long, everyday at home...and everywhere else. You're a mom on a mission! Therefore, instructing those you love most in the things of the God you love supremely should be—or become—a passion and a pleasure.

And remember, if you begin to wonder how much to teach or waver in your teaching, your children can *never* get enough teaching from the Bible! So set a regular time to instruct your kids in God's Word and His principles. Even if you are getting a late start, start now. If your children are older and wonder, "What happened to Mom?" be bold. Tell them there's been a wonderful change in your heart, and you want to start a little Bible time because it will help them too.

Mom, the particular stage of your life or your kids' lives doesn't matter. Just read! Read God's Word together until it becomes familiar to your boys and girls, until the Bible becomes a cherished friend and a trusted guide. Read it to them until, hopefully, it is written—burned, etched, and recorded—deeply on the tablet of each of their hearts (Proverbs 3:3). A child after God's own heart is shaped and formed as the Word of God becomes embedded into his or her heart, mind, and character. As a poet expresses it,

> Whatever you write on the heart of a child
> No water can wash away.
> The sand may be shifted when billows are wild
> And the efforts of time may decay.
>
> Some stories may perish, some songs be forgot
> But this graven record—time changes it not.
> Whatever you write on the heart of a child...
> Will linger unchangeably there.[9]

From a Dad's Heart

What a wonderful privilege you have as a mom after God's own heart! You are blessed to not only bring your children into the world, but also to bring them up in the nurture and admonition of the Lord! So regardless of where your husband is on the "religion scale," you must do all you can to teach your children about God with the following cautions in mind.

If your husband is not a believer, make sure you are discreet about your teaching. Don't be an in-your-face Christian wife. Also don't purposefully use your children to manipulate your husband into some kind of faith. If the children are excited about what you are teaching them and they naturally share it with their father, let the Holy Spirit do His work through your children's enthusiasm. Otherwise, quietly, behind the scenes, instruct your children in the things of God. You have many opportunities when your husband is not at home or is busy at home. This instruction should include showing loving respect to their dad, whatever he does or doesn't believe about God.

If you do have a believing husband, thank God every day for this man! Your job of teaching becomes a little easier. Most men are busy providing for their families, so they don't always think about the teaching aspect of being a parent. I know Elizabeth was very diligent to assist me in doing my part in training up our girls. She would have the Bible and our daily devotional book at my place at the breakfast table each morning. The next devotional reading was well marked—just in case I had forgotten the place from the day before. She would always structure the early morning so there was time for family devotions before we all went off in a hundred different directions.

Then in the evenings when I was home, Elizabeth would schedule my time with the girls as part of the evening ritual. No pressure. Just simple nonverbal reminders of my responsibility to be part of the "team" of teachers to train up our girls.

Why not sit down with your husband and agree on the part each of you is to play in the exciting role of teaching your children about God? The reward is great! I'm so blessed as I see my daughters now doing many of the same things with their husbands that my wife (and their mom) did with me! And the ultimate reward? My grandchildren are hearing the Word of God not only from their moms but also from their dads.

Little Choices That Reap Big Blessings

1. Read God's Word regularly yourself.

Oh, dear mom! Your personal love of and familiarity with the Scriptures will be a driving force in your desire to share it with your children and in your faithful follow-through on God's calling to do so. When God's Word fills your heart, you won't be able to wait to pass on the most important thing in the world to your little and big ones! As you fall more in love with God's Word, you'll want your children to do the same. So be sure the first little choice on your to-do list each day is your own heart-filling, soul-refreshing, strength-producing time with your Bible. Choose to do it for yourself...and choose to do it for your family.

2. Read from the Bible first.

As a busy mom of a family that runs on a variety of schedules, there's only so much time that can be found for reading together. So when that precious (and scheduled!) time comes around, be sure you treat the Bible as the most important book in the world. After all, it is *The Book!* Even if you read Christian books and literature to your brood, make sure the Bible is treated as the most important book they will ever hear or read. And if you only have time to read from one book, you know what to do—make sure you choose the Bible! Other books, as good and solid and helpful as they may be, are, quite simply, not the Word of God. They are about the Word of God or drawn from the Word of God. Nothing can take the place of the God-breathed, God-inspired, written-by-God-Himself Scriptures (2 Timothy 3:16). They and they alone are quick and powerful and "sharper than any two-edged sword" (Hebrews 4:12). And they and they alone are "profitable for doctrine, for reproof, for correction, for instruction in righteousness, that the man of God may be complete, thoroughly equipped for every good work" (2 Timothy 3:16).

And here's something else—Be sure each of your children has a Bible, no matter what their ages. They can bring it to the table, take it to church, carry it around all day, sleep with it...whether they can read it or not! (What a great baby shower gift!)

And something else—Read the Bible to your kids, no matter what their ages. Remember, even an infant responds to its mother's voice. If you begin early, your child will never know what it's like to not hear the Bible being read out loud.

3. Read Christian books to your family.

Borrow good Christian books that reinforce and illustrate the truths from the Bible. Check them out from your church library or borrow them from friends. Get your hands on anything that is centered on the Bible and appropriate for your children's ages. Every child—even teens—loves to hear about God's "superheroes" of the Bible. And children are mesmerized by rhymed versions of the Bible and its exciting truths. Read these books over and over with your children until they are familiar favorites and their messages become a point of reference for their actions, choices, and character. Make it a point to read them at meals, at snack times, after school, at bedtime. Again, your little—and big ones—can never get enough teaching from and about the Bible. In time, you may even want to build your own library of cherished favorites.

4. Read to everyone.

I urge you, don't leave anyone out! Pay no attention to your children's ages. And if they have friends over, include them too. Just pile the whole kit and caboodle of kids into the room, on the bed, the floor, the couch, or around the table, and read away! One of my favorite pictures of my family is my son-in-law reading to five of our grandchildren on a little toddler bed. All the kids, representing a rainbow of ages, are enveloped into Paul's arms and leaning on one another...and hanging on every word out of his mouth. I call this picture "Paul's Bible Club." He does this every bedtime with his children and is always faithful and happy to include all of the family members whenever we get together.

5. Read from Proverbs.

God states the purpose of the book of Proverbs right up front in chapter one, verse four: "To give...the young man knowledge and discretion." From that point on, Solomon (the writer) addresses "my son" at least 23 times. You see, Solomon wrote the book of Proverbs to teach his child—his young son—wisdom, to instruct him in the disciplines he would need throughout life. So give your children the gift of the proverbs. Give them godly wisdom. How? Read out loud from the proverbs at every opportunity.

3

Talk to Your Children About God

*And these words
which I command you today
shall be in your heart.
You shall...talk of them
when you sit in your house,
when you walk by the way,
when you lie down, and
when you rise up.*

DEUTERONOMY 6:6-7

What does your average day look like? It's very, *very* busy, right? But despite a hectic pace, it also probably falls into some sort of schedule or routine. Most moms' days begin with the sound of an alarm clock...or a crying baby. Then things begin to rock and roll! There are others to wake up, breakfast to fix, people to get settled or out the door and off to work or school, household tasks to take care of, not to mention errands, evening meal preparations, carpooling, extracurricular activities for everyone, home-schooling...and perhaps even your own job.

Well, in the midst of all of the above—and more!—God helps you do two things at the same time. All of the busyness of your personal and family life must be managed and taken care of, but so must teaching your children about our almighty and awesome God. How can a swamped momma fit this assignment into an already brimming and impossible schedule? Well, thank the Lord that He comes to the rescue and prescribes His all-wise solution! He says:

> And these words which I command you today shall be in your heart. You shall...*talk* of them when you sit in your house, when you walk by the way, when you lie down, and when you rise up (Deuteronomy 6:6-7).

God doesn't ask or require that you have any special giftedness, training, degrees, or abilities to further instruct your children in the things of God. No, regardless of your background, upbringing, or education, you can effectively point your little (and big!) ones' hearts toward God. All you have to do is *talk* about Him all day long. Just talk about God in the ebb and flow of the day-in, day-out rhythm of normal (albeit chaotic!) home life. (Now we're talking, because "talking" is something we women excel at. And it's something God is asking us to do for Him and for our children's sakes!)

Speak Up!

God tells us moms clearly and simply what He wants us to do. He says "you shall...*talk* of them." And what is the *them?* "These words which I command you" (verse 6). And who is it you are to talk to? Primarily, your children...and anyone and everyone else who will listen. With these instructions God is asking you and His corps of godly moms to constantly focus all of everyday life on Him and His teachings. And how is this done? It's easy! By *talking* about the things of God with your children *while* you go through the bedlam of each crazy day.

> *It takes dedicated parents to produce consecrated children.*

Again, looking to the Jewish model, we learn that the Hebrews made religion a built-in part of life. And the reason for their success was that religious education was life-oriented, not just information-oriented. They used the context of daily life as opportunities to teach about God and to talk of Him. They purposefully pointed all of life back to God, ingraining God's teachings into their children's hearts.

Do you want your children to love God? Then simply talk about Him. Why talk about God? Because we talk about what's important to us. And when we don't talk about God, we send a loud message to our children that God really isn't that important. So make God a part of your everyday life and chit-chat. Talk about Him and His ways. Talk about His Word and His Son. Talk about the wonder of His creation. This act of talking will make God a part of your children's everyday experiences and conversations.

So take note: God is asking you to commit yourself to teach your children diligently to see Him in all aspects of life, not just those that are church related. Your teaching is to go on no matter where you are physically with your children.

And what will happen? You never know! But here are a few assurances. When you speak of God,

♡ You honor and glorify Him.

♡ You obey His teaching to talk of Him to your children.

♡ You are spiritually uplifted as you voice your heart for God and your knowledge of Him.

♡ Your chances for positively affecting and infecting your family by your communication go sky high!

As I said, you never know what wonderful things will happen as you faithfully obey God, so speak up! It's been reported that the renowned and eloquent preacher Dr. G. Campbell Morgan had four sons who all became ministers. At a family reunion, a friend asked one of the sons, "Which Morgan is the greatest preacher?" While the son directly looked at his famous father, he replied, "Mother." Obviously this man-of-God had a mom-of-God who followed after God's own heart and Deuteronomy 6:6-7...and spoke up.

Dear mom, speak up!

Speak Up Day and Night

God goes on and tells you *when* to speak up and talk to your children. It's to be done "when you sit in your house, when you walk by the way, when you lie down, and when you rise up" (Deuteronomy 6:7).

In other words, as you and your little family sit in your house, while you do your work, when you are relaxing, when you are eating...talk about the Lord. Or when you are resting, or when you tuck in the kids as they lie down at night to sleep, or when someone has a bad dream in the night or is sick...talk about the Lord. And when you first awake to the gift of yet another glorious day God has given...talk about the Lord. Even when you visit or talk with others, when you walk by the way and go through your day, when you run your errands, and when you do your housework...talk about the Lord. Take every occasion as an opportunity to talk with your children about divine things, about the plain and simple truths and laws of God. For instance...

Did you see a rainbow today? Are the seasons changing? Did it snow? Was the sky clear at night, giving you a glimpse of the moon and the stars? Remark with wonder, "Only God can make a rainbow! It's a sign of His goodness!...For everything there is a season!...God's heavens declare the glory of God!"

Are you doling out, checking up on, or praising your kids' work chores? Spout out the teachings of Proverbs and God's work ethic—"There is profit in all labor!...The hand of the diligent will rule!"[1]

Are you fixing a meal together or setting the table with the children? Remind them that God takes care of His own, that He promises to supply all their needs...

forever. Share with them that they will never hunger or thirst and that God promises He will even prepare a table for them in the presence of enemies!

Is everyone under your roof getting along with each other? Whether they are—or aren't—speak constantly of God's instructions to be kind to others, to do to others (including their brothers and sisters!) whatever they would want done to them.

The Bible says the godly (that's you, mom!) are to meditate on the scriptures at all times. And "blessed" is the one (you again!) whose "delight is in the law of the LORD, and in His law he meditates day and night" (Psalm 1:2). And the Bible says you, precious mom after God's own heart, are to talk of Him day and night to your children.

That's the picture in Deuteronomy 6. And that's what God wants to be true of you and your family. What a great way to spend every day of your life—reveling in the God you love and talking about Him all day long with those you love most!

It's Never Too Early...

I was struck to the core as a young mom (...who got a late start on Christian parenting!) when I read a devotional that began with a United Press newspaper release that heralded "the time to start a child on a musical career isn't too far beyond the bootie and bottle age." I read on to discover that a world-famous violin teacher in Japan believed that the earlier a child is exposed to music, the better a musician he will be. Dr. Shinichi Suzuki stated that "just as a child imitates gestures, he can also imitate music." He then prescribed, "For this reason it is extremely important that a child hear *nothing but good music from a very early age.*" Therefore, although Dr. Suzuki likes to start his students in classes between the ages of two and four, he begins exposing them to music even earlier.[2]

And then I thought about my two little ones...who were one-and-a-half and two-and-a-half before I even became a Christian mom. Oh, how I wanted to begin to influence them for Christ right away. And I didn't have a second to lose! I prayed to God that, being a late-bloomer in the Christian Education Department at home, it wouldn't be too late!

I mean, here was a man, a teacher of *music*, saying that "it is extremely important that a child hear *nothing but* good music from a very early age" so that he will mimic only the best! How much more important—no, critical!—it is that our children who come to us from the mind and heart and hand of God hear *nothing but good* in our Christian homes. The apostle Paul wrote concerning Timothy, "that from *childhood* you have known the Holy Scriptures" (2 Timothy 3:15). I pray the same will be true of you and your beloved family. May your children hear and learn about God from childhood!

All of this to say, dear mom, start them early. It's never too early to begin sharing God's words and teachings with your little ones. Go ahead...talk your head off!

...And It's Never Too Late

And, at the same time, it's never too late. Did you know that...

> Ninety-one percent of all 13-year-olds, whether they are exposed to Christian truth or not, pray to God during a typical week?
>
> Most adolescents are involved in religious activity of some sort?
>
> Nine out of 10 young people accept the existence of God, and 91 percent accept the fact that every person has an eternal soul?
>
> More than 4 out of 5 youths want to have a close relationship with God as a cornerstone in their lives?
>
> Two-thirds of American teens are at least somewhat persuaded that the Bible is totally accurate in its teachings.[3]

This survey data reveals that teens—and even college-age young adults—do want to know what to believe and also want to believe what their parents believe.

Dear mom, others—including the enemy!—will be happy to tell you it's too late to begin teaching your older kids about God. But never ever forget that with God nothing is impossible. He will be faithful to honor and bless your faithful obedience to follow His Word.

So determine right this second to begin talking about the things of God "when you sit in your house, when you walk by the way, when you lie down, and when you rise up." Then, hopefully, your little—and big—ones will mimic what they are hearing and learning from your heart and lips about your Lord.

How Important Is God to You?

But there is a core issue. As a mom and grandmom, I ask myself these questions regularly, and now I share them with you: How important is God and His Son to you? And how important is nurturing godly character in your life? Are you emulating God's standards to your family?

An author shared this frightening information: "One survey I read asked parents...which quality they most desired in their children. *Intelligence* topped the list, followed closely by *personality*, then *creativity*, and *imagination*." He then wondered, "What ever happened to trust, love, faith, honesty...? Aren't those the real building blocks for maturity?"[4]

I know this is soul-searching. But go ahead and ask—and answer—the tough questions. Think about what you talk about with your kids. What do you point them toward? (Do you ask "What will others think?" or "What does God desire?") What activities do you reward the most? (Excelling at school or kindness to brothers and sisters?) What achievements thrill you most? (A's or another memorized verse?) What groups do you encourage them to follow? (Being on the pep squad or being faithful to attend their Christian youth group?) What endeavors do you push them to pursue? (Soccer/gymnastics or the Bible programs or clubs at church?) What accomplishments make you happiest? (A good report card or a consistent personal quiet time?)

Don't get me wrong. There is nothing wrong with excelling at school, or being a part of school programs and activities, or participating in sports and physical

Imitate me, just as I also imitate Christ.

1 CORINTHIANS 11:1

activity. But do lay your answers next to the teaching of Deuteronomy 6:6-7. Then pray and make any changes that are needed...right away. Remember, it's not too late for you to change the direction of your emphasis at home. (I'll be sharing my own turnaround story in a little bit.) It's not too late to commit yourself to the priority of teaching God's Word, of talking about Him, of pointing all of life toward Him. Doing so will affect your children's hearts and lives!

Of course we should talk *to* God about our children. That's a given. But we should—and must—also talk to our children *about* God. That's the instruction of Deuteronomy 6:6-7. God expects—and assigns—us to talk to our sons and daughters about God at all times. He asks us as moms to take every opportunity to talk about Him—and also make the instances in life an opportunity to talk about Him and His Son.

Talk about "home" schooling! Many moms today are choosing to school their children at home. In fact, one of my daughters is taking this route with her oldest. But whether you homeschool or not, you are called to "homeschool" your children in the things of the Lord. Home is the best school for teaching the biblical precepts

the Bible teaches and those your family stands for. And
again, you are to teach and to talk of God and His Word
to your kids all day long...every day...as often as you
can...and for as long as you can.

And there's an urgency! In the context of
Deuteronomy 6, God is expressing the absolute importance of His Word to His people through Moses. It was so
important that He instructed His people to do everything
possible to know, keep, and remember His commands.
He wanted them incorporated into everyday life. And He
wanted all parents to pass them
on to the next generation...who
were to pass them on to the
next...and the next...and the
next.

So, you see, now, as well as
then, the spiritual education of
children was the responsibility
of the parents. Sure, others
help. Godly pastors and Sunday-
school teachers and youth lead-
ers and mentors contribute mightily. And Christian
schools partner with you in teaching God's Word and
ways to your children. But *you*, dear mom, as a parent
are the one (along with your husband if he participates
in your passion for Christ) who is called to wholeheartedly embrace God's instruction to teach and talk to your
children about Him...and to faithfully live it out in the
everyday setting of life at home and in the world.

> *Spiritual
> and moral
> principles are
> best conveyed
> in the labora-
> tory of life.*[5]

So, once again, we've come full circle, right back to
your love for God, Mom, haven't we? "*You* shall love the
Lord your God with all *your* heart, with all *your* soul,

and with all *your* strength. And these words which I command you today shall be in *your* heart" (Deuteronomy 6:5-6). That's Step One.

And here is Step Two: "*You* shall teach them diligently to your children...and *[you]* shall talk of them when you sit in your house, when you walk by the way, when you lie down, and when you rise up." And when you do, my precious fellow-mom, you show forth *your* love for God. For as His Son said, "If you love Me, keep My commandments" (John 14:15).

From a Dad's Heart

I can still remember the day Elizabeth learned about the importance of singing hymns and praise songs and talking openly about God with our little girls. She came home from her mom's Bible study and immediately shared it with me. As we began to follow this wise advice and establish this practice, I was amazed to discover that our kids' little minds were sponges. They soaked up everything they came into contact with.

I was also shocked after we became a Christian family to learn that, at one-and-a-half and two-and-a-half, our girls had already missed out on some vital years of Christian training! (As Elizabeth said, it's never too early to begin talking about God.)

But I'm also grateful that by God's grace it's never too late. Even though Elizabeth and I felt we were behind in talking about God, we started where we and the children were. And this is my advice to you too. Don't become immobilized by past mistakes, failures, or inactivity. Thank God for what you are learning now...today. Then with newfound vitality and renewed vigor and excitement for the Lord, start "talking up God." Your enthusiasm can't help but rub off on your family!

And here's another suggestion: If your husband is interested, and the timing is good (that's very important when talking to us guys!), share this chapter with him. A father can contribute much emotionally and physically to the children and to the home. But everything he does around the home *spiritually* seems to get double mileage. When Dad comes home, the children listen. And because he's Dad, they *really* watch what he does and says. So, in your sweet way, try to alert him to the importance of talking about God, talking about Jesus, talking about being a Christian. Ask him to speak up. Believe me, it will make a lasting impression on the kids!

Sometimes it's hard for a guy to think of something spiritual to say. (That was me!) So one of the ways I became involved with the everyday Christian "talk" around our house was to help the girls memorize their verses for their church programs. I did this for more than a decade. Every day the girls and I would attempt to say "our" memory verses to each other. That would get us talking and sharing about what the verses meant and how each one could apply the verses in her personal life and at home and at school.

And here's another thing I did. I said earlier that I began to lead devotions each morning. And many times the daily devotional would spark a lively conversation at the breakfast table too. And there were also times when we would continue the discussion at dinner.

Even if your husband is one of those "stay silent type" guys, ask him to assist you spiritually when he is home. Ask him to simply talk about God to the children. Just maybe after he talks about God around the house, his faith will be strengthened and he'll want to go to work and talk about God there too!

Little Choices
That Reap
Big Blessings

1. Ask God to help you be more aware of Him.

In Deuteronomy, God begins with your heart, mom. He then moves to your calling to pass your heart for God along to your boys and girls. Ask Him for His help in making you more aware of Him—of His goodness, of His creation, of His love for you. If you want your children to follow God, make God a part of *your* everyday experiences.

2. Purpose to talk about the Lord.

Create an environment and a schedule or routine for teaching your children about God and the principles of Scripture. But go the next step and purpose to intentionally talk about God. One thing that has helped me as a mom (and as a Christian) has been trying to begin my sentences with the word "God" or with "the Lord." If you do this, you'll most definitely be talking of the Lord and relating all of life to Him.

3. Examine your daily routine for opportunities.

How do your waking-up hours go each morning? And how can you introduce and interject God into that portion of the day? And how do things generally flow when others are leaving the house in the morning for school or work? What could you do to leave them with some reminder of God? In our routine, we had a prayer circle at the front door every day when the first member of our family left for the day...followed by a group hug.

Are any little ones at home during the day? How can God be the center of their at-home time? You could have verses for them to memorize and illustrate with crayons or markers. Another option is to have a CD of children's hymns that can play in the background all day. Keep a plethora of Christian children's books lying all over the place (even if they come from the church library). Do you play videos or DVDs in your home? If so, do you have a storehouse of Christian videos to further fill their minds with teaching about God?

Are your children going off to public school? Oh, then you *must* send them off with some reminder of God. Send them into the world with a 3″ x 5″ card or a sticker or a bookmark or a verse in their lunch. And don't forget to pause and pray with them in the car as you drop them off. Then, when you pick them up after school or they come through the front door ask, "How did God bless your day?"

4. Center on God at mealtime.

Examine your mealtimes. Are you praying and saying "grace" and asking your children to participate in the praying? A word of caution: Do be sensitive to your husband's desires. If he is not a Christian, don't push this issue. Just be sure you pray with your children of all ages at mealtime and snack time when your husband is not present.

5. End the day with God.

And how about the evenings? Again, be aware of your husband's desires for the nightly routine when he's there. But you can still have a quiet little individual talk with each of your loved ones, even your teens, when they go to bed. Remind them of a memory verse or truth about God. I especially loved ending each little bedtime talk with "Jesus loves you, and so do I." And today, I'm doing the same things with our next little generation!

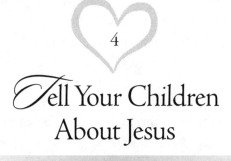

4

*T*ell Your Children About Jesus

We are ambassadors for Christ,
as though God were pleading through us.

2 CORINTHIANS 5:20

'm looking at the cover of a book that's lying here on my desk as I write. It pictures a large archery target with an arrow imbedded in the target's bull's eye. The book addresses a different subject than we're focusing on in our book. But the graphics of the target, arrow, and bull's eye hit the mark when it comes to depicting the message of this chapter. It's right on! There are many "things" we moms must do to love our children. In fact, we're addressing ten of them in this book. But *the* most important one—"the bull's eye"—is that we must tell them about Jesus!

87

Aim for Your Child's Heart

First, there's the target. I know you live a multilayered life. I also know it's filled with the challenge of multitasking during every waking minute of every day! Your list of responsibilities is long. And so is the list of people you must care for. Truly, the number of hats you regularly wear is staggering!

But somewhere in the midst of all you do, want to do, and need to do, there should be this aim: to educate and introduce each of your children to Jesus Christ. You can't "save" them. Only God can do that. That's His job. But your job is to instruct young hearts in the truth about Jesus and His importance in their lives. You need to do everything imaginable to make them aware of God's Son and His message of salvation.

I'll go a step further and say, *You must see telling your kids about Jesus as your Number One priority and purpose in life as a mom.* Of course you're going to love them, feed them, and pray for them. But as a Christian mother who's been saved by Christ's sacrifice and God's grace, you are to be a full-fledged "ambassador for Christ" (2 Corinthians 5:20). You are a representative of Christ to your children, a spokesperson for God. And what is the message you are to bring to them? It's the same message Paul was sent to deliver in 2 Corinthians 5—"We implore you on Christ's behalf, be reconciled to God" (verse 20).

Here's a thought-provoking question: What do you consider to be the target of all that you do for your kids? What is the purpose and aim of your parenting? Take a look at your life and your priorities. What are you intent on teaching your children? How to tie their shoelaces?

Techniques in brushing and flossing? Good manners? How to catch, kick, or hit a ball? How to make an A? How to play an instrument? Respect for others and for property? The list could go on and on. But as good and as necessary as these issues and activities are in your kids' lives, what you must be asking your heart is, Am I making sure I tell them about Jesus? Until you and I wake up every single morning and know without doubt that "Today, if I don't get anything else done, I must teach my children about my Lord Jesus," we are aiming at the wrong target. So take aim!

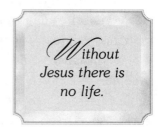

Without Jesus there is no life.

Directing the Truths About Jesus

Next come the arrows. What are the piercing arrows we want to sink into little hearts?

Obviously, they are the Scriptures. The truth. The Word of God. The Bible. And especially the Bible's account and stories about Jesus' life. Teach your children about Jesus—His miracles, His teachings, His birth, death, and resurrection, His interactions with His Father and His disciples, His goodness, His perfect, sinless life.

And what is the best way to accomplish this goal? It's simple! Read out loud to your children daily from the four Gospels—Matthew, Mark, Luke, and John. Have your kids share in the reading if they can. Also have them write out and memorize key verses such as, "Jesus said to him, 'I am the way, the truth, and the life. No one comes to the Father except through Me'" (John 14:6).

Even if your three-year-old can only scrawl out a few letters of the alphabet, have those letters be J-E-S-U-S. (And, of course, Step 2 could be "Jesus loves me.")

Also have your family work puzzles and anagrams. Encourage them to write letters and prayers to Jesus about what they are learning. Start a Jesus scrapbook. Set up a time for them to draw or color pictures of the stories you are reading to them about Jesus. Create a full-on craft time aimed at illustrating the day's story and truth.

For instance, this Christmas when our family got together, our focus was on the Christmas story in the Bible. To reinforce our emphasis I had purchased five sticker sheets (one for each little person) with stickers of the figures in the nativity scene. So one day our "craft for the day" was to use the stickers to recreate the Christmas story on a piece of construction paper.

You can well imagine the hodgepodge of places where Baby Jesus, the donkeys, camels, shepherds, and wise men ended up! And God's star did not always "appear" in the upper half of the paper. But this fun time served to reinforce the Bible's account of God sending His Son to live—and die—for us. What a joy to see five little minds and ten little hands (and, I pray, five little hearts!) handling each person and animal that had a part in Jesus' advent! And it only cost pennies.

Now, what will you do today or this week to direct the truths about Jesus toward little and big hearts?

Hitting the Bull's Eye

And what is the bull's eye? For me as a mom, I wanted my children to know God, to love my Jesus, and to enjoy the eternal life spoken of in 1 John 5:12:

He who has the Son has life; he who does not have the Son of God does not have life.

So I prayed (and prayed and prayed!) for my girls to have a relationship with God through Christ. And I know you want the same for your flesh and blood. Therefore, to hit the bull's eye, take care to share vocally and repeatedly the facts about "the gospel."

> *Faith in Jesus is the most important event in the history of a child's life.*

What is the gospel? Here's a short answer. Paul, who received the gospel message from Christ Himself, was faithful to pass it on to others in 1 Corinthians 15:3-4. He put it this way, "For I delivered to you first of all that which I also received: that Christ died for our sins according to the Scriptures, and that He was buried, and that He rose again the third day according to the Scriptures."

As you can imagine, whole volumes have been written on these two verses. But for our sakes, think of the gospel truths presented in these three statements:

> *Christ died for our sins*—The sinless Jesus Christ bore the punishment of sin so that those who believe have their sins removed.
>
> *He was buried*—Jesus Christ died on a real cross and was buried in a real tomb.

He rose again the third day—God the Father raised Jesus Christ up from the dead, permanently and forever.

What does this mean to us and to our children? First of all, the Bible says that "all have sinned" (Romans 3:23). Clearly, then, we and our children are in need of forgiveness for sin. We need a Savior! We need Jesus! The Bible also says "godly sorrow" over sin "produces repentance [a desire to turn from sin and restore one's relationship with God] leading to salvation" (2 Corinthians 7:10).

All of that said, mom, speak from your heart and from God's Word to your children. Make it a point every day. See it as a sacred, nonoptional, daily duty. Praise your children's good deeds, but be faithful to point out any behavior that goes against God's standards. And at the same time, point them to Jesus as the One who can forgive their sins and help them do the right things. Talk to them about Jesus' death for their sins. And share the good news that He is alive—that they can have life in Him and live forever in His presence. Let them know the promise of John 1:12: "But as many as received Him, to them He gave the right to become children of God, to those who believe in His name."

> *Build a bridge of truth to your child's heart and pray for Jesus to walk over it.*

Here's what Jim and I did with our little ones. For several years our family sang in unison and with gusto the hymn that expresses, "When we all get to heaven what a day of rejoicing that will be!"...until one day Jim said, "Wait a minute! How do we all get to heaven?"

That's when we began teaching and telling our girls more about Jesus. We started to share the truths I've mentioned, as well as what I call "either or" truths:

> Enter by the narrow gate; for wide is the gate and broad is the way that leads to destruction, and there are many who go in by it (Matthew 7:13).

> He who has the Son has life; he who does not have the Son of God does not have life (1 John 5:12).

> Unless one is born again, he cannot see the kingdom of God (John 3:3).

Again, only God can save your child's soul. And only God can work in your child's heart. But His Spirit works through His arrows—His Word and His truth. Be ever faithful to do your part. You must preach Christ! As the apostle Paul remarked, "How then shall they call on Him in whom they have not believed? And how shall they believe in Him of whom they have not heard? And how shall they hear without a preacher?" (Romans 10:14).

Well, that's you, mom. You are to be one of God's "preachers of the gospel." And your little flock is right there at home! So make telling your children about Jesus the priority purpose and aim of your parenting. Be faithful to open your mouth. Be faithful to prepare. Be faithful to teach. And be faithful to preach! Be faithful to hang in there and persist...while being faithful to live out genuine faith. And, of course, be faithful to pray!

But What If...?

Are you wondering, "But what if my child has already prayed to receive Jesus as Savior?" First, that is great news! But now "the target" becomes spiritual growth. And spiritual growth is progressive and ongoing. Each new day and trial will bring you more opportunities to teach your child about Jesus—how He grew, how He knew the Scriptures, how He walked through life and trouble, how He treated others, how He prayed, how He loved and obeyed—and trusted—the Father, how He lived fully for God, how He fulfilled God's purpose for Him.

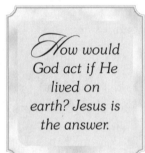

How would God act if He lived on earth? Jesus is the answer.

The Bible says, "But grow in the grace and knowledge of our Lord and Savior Jesus Christ" (2 Peter 3:18). Let your family members respond to each truth along the way. Also have them articulate their understanding of the gospel and their beliefs to you. This way you can keep your finger on the spiritual pulse of each child. You'll also gain insights into the level of their understanding, which will lead and guide you in further conversations about God.

When Should You Start?

Moms ask me regularly if such-and-such age is too soon to begin telling little ones about Jesus. And my answer (as you know by now!) is always the same—it's never too early to start. In fact, may your children never remember a day when you didn't talk to them about Jesus, your Best Friend and Savior!

Consider, too, these survey results: "People are much more likely to accept Christ as their Savior when they are young. Absorption of biblical information and principles typically peaks during the preteen years....Habits related to the practice of one's faith develop when one is young and change surprisingly little over time."[1]

Your goal, then, as a Christian mom is to teach and teach and teach your children about Jesus. To share and share and share with them about Him! To talk and talk and talk about the Savior. English preacher and evangelist C.H. Spurgeon rhymed it this way:

> Ere a child has reached to seven
> Teach him all the way to heaven;
> Better still the work will thrive
> If he learns before he's five.

Never Give Up!

Is your child older than five? Or seven? Or the preteens? Don't despair! Instead check your heart (and emotions!) and do the following:

> *Remember*—salvation is God's job, His work in your older child's heart.
>
> *Pray*—fervently for your older son or daughter and faithfully to "God our Savior, who desires all men to be saved and to come to the knowledge of the truth" (1 Timothy

2:3-4). And pray for him or her until you die. Aim the arrows of your prayers for any wayward or lagging children heavenward until your last dying breath. It's never too late to pray! And it's never too late for the miracle of salvation!

Talk—to your teens and young adults about Christ. Point the issues in their lives back to Jesus—His teachings, His life, His wisdom, and His ability to help...and to save. Even if they say, "Oh, mom, there you go again!" go right ahead and talk about Jesus. They act like they couldn't care less but, believe me, it's going in! And they are having to process it. I ask you, if they are not going to hear it from *you*, the one who lives with them and loves them most, then *who?* You, dear faithful mom, are the one closest to any of your children who desperately need to hear and know about Jesus.

> *The gospel breaks hard hearts.*

I've shared before in one of my books about Augustine, cited to be "one of the greatest of the Church Fathers."[2] For 33 years Augustine scorned the Christian teaching and prayers of his mother, Monica. And yet Monica never gave up. She preached. She prayed. She pursued...until one day, at age 33, Augustine cried out in agony to God, "How long? Remember not the sins of my youth!" When he told his mom he had at last embraced the Savior, Monica said, "Now I can die in peace." Her son's salvation was the only thing on earth she had desired. Monica died five days later, and her son went on from having been a prodigal to becoming a pillar in the church.

Never give up!

As a mom after God's own heart who's been blessed by Him to have children, you are also appointed by Him to share the knowledge of His Son with each child under your roof. If you never get beyond this one priority—this one target!—in your lifetime, you will live a full and meaningful life. Even if all your other dreams pass you by, doing this one thing will be enough...because *this* is what God asks of you as one of His moms.

And, whatever you do, don't get caught up in worrying about your children's responses to the truth about Jesus. I know you care passionately and pray fervently about their eternal souls, and that's natural...and a good thing! But again, salvation is God's job. But here's what you can do: Open your heart to God and own His assignment to you to tell your children about Him—about His love—and about His precious Son. Accept this as a calling from God. Embrace it and go forward full-speed ahead. And do so with confidence and zeal!

Dear mom, this is *the big why* when it comes to all we do for our children. Why do we teach them God's Word, talk to them about God, take them to church, train them in God's ways, teach them to pray, and talk to God about them? We do it because it's our God-given responsibility, our role, our duty, and our mandate from God. Our heart's desire—indeed, the goal of our life—is that our children hear the truths about Christ. And then, Lord willing and by His grace, we pray that those truths will strike deeply into their hearts, that they may come to know Christ personally and enjoy the promise of eternal life!

So roll up your sleeves and move out heartily on your mission! Take great care—and exact aim—and target the heart of each of your loved ones. Pummel the hearts of those under your roof again and again with truth after truth about Jesus. And do it for years! Pray with each truth that the knowledge of sin, salvation, and the need for a Savior will sink deeply into soft young hearts...until, by God's grace, they respond positively.

From a Dad's Heart

As a former pastor I conducted many sessions of marriage counseling. As a general rule, the couples I talked with fell into two groups.

The first category was what the Bible calls being "unequally yoked" (2 Corinthians 6:14), where one partner is not a Christian. If your husband is not a Christian, he won't be all that interested in hearing about Jesus. But he is probably very interested in knowing that the children are under control. He likes knowing that the home is clean. And he *loves* knowing what's for dinner! For this dear guy, make sure you are living out before him the reality of the Jesus you want him and your children to know. Communication takes on many forms. Often we teach the loudest by what we do rather than what we say. Your actions will teach your husband about Jesus too! As the Bible says, "without a word" husbands "may be won by the conduct of their wives" (1 Peter 3:1).

The second category is a couple made up of two Christians. Now, and always, if you have a believing husband, thank God every day for this man and pray daily for growth and wisdom for him. Then beyond that, sit down with him in a quiet place and share what you are learning about being a mom after God's own heart. Let him know of your commitment to tell your children about Jesus. Share your dreams that they come to a genuine faith in Christ. Enlist his support in helping you talk about Christ.

Also be sure you thank him for all that he has already done to lift up the name of Jesus in the home. Thank him for the support and encouragement he has already given you in this critical task.

And if he is lagging behind in his understanding and efforts, tell him how important this assignment from the Lord is to you and how it should be to the both of you. Ask him for suggestions as to how the two of you can get the message of Jesus across to the hearts and minds of your children. Neither of you has all the answers and wisdom. However God has given you both the resources of godly men and women to help. Let your husband know you are willing to meet with a more seasoned woman for advice and wisdom. Then ask him if he would consider seeking out a more mature man in the church who has been down this road in the past.

I know this is where Elizabeth and I found ourselves in our early days of Christian parenting. We didn't have a clue about how to be godly parents. And we sure didn't know how to begin teaching our girls about Jesus. Elizabeth and I determined to go to as many parents as we could to ask for advice. And we did that until they got married.

Don't limp along in your parenting. Don't go it alone. Enlist your husband's help and the help of others in your church.

Little Choices That Reap Big Blessings

1. Concentrate on the gospel.

Now that you've thought about the power of the gospel message to salvation, do what my Jim did. Ask your kids, "But wait a minute! How do we all get to heaven?" Then choose to aim the arrows of the gospel more precisely, to pull the bow with more force, and to fire away more often. Consider this:

> The Gospel is God-given.
> The Gospel is what God does for man.
> The Gospel is good news.
> The Gospel ends in inner transformation.
> The Gospel is...a force—the power of God unto salvation.[3]

2. Share the lives of God's saints.

As you read Christian biographies with your kids, you'll find positive answer after positive answer about the difference knowledge of Jesus makes in a child's life and heart. For instance, think about the life of G. Campbell Morgan. He was a little boy who grew up to become a famous British minister and later the pastor of the Tabernacle Presbyterian Church in Philadelphia. Of him it is written that he was "a great organizer, a powerful preacher, a prince among evangelists, a teacher and leader amongst ministers and student of Holy Scriptures."[4]

But hear Mr. Morgan's own words: "My dedication to the preaching of the Word was maternal.... When but eight years old I preached to my little sister and to her dolls arrayed in orderly form before me. My sermons were Bible stories which I had first heard from my mother."[5]

Read on, mom! Tell your children the stories about Jesus from the Bible!

3. Sing about Jesus.

I was appalled one Sunday at church when I went to check on one of my small grandchildren. And there he was, sitting on the lap of a young girl who was assisting in the class. She was holding my grandson's hands and clapping them together singing "MIC-KEY M-O-U-S-E" to him. I smiled and quietly (I hope!) asked, "Do you know "Jesus Loves Me"? When she answered "Sure," I said, "That's one of his favorites. Why don't you sing that with him? He loves that one."

Oh, how my heart hurt! Here we were, as a Christian family, bringing everyone to church so they could learn more about Jesus. But I got a message too: When at home sing about Jesus! I wondered how many times I missed an opportunity to sing or tell that same toddler more about Jesus!

4. Budget for books.

It's staggering how much a family can pay for cable TV service, videos, and CDs. So don't hesitate to have a budget for Jesus books. Schedule regular visits to your Christian bookstore and keep a list of the titles you spot on your outings that would teach your children the truths about Jesus. Also note the books your kids particularly like. A special book purchased every so often that they picked out will surely become a favorite and an heirloom. And just think what it can accomplish in your child's heart!

5. Ask others to pray.

Being a mom is the same as being in a battle. You're a warrior! And the battle for your child's heart is a spiritual one! So enlist the prayer support of any family members who are Christians. If your parents or your husband's parents are believers, personally ask them to commit to becoming prayer warriors on behalf of your children. Ask them to pray for each of your children every day. And if there aren't any prayer warriors in your family, enlist a godly older woman or your best friend to join you in battle. Storm the gates of heaven for the souls under your charge!

5

*T*rain Your Children in God's Ways

*Train up a child
in the way he should go,
and when he is old
he will not depart from it.*

PROVERBS 22:6

'*ve* shared before in my books about my friend, Judy-the-gardener, and her incredibly beautiful garden. Well, delight of delights, Judy (also known as Judy-the-artist) and I collaborated on a children's book entitled *God's Wisdom for Little Girls.*[1] We weren't surprised that everyone's favorite painting is Judy's "little girl" busily working away in a corner of Judy's actual garden. To guide girls and their character development, I wrote:

> The garden of God's little girl—how grand!
> It began with a dream, a prayer, and a plan.

105

Nothing this splendid just happens, we know:
It takes time and care for flowers to grow.

How did Judy's garden come to be so magnificent? Multiple words are rushing in as I search for an answer. Commitment. Hard work. Dedication. Attention. Diligence. Creativity. Time. And I can't leave out...love! And all of these qualities and attitudes of heart have been worked out day after day for years on end.

Judy's training efforts go something like this. Each day, in the early-morning stillness she faithfully feeds, tills, and waters the roses that gift-wrap her arbor. Then, with sharpened shears, she cuts away any unruly growth, prunes off all unnecessary shoots, and removes every dead blossom. Surgically, Judy (who also used to be Judy-the-nurse!) removes any and every thing that would hinder the growth and development of her roses.

Oh, but she's not done yet! Next is the training process. Judy mounts her ladder and wires and tacks down her rose vines, carefully directing and redirecting their growth. She works away at this until she gets the results she wants and sees the design and beauty she has in mind emerging. Judy knows that growing a garden— even a single plant in a garden—is work. But it's a labor of love. And work is required of anyone who wants something grand.

Are you with me, mom? Are you guessing where we're going in a section about training children for God...and for life? We are going straight to the heart of what it means to train our children in God's ways!

Growing a Child

God wrote *The Book* on raising children, and He has much to say on the subject of training them. To begin, He expects us to actively prepare our children for life. In Proverbs 22:6, God gives His command—"train up a child in the way he should go." He also gives His encouragement—"and when he is old he will not depart from it." As moms with a heavenly charge to "train" each child, two efforts are required:

- ✓ *Educate*—One definition of *train* is to "educate," or "give instruction." This incorporates all parts of true religious education. How does this education take place? Do we wait until our baby can sit, walk, or talk, until our child reaches a certain age? Do we wait until we spot some glimmer of desire in the child? Do we count on a Christian school to do it for us? Or do we wait until our child gets into the Sunday-school system or the youth group at church?

- ✓ *Initiate*—This next definition answers these questions: To train also means to "initiate." You see, we as the parents must do the training and the educating. And we must be aggressive and take the initiative. Our training should be willful and on purpose, something we commit to, schedule, plan, and do, taking every opportunity to

educate our child "in the way he should
go."

And what happens if we don't initiate and educate our
children in the way they should go? They will go in the
way they want to go! Children left to choose their own
direction will be spoiled and self-centered in later life.
And the book of Proverbs teaches us "a child left to himself brings shame to his mother" (Proverbs 29:15).

Proverbs 22:6 (train up a child...) is also a warning
from God to parents: If we fail to train up our child, or
allow a child to train himself according to his own
wishes, we should not expect that child to want to
change this pattern in later life. That's because "children
are born sinners and, when allowed to follow their own
wishes, will naturally develop sinful habit responses....
Such habit patterns become deep-seated when they have
been ingrained in the child from the earliest days."[2]

Mom, realize you're on a mission to train up your children from the earliest minute possible. This training is
accomplished in two ways that never change.

Hands-on training—Like Judy with gloves, shears,
and wire, you are to actively and aggressively instruct
your "young plants" by hands-on training. Yes, you teach
your children the Bible. And of course you're teaching
them the rules to live by and how to do necessary, practical tasks. But are you teaching them how to make wise
choices? It's one of your jobs as a mom. So, as hard as it
is, don't give in to your natural mom instincts and make
all the choices for your child (which is easy to do but

damaging in the long run). Instead train them and show them how to make good decisions (for the long run!).

Active training also involves training your children through correction, which includes discipline when necessary.[3] One source put it something like this: Education commences at the mother's knee. You have to not only train your children *at* your knee but also, on occasion, *over* your knee! It takes *both* knees to train up a child in the way he should go. (More on this in a minute.)

Live-it-out training—This nonactive training process involves providing training and instruction by modeling right behavior. It's much more personal...and much more difficult. It's walking the walk in addition to talking the talk! To me the most frightening "mom" verse in the Bible is Proverbs 23:26: "My son, give me your heart, and let your eyes observe my ways." As the saying goes, It is noble to train a child in the way he should go, but better still is to walk that way yourself. While studying in college to become a teacher, I was constantly told, "You teach little by what you say, but you teach most by what you are." And the same is true of you as a mom. Your children will follow your footsteps more easily and often than they will follow your advice!

> *Train up a child in the way he should go, and go that way yourself!*[4]

The apostle Paul told other Christians to "imitate me, just as I also imitate Christ" (1 Corinthians 11:1). He reminded them that "the things which you learned and received and heard and saw in me, these do" (Philippians 4:9). We, as moms after God's heart, should be able to issue these same charges to our family too. Our lives should be a "copybook" they can follow.

I was so touched by this poem that I forwarded it on to my daughters. The wording is for parents of little boys, but it applies to raising little girls too.

> A careful [mom] I ought to be,
> A little fellow follows me.
> I do not dare to go astray,
> For fear he'll go the selfsame way.
>
> Not once can I escape his eyes;
> Whate'er he sees me do he tries.
> Like me he says he's going to be,
> That little chap who follows me....
>
> I must remember as I go
> Through summer sun and winter snow,
> I'm molding for the years to be—
> That little chap who follows me.[5]

From a Seedling

When is the best time for a mom to begin to "train up [her] child in the way he should go"? Obviously sooner is better. Like gardening, if we can begin from the outset with each little seedling, the training usually goes more smoothly. Reformed pastor and preacher Henry Ward Beecher well observed, "It is not hard to make a child or a tree grow right if you train them when they're young, but to make them straighten out after you've allowed things to go wrong is not an easy matter."

I'm always amazed at moms (and grandmoms too) who come through an autographing line and share that they think it is too early to begin reading my children's books—or any children's books, and even the Bible!—to their children. Why, they explain, they're only 9 or 12 months old, 18 months old, 2 years old, 4 years old! I try to be a lady, and I hold myself back as I let them know that I fiercely believe that it's never too early to begin training up little ones. Never. (Remember little Samuel in the Bible? At around age three he was already separated from his mom and serving God in the temple.)

So, whatever ages your little seedlings are, start the reading, teaching, and instructing...now. Initiate the training and teach your heart out. No matter what they do or don't understand, they will sense your love and passion. They'll also become accustomed to your voice and to your teaching. Believe me, they pick up much more than you can imagine. Think about this...

During a recent Thanksgiving holiday, Jim and I stayed in the basement/playroom/guestroom at our daughter Katherine's home in New York. We knew Paul had just painted the room in anticipation of our arrival, so we were surprised to see some dirt smudges on one wall in our quarters. But as we took a closer look, we saw the pencil markings of dates and the names of Kath and Paul's children...and lines with recorded height measurements! This, of course, brought smiles to our hearts and faces.

But here's what's alarming. Many parents (Jim and me included) are faithful to record their child's growth and development on walls, doorjambs, or journals. But long before that child can physically stand up to be measured, massive growth has been going on mentally, spiritually, and morally in that little person. Some parents don't even measure their children's growth until after their third

> *The kind of person your child is going to be, he is already becoming... and becoming quickly!*[6]

birthday. And yet, when it comes to a child's heart and soul, "let every father and mother realize that when their child is three years of age, they have done more than half they will ever do for its character."[7]

Which Way, Lord?

Thank goodness when God said "train up a child" He didn't leave us moms with a vague job assignment! He didn't leave us wondering or worrying about the direction and desired outcome of our training. No, He told us in Proverbs 22:6 exactly what our purpose and objective is—to "train up a child in the way he should go." The "way he should go" answers our heart cry, "Which way, Lord?"

God's way—What do you think the right way is? If you said "God's way," you're correct. Proverbs tells us "the way of the Lord" is "the way of life," "the way of wisdom," and "the way of righteousness." This is more ammunition for making sure we teach God's Word to our children. Then they will know His way! And (again!) that's our job, mom—to teach our children God's way, train them in God's way, and insist that they follow God's way. Proverbs 6 says the law of the mother and her instruction "are the way of life" (verses 20-23).

So instruct your heart out, dear mom! Live out God's way continually, teach God's Word constantly (Deuteronomy 6:7-8), and enforce God's wisdom con-

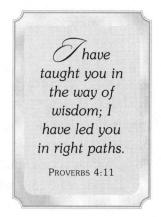

I have taught you in the way of wisdom; I have led you in right paths.

PROVERBS 4:11

sistently with loving discipline throughout your child's upbringing (Ephesians 6:4).

God's wisdom—Did I say "discipline"? Yes. Actually, God said it. And as moms after God's heart we do what He says. He says we are to teach our children, so we do. And He says we are to train our children, so we do. And part of that training involves His commands to correct and discipline our children, so we do.

Discipline the child in whom you delight (Proverbs 3:12).

Discipline while there is hope (19:18).

Discipline diligently the child you love (13:24).

Discipline a child in the way he should go (22:6).

Discipline foolishness out of your child's heart (22:15).

Discipline evil out of your child's heart (20:30).

Clearly the Bible teaches that to love your child is to discipline your child. Proverbs 13:24 states "he who spares his rod hates his son, but he who loves him disciplines him promptly." And Ephesians 6:4 cautions, "Do not provoke your children to wrath, but bring them up in the training and admonition of the Lord."

Oh did correcting and disciplining my two toddlers—my precious, darling little girls—ever come hard for me! In my book *A Woman After God's Own Heart*, I describe how I first heard this teaching from the Bible. How I didn't believe the teacher who taught it...until I read it in the Bible for myself. How I fought this truth, cried over it, and prayed through it. How I talked it over and hashed it through with Jim until we reached a mutual plan for implementing this wisdom from God. And then, how we dove into training up our little loved ones in the way they *should* go...not the way they *would*—and already were at such tender ages—go!

Those were hard days...and years! And if you need help getting started with biblical discipline—or encouragement to keep on or a fresh reminder to stay faithful—I've dedicated the entire "Little Things" section to a few "little" basics.

The child's way—Properly training up a child is a two-edged sword. On the one side, you must point them to God's way. And on the other, to enjoy any success at all in training your child for God and for life, you have to know your child, to know what makes him or her tick. That's another message from God to His moms in Proverbs 22:6. This verse has been translated "educate a child according to his life requirements," "train a child for his proper trade,"[8] and point him in "the way"—his way, "that way selected for him in which he should go"[9]

In other words, each and every child is fearfully and wonderfully made and has his own "bent." There is a way or direction each is meant to grow and go in. Each of your little—and big!—ones has natural talents and personality traits that must be encouraged. For instance, maybe, like me trying to raise children who were only 13 months apart in age, you are trying to raise all of your children alike and train them all in the same way, with the same methods, and in the same direction.

And yet your children are individuals. For example, one of my girls is right-handed and the other a lefty. One is blessed to be a neatnick and the other is "a free spirit." One could be moved to tears of remorse by a stern or displeased look...and the other required stiffer consequences...again and again and again! Today both of these wonderful, unique, grown-up individuals and women of God love the Lord (and Jim and me!) and are moms themselves, but one is more on the artsy-craftsy, designer side and the other enjoys organizing and accounting.

My experience is just a thumbnail sketch with a few differences in "bent," but I'm sure you get the point. Your children are individuals with special strengths and capabilities—their own bent—that should be developed. God asks you to join with Him in the adventure and help them each discover, choose, and walk in the right path.

Harvesting the Fruit of Your Labors... and Love

At last we come to the hope of the fruit we may well reap in time—"Train up a child in the way he should go, and *when he is old he will not depart from it.*" Of course, there are exceptions to this "promise," but it still stands as a general rule. This favorite verse of Christian parents is not making an ironclad guarantee. But it is laying down a general principle. It's like this—just as a tree grows to be straight and healthy with a gardener's help (help like Judy gave her roses), so a child grows in the direction in which they are trained at home.

> *'Tis education forms the infant mind; Just as the twig is bent, the tree's inclined.*[10]

And, yes, children raised in the nurture and admonition of the Lord can stray from God. But they can never get away from the prayers of their mom watering the seeds of God's Word and love that have been planted in their hearts through a lifetime. Chances are high that the seeds of faithful instruction will one day burst forth into life. The Scriptures, learned by heart, will move lost loved ones to remember their father's house, come to their senses, and return home (Luke 15:11-20).

Do you know what I want for you? It's the same thing I want for me. I want us to reap the harvest God is pointing to here in Proverbs 22:6. I want our children to "rise up"—to go out into public and go on with their lives as full-grown adults—and "bless" you, not verbally but by their lives (Proverbs 31:28). I want our children to be the next generation God and Moses were so concerned about in Deuteronomy 6. I want them to carry the baton of faith in God to yet another generation as they too train up their children in the way they should go.

Heart Response

Our chapter is running long, and part of the reason is because being a mom is one of my "hot buttons." I want you to take God's command to train up your children to heart. But I also want you to take heart, dear mom. How I wish I were right there with you. To listen. To share. To encourage. To rejoice...or to sorrow. To hug. To pray. But after all of the camaraderie and after the tissues are put away, I would tell you this....

Please, roll up your mothering sleeves and dive in. Give being a mom your heart, your all, your best, your time, your blood, sweat, and tears...and above all, your prayers! Learn all you can. Do all you can. Hang in there. Don't get discouraged. Don't even think about giving up. And pray always!

God has entrusted you with a new generation. And He's also given you all of the grace and strength and power and wisdom and love you will need for every step and second along the way. Believe it and own it. Never forget—you are a mom after God's heart. For this you were born.

From a Dad's Heart

As I just read this chapter in preparation for my "From Dad" section, I couldn't help but think back on something I wrote to teen guys in my book *A Young Man After God's Own Heart*.[11] I compared the training of soldiers at "boot camp" with the training of young men at home. Here's what I said in the chapter called "Training at Camp Home." (And by the way, this would apply to young girls as well.)

> Your home is God's training ground for your future. Train well, and you will have the tools and will develop the skills for a productive and influential life. Fail in your training at Camp Home, and the possibility of a lifetime of failure is greatly magnified.

Now, what should be of interest to you is that authentic training at military boot camp requires not only a willing recruit, but also a combat-hardened veteran drill sergeant for the training to be successful. (Do you see where I'm going with this analogy?) Your young recruits, whatever their ages, may or may not be willing, but that doesn't matter. God is asking you to do your part by becoming His "drill sergeant" in the home. He's asking you to take your young recruits and give them instruction for life and living, "to train them in the way they should go." Their future is partially dependent on how well you do your job at "Camp Home."

If your children are even as old as two or three, you probably already feel like a drill sergeant. All day long you are barking orders, giving instructions, inspecting bunks, and moving the troops from Point A to Point B. And in the evenings you try to hand off the responsibility to the master drill sergeant over your family, your husband, also known as Dad.

It's great when the "transfer of power" is successful and Drill Sergeant Dad takes over with the orders and the discipline. But, unfortunately, the ball gets dropped by Dad at times. Or, for whatever reason, he doesn't want the ball. Or he's away on business and not there for the hand off. What do you do then?

Whatever you do, don't go AWOL (Absent Without Leave)! Continue to stay at your post. Continue to carry out your orders and fulfill your duties. Ask God (your Commander-in-Chief) to sustain you in your role of trainer and drill sergeant. And pray for reinforcements!

And what if you're a single parent and there is no other drill sergeant? Then look to your church or family for reinforcements. Ask other godly men to be on call for those occasions when a man might help out, especially with training your boys. I do this for my daughter Courtney when her Navy husband is out to sea. One day she called and asked, "Dad, can you come over and talk to Jacob? He just needs a man in his life." Whom has God provided to assist you?

Little Choices That Reap Big Blessings

1. Start today!

It's never too early to start training your children. And it's also never too late. So whatever you do, do something today. Present neglect leads to later risk. And present neglect can also lead to future regret. It's easy to begin our work as a mother too late, but we can never begin it too soon. I once heard a godly dad share that his goal was to discipline his children so early in life that they not only got the message of right and wrong early on, but they also never remembered being disciplined!

2. Talk to your husband.

Seek to agree with your husband on the manner and methods you as a team will use for discipline and correction. Consistency is the goal. It's good for the parents, and it's good for the kids. It creates less confusion in your children...and sends them a loud, solid, unified message not to play one of you against the other.

3. Enroll in a parenting class at church.

When our girls were two and three, Jim and I took an invaluable class (it was only four sessions!)

on biblical child-raising taught by one of our church elders and his wife. We followed many of their principles for almost 20 years, until our daughters married. Coming from the Bible, their advice stood the test of time. Don't miss out on the wisdom that's available in your church. And if scheduling and classroom time is a problem, check out a parenting video or DVD from your church library. Just be sure you are growing in this sometimes perplexing part of life.

4. Be flexible.

Every minute of every day of every week of every year, your children change. So plan to review and adjust your child-raising regularly—at least weekly. Changes will always have to be made. *Always!* Constantly evaluate your training and discipline. What's working? What's not? What forms of discipline can be dropped? Which should be intensified or kicked up a notch?

5. Be generous with praise and encouragement.

Speak up when you see godly behavior in your children. When positive changes are made, praise God...and then praise your children. Let them know that you noticed. Celebrate! Brag on them. Tell dad what great things they have done. This is a terrific way to balance discipline with love.

Martin Luther, whose father was very strict, once wrote: "Spare the rod and spoil the child—that is true. But beside the rod keep an apple to give him when he has done well." Check yourself, mom. Do you encourage and praise at least as often as you reprove or correct?[12]

6. Pray like you've never prayed before!

We'll have an entire chapter on this "little choice" that reaps big blessing, but start praying now. Don't wait another second. These are *your* children! No one (other than God Himself) wants them to walk in God's ways more than you do. You'll need strength, wisdom, obedience, love— and lots of patience!—and these all come from God. So ask!

7. Have lots of fun!

One of my principles for being a mom was "Have a ball!" Training takes time, effort, and planning. And so does having fun. So create a page for every day this next week and plan in one element of fun. Let the party begin!

Ten Commands for Guiding Your Children

♡ Teach them, using God's Word
(Deuteronomy 6:4-9).

♡ Tell them what's right and wrong
(1 Kings 1:6).

♡ See them as gifts from God
(Psalm 127:3).

♡ Guide them in godly ways
(Proverbs 22:6).

♡ Discipline them (Proverbs 29:17).

♡ Love them unconditionally
(Luke 15:11-32).

♡ Do not provoke them to wrath
(Ephesians 6:4).

♡ Earn their respect by example
(1 Timothy 3:4).

♡ Provide for their physical needs
(1 Timothy 5:8).

♡ Pass your faith along to them
(2 Timothy 1:5).[13]

Susannah's Rules for Rearing Children

Can't think of any guidelines for your children? Let Susannah Wesley get you started. As the mother of 19 children, this noble mother developed these guidelines. Though 200-plus years old, her rules for teaching a child to be obedient are still helpful today.

1. Allow no eating between meals.

2. Put all children in bed by eight o'clock.

3. Require them to take medicine without complaining.

4. Subdue self-will in a child and thus work together with God to save his soul.

5. Teach each one to pray as soon as he can speak.

6. Require all to be still during family worship.

7. Give them nothing that they cry for, and only that which they ask for politely.

8. To prevent lying, punish no fault which is first confessed and repented of.

9. Never allow a sinful act to go unpunished.

10. Never punish a child twice for a single offense.

11. Commend and reward good behavior.

12. Any attempt to please, even if poorly performed, should be commended.

13. Preserve property rights, even in the smallest matters.

14. Strictly observe all promises.

15. Require no daughter to work before she can read well.

16. Teach children to fear the rod.[14]

6

$\mathcal{T}$ake Care of Your Children

If a son asks for bread
from any father among you
will he give him a stone?

LUKE 11:11

y good friend Lisa is known as "Dr. Tatlock" to her students at The Master's College where she teaches home economics. In the book she authored with Dr. Pat Ennis, *Designing a Lifestyle that Pleases God,* Lisa shares about "the culture shock of motherhood" and her struggle to adjust to her role as a new mom. (Sound familiar? Bring back any memories?) To help make the transition from being a professional with a doctoral degree to mommyhood, Lisa made this list in an attempt to keep her sense of humor.

You Know You're a Mommy When...

"Sleeping late" on a Saturday morning is 7 A.M.!

You get up on Sunday mornings at 5:30 A.M. and are still late for church!

You know the location of every drive-through bank, pharmacy, and restaurant (so you don't have to do the car-seat-to-stroller/stroller-to-car-seat workout routine on every errand)!

The grocery store is an exciting family outing!

Weekly menu plans and recipes come from the *20 Minutes or Less* cookbook!

You have your "quiet times" with the Lord during the 2 A.M. baby feeding!

Macaroni-and-cheese or peanut butter-and-jelly sandwiches become your lunch delicacies!

You discover you really can talk on the phone, give the baby his bottle, and play cars with your toddler all at once!

You used to need an hour to get ready to go out but now are excited about having ten uninterrupted minutes to fix your hair and change your clothes!

Staying up late is 9 P.M.![1]

I love it! Lisa's list illustrates the amount of time, effort, and love involved in taking care of your children. If you were to make your own "you know you're a mommy when" list, I'm sure it would point to this same common denominator: We love our children by taking care of them. It's a more-than-full-time job...beginning with food! (Did you notice five of Lisa's ten mommyisms dealt with food?)

What's for Dinner?

Some say love is spelled t-i-m-e, but just maybe it's spelled f-o-o-d. How many times have your kids of all ages (and their dad too!) come in and asked in whatever vocabulary they have, "What's for dinner? When's dinner? Eat?" Mealtime is a fact of life. No matter when you made the last meal, it's already time for the next one! I know as a mom with a thriving, growing family, I had to face this daily fact head on. Just because I wasn't hungry didn't mean my little ones weren't. And just because I was in a time squeeze didn't mean time could be squeezed out of mealtimes.

Luckily, the Proverbs 31 mom in the Bible showed me how to take care of my family's food needs. From her I learned a mom "watches over the ways of her household," including the Food Department (verse 27). She also taught me that to put food in front of a family often means a mom "rises while it is yet night, and provides food for her household" (verse 15). In other words, food for my family was to be a top priority each day, and I needed to do whatever it took to obtain it, fix it, and serve it each day.

As I began spending the time and effort required to feed my family, I discovered two main benefits that made a super impact on both them and me.

Tiger's milk—First, nutrition is the key to growth and development. I began to think of myself as serving up "Tiger's Milk"[2] to my cubs—food that promoted their good health. The body of every person, even an unborn child, thrives on nutrients and minerals. That's why we moms put on yet another hat and study nutrition. We become experts on what's best for our family's health and how to maintain each person's ideal weight.

Feed me with the food that is needful for me.

PROVERBS 30:8[3]

Get-up-and-go power—Next, energy. You know that eating the right foods shoots both quick and sustaining energy through your system. Food is jet fuel to the body. We see this in the story about Jonathan, the son of King Saul (1 Samuel 14:24-32). Saul gave a rash order that the people under his command could not eat. Obviously the longer they went without food, the weaker and more downhearted they became. But Jonathan, unaware of the command, touched the point of a stick into a honeycomb. When he tasted the honey, his eyes brightened, and he was refreshed and energized. Sadly, the people's need for food was so great they ate what God had forbidden.

As moms with a heart for doing the right thing for our family unit, we feed them the right things and at regular intervals. This boosts blood sugar and protein levels, creating a higher level of sustained energy...no matter how big or little a person is.

Give us this day our daily bread.

MATTHEW 6:11

As I grew as a mom, TLC—Tender Loving Care—took on new meaning. I went to work learning what it took to fuel my family. I learned to plan ahead for meals and snacks. I learned to make a weekly menu every Sunday afternoon. I learned to make a schedule for each day that included all meals and snack times. And I learned to back that schedule up and factor in prep time.

How are you doing in this vital area? I know you're busy. I know there's a permanent dust cloud behind your car as you race here and there to fulfill all your responsibilities. But if you wrote down what you served your brood during the past seven days, what would it reveal? Our goal as moms is to see that those in our family are not deprived of the food, nutrition, health, and energy they need to handle daily life, prevent melt-downs, and stay happy.

And don't forget to balance out the nutritionally correct foods with a few family favorites. Do you know each child's three favorite foods? And are they on hand for special times? (And why am I thinking about pizza!)

And another don't forget: Eat together! It's the secret to food in any family. I recently read a list of 50 ways to love your children, and one of them was to "eat meals together." It was followed by 25 ways to enjoy your family, one being "eat dinner together as a family for seven days in a row."[4]

Will I Be Safe Today?

Are you surprised to learn that of the 12 things kids of all ages worry about every day, "Will I be safe today?" ranks near the top?[5] I was! But as I researched the Proverbs 31 woman for my book *Beautiful in God's Eyes,*[6] I discovered that many of the descriptive Hebrew images of her care for her family pictured her as a lioness tending and watching over her cubs. She not only fed her babies, she also protected them...fiercely! Let's take this imagery into our homes. How can we fiercely protect our cub-children? At home they need...

Protection from siblings—Home is a shelter for every family member. Teach your children that home is where peace reigns. Sure, you can have fun and engage in friendly roughhousing. And joyful laughter is the rule of the day. But don't let things get out of control. And make sure your kids don't hurt or harass or threaten their brothers and sisters.

Protection from accidents—Do your best to set up and reinforce safety practices. It's an ongoing job, but teach your children to put away toys, both inside and outside, to prevent falls, scrapes, and broken bones. Tuck electric cords out of harm's way and cover empty sockets. Childproof your drawers and cupboards with safety latches to protect little inquisitive people and happy wanderers. Establish rules—with consequences for violators—for going into the street, for bike-riding without a helmet, and so forth. Have an "everyone buckles-up!" seatbelt policy.

Protection from incidents—Do your children know their name, address, and phone number, and what to do if they get lost? (Our granddaughter, Taylor, as a toddler in New York City, learned this information right along with the lyrics to "Jesus Loves Me" and the alphabet song. It was a must!) Do your kids know to dial 911 for help? Do they know what to do, say, or not say when approached by strangers?

Deliver us from evil.

MATTHEW 6:13 KJV

Protection through education— Much protection of our children is accomplished by faithful instruction. Another of our mom assignments is instructing each child about the dangers of being in the wrong places or with the wrong crowd, about talking to strangers, about sexual purity.

The first time I read the book of Proverbs, I couldn't believe it. The writer of this book of wisdom—a father— addressed "my son" at least 21 times! His advice spells out the "how-to" and "do not" instructions we must give our kids to protect them. This passionate parent pleaded,

"My son, if sinners entice you, do not consent." "My son...the lips of an immoral woman drip honey....Hear me now, my children...remove your way far from her, and do not go near the door of her house." "My son...keep my words...that they may keep you from the immoral woman....Listen to me, my children...do not let your heart turn aside to her ways."[7]

We learn a valuable parenting lesson from this concerned dad and writer of biblical wisdom. His instruction for his son and children was

> from the heart,
> to the point, and
> filled with specifics.

He gave explicit details and clear instructions. This dad wanted his son to know *exactly* how a prostitute or loose woman dressed, talked, and acted. And he wanted his son to know *exactly* what happens to the one who falls under her spell. And he wanted his son to know *exactly* what to do to avoid temptation and destruction.

Protection from the internet—This new front requires a parent's protection. Our kids need our serious instruction and involvement. I still grieve with the mom whose little boy viewed pornography on an educational internet hookup at school. It seems another second grader wanted to show everyone what he could do online. The bottom line is, We can't think this couldn't happen to our children. It could even happen right in our own homes! So we need to aggressively do our part and take precautions. What can we do? Purchase a computer program that restricts risky websites and dubious infiltrators. Set up a super-thick parental firewall with multiple restrictions, blocks, passwords, and filters. Make a rule that a parent must be present for any school-aged child to use

I will set nothing wicked before my eyes.

PSALM 101:3

the internet. Keep the home computer in the family room where we can monitor activity. Limit the number of minutes and set a cut-off time for each family member's online time. Regularly look over the file names of the sites our kids are visiting.

Protection from TV—TV can become another violator of our children's mental health and moral purity. So again we go to battle. Block questionable channels. Stand strong against the trend of putting a TV in each child's room; have everyone watch TV in the family room. We can also set limits on TV time and programs.

Be careful, little eyes, what you see; be careful, little ears, what you hear.

I recently heard a CD by a dad who limited his children to one hour of TV a week. He sat with them while they watched what they selected and he approved. Afterward, they followed up by talking about the program. He finished his story saying today, as adults, his children have TVs that they seldom watch. During the years of limited TV, they learned to spend their time and minds on much more interesting activities.

Protection from the opposite sex—Have you noticed the progression in this chapter from the dailies of food and safety at home to the biggie—to sex? The faithful watchcare over our flocks stretches far beyond putting meals on the table. Yes, we moms take care of our children's physical well-being, but we also keep an eye out for their sexual and moral well-being. No scar is as deep and as permanent as the loss of sexual purity.

Several of our topics have already addressed this big area in children's lives, an area which calls for high-gear parental involvement. We must never forget we are in a serious battle for the purity of our children. True, we live in the world, but we don't have to succumb to its lures, temptations, and lack of standards.

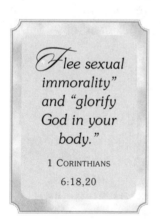

"Flee sexual immorality" and "glorify God in your body."

1 CORINTHIANS
6:18,20

As a member of God's brigade of moms, set the highest standards for your children. (I mean, as high as the heavens! As high as God's Word!) Work relentlessly at communicating those standards clearly. Enforce them sternly, and hold any and all lines. If ever there was a place for you to get tough, to be passionate and fierce, this is it. Your kids need to know their purity is 100 percent important to God, 100 percent important to you, and it should be 100 percent important to them too.

Fellow mom, share your heart earnestly. Don't be afraid to be thought of as strict or prudish, or old-fashioned. You can take it! Regardless of what happens, you'll be glad to know that you did all you could. That you spoke up. That you cared.

Keep your growing kids in the Bible, and keep on having devotions at home. Take them to church. Help them develop relationships with solid believers, peers, mentors, and youth leaders at church. Talk openly and regularly about the details of their daily lives, about their standards and their relationships. Let them know you love them and care about them. And above all else, keep on praying!

Why Do I Have to Rest?

Do you wish someone would make you take a nap? While we tend to function on sleep-deprivation mode, each of our little ones needs to rest, yet constantly asks, "Why do I need to rest?" Everyone gets tired, run down, and stressed out. And if time out for rest isn't taken, prepare for a complete meltdown! Lack of sleep robs everyone of the rest needed for health, for coping, for energy, for clear thinking. Even Jesus, in His humanity, was weary (John 4:6). He also understood His disciples' need for rest and initiated a time of R & R for them (Mark 6:31).

So we, like Jesus, look out for the rest needed by our "disciples" at home. For the baby, sleep is essential for growth and development. That means we moms need to create schedules that factor in that needed sleep time. For preschoolers, it's a full out tug-of-war! That means we need to be the boss, to assert ourselves, and ensure that whether they sleep or not during nap time, they at least get some rest and a little down time. For school-aged family members, adequate rest comes down to getting them into bed good and early.

For older kids with homework, commitments, and jobs—and, of course, lots of friends!—we definitely enter into a whole new scene. In their case, we watch out and watch over what keeps them up at night. (Remember the woman from Proverbs 31 who watches over her household? That's you, mom!) What—and who—are the culprits? Phone calls? The internet, email, or text messaging with friends? TV programs? Caffeine? Sugar? For everyone's sake, especially your teen's, be firm. Set house rules. Go to work on eliminating or curtailing whatever is interfering with them getting their homework done and getting to bed.

Obviously there's more—much more!—to taking care of your children than these few pages allow me to highlight. And more will be addressed in the "Little Choices" that follow. But in this section we're dealing with the heart of a mom after God's own heart. It's true, we may not get too excited about running our home on a schedule or cooking another meal or doing another load of laundry or being on parental patrol duty. But a heart filled with motherly love does all of the above.

And what if you are a working-outside-the-home mom? Taking care of your children is just as important but even more difficult. And you know why, don't you. Because you're not with your children as much as you would like, and they are under the care of others part of the time. Some caregivers have your same convictions and standards, but unfortunately many don't. This means you'll have to redouble your efforts when you are with your children to ensure that when they are away from you, they still have your standards, which are God's standards.

And what if your older kids are home alone for a time before you or your husband arrive? Again, you'll need to really impress upon them what the boundaries and standards are at home—and what the consequences are for not following the house rules.

Dear mom, I know the things covered in this chapter are your heart concerns too. I probably haven't brought up anything you didn't already know. My intention has been a little like the apostle Peter's role in his letters. He saw himself as a *reminder*. He wrote his readers that he would "not be negligent to *remind* you always of these things, though you know and are established in the present truth." He desired "to stir up by reminding" (2 Peter 1:12-13).

I'm not in any way suggesting that you're not doing your best. What I am doing is reminding you (and me too!) of God's privileged calling to take care of your children...in the best way you know how, with as much zeal as you can gain from the Lord, for as long as you have the opportunity.

From a Dad's Heart

"How many children do you have?" I'll bet you've been asked that hundreds of times. You think for a minute and reply in jest, "I have three children. Two boys, ages 6 and 10, and one aged 35." Sometimes that's half true. I don't know what it is with us guys when it comes to our families. We are dynamos at work. We can keep three secretaries busy all day, move ten men forward on a construction site, provide service for others all day and into the night.... But when it comes to our kids, we can be clueless!

As one who was raised in a home with a hard-working, unbelieving father who didn't provide a lot of modeling in the Care Department, let me give you a few suggestions on how to help your husband in this area.

1. Consider yourself blessed by God if you have a husband who helps care for the children at all. He is a rare breed! Be sure to thank him.

2. If your husband isn't as concerned as you are, don't see it as a character flaw. See it more as an educational flaw. Elizabeth steadily

encouraged me in the direction of being a more caring father. How? See #4.

3. Make sure you are doing all *you* can to care for your children in the areas you are in charge of: nutrition, safety, hygiene, manners, sleep, playmates, daytime TV, to name a few.

4. Once you have evaluated your heart and your level of commitment, sit down with dad. Share your concerns for the children. Ask him what you, he, and both of you should do about your concerns. Ask for his input and suggestions. What does he see being done, not done, needing improvement?

5. Many areas of childcare are your responsibility. So it's important that you get a report card of how well you are doing. Who better to ask than your husband and the children's dad? He sees you day in and day out. Ask for his evaluation. And don't react if he gives you a little constructive criticism. Respond positively. Thank him for his observations and suggestions. Then go to God and prayerfully evaluate his comments. Take them as coming from the Lord and act on them. Then later on, ask for another progress report!

6. Enlist and encourage your husband's support and leadership, especially as the children get a little older. Let him be the point man regarding school friends, school curriculum, relationships with the opposite sex, dating standards, curfews, house rules.

7. Ask your husband to read Job 1:4-5 with you. Job was concerned for the spiritual condition of his adult children. He prayed and offered sacrifices for them just in case they had offended God. That's the model of daily care and concern God is asking of you and your husband. Together, make a covenant to pray for your children, whether they are one or twenty-one. God sees your care starting when those children are conceived, and He desires that you continue that care as long as you can, even if it's just to pray for your long-gone-from-home adult children.

Little Choices That Reap Big Blessings

1. Bone up on diet and nutrition.

(And I don't mean a weight-loss diet...unless one is needed!) Diet means "a way of life." Every mom, including you, can always learn more about diet and nutrition. After all, you're the head of that department. So go online or to the bookstore and bone up. Discover how you can improve the health of your loved ones.

2. Eat dinner together tonight.

If it's possible, gather everyone together—at the same time. (That may count as a miracle!) What will you serve? When will you eat? And where? How can you jazz up the table a bit? And what can you do to make the meal special, whimsical, fun, a time of sharing? Then work on one of the suggestions in this chapter—plan to eat dinner together seven days in a row.

3. P.E. anyone?

Physical Education class was always a welcomed break in a long school day, wasn't it? So factor in physical activities for your restless—or sedentary—ones. Keep the kids physically active. What can they do outside? Is there a park nearby? A walking path? A sprinkler on a hot summer day? Be creative. Make sure your kids get lots of exercise. And, amazingly, if the TV is off, children always find something to do and usually end up outside...playing. The exertion increases health, helps guard against weight gain, and burns up excess energy in your young ones.

4. Limit TV time.

There's no doubt the TV can be mom's helper when it's crunch time—you know, between four and five in the afternoon. But just for today, set a limit on the time and times the TV will be on.

After a few days of limited viewing as a break-in time, design a workable plan for the household. What are the best programs for your children to watch? And which ones are absolutely out? What is each child's favorite program? How many minutes a day should the kids spend in front of the TV? And consider this: I read about one family that selected three nights per week they would not even turn the TV on.

And don't forget to follow-up on something most important: Find the instructions for how to block or remove certain channels on your TV. Don't know where they are? They're available online through your TV's brand name.

5. Establish a daily routine.

Everyone—including moms—are more productive and feel better about their lives when they have a consistent daily routine. It's called "horizontal planning"—trying to do the same thing at the same time each day.

Children do better with a routine too. They thrive on knowing what's next, knowing what to expect. It gives them confidence and a sense of order. Establish a schedule for your family for Monday through Friday. (Saturday and Sunday are always another story!) There will be less tension and confusion, and attitudes and productivity will improve, both at home and at school.

6. Double-check reasons behind misbehavior.

Are the kids acting up, talking back, grumpy, and requiring additional discipline? Are they getting the basics of nutritious, scheduled meals, and adequate sleep and rest? Check out what's not going on at home to make sure you're doing all you can do in providing for their needs.

7. Factor in some fun.

Where does family fun come from? Out of mom's happy heart. This book is about ways to love your children. Don't forget to plan in some fun time with your children every day.

8. Enjoy Proverbs 31:10-31.

Plan a special break in your mommy madness, set out your favorite drink, curl up, and read through this poem. Notice the ways this mom who, just like you, took care of her children. You'll be encouraged in your role of being a mom after God's own heart!

7

Take Your Children
to Church

*Let the little children come to Me,
and do not forbid them.*

MARK 10:14

Good things happen to the family that goes to church—good things that pay dividends for generations and generations. Do you believe it? It's hard to imagine—and understand—what attending church can mean eternity wise. Sundays are just a small commitment of a tiny slice of time each week, yet this one little practice, slowly, steadily, and surely, over time, supernaturally ingrains something into a soul. Sooner or later it makes a difference in a life, a heart, and in a family.

I know that's certainly been true for our family. And it all began with parents who were faithful to take Jim and me to church when we were growing up. I only share our stories to point out how this one activity on our parents' parts paid the highest dividends—that is, eternal dividends—in each of our lives years and years down the line, extending now to two more generations.

One Little Girl

In my case, my parents took me and my three brothers to church every Sunday. I don't remember ever not liking to go or not wanting to go. I mean, it was *somewhere* to go! And that's always appealing to a child, even (and maybe especially!) to a teen. I personally couldn't get enough of church. I loved my teachers there, and my youth leaders who came later on. I enjoyed participating in all of the activities and gatherings, including the youth choir. The more the better! And I looked forward to summer church camp all year long.

> *Please take me to Sunday school and church regularly... I enjoy learning more about God.*[1]

A child's heart is tender and receptive to spiritual truths and experiences, and mine was no different. As a little one with petticoated dresses, black patent leather shoes, and bows in clean curled hair, I looked forward to sitting around the little low tables with kid-sized matching chairs and hearing another story about Jesus, followed up by working on activities and projects, coloring lesson papers, and singing. I loved learning about God and Jesus and heroes like Joshua (and the walls that fell down!) and David (killing the awful giant with a mere rock in a slingshot!). And I still recall my teen years and how I loved to pray. I hung out in my room and journaled about my love for God. I wrote out my prayers. And I loved going to each and every activity for my age group, where there were caring people and friendships formed in small groups.

As you'll see in a second, I didn't become a Christian during those going-to-church-years. But, praise God, seeds were sown and watered!

One Little Boy

Jim too grew up going to church several times a week. As he's already shared, in his family only he (an only child) and his mother (a true mom after God's own heart!) went. Like every little boy, Jim couldn't wait to get out of the house and go somewhere—anywhere! His Sunday school teachers were like part of his family. And at church he participated in a Bible club where he memorized 600 Bible verses and won the highest possible award. (That's always good for any kid. Just think of the lessons learned. The discipline. The thrill of achievement. And the priceless, eternal, living Word of God in a tender young heart!)

The Difference Church Can Make

I must tell you that when both Jim and I left our childhood homes to go to college, neither of us continued to go to church. And when we met on campus, fell in love, and married, Jim was a Christian and I was not.

As a newly formed family unit, we thought, What a good time to begin going to church again! So we attended church...exactly two times—the first two Sundays after our wedding. We went exactly once to Jim's childhood church denomination and once to mine. But because we couldn't agree on either, we never went to any church again...

...until our two little girls were one and two years old. And then, because church had been a part of our childhood years, Jim and I wanted to provide the same experience for our little ones. (You understand, *they* needed it, right?) So we started taking Katherine and Courtney to church. It was quite an adventure as we turned again and again to the phone book and selected churches to visit...until we found one we all liked.

Oh, dear reading friend! There isn't space for sharing the details. It would be a very poor attempt at trying to describe the by-God's-grace-transformation that the "little choice" to go to church launched in our family. But, please, let me just state this: In both Jim and me, God used our parents' dedication to taking us to church ...to cause us to want to go to church...to cause us to want to take our children to church... where I became a Christian and Jim renewed His commitment to Christ.

> *Putting God first puts a powerful example before our children.*

And then what happened? You guessed it! In time, our little

ones became believers in Christ...and they are now taking *their* little ones to church.

Jesus and Church

According to the Bible, our Savior was "taken to church" (so to speak) by Mary and Joseph, a set of righteous parents who sought to keep God's law. In Luke 2:41-42 we learn that Jesus' "parents went to Jerusalem every year at the Feast of the Passover. And, when [Jesus] was twelve years old, they went up to Jerusalem according to the custom of the feast."

Jesus, of course, was the fullness of God and the perfect Son of God, so our focus right now is not on Him, but on His parents. The Bible says His "parents went to Jerusalem every year at the Feast of Passover" (verse 41). We note here *their* faithfulness to take their child—even "that Holy One" (Luke 1:35)—to worship in Jerusalem. Why would they bother to make the strenuous journey from Nazareth to Jerusalem to attend the Passover? Because of their commitment and love for God, and because it was the right thing to do.

The Savior grew up in a home where God's laws were obeyed and the prescribed annual festivals were faithfully observed. In Jesus' family and culture, families worshiped together. There was no such thing as dropping your kids off at church and going out shopping or for brunch or coffee. No, the parents took the children to worship with them.

Why Is Church So Important?

As New Testament believers, we are not bound to the Old Testament law. However, the kind of love Joseph and Mary had for God as a man, a woman, a couple, and parents after God's own heart burns in our hearts too. And such a love for the Lord leads to following His instructions (John 14:15). The Bible urges us to "consider one another in order to stir up love and good works, not forsaking the assembling of ourselves together, as is the manner [or habit] of some, but exhorting one another, and so much the more as you see the Day [of the gathering together of the elect to Christ at His coming][2] approaching" (Hebrews 10:24-25).

What's so important about gathering together with other Christians at church? It strengthens us because of the like-mindedness of the faith of those present. As we come in out of the world and gather together with other believers, we grow in our faith in Christ and in our trust in God. We are bolstered and boosted in our Christianity. We receive encouragement and advice from others and strengthen them in the same way.

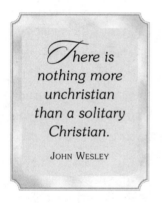

There is nothing more unchristian than a solitary Christian.

JOHN WESLEY

I began this chapter by stating "good things happen to a *family* that goes to church." But, mom, good things happen to *you* too. For instance, going to church...

> is an opportunity to hear the heart, mind, and voice of your pastor (Colossians 4:16).

is a time to join your heart with others in unified worship (1 Timothy 2:8-12).

is a time to blend your voice together with others in praise to God (Matthew 26:30; Ephesians 5:19).

is a time to give sacrificially to the Lord (1 Corinthians 16:2).

is an opportunity to have a shared experience with both young and old (Acts 2:42).[3]

No church is perfect, and going to church doesn't make you a Christian. But as I've already said, it's a supernatural experience and good things will happen because of your obedience.

Jesus' Take on Children

Jesus-the-boy grew up to be revealed and recognized as Jesus-the-Savior. And He too speaks of the importance of children being exposed to Him, His life, and His teachings. In one scene in the Bible, we witness parents who were eager to bring their little ones to Jesus. Note what happened in Mark 10:13-16:

Then they brought little children to Him, that He might touch them; but the disciples rebuked those who brought them.

But when Jesus saw it, He was greatly displeased and said to them, "Let the little children come to Me, and do not forbid them;

for of such is the kingdom of God. Assuredly,
I say to you, whoever does not receive the
kingdom of God as a little child will by no
means enter it."

And He took them up in His arms, laid His
hands on them, and blessed them.

Do you wonder why Jesus rebuked His disciples who
thought it best to protect their Master from annoyances
and interruptions? It was because they erroneously
thought that babes and young ones were incapable of
receiving anything from Jesus. But they were wrong.
Besides holding and blessing the infants and toddlers,
Jesus used them as an exhortation to those present that
they must receive the kingdom of God with childlike
trust.

There's something else here in this sweet scene. It's a
strong admonition to parents too. "Jesus' words forcefully
confront parents and all those in contact with children:
Are we helping or hindering children from coming to
Christ? Are we, ourselves, receiving the kingdom of God
with childlike trust?"[4]

Are you, mom? Are you helping your children come to
know about Christ? Are you taking them to church regularly? Faithfully? I want to repeat Dr. George Barna's
survey results here: "People are much more likely to
accept Christ as their Savior when they are young.
Absorption of biblical information and principles typically
peaks during the preteen years."[5]

But What If...?

It's "But what if...?" time again. Amazingly, a little thing like going to church can become a big issue!

*What if...*my children don't want to go to church? First of all, pray! Then stand firm. You're the adult, the parent, the one God has given authority to train up your children for life and for Him. You're in charge. One book I read included a section that covered "the principle of relentless parenting."[6] I like that. You're not a best friend or a buddy to your kids. There's a place for that, but you are primarily their parent. So hang in there. Don't coast, back down, or back out. Make the decisions and rules, and hold the line. And if you decide (along with your husband, of course) that your family is going to go to church, then your family is going to go to church.

*What if...*I'm a new Christian and my children are older and don't want to go to church? Again, pray! Then tell your family what's happened to you, about who Jesus is and what He's done for you. Let them know going to church will benefit everyone, including them, that it's been a missing element in your family, and you're sorry about that. Ask them to come along with you and see what's happening. And keep praying!

*What if...*due to a divorce, my children are with their other parent(s) on weekends and don't go to church? This time, pray, pray, *pray!* The time you do have with your kids is critical. Take time to nurture your heart and their hearts, teach them God's Word, talk to them about

God, tell them about Jesus, train them in God's ways. Be sure you prepare your kids for each time they'll be away from you. You must do your part, and then trust the Lord for them. He knows your situation. He knows your children's situation when they're away from you. And prepare to receive them back...and continue the loving and godly training.

Heart Response

"Take them to church." This one decision harvests positive fruit for a lifetime (and Lord willing, for eternity!) in the hearts and lives of our children. As we prepare to leave this tiniest and easiest of all commitments—that of simply taking our children to church—let's examine our mom hearts.

✓ How's my attendance and my zeal?—
Church isn't the worst thing you have to do, but the best. It's your greatest privilege and something to look forward to all week. The psalmist declared, "I was glad when they said to me, 'Let us go into the house of the LORD'" (Psalm 122:1). Is this the attitude of.your heart?

✓ How regularly are my children getting to church?—The story's been told that near a church in Kansas, the prints of two baby feet with the toes pointing toward the church are forever implanted in a cement sidewalk. It's said that scores of years ago, when the sidewalk was being laid, a mom after God's own heart who wanted her little boy to start out right, secured permission to stand her baby boy on the wet cement. The tracks are plainly seen today.[7] In what direction are your children's feet pointed?

✓ What's keeping my children from going to church?—Is it the time and effort it takes to get the family up, dressed, fed, and out the door a *sixth* day in your week? Is it late-night Saturdays? Is it other commitments your family's made for the Lord's Day? What part of this are you responsible for?

✓ Am I giving my children minimum or maximum exposure to church?—There is church...and then there is *church!* For instance, instead of one service for your children, most churches provide two services of teaching and activities for kids. As long as you're going to the trouble to prepare and get everyone to church, get twice the mileage out of your efforts. Stay as long as possible.

Go to the limit when it comes to church and your children. Ambassadors, Awana, Cubbies, Sparks Bible clubs?

They'll be there! Church camp? They're going! Gym nights? Sign them up! Backyard barbecues and get-togethers? Send along some hot dogs! Campfire times at the beach? Youth fellowship night? Saturday gatherings? There's no way they're missing out on spiritual growth opportunities!

Dear busy mom, I went through this entire checklist—and more!—as a going-to-church-beginner when my girls were little. Our family knew what life was like without church...and it wasn't all that good. In fact, it was empty. Sunday mornings consisted of sticking our little ones in front of the TV, sleeping in, reading the *Los Angeles Times* for hours while sipping coffee in our pj's until the ball games started on TV.

And oh do I ever remember the first time we set the alarm clock(!) on Sunday morning. But the blessings! They are countless, life-changing, and eternal. Going to church focused us on good things that carried us into and through the next week. It anchored our family on biblical principles. It flavored the daily atmosphere at home with the sweet aroma of Christ. It introduced us to other Christian families and friends. It brought meaning to the days of our lives. And it turned our feet, hearts, and minds away from the things of this world and set our affection on things above—on Christ.

I'm still thanking God daily for His gracious intervention in our lives, for the Christian friends Jim and I have, for the friends and teachers who positively influenced our children, for the mates they met at church, and for our seven little grandchildren who are now toddling off to church to their classes and teachers and lessons about Jesus.

What a blessing it is for you and your family to be part of a greater family—the body of Christ, the family of God!

From a Dad's Heart

I have to say, when it comes to taking children to church, the mom is a key player. The dad can definitely help, but you, mom, are usually the one who sets and runs the schedule for Sunday and for pacing the week as it leads up to going to church. Because you live for Sunday and for seeing your family at church together, you plan for it all week long. By Sunday you have planned your meals, set out the clothes for the children, and tried to get everyone into bed early on Saturday night. And all of this with at least some help from your husband, I hope...which brings up a couple of "what ifs" that I want to cover.

What if...my husband doesn't want to go to church with us? I'm a resident expert on this one. As you know, my dad wasn't a Christian. But somehow my mother made his life so pleasant that he didn't mind her going to church and taking me along with her. Even during the summer, my mom and I drove 30 miles each way to go to church from our cabin on the lake where my dad liked us to go as a family every weekend. Then we were right back on that lake by one o'clock to fix lunch for my dad.

I'm sure my mother invited my dad to go with us, but I can't remember him ever going to church, except when his mother died. So, like my mom, be the best wife you can be. Your husband will see a correlation between your church involvement and your life at home and will more than likely gladly give you and those sweet children up for a few hours each week.

What if...my husband doesn't want me and the children to go to church? This is a difficult place to be in as a wife and mom. You know what church means to you and the kids, and it's unfortunate to have an antagonistic husband. First, check your own heart, and evaluate your conduct around your husband and at home. Is he upset with your *faith* or with *you?* Are you portraying a form of Christianity that's unbiblical? Is your husband feeling neglected? Does he see your church attendance as driving a wedge between him and you and the children?

Ask God to show you areas where you can better demonstrate Christ's love to your husband. Also ask your husband what bothers him about your going to church. Try to reassure him that church will help you become a better wife and mother and that his children will be better for it as well.

*What if...*you work on Sunday? This is sometimes unavoidable. But if taking your children to church is a priority, then you will want a schedule where you have time for church, even if it means a pay cut. God will honor your commitment and, Lord willing, your children will grow up with a love for God and the things of God, including going to church.

One of the greatest blessings of a parent is seeing your grown children following in your footsteps and making an effort to be regular at church. It's at these times that you thank God you made the effort to take them to church throughout their formative years.

*L*ittle *C*hoices That Reap Big Blessings

1. Debrief Sunday school lessons.

My favorite part of going to church as a family is when the little ones run out of their Sunday school class waving their lesson paper in their hands. They can't wait to give it to their moms! Listen as your kids blurt out something on the run. Be sure in the fuss and flurry of visiting with others and getting to the car and home that you don't misplace this paper treasure!

Then make this one little choice when you get home: Sit down with your children individually and go over the story or activity featured in their lesson activities. Let them tell you the lesson... about Jesus healing blind eyes, about how the stone got rolled away from the tomb, about the handmade scroll with "all scripture is given by inspiration of God" copied on it. Don't miss the opportunity to reinforce these truths in young hearts. And with the older kids, tap on the door, plop on their beds, and ask what their teacher or youth pastor talked about today. Just listen. Punctuate often with, "That's good!...Oh, I like that!" What a blessing you receive as you hear firsthand

how God's Word is working in little—and big—
hearts!

2. Begin the night before.

Guard the evening before church. Consider
making it your "family night" at home. Begin
bath time early. Select and lay out church clothes
and Bibles. Set an early curfew for teens. Get the
kids to bed a little earlier than usual. (And don't
forget to make all these same little choices concerning yourself too. Things will go more
smoothly the next morning.) Then let the blessings begin!

3. Have a teacher's meeting.

How many parent–teacher meetings have you
had in your lifetime? If you have school-age
kids, probably a lot! So why not schedule a
meeting with your child's Sunday school
teacher? Or make an appointment to visit for a
few minutes after class to talk about your child's
spiritual development? Or have this saint over
for dinner with your family? You want to be as
much or more interested in the spiritual side of
your child's life as the academic side, don't you?
So find out, How does your child act in class?
What questions is he or she asking about spiritual things? What can you do to reinforce and
complement the Bible curriculum at home? And
most important, how can you assist the teacher
in leading your little one to a knowledge of
Jesus?

4. Double your pleasure.

Make the most of your time at church. God has given you a tremendous resource in your church, so be sure to take advantage of it. Most churches have both a worship service and a Sunday school program for both adults and children. Stay for both teaching times. If your child is old enough, sit together in church. Then during the next hour, split up as a family and go to your personal classes. Church has so much to offer you and your children. Go the extra mile and make the little choice to participate in extra times of worship, teaching, and fellowship. For a fraction of your total week, you get so much! What's an extra hour compared to the multiple benefits and blessings of going to church? That's not much out of the total week, but it means a lot when viewed from an eternal perspective.

5. Talk about church.

What you talk about in front of your children will give them a good indication of what's on your heart and mind. If church is important (and it is, right?), then talk about it all week. "Hey, kids, it's only three more days 'til youth night, Awana, Bible study. Let's go over your verses and look at your lesson." Take every opportunity to make going to church something your kids look forward to. "You're going to see your good friend Tommy...or Suzie...or hear your youth leader teach." If you do your part, what's important to you will be important to your children. So talk it up! Open your heart and lips and bless your kids of all ages by talking about church.

6. Read "Generations of Excuses."

I've added this insightful and clever article on the pages that follow. With your favorite cup of tea or soda, relax and read it for yourself. Look at the "little choices" made along the way—subtle little choices—and the effects that lasted for generations to come. Pause, pray, and see if your family might be making any of these same little choices. And then...well, you know what to do. Take your family to church!

Generations of Excuses[8]
by Mary Louise Kitsen

Dear Joan,

What a beautiful baby boy Ben and I have been blessed with! I cannot begin to tell you the joy he has brought to us.

You asked how Mrs. Miller is doing in church since her accident. They tell me she manages her wheelchair with amazing ease. She's still teaching Sunday school too. To tell you the truth, Ben and I haven't been to church since Timmy was born. It's just so difficult with a new baby. And I worry that he'll catch something. So many people have colds right now. When Timmy is just a little bigger, it will be so much easier.

Love, Sarah

Dear Joan,

Can you believe our Timmy is a year old already? He's so healthy and active—just beautiful.

No, we haven't really started attending church regularly yet. Timmy cried so hard when I tried to leave him in the nursery that I just could not do it. But he was just too noisy and active in church with us so we finally left early. The pastor came to visit. He assured us Timmy would be fine once we left him at the nursery, but I'm just not ready to force it yet. When he's just a little bigger, it will be so much easier.

Love, Sarah

Dear Joan,

However do you cope with three lively children? Timmy is into everything, and I simply cannot control him.

We still aren't attending church regularly. I tried leaving Timmy in the nursery a few Sundays back, but he didn't get along with the other children. The next week we took him into church with us, but he was all over the church. He'd be out of our pew before I could stop him. Several of the members sitting nearby were annoyed, but after all, Timmy's only three. It will be easier when he's just a little bigger.

Love, Sarah

Dear Joan,

I must be a perfectly dreadful mother! But Ben and I cannot keep our little boy under control. Last week he slipped out of our booth at a restaurant and caused a waitress to drop an entire tray of food. And last Sunday he slid out of our pew at church, and before I knew what was happening, guess where he was—right up front with the pastor! I could have fainted from embarrassment.

The pastor thinks a few hours at a preschool would be good for Timmy, but he's just four. He'll quiet down when he gets a little older.

Love, Sarah

Dear Joan,

It seems so funny to see our little boy walking off to school each morning. I thought starting him in school would be an ordeal, but Mrs. Foster must have a way with children. He seems happy as a lark.

No, Joan, we haven't started Timmy in Sunday school yet. It's just that his sister is still a new baby. And you know how hard it is getting ready to go to church with a new baby. When Sally is just a little older, it will be easier.

Love, Sarah

Dear Joan,

How the years fly by. Tim is in the fifth grade now, and little Sally just started kindergarten.

No, I'm afraid we aren't as faithful about attending Sunday school and church as we should be. With work for Ben and the children in school, we just don't get a chance to be together much during the week. And on Saturday there are always so many errands to run. Sunday is really the best time to spend some time together, and we like to start early. Last Sunday we drove to Lake Manaware. It's quite a distance. You really cannot wait until after church. These years are so special.

Love, Sarah

Dear Joan,

Teenagers certainly have a mind of their own! I simply cannot get Tim to attend Sunday school and church at all. He doesn't even want to go to youth fellowship. He thinks their activities are "dumb." He isn't getting along as well in school as Ben and I would like either. He doesn't seem to get along with his teachers or the other students. I wish we lived in a different town. There just seems to be something missing in this one.

Sally? She goes to Sunday school sometimes, but you know how little ones are. She thinks everything her brother does or thinks is perfect. But after all, the teen years are so difficult. It's a time of adjustment. When Tim matures a little more, he'll see things differently, and then his adoring little sister will too.

Love, Sarah

Dear Joan,

How I wish you and Tom could have made the wedding. It was so very beautiful. Tim looked so handsome, and his bride was just a vision. The church was filled, and everything was so lovely.

No, Tim and his bride haven't started attending church regularly yet. But after all, they are newlyweds. They enjoy just being together. So young and so in love. But they'll settle down in a little while, and then church will become a part of their lives.

Love, Sarah

Dear Joan,

Ben and I are grandparents! Tim and his Margie have the most darling baby boy you could ever hope to see. We are all so proud of him.

Church? Well, Ben and I just don't seem to go as often as we should. Ben's been promoted at the office again, and he sometimes plays golf with his boss on Sunday morning. And Sally is a teen now, and she's got her own interests. When things change, we'll get to church more often.

Tim and Margie? Oh, they can't really manage church right now. You know how hard it is with a new baby. And I warned Margie about letting the baby get exposed to colds that seem to be going around right now. When the baby is a little bigger, it will be easier. I'm sure they'll become active in church. After all, Tim was raised in a Christian home by Christian parents....He has a good example to follow....

Love, Sarah

8

$\mathscr{T}$each Your Children to Pray

One of His disciples said to Him,
"Lord, teach us to pray."

LUKE 11:1

Children seem to naturally desire to pray. Very few little ones will not gladly bow their heads to pray "grace" or say bedtime prayers. They want to pray! Even the baby in a highchair loves the ritual—fold hands into a fist, scrunch eyes shut, press head on folded fingers, take a peek or two, and spout out something resembling "Amen!" when the prayer is finished.

In times of fear or bewilderment, children sense the need to pray too. Again, they want to pray. I well remember an elementary schoolteacher in the Los Angeles public school system telling me that on the first day school reopened after the killer 6.8 Northridge earth-quake, her little students gathered around her. They clung to her as large aftershocks continued to roll through the area. One or two of the children even asked her if she could please pray for them, pray with them.

Because it was unlawful for my friend to pray with her students, she did what she *could* do. She gathered the children together and let them bow their heads and close their eyes for a moment of silence so they could pray as they knew how during that time.

I'm sure you scraped a knee (or two!) as a child, or took a bad fall (or two!). And you probably did what I did and turned to a parent. Somehow mom or dad made things all right, and you felt better right away. And if you were really fortunate, that parent also prayed with you.

In our family, our two little girls, with all the normal wear-and-tear of falls, scrapes, and bruises, came to either Jim or me. And we listened. We cared. We kissed boo-boos. We doctored cuts and wounds. We went to the emergency room for stitches. And we prayed. As time went by, the "falls, scrapes, and bruises" came more under the interpersonal relationship category and the resultant hurt feelings, broken friendships, break-ups, and losses.

And still today when our grown daughters have very good news to share or suffer a devastating disappoint-ment, we get a phone call. And then, once again, we listen, we rejoice or weep, we care, we seek to mend or help or comfort—whatever is needed. And we always pray, right on the phone.

Dear mom, prayer is important to our children at all ages and stages. And we bless and better their lives when we let them see and hear us pray—when we pray for them, when we pray with them...and especially when we teach them to pray. It's one more way we love them. And it's one more way we train them up for life, especially for the future when we won't always be available and they're on their own. And, blessing upon blessing, it's one more way we train them to serve God as they enter into the personal privilege and ministry of prayer.

The Optimum Mom

We've already met the optimum mom in this vital area of being a praying mom and a mom who teaches her children to pray. Her name was Hannah, and Samuel was her little guy. Hannah poured out a magnificent, powerful worship prayer to God when she left little Samuel at the temple in Shiloh (1 Samuel 2:1-10). And it's probable that, kneeling beside her, was three-year-old Samuel.

It's no wonder that the little boy Samuel—who more than likely eavesdropped on that mighty prayer from his mom's heart after God—grew up to be a great man and a man of great and mighty prayer himself. We first see the boy Samuel praying and talking with God in the sanctuary as a youth (1 Samuel 3:3-20). Commenting on this scene, Matthew Henry writes regarding Samuel: "He worshipped the Lord

> *May each of us be saved from the sin of prayerlessness!*[1]

there, that is he said his prayers. His mother, designing him for the sanctuary, took particular care to train him up to that which was to be his work in the sanctuary."[2]

Later we witness the boy-become-man-become-prophet-and-priest praying...

> ...for the nation in a time of grave trouble (1 Samuel 7:9).
>
> ...for a king for God's people (1 Samuel 8:6).
>
> ...for God to justify his displeasure with the people over their desire for a king (1 Samuel 12:17-18).
>
> ...with a grieving heart due to King Saul's disobedience (1 Samuel 15:11).
>
> ...for discernment of God's will in anointing a new king, David (1 Samuel 16:1-12).

Where, we wonder, did he learn to pray so faithfully and fervently? Probably at Momma Hannah's knee!

Other Praying Moms

One of my red-letter days as a mom was the day I first read this appeal to moms:

> The heathen mother takes her babe to the idol temple, and teaches it to clasp its little hands before its forehead, in the attitude of prayer, long before it can utter a word. As soon as it can walk, it is taught to gather a few flowers or fruits, or put a little rice upon

a banana-leaf, and lay them upon the altar before the idol god. As soon as it can utter the names of its parents, so soon it is taught to offer up its petitions before the images. Who ever saw a heathen child that could speak, and not pray? Christian mothers, why is it that so many children grow up in this enlightened land without learning to pray?[3]

I admit, I was letting my little ones grow up without learning to pray. I was allowing the days, years, and opportunities to slide by without teaching my girls to pray. This example hit me so hard as a mom of little people that I saved it. And frankly, it was just the fuel I needed to get the flame of prayer going in their hearts.

Other moms helped to show me how to teach my children to pray. (And, you guessed it, I also saved these inspiring words as I read them.)

> Valerie Elliot Shepard (a mom herself to eight children) wrote this of her famous mom, Elisabeth Elliot: "Every night when she put me to bed, she sang and prayed for the two of us."[4]

> Billy Graham's biography reports that "Billy's mother encouraged him to take part—beginning with a sentence prayer rehearsed in advance—in the family's daily devotions and to memorize scripture verses."[5]

No matter what they say or how they act, kids of all ages want to know about prayer. In fact, as we noted earlier, 91 percent of 13-year-olds pray to God during a typical week.[6] One teen, when asked what he wished his parents had done differently, said, "We should have had a family devotion time on a consistent basis, or at least prayed together each night." Still another added, "Step-by-step help in methods of Bible study and prayer would have better equipped me for life on my own."

Teens generally live lonely lives, despite the gang that's always around. So be sure to impress on your teens that God is interested in them and in whatever bothers or stretches them. When they enter new phases or must decide about their activities, encourage them to pray.[7]

> *You cannot lift your children to a higher level than that on which you live yourself.*

Yes, you'll pray with them. But point them toward personal prayer. Give them the gift of a super-special journal that reflects their personality and interests, a pen you know they'll like, and show them how to make and keep a prayer list. Help them to also create a schedule that contains a 5- or 10-minute slot for prayer. And above all else, let them see and hear you pray. Your example and your dedication is a priceless teacher.

Moms ask me all the time how Jim and I handled teen quiet times in our household. One thing we did was have everyone get up—and wake up! Then we had a set time of 30 minutes for each person in the house to be alone for "devotions." It was the household "quiet time." Doors were shut, and all was still.

And no, we didn't know what our teens were doing behind the doors. And no, we didn't surprise them or knock on their doors to check up on them. But we did provide the instruction, structure, books, tools, and time for spiritual growth to take place—spiritual growth that included praying about the issues of their lives.

A Walk Through Your Day

When you get a minute to yourself (and I'm smiling as I say that!), walk through your normal (there goes another smile!) day. Think of what you and your children have to give thanks for and where you need God's help. Then show them the way. Is it...

> ...breakfast time? Thank God for food and pray for a good day.
>
> ...devotional time? Verbalize to God what's been learned and ask for His help in applying it.
>
> ...work or chore time? Ask for God's help with character development, for your kids to do their work heartily to the Lord—not just for mom (Colossians 3:23)!
>
> ...leaving for school time? Share in a brief group prayer and a group hug in the doorway.

...homeschool lesson time? Pray for God to help you to teach clearly and your child to learn, for both of you to do a good job.

...homework time? Teach your children to ask God for help with any and all projects.

...arriving home from school time? Praise God for another day of education and a safe return to home-sweet-home.

...snack time? Give thanks for food (again!) and pray about what's happening next, what each one of you is preparing to do next.

...go to work time? Send your older kids off to jobs with a prayer and a kiss. They'll need it! Things are tough out in the world.

...another meal time? At any and all meals be faithful that "foods which God created [are] received with thanksgiving" (1 Timothy 4:3).

...bedtime? Pray something like the sentiment of Susanna Wesley's end-of-day prayer: "I give Thee praise, O God, for 'a well-spent day.'"[8] (And P.S.: Don't just pray with your children. Send them to sleep with a kiss!)

As a mom I aim for the apostle Paul's attitude. He told those he prayed for, "I have you in my heart" (Philippians 1:7). And because I carry my children in my heart (just like you do), I find myself praying always...and fervently...for them.

Prompting Prayer

As you teach your children to pray, prompts from you help. Be creative and proactive. Ask them questions. Not only will you be prompting them to pray, but you'll get a glimpse into what's going on in their lives. Begin small. For really little ones, begin with a muttered or hearty "Amen!" Then move to sentence prayers during grace at meal times. Teach them to answer your prompts,

> *Pray that your children will "continue in the things which [they] have learned... knowing from whom [they] have learned them."*
>
> 2 TIMOTHY 3:14

"Jesus, thank You for..."

"Jesus, please help me to..."

"Jesus, please help

to..."

Have them pray sentence prayers for any big or small blessing in their little lives. Then advance the level of depth as their ages advance.

Ask, "What would you like to thank Jesus for tonight? Today? Right now? Let's not forget to say 'thank You' to

Jesus!" No matter the age, from toddlers on up, they can answer this question...and pray about it.

Ask, "What are you worried about? Sad about? Let's tell God about it right now. He can take care of it." And away you go, sharing in the scary issues in their little—and big—lives...and helping them learn to cast their cares upon the Lord (1 Peter 5:7).

Ask, "What is your biggest challenge today? What would you like to ask God to help you with? Let's ask Him now." Older kids have school pressures (tests, grades, performance), peer pressure (friends—both boy- and girlfriends!), job pressures, and pressure to stand up for what's right and speak up for their faith in Christ.

Ask, "Can you think of a special friend we can pray for? How can we ask God to help him or her?" This prompt pushes children to think beyond themselves, to begin to take notice of others and their needs, to be concerned for others. As they add praying for others to their daily prayers, their character grows.

Ask, "What do you think your dad/brother/sister needs help with? What kindnesses can you do for them to make their lives easier? Let's ask God to help us all." It's never too early to work on family love.

Praying Always...for All Things

The New Testament writers summed up the importance of prayer best for us: We should...

> pray always with all kinds of prayers and requests (Ephesians 6:18),
>
> pray without ceasing (1 Thessalonians 5:17),

pray one for another (James 5:16),

pray about everything (Philippians 4:6),

pray fervently (James 5:16), and

pray continually (Acts 6:4).

The goal is to teach our children to do the same as we strive to fulfill these instructions ourselves.

As you and your family deal with the everyday cares of life, make it a point to pray. As my former pastor loved to say, "Prayer is spiritual breathing. Every breath in should result in a prayer out." That, mom, is your goal with your children. Let them see that prayer is a natural, first response to everything. Here are two more scenarios that merit your spontaneous prayers, your "spiritual breathing."

Pray with their friends. When your kids have friends, neighbors, or schoolmates over, no matter what their ages, pray grace with them at the table or with a snack. If your kids have guests sleeping over, pray over everyone when you "tuck them in." If their friends share a problem or a worry in the midst of a conversation, pray with them...just like you would your own. You see, you're a praying mom! You can't do otherwise!

Pray on the phone. When our family arrived home from the mission field, our girls were junior high age. As "missionary kids"—MKs—back in America, they suddenly seemed like they were from another era of time. They were out of it, behind the times culturally. When they entered junior high, surprisingly, they began to call home during the day, usually during lunch. At first I couldn't figure it out, but at last I got it. They had no friends, no one to eat with or talk to. So if they "had to make a phone call," their loneliness, confusion, and awkwardness didn't stand out. So I began praying with them on the phone...for a good rest of the day...and telling them I'd see them in just a few hours.

Jim too prayed with our daughters on the phone. Even to this day, when they call he always says something like, "Let's thank God." Or "Let's pray about this." Or "I don't want to hang up until we pray."

Even though it may not be verbalized or requested outright, kids phone home for assurance, to touch base, to talk to someone who loves them and cares about the details of their lives, for something familiar, for love, for wisdom. When you and I don't pray with them...why, they could have called anyone in the world and gotten advice! They could have dialed 911 to *talk* to someone, but they dialed you so you could *pray* with them. You can give them something no one else can—your prayers.

Here's a principle I've tried to live by that was passed on to me from an older mentor. She said, "Elizabeth, remember that everything you do and don't do teaches." So, dear mom, when you pray, you teach your children to pray. When you pray with your kids, you teach them to pray. When you pray with them on the phone...in the car...at the door...when they eat...when they get home...when they go to bed...with their friends, you teach them to pray.

And when you don't pray with them, you are teaching them that prayer isn't that important. So speak up. Open your mouth and pray...and pray...and pray. Don't give your prized children even the slightest opportunity to think you are not a praying mom. You are...and they must know it. Let them see—and hear—your passion for God, for praying to God, for them, and for praying for them. As a mom after God's own heart—a mom who prays—you will teach them much about prayer.

From a Dad's Heart

Some years ago I attended a pastor's conference and was again challenged with the importance of teaching my children to pray. One of the speakers gave a testimonial of how his father had spent quality time with him and his two sisters every night as they were growing up. The man's father wasn't a pastor or seminary theologian. He was just a layman in his church, an ordinary guy who would gather his children around him every bedtime and read a small portion of Bible to them. He would ask each child what the passage meant, and he would give his thoughts on the passage. Finally, the father would have each child pray about the happenings of his (or her) day and anything he was to face the next day. The godly father would finalize the bedtime ritual with an all-encompassing prayer.

The speaker went on to say that this nightly routine lasted for as long as any of the children were living at home, some into their twenties. Needless to say, it wasn't surprising to hear that, by God's grace, all three children grew up to be strong, vibrant Christians.

I want to encourage you to do two things. First, be sure you are praying with your children.

You don't have control over your husband, over whether he is a Christian or not and over his desire to be involved with parental and spiritual input. But you do have control over *your* time and priorities. Like my mom did with me, while dad is in the living room watching TV, tuck your little and big ones into bed and pray with and for them. It only takes a few minutes. Like the parent above who made a dynamic impression on his son and two daughters, do whatever it takes to spend quality time with your kids.

Then, with much prayer, if your husband is a believer, move toward helping him understand the importance of his involvement with teaching the children to pray. He may already be doing this—and that's ideal! Don't fail to give him a regular pat on the back for his participation. However, if he is not as involved as he should be or could be, share with him what you are learning, and ask for his help in this most important child-raising activity.

The father I mentioned wasn't a dynamic preacher or church leader. He was just a man— a dad—who loved his children, loved God, and wanted his children to love God too. So pray that together you and your man will consider "teaching your children to pray" one of your highest and most sacred duties as Christian parents.

*L*ittle *C*hoices
That Reap
Big Blessings

1. Memorize "The Lord's Prayer."

Are you wondering where to begin? Begin where Jesus began with His disciples, His children (so to speak). Jesus' disciples repeatedly saw and heard Him praying. Finally they asked, "Lord, teach us to pray" (Luke 11:1). And Jesus answered them by showing them exactly how, even providing the words for them. He said, "When you pray, say" and then He gave them what we call The Lord's Prayer (Matthew 6:9-13).

If that prayer is what Jesus' own family of disciples needed, then it's a good thing for your children too. Make a group project of memorizing and praying this prayer with your children. Pray it occasionally at mealtime, at bedtime, and on special occasions to keep it fresh in everyone's heart and mind.

2. Pray as a lifestyle.

The Bible says "pray without ceasing" (1 Thessalonians 5:16). Make this command your personal prayer motto, not only because this is to be your attitude as a Christian, but also because of the model you provide for your children.

To follow-through on this constant attitude of prayer, pray all day long with an eye on the clock. Where are your children? What classes are they in? Are they taking their test, giving their speech? Is it lunchtime? Recess? Are they on the school bus? At practice? In a study group? At work? At youth group or Bible study? Driving the car? Be known to your children as a praying mom.

3. Share sentence prayers at the dinner table.

If it's okay with your husband, and he doesn't feel awkward about it, have him ask everyone to go around the table and in one sentence thank God for something that happened in their lives that day. (And here's a hint: It helps if you've prepared everyone to be on the lookout during the day for what they want to especially thank God for in the evening.) If you do this on a routine basis, your children will begin to automatically notice and think all day about what God is doing in their lives. They too will become trained to "in everything give thanks" (1 Thessalonians 5:18).

4. Read from a book of prayers.

There are many books of "Common Prayers," or books of the prayers of great men and women of the past. The Puritans were famous for their books of prayers, *The Valley of Vision* being one of them.[9] If he's up for it, have dad read one prayer each morning and then ask each person to pray a sentence prayer reflecting the theme of the written prayer. That's all he has to do! If dad would rather not be a part of the prayer, then do this exercise privately with your children when dad is gone or busy.

5. Create a family prayer list.

What better way can you think of for teaching your children the importance of prayer and how to pray than by showing them the answers to their very own prayers! How is this done? By creating a family prayer list. Each day as you discuss the activities of the day and the needs of others, you, or one of the older kids, become "recording secretary" and create a list as you ask, "What would you like to ask God to help you with? Can you think of a special friend we can pray for? I heard about someone at church who needs our prayers. How can we ask God to help him or her?"

Again, prompts like these cause kids to think beyond themselves, to care about others and their hurts and needs. As your family prays for others, personal and spiritual growth occurs. Then at the end of the day, at dinner or at bedtime, or the next morning, follow-up on the prayers. Ask, "How has God answered your prayers about...?" Then write the answer next to the prayer request. Save the answers and review God's goodness often with the children. Show them how He is working in their lives through prayer.

6. Pray daily with each child at bedtime.

Whether it's you or your husband or both, relish the nightly ritual. Even plan for it—what you want to say to each child, any verses you want to share, what you want to pray over each child. In the years to come, your children will look back and say how much they appreciated these times. And they'll do the same for their little ones. Again, your kids may protest at first, but go ahead. They'll go to sleep and then wake up the next day knowing *someone* is concerned for them...and that God is watching over them.

Bedtime prayers will also become a time when your children often open up and share their heart concerns, fears, and joys with you. Why? Because they know you'll pray about it right there on the spot. And the blessing is often reversed: One teen shared, "My mother would kneel beside my bed at night and pray for me before telling me good night. It was often during the prayers that she was able to communicate her feelings or concerns to me."[10] Don't miss out on these priceless times.

9

*T*ry Your Best

And whatever you do, do it heartily,
as to the Lord and not to men.

COLOSSIANS 3:23

love the verses in the Bible that point to
God's grace. Maybe that's because I need so
much of it! Especially in the Mom Department. I'm guessing that's true of every mom because of
the delicate nature of child-raising. We love God. We love
our children. We want to follow God's instructions for us
as moms. And we want to do our best. We really do!

But here's how it goes for me. I have so many passionate desires, dreams, and prayers for myself as a mom
and for my children. So I move forward, full-steam
ahead. I do everything I think I'm supposed to do—and
more!—for a while. And then there's a bad day. I slip up
or parenting seems more demanding or less rewarding

than it was yesterday. Somehow something got acceler-ated or something went wacky. Something changed and, amazingly, what worked yesterday didn't work today.

And then I'm right back down on my knees. Again I'm lifting up my prayers and cries to God for wisdom, for discernment, for His love-joy-peace-patience-self-control, for His strength...and, most of all, for His grace.

And I start all over again. After my flop or lapse or wake-up call, God points me once again to square one, to my priorities as a woman and my purpose as a mom.

Dear fellow mom, these are the facts of life for any and every mother. Being a mother is a commitment, a responsibility, and a calling from God...for a lifetime. And being a mom is our highest joy *and* our greatest challenge. So what can we do? Every time I ask myself this question, the answer is always the same—we can only try to do our best. It's one more way we love our children.

As we head into this subject in this most important chapter, let me share six attitudes and approaches that will help you do your best. And notice I said "attitudes and approaches." These will not be things to *do*. No, they will be more like things to *think* as you approach your "Mommyhood"[2] each new day.

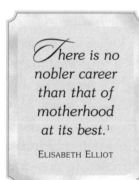

There is no nobler career than that of motherhood at its best.[1]

ELISABETH ELLIOT

1. Know Who You Are

A red-letter day in my life arrived on a Sunday afternoon.

That's the day Jim and I sat down to write out some life-time goals. Our hearts were searching for direction for our service to Christ, for our marriage, and for our family and us as parents. Our girls were young—still in diapers. Jim and I eagerly wanted to do the right thing, so my husband prayed...and away we went, off with the Lord for a few hours of brainstorming and goal-setting while our little ones napped.

Well, at the end of the afternoon, I emerged with three life goals in mind—goals that would definitely have to be accomplished by the energizing power of the Holy Spirit if they were to happen at all. And there was no doubt as I looked at them that they would demand some tremendous personal growth—like a 180-degree turn-around!

My Number One goal that came out of that afternoon of prayer and heart-searching was stated this way: "To be supportive and encouraging to my husband and chil-dren." These are simple words. There's nothing earth-shattering here (unless you had been living for yourself and neglecting your family...like I had!). But since that memorable day, I have known exactly who I am and what it is I'm supposed to do—I am a wife and a mother. I am to love my husband and love my children. In short, on that sunny Sunday, my life became, for the first time, focused.

And today, as I'm sitting here thinking about where I was...and where I wanted to go...and thinking about you...and where you might be...and where you might want to go, I realize that any lifetime goal is just that—a goal that will require a lifetime to accomplish. But this one goal forced me to answer a most significant question: "Who am I?"

I believe with all my heart that your best—or my best...or anyone's best—is born out of knowing who you are. So I'll ask: Do you know who you are? If you have children, you are one of God's moms. That's who you are.

2. Know What It Is You Do

I addressed what it means to love God first and foremost in *Loving God with All Your Mind*.[3] Loving God with all your heart, soul, and mind is—and always will be—our ultimate priority (Matthew 22:37). And being a loving wife is covered in other books I've written.[4] But my role as a mom is what this book is all about. My goal to focus on my family forced me to realize that, based on Titus 2:3-5, next to loving God and loving my husband, loving my children was my highest human priority and responsibility.

The young women [are]...to love their children.

TITUS 2:4

Oh, what freedom! To finally know who I am *and* what it is I am to do! From that point on, I began to focus my efforts and energies into being the best mom I knew how to be. And you know, with this focus life got a lot easier. Before knowing who I was and what I was to do, I was trying to be all things to all people—including myself—and I was failing miserably. I realized I couldn't serve all those people and interests at the same time. I couldn't please everyone and do everything. I was going to have to make choices about who I needed to serve.

So I chose to focus on my family. And that choice also meant I needed to focus on myself and growing in Christ—so I did just that. I focused on growing in God's grace and in my knowledge of Him through His Word and in my walk with Him. And I soon grew to better understand the amazing assignment God had given me— that of being a mom—a mom after His very own heart! I began (like you are right now) to read books about Christian parenting, about training my little ones, about teaching them godly wisdom and character.

It's now been 30 years since that bright goal-setting day. And I have to say, the goals I laid out that afternoon have never budged, changed, shifted, or evolved. Yes, my nest is empty as I'm sitting here pouring out my heart to you, but I'm still a mom to this day. That will *never* change. And glory-upon-glories, I'm a grandmom to seven little ones too.

And I have to be honest, if I really want to move into fear-mode, all I have to do is start wondering, "What if…I hadn't set those goals? What if…I hadn't gotten things straight with God? What if…I hadn't made some hard and important decisions? What if…things had continued to drift along…in the wrong direction?"

All of this to say, I want to encourage you to take your own hour or two (yes, I'm smiling!) and think through who you are and what it is you do—or what you are supposed to do. Putting your answers on paper will simplify your life, clarify your purpose, and revolutionize your life as a mother. It will provide the focus that is required for trying to do your best as a mom. It will provide you with 30, 40, 50 years (only God knows how many actual years) of knowing, every single day, exactly who you are and what it is you are to do.

Dear one, realize too that on every single one of your days, the world will be sending you signals that you are a nobody unless you are a focused, sold-out working woman. The world says being a mom is old-fashioned. That you need to take care of yourself. That you're supposed to be Number One. That your kids will make it just fine without your constant care. But the world is wrong! You can rest in your heart and know with all of the confidence and strength in the world who you are and what it is you are to do.

3. Realize You Cannot Serve Two Masters

I now understand that I was learning the value of the principle Jesus laid down for us that applies equally to all areas of life: We cannot serve two masters equally. Jesus stated, "No one can serve two masters; for either he will hate the one and love the other, or else he will be loyal to the one and despise the other" (Matthew 6:24). Although Jesus was speaking of loving God or loving money, His remarks regarding divided loyalties apply to many areas in a woman's life—even that of being a mom.

Here's how this principle worked in my life. I had two little girls, ages one and two...but I also had a desire for an advanced education degree. So I enrolled in college with a full load of classwork, found a babysitter, began dropping my babies off at daycare before daylight, and picking them up after dark. I was definitely serving one master (going to school) over another (being a mom).

Then, when I became a Christian and wrote down my goals, I realized that to serve my new and forever Master, Jesus, meant I also needed to serve my husband and children. So I dropped the master's program and began the real "Master's Program"! You might say I began earning a Master's degree in Mothering.

Please, don't get me wrong. I'm not saying you can't or shouldn't have a job or a career or be enrolled in school. We moms are the absolute best when it comes to managing, juggling, and balancing life's demands. We are the world's finest. That's something else we do! But what I am saying is that if you find yourself (like I did) viewing your job or career, schooling or hobbies, even your ministry, as your master, as the focus of your life, time, and energy, then you've drifted over a line that will make it next to impossible to give your best to your children.

Oh, there'll be good times. You'll have some quality spurts with your children. But you'll find this *other* thing tugging at your heart and mind. Your ener-

Divided loyalties lead to diluted living.

gies will quickly turn elsewhere. Believe me, I know what I'm talking about, both as a mom who fell into this category for a while and as a child of a career mom.

I'm praying that, with God's help and by His grace, you will begin to understand who you are—a mom—and that what you do is give your best to your kids. Except for God and your husband, everything else is secondary.

4. Keep It Simple

I recently read some startling statistics about moms. Did you know that "70 percent of American moms say they find motherhood today 'incredibly stressful.' Thirty percent of mothers of young children reportedly suffer from depression. Nine hundred and nine women in Texas recently told researchers they find taking care of their kids about as much fun as cleaning their house, slightly less pleasurable than cooking, and a whole lot less enjoyable than watching TV."[5]

Oh, do I ever see myself here on certain days (you know, those crazy loser days every mom drowns in once in a while). All I can say is it helps to keep things simple. That's perhaps the greatest survival tactic for moms. The word "stressful" means strained. It's a condition of tension caused by too much pressure. To relieve the strain and reduce the tension and pressure, simplify things. For instance...

> ...make fewer trips out in the car. Run less personal (notice I didn't say needful) errands when the kids are with you. Choose one or two days to go out for errands each week...instead of every day.

> ...make simpler meals and serve them in a simpler manner. Eat earlier at night. Get the kids ready for bed—and in bed—earlier. End your day earlier.

...well, I could go on and mention things like organizing and cleaning out clutter, but for most of us that might put us over the edge by adding even more pressure!

As you think about keeping things simple, picture the classic fable of the tortoise and the hare. Who won the race between these two? The tortoise. Why? Because the tortoise was steady, easy going, forward moving, and unpressured. The hare, however, was all over the place, running here, running there, frazzled, and unfocused. In all of the hustle and bustle, the hare lost sight of the goal. I'm sure you get the message: Keep it simple, steady as she goes, and don't lose sight of the goal—of being a mom after God's own heart.

5. Don't Go It Alone

In the Bible Mary, the mother of Jesus, had Elizabeth (Luke 1). Paul had Timothy. Elijah had Elisha. Moses had Aaron. All these mighty-for-God men—and moms!—needed the encouragement and the camaraderie of like-minded people. There will be more on this important aspect of survival for moms in the final chapter. But for now, remember that God has surrounded you with other moms. Surely in your church there are those in your same boat—the mommy boat. There are also older women who are a step or two ahead of you in the mothering game, and maybe even some who have finished the course.

God has set the church up to include younger women and moms who can and need to learn from older women and moms, and also older women and moms who can pass on their wisdom and lend support to those who are younger and less experienced. Hook up with other moms. Let them steer you in the right direction—God's direction. Allow them to provide you with wisdom—God's wisdom. Welcome any and all helping hands, praying hearts, and much-needed encouragement.

6. Take One Day at a Time

If you think about it for even a millisecond, you might begin to see mothering as an overwhelming task. Here you are, entrusted with a human soul that will live for eternity. Of course, God is ultimately responsible for the eternal destiny of that child, but humanly speaking, you and your husband are responsible for his or her physical, mental, and spiritual development. Now before you get too anxious and have a nervous breakdown, take to heart Jesus' calming advice about focusing your efforts on today only: "Don't be anxious about tomorrow. God will take care of your tomorrow too. Live one day at a time" (Matthew 6:34 TLB).

My friend and fellow mom, just focus on making today count. Try your best to be the best mother you can be...just for today. Oh, believe me, you will fail on some days, but don't give up. The reward is too great to not give it your all each and every day. Cherish your one day. Welcome it. Plan it. Live it. Enjoy it. Evaluate it. Adjust it. (I just received an email from a first-time home-school mom who admitted she was very task-oriented, but, after some evaluating, planning, and adjusting, was learning to "have fun" with the kids. She wrote, "We are having a blast!")

And what will happen when you begin to live one day at a time? You'll find yourself stringing one "best" day after another. Don't get in a hurry to have a season pass. Pass it will! Don't wish away the nursing infant at your breast and the fact that his or her care takes your time away from other activities. Don't wish away the crawler or toddler who's into everything. Don't wish away the "terrible (or is it terrific?) twos," the troublesome teen years, or hectic summers. What matters is where your heart is and enjoying the days you have with your children.

> *Sow your best efforts today, and reap God's abundant blessings tomorrow.*

Then when you have finally fashioned, with God's help, your child into a beautiful, godly life, you can stand back with amazement and thanksgiving. What you will be looking at is a life that is ready to take his or her place in society as a strong, vibrant Christian. A life that represents God's next generation. A life that will start the process all over again in another home with other new little souls. As the psalmist declared, "[The LORD's] truth endures to all generations" (Psalm 100:5).

Heart Response

I'm sure I've said this before (and may again!), but it's worth repeating. When it comes to your mothering, it's a matter of the heart. Focus your heart firmly on giving your all to each day as it arrives, and don't worry about your entire life. All God is asking is that you give being a mom your all...just for today. It's just a 24-hour span. And even some of that span (though never enough!) will be spent sleeping (if all goes well!).

And remember, giving all your heart to practice right priorities begins with God. Therefore, seek Him first thing each new day. Acknowledge Him. Spend time with Him. Pray and present your day to Him, along with its "trouble" (Matthew 6:34)—you know, all the accidents, curve balls, interruptions, and Plan B's that will most surely arise during your day. Draw energy from Him. Sharpen your focus before God into a settled determination.

Next, lay your priorities as a wife before God. Then put your high calling of Mom before Him. Reaffirm who you are and what it is you are to do...just for today. Review your priorities—what's important to you, and most important, what's important to God. Turn every area of life over to Him...just for today.

Finally, as you walk through your day, "in all your ways acknowledge Him, and He shall direct your paths" (Proverbs 3:6). As each issue and option comes at you, stop, think, and pray—even if it's just for a split second. Ask God's advice. Ask for His wisdom (James 1:5). Involve Him in your every thought during the day, your every word spoken to your little male and female treasures. Make Him the center of all that you do. When you follow this practice, you'll discover that He is truly guiding you step-by-step through your day, assisting you as you do your best...just for today. He will lead and empower you to work to accomplish His purposes, one of those being that you are a mom.

I have a few verses that keep me going as a mom and inspire me to keep on giving my all. I use them almost as one, and I use them every day, all day long: "But one thing I do... [and] I can do all things through Christ who strengthens me" (Philippians 3:13 and 4:13). You see, the apostle Paul, who wrote these words, had a goal. And that goal required—and consumed—all his energy. He never took his eyes off the goal...nor should we. He gave his all...and so should we. And what did Paul do when things got tough, when the path turned uphill, when his energy waned? He simply drew on his riches in Christ Jesus (Philippians 4:19). Why, he could do *all* things through Christ, his power source! And so can you.

From a Dad's Heart

Before you were a mom, you were a wife. Hopefully, you do everything you can to support and love your husband (Titus 2:4). You do your best. You try to do him "good and not evil all the days of [your] life" (Proverbs 31:12). Well, keep up the good work! Your marriage will be blessed by God, and you will have a great friend in your husband long after the children are grown and gone.

But what about Proverbs 31:27: "She watches over the ways of her household"? Are you also continually "watching" as a sentinel over your home and your children? In Bible times a "watchman" had one function, one purpose—to watch and warn. You, as a mom, have an important purpose as ordained by God—love your children (Titus 2:4). How is this to be done?

Elizabeth has been helping you see how this calling fleshes out in your life. You love your children by guarding them from the evils and pitfalls they encounter outside the walls of your home. And the best way to do this is to train them in the ways of God so they are prepared when they leave the house. And this training starts early. The communists said, "Give us a child for the first six years of life and then you can have it back." Why six? They knew, along with science and educators, that the majority of foundational learning comes by age six. In six years the communists could so thoroughly indoctrinate a child in their ideology that he or she was theirs for life.

Most parents, even Christian parents, put off training until their child "gets older." By the time many Christian parents put spiritual training into full gear, humanly speaking, it's almost too late. The child is already set in the world's ways.

Christian mom, are you trying your best to love, train, watch, and warn? Or are you a little preoccupied with other things? Have you gotten side-tracked? Has your primary focus in life been diverted? Have you subtly stopped watching over your children? Have you relied on others to teach and train your children? Don't give your children over to the world. Fight for their souls! Do battle with the forces of evil. Watch and warn, pray and act. Jobs and hobbies and other activities come and go, but the soul left to the world's pull can be lost for eternity. Pray, do your best, and trust the results to God.

And what if you are having to go it alone? What if you are a single mom having to raise your children for life and for God alone? Or

208 A Mom After God's Own Heart

what if your husband travels a lot, or is deployed by the military, or works long or odd hours, or is unsupportive in child-raising efforts? Never forget that in reality, you—and every mom—are never alone. God is there! He knows your situation. He knows what every one of His moms is up against and the difficulties you encounter. He knows your children and their struggles. But He still asks one thing of you—that, as a mom, you try your best. Thank Him that His "grace is sufficient for you" and His "strength is made perfect in [your] weakness" (2 Corinthians 12:9)!

Little Choices That Reap Big Blessings

1. Evaluate your normal weekly schedule.

Mentally list your many roles and responsibilities. What little choices have you been making in terms of activities, time investments, and personal pursuits that are consuming the majority of your physical time? Your mental energies? How do these choices compare with God's choices in Titus 2:4: "The young women [are] to love their husbands, to love their children"?

2. Make a fresh start today.

As a busy mom, I'm sure you are shocked at the amount of time you can sometimes spend on pursuits other than that of being the best mom you can be. But as you evaluate your schedule, start turning things around. What little choices can you make today to say "no" to other activities in order to say "yes" to your children? The great preacher, Charles Haddon Spurgeon, put it this way: "Take care of your lambs, or where will you get your sheep from?"

3. Lavish them with love.

Write "Three Ways I Can Love My Children Today" on a 3″ x 5″ card and list three choices you can make today that say "I love you, I cherish you" to the little and big people who make up your family. Make a fresh card each morning for the next few days. God's love for you is fresh and new every morning...and your love for your loved ones can be too. Look for new and personal little ways to demonstrate your love to your children.

4. Start being a more involved mom.

If your schedule is keeping you from being more involved in your children's lives, pray, and start making the little choices that will result in a dramatic turnaround. Start by choosing to be more involved in the daily process of their lives. Choose to be a part of their daily training. It's only natural for people—and especially children of all ages—to stray and run wild when left to themselves. As the proverb puts it, "A child left to himself brings shame to his mother" (Proverbs 29:15). A mom needs to remember that children thrive in their mom's very presence when given strong, sure limits. The limits you set are an indication of your love.

7. Schedule your own goal-setting session.

Pardon my smile for putting this as a "little choice"! But really, it's a little choice to take out your calendar and choose a time to meet with God to evaluate your life. It's no problem getting to the beauty salon for a makeover that takes two hours or traveling to attend a special craft seminar to learn something new. So go for the ultimate makeover! Learn the ultimate new skills! Make the all-important little choice to reserve your own personal appointment with God. Who knows? It may just well be your own red-letter day!

10

$\mathcal{T}$alk to God About Your Children

Be anxious for nothing,
but in everything by prayer
and supplication with thanksgiving
let your requests be made known to God.

PHILIPPIANS 4:6

've often heard Jim teach about "the whole man." In the Greek culture of Bible times, the whole man was one who was complete in three areas of life: body, soul, and spirit. All three parts were to be trained and matured. The Greeks worked on their bodies, developed their minds, and sought a fine-tuned spiritual awareness and religious understanding. Excellence in all three areas was required in order to be considered complete or whole.

The Whole Child

This same concept applies to child-raising. We are to prepare, educate, and train "the whole child," neglecting

none of these realms. Physically, we take care of our
children to ensure, to the best of our ability, that they are
healthy, strong, and fully developed. Mentally we make
sure they are educated and trained for life. But spiritually
we teach, train, show the way, *and* pray! That's because
spiritual development is a battle. As the apostle Paul
explained, "We do not wrestle against flesh and blood,
but against principalities, against powers, against the
rulers of the darkness of this age, against spiritual hosts
of wickedness in the heavenly places" (Ephesians 6:12).

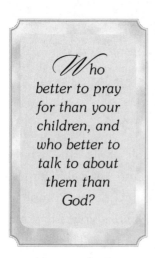

*Who
better to pray
for than your
children, and
who better to
talk to about
them than
God?*

This is where praying and
being a praying mom comes
into focus. In this chapter we
move to the area that accomplishes more than all of our
doing for our children does. It's
private. It's personal. It's done
alone. And it's spiritual. I'm
talking about spiritual warfare!
It's nothing we do *with* our children because we do it alone,
yet…somehow…it seems to
accomplish amazing things *for*
our children. Dear mom, it's
prayer, and here are "The Top Five" items for your prayer
list…the prayer list of a mom after God's own heart.

1. Pray for Your Child's Salvation

This week, while Jim and I were at a speaking event,
our little grandson Ryan entered this world…four weeks
early! Although we had arranged our schedule to cover

his mom and family for two weeks before and after his due date, he chose to surprise us. I'm so thankful to the event coordinator who was able to print off a picture of this new little grandson for Jim and me so we could see what he looked like. Well, from that point on I found myself kissing his picture and saying, "There's the little one whose salvation I've been praying for!"

That's the way it is with our children. As my own children were growing up, I prayed daily for my two girls to become Christians, to believe in Jesus Christ as their Savior. I also prayed daily for 20-plus years for their future mates, that they would love and belong to Christ as well. And, by God's grace, our daughters and their husbands have become two Christian families with seven children. And, you guessed it, we are now in the throes of praying for God's gracious salvation of the next generation...and their spouses...and... Well, you get the picture. It's one that extends into eternity!

Dear mom, I don't know how many minutes a day you have or can set aside for prayer for your children and the salvation of their souls, but we can never underestimate its value and importance. The way I made praying for my girls through the decades happen was by creating a special tab in my prayer notebook. The tab didn't say "Children." No, it said "Katherine & Courtney." Using their names was much more

Who better to pray for a child's second birth than the mom who gave birth to that child?

personal. You see, they were (and are) a passion of mine, and my prayer time for them was (and is) an eternal investment. They were and are vitally important to me. Within that section in my notebook I had three pages that I wrote on daily:

> Page 1—General prayer requests for both.
>
> Page 2—Specific prayer requests for
>   Katherine.
>
> Page 3—Specific prayer requests for
>   Courtney.

With this setup I could pray for general issues for both girls—salvation, spiritual growth, safety at school, friends, godly character qualities, involvement at church. These kinds of prayers rarely change and apply to all our children, both yours and mine.

After covering the "biggies"—with eternal life being the Number One biggie—I then moved to the individual pages and prayed specifically for the concerns of each of my girls—respect for Jim and me as their parents, medical problems, habits, attitudes, any difficulties at school, problem relationships, a job interview, acceptance of their applications for college. As individual as each of your children is, that is how unique you can tailor your list for each one of them.

There are many things we moms can pray about for our children, but there's absolutely no doubt that their salvation is tops on the list. Pray what I call "The Lydia Prayer" from Acts 16:14:

Lord, please open [your child's name] heart to accept the message of the gospel.

If and when, by God's grace, this becomes a miraculous reality, then you move right on to praying for their "sanctification"—to praying for their spiritual growth, for their Christlikeness.

2. Pray for Your Child's Friends

Beyond the preaching and teaching that must accompany and prepare the way for this key area in every child's life—their friends—prayer is the order of every day! Constant prayer for years and years and years! That's because friends are such a vital area in a child's life. As Paul stated, "Do not be deceived: 'Evil company corrupts good habits' " (1 Corinthians 15:33). Proverbs, too, teaches, "Make no friendship with an angry man, and with a furious man do not go, lest you learn his ways and set a snare for your soul" (Proverbs 22:24-25). And so we moms pray!

Here's how praying about friends went for me as a mom. As I listened to my daughters talk about their friends and as I met them one by one, I put their friends' names on my prayer list for each daughter. I prayed for their friends' salvation and Christian character. I prayed for their situations at home. I prayed that they be a good influence on my girls…and my girls on them!

Also, whenever my girls were invited to a friend's house or to do something with a friend, I prayed for wisdom. Was it the right person? The right kind of activity? The right amount of time (or too much)? The right timing in their lives? (For instance, when should sleepovers and trips to the mall begin?) The right time of day? Of course I talked everything over with Jim, but I also talked everything over with my Heavenly Husband.

And friends of the opposite sex? All of the praying mentioned above goes double—and triple!—for this delicate area that calls for utmost carefulness on a mom's part. One thing that helped us tremendously was my husband's foresight. He had both of our daughters write out in their own words the Bible's standards for the kind of boyfriends they should have. These lists were written before adolescence and hormones and peer pressure set in, and they were carefully filed away. Then, when some guy came along, Jim would say, "Let's get your list, honey, and see what the standards are that you set for a boyfriend." And out came the list from the file cabinet,

> *Anyone who pushes you nearer to God is your friend.*

and together we would all go over it. Did the young man measure up to God's profile? As the girls answered that question, decisions became obvious... regardless of emotions.

Those handwritten lists, my friend, became the guidelines we *and* our children prayed over...and over. And then, of course, if some boy did qualify, his name went right on top of Momma's Prayer List—and I mean with capital letters! Now here was *ultra*-serious business I needed to tend to with God!

If I had my way, I would ask you to *please* read daily from Proverbs with your child. Why Proverbs? First, because the dual purpose of the book of Proverbs is "to produce the skill of godly living by wisdom and instruction...and to develop discernment."[1] As the writer of Proverbs explains, the purpose of the book is "to give prudence to the simple, to the young man knowledge and discretion" (Proverbs 1:4). What a blessing for our kids! And second, because so much of this little book of wisdom has to do with different types of people and situations and how to recognize them. In everyday language, Proverbs describes those who are good and evil, righteous and unrighteous, wise and foolish. With any exposure to Proverbs, your children will have God's wisdom concerning the kinds of friends to choose to be with and those they should avoid at all costs.

But don't leave it all up to Proverbs. Pray like only a mom can! Pray the contents of Psalm 1:1-2:

> Lord, grant that [your child's name] would walk not in the counsel of the ungodly, nor stand in the path of sinners, nor sit in the seat of the scornful, but that his (or her) delight will be in the law of the Lord.

3. Pray for Your Child's Purity

I shared 1 Thessalonians 4 earlier. It's a wonderful purity verse for you to preach and teach...and pray for your kids: "For this is the will of God, your sanctification: that you should abstain from sexual immorality; that each of you should know how to possess his own vessel in sanctification and honor, not in passion of lust, like the Gentiles who do not know God; that no one should take advantage of and defraud his brother in this matter....For God did not call us to uncleanness, but in holiness" (verses 3-7). Briefly, based on these verses, you can teach, preach, and pray as follows:

- ♡ God has revealed His will concerning sexual purity.

- ♡ Steer clear of all sexual sin.

- ♡ It is possible to control your body.

- ♡ God's standards are the opposite of the world's.

- ♡ Sexual expression is reserved for marriage.

- ♡ Never tempt, tease, or take advantage of anyone sexually.

- ♡ We are called to holiness, and God will help us fulfill this calling.

Fellow praying mom, this is why we pray first for salvation for each child, and then for their friendships. Both prayer processes pave the way for this one. Turn these verses from 1 Thessalonians 4:3-7 and their instruction into a prayer that goes something like this:

Lord, I pray that [your child's name] will keep himself (herself) from all sexual sin, that he (she) will learn how to master his (her) own body in holiness and purity, that he (she) will not succumb to temptation or take advantage of another person, that he (she) will understand that God has called us to dedicate ourselves to holiness and the most thorough purity.

4. Pray for Your Child's Schoolwork

Are your children young? Then you as a mom get to make learning fun. But to do this requires time. So pray for the time to be with them and that learning will be a joy when you are together.

As your children get older, they probably won't be quite so motivated to learn. This poses another opportunity for you to pray for them, to talk things like their education and schoolwork over with God. What generally motivates you to do something? Usually it's knowing why something is important, right? If you have a reason, you're more motivated to get the job done. So again, pray that you can help your children understand the importance of learning in general and their schoolwork specifically. Sit down and explain God's desire that we do all things well, including schoolwork, that it's our way of preparing for the future—for a future of serving God and for the future He has in mind for each of us. In other words, that's the "why."

So in all your praying, pray for your children's willingness to work and desire to do well. Then follow-up to see how they're doing with their schoolwork. Let them know by your involvement that you love them

No work is too small to be done well.

and care how they're doing. And as a reminder, also pray
for wisdom for them—and for you—as together you
assist each child in determining the way he or she should
go practically and vocationally.

For decades I prayed for my daughters' teachers. It's a
must for a mom after God's own heart, whether your kids
are in secular or private schools. Pray for God's saving
grace for their teachers. Pray for your children to be a
consistent witness of their faith in God. And if your child
is in a Christian school, pray for their teachers and their
walk with God. Also pray about what their teachers are
teaching. School is a huge part of every child's life, and it
makes up a huge part of your life and your prayer life.
And if you're homeschooling? Pray for your diligence as
you faithfully prepare and for your children to hear what
you have to say as a teacher. Your prayers need to cover
every educational scenario. Pray the content of Colossians 3:23-24:

> Lord, whatever [your child's name] does,
> including his (her) schoolwork, motivate him
> (her) to do it heartily, as to the Lord and not
> to men.

5. Pray for Your Child's Church Involvement

Amazingly, when children are little, they want to be
involved in whatever you're involved in, especially at
church. But as they age, it takes a little more than that.
That's why, from an early age, Jim and I prayed for the

salvation of our two children. Without the indwelling Holy Spirit, a child will become less and less interested in church. So again, a relationship with Christ as Savior is the starting point for your prayers.

And while you're praying for God to open young hearts, keep taking them to church. This will help develop in them the pattern of going to church. As parents, we made it a habit for our family to attend every worship service at church. We also made sure that our girls participated in every activity for their age group, including camps. We sacrificed whatever it took, whether time or money or inconvenience. We didn't want them to miss out on any and every opportunity for God's Spirit to work in their young and impressionable lives.

You and I can—and should—pray long and hard about our child's participation at church. But we should also remember that their involvement is influenced by our involvement, especially as they get older. Pray for their Bible clubs, church activities, youth groups, service opportunities, and camps. Treat them as being even more important than their schoolwork. And put their Sunday school teachers or youth pastors on their individual daily prayer lists too. These are important people in your kids' lives, and you'll want to pray earnestly for them as they teach your children about God and their walk with Him.

When it comes to your children and their involvement and instruction at church, pray along with 2 Peter 3:18 and Ephesians 4:15:

> Lord, may [your child's name] grow in the
> grace and knowledge of our Lord and Savior

Jesus Christ. May he (she) grow up in all things into Him who is the head—Christ.

Think about prayer for a moment. As we've journeyed together through these ten ways to love our children, there has been much for us to *do*. For instance, we are to take time to nurture our own heart. Then we are to teach, talk, tell, train, and take care of our children. And we are also to take them to church, teach them to pray, and do our best. That's a lot of *doing*.

But in this chapter, with this most important way to love your children, in this utterly heavenly category, we don't *do*. Instead we *pray*. It's spiritual labor. It's the mighty ministry we perform when we talk to God about our children. It's the time when we plead, supplicate, importune, appeal, and ask God to work in our children's lives. It's when we come boldly before our God and His throne of grace and talk over our concerns about our children with Him.

So who is a mom after God's own heart? She's a mom who's devoted to preaching and praying. No matter what your children's ages, you will be teaching your children the scriptures that will train them for God and guide their lives. (This is the preaching part of the formula.) And, of course, you are going to be talking to your child about God at any and every opportunity. (This might be considered to be even *more* preaching.) But most of all, you are going to be talking to God about each of your precious ones. And this is the praying part. And, mom, we do it with all of our heart...for life! It's what a mom after God's own heart does.

From a Dad's Heart

In the first chapter of this book, Elizabeth suggested that, if it was appropriate and your husband was interested, you might invite him to read my "Dad" pages. I have written these sections to suggest how you can help your husband to assist you in raising your children. Prayer is one of the most special ways both of you can love your kids. Prayer is not like feeding or clothing or sheltering your children. But prayer is as important or more important than anything physical you can do for them. Prayer is also a unique opportunity for a dad. As a Christian, God has ordained that your husband be the spiritual head of the family. Part of that responsibility involves praying for you and the children.

When I think of a parent or a father in the Bible who prayed for his children, I immediately think of Job in the Old Testament. I know I mentioned him before, but if your husband is interested in having a model to follow for his own prayers for the children, ask him to read Job 1:1-5. As you or he reads, you'll see Job's prayers as a parent involved three elements:

♡ First, Job prayed with *focus*. He probably prayed for many other things, but in the opening verses of the book that bears his name, God wants us to know that Job's family was a priority for his prayer time. He had seven sons and prayed for each one by name (Job 1:4-5).

♡ Next, Job prayed with *frequency*. He didn't pray for his children on a hit-and-miss basis. He prayed "regularly" (verse 5).

♡ Finally, Job prayed with *fervency*. He rose up early to pray for each of his children. Job was concerned for their spiritual condition. His thoughts centered around their conduct. Job reasoned in his mind, "Perhaps my children have sinned and cursed God in their hearts" (verse 5 NIV). So he prayed.

Job provides a model for all parents—especially dads—to follow when it comes to praying for our children. However, you, as a mom, should never fail to pray for your children. Don't assume your husband is praying for them. Pray that he is, but be sure you are praying. And if you can, pray together with your husband for the children.

As you can see, there is always much to pray for your husband too, for the father of your children. Pray for his sensitivity toward the children. Pray that he will assume his position as spiritual head of the family if he isn't already doing that now. Also pray that your husband will read these few verses about Job's prayers for his children. Obviously, if your husband isn't a Christian, he won't have a great desire to pray, so pray for him to become a Christian. As I've heard Elizabeth encourage women so many times, "the effective, fervent prayer of a righteous *[wife and mom]* avails much" (James 5:16).

Little Choices That Reap Big Blessings

1. Create prayer pages for your children.

Make one general page and one personal page
for each child. Then begin recording your concerns. We only covered "The Top Five" in this
chapter, but obviously there are many more concerns we moms have for our precious ones. So
make your own lists...and pray, pray, pray. As
God's goodness and grace are revealed in
answers and your pages are filled with His will
concerning your prayers, file them away. For me,
these pages were placed in a file folder. Then, as
the filled pages continue to come along, they
soon required an entire file drawer for storage!

As the years of mothering pass, even the dark and
baffling ones, be sure to go back and revisit the
answers to previous prayers. Be blessed again and
again. Have your faith strengthened over and over
as you remember each situation and how God
worked in your life and in the life of each child.
Give Him thanks for His goodness and faithfulness.

2. Enlist the prayer support of others.

Do you have godly relatives or very close friends?
Who better to pray along with you at every stage

of your child's spiritual and physical development than a grandparent, or a special aunt, or a trusted and longtime friend? But do be careful not to be too specific about some areas of your child's life. You don't want to betray the trust of your child and permanently mar another person's opinion and memories of your child.

3. Set aside some time each day to pray for each child.

Let me ask you a question: If you aren't praying for your child, who is? Maybe a godly dad or a godly grandparent? But it's possible that on any given day, you are the only one praying for your child. Please don't miss a day. Your child needs your prayers. Do you have ten minutes? That's a fairly "little choice."

But also be aware that the more children you have, the greater the time commitment will become. I met one faithful grandmother who committed to pray 10 minutes when the first grandchild came along. Now she has 24 grandchildren and is praying 4 hours a day! Is praying for your child important to you? If it is, then you'll find the time...no matter how many children you have.

4. Pray with each child every day.

This great privilege usually comes at bedtime. Ask each child privately about his or her day. How did things go? Any problem relationships? Together pray for what happened today and what's going to happen tomorrow. Don't send your children to bed without prayer. These precious opportunities will soon be gone. Take advantage of these times to teach your children the importance of prayer as together you see how God is going to answer your combined prayers.

5. Pray for your child's schedule.

This won't be too difficult for a two- or nine-year-old, but a 16- or 17-year-old's life and schedule can get pretty hectic. By knowing their schedules (which you found out while you prayed and tucked them in the night before—and yes, I mean your teens too!), you will know how to be praying as events unfold throughout the day. Then ask how things went when the children return home at the end of the day. And don't forget to seal the report with yet another prayer.

6. Find scriptures to pray.

I've shared some of the prayers I prayed for my children—and still pray!—that use scripture. Please help yourself to them. Write them on 3″ x 5″ cards and carry them with you...everywhere. When you are reading your Bible or attending church or Bible study, keep your ears open to other scriptures to pray. Jesus prayed for His own in John 17. You can draw rich scripture text here from the heart of the Master Pray-er and Lover of our souls. And Paul prayed for his disciples. The epistles contain multiple prayers from his heart that you can use for your little and big "disciples." Colossians 1:9-14 is a great place to start. When you pray using scripture, you can have confidence that you are praying according to God's will...and that He hears you (1 John 5:14).

MAKING THE CHOICES THAT COUNT

Making the Choices That Count

In all your ways acknowledge Him,
and He shall direct your paths.

PROVERBS 3:6

Have you ever been at a place in your life where you began to think that the churning of the turbulent sea of life had finally calmed (or at least was calmer!), and you just might sail into some calm water? Well, that's the way I felt just after we became a Christian family. Jim had a good job. Our children were healthy. We had just returned from our first church service with brand-new Bibles in hand. We at last had purpose in our lives and a direction for our family. As a unit, we wanted to follow Jesus.

That was on a glorious Sunday.

Then came Monday. That's the day Jim came home from work and informed me he wanted to quit his job, go back to school, and prepare to enter the ministry.

Needless to say, that churning, turbulent sea started right back up again! But this time something was different. I now had the Holy Spirit to help me (you know, with things like patience and self-control!). My immediate response was, "But what about all that we've worked so hard for up to this point—a nice house, furniture that's paid for, your job advancement, medical coverage, a regular paycheck?" Obviously I was only thinking of myself. But it wasn't long before I came around to God's plan for our family…and His peace. Together Jim and I made the choice to basically sell all and follow Jesus. We made the choice to leave everything behind and follow God's call on Jim's life to go into the ministry.

Now I am not sharing this to say you should do as we did. No, God leads each person, husband, wife, mom, and family in different ways and in different directions. I share it to illustrate the impact one choice—just *one* choice!—to follow God's leading had on my life and the lives of those in my family. That choice set in motion the most remarkable 30 years. And that's just one of many choices (hopefully right ones) we've made during the following decades as we attempted with all our hearts to follow Christ. And choices are never made in a vacuum. Yes, they affect us personally, but they also affect others…like our children. This childhood saying underscores the direction of our little choices: "Little choices determine habit; habit carves and molds character, which makes the big decisions."

The Results of One Little Wrong Choice

Abraham, in the Old Testament, faced a problem...but it was a good problem. You see, God had blessed. As Abraham and his nephew, Lot, wandered throughout the land of Canaan in answer to God's call on their lives, they amassed herds and flocks. These herds were a sign of wealth for nomads like Abraham and Lot. But the land could not sustain both men and their herds (Genesis 13:5-7). What to do was Abraham's dilemma.

Graciously, Abraham decided to allow his nephew to choose between two directions and two different types of land for his herds, herdsmen, and family. Abraham explained to Lot, "If you take the left, then I will go to the right; or, if you go to the right, then I will go to the left" (verse 9). In one direction the land was "well watered...like the garden of the LORD" (verse 10). The Bible doesn't say, but the land in the other direction had to be less desirable in its desert setting.

By offering Lot his choice, Abraham was risking the first and best choice, a choice rightly his as the elder. And sure enough, the nephew took advantage of what seemed to be a good business decision: Herds need grass and water to survive, right? So he chose the well-watered, garden environment.

History is made every time you make a decision.

Unfortunately, however, this wasn't the best choice spiritually. Lot separated himself from the godly Abraham and moved his herds and his family to the green pastures near Sodom and Gomorrah. (Do these towns sound familiar?) In the end, Lot's choice—a little choice between going right or going left—had disastrous consequences. God judged these two cities filled with wicked people, but spared the lives of Lot and his family. But in the process of the purging, Lot lost everything—his herds, his wife, and eventually his children, so to speak, when his daughters' lives were ruined as they lost their moral and sexual purity (Genesis 19:1-29). Why all of this devastation? Because of one little wrong choice.

Making the Right Choices

We've been talking throughout this book about becoming moms after God's own heart. We started by looking into the depths of our own hearts to make sure we were truly desiring to follow God's design for us as His moms. Now it's time to put that love and desire for our children to work and make a few more choices—hopefully the good, better, and best choices—the choices that really count.

Throughout time, God's moms have been making right choices—and sometimes hard choices. For instance,

♡ Moses' mother risked her own life to make a choice not to follow the king's edict. Instead of killing her baby as ordered, she held onto him and preserved his life (Exodus 1:22–2:10).

♡ King David's great-great-grandmother, Rahab-the-harlot (Matthew 1:5), risked her life and made a choice to hide Joshua's spies rather than turn them in to the king (Joshua 2).

♡ Samuel's mother, Hannah, made a choice to follow through on her vow to give up her only son to God's service (1 Samuel 1–2).

Like these moms in the Bible, not all of the choices you make will be easy. Some, in fact, may be costly to your own personal ambitions. And many of your decisions may go against the culture of our day. Others will require more of your already nonexistent time. But in the long run, and in God's economy, they will be the right choices—God's choices—choices that will count for your family now, in times to come, and also in eternity.

As we begin to wrap up our time together as moms, please make the choices that follow a matter of prayer. Talk them over with God. Talk them through with your husband. This list is in no way exhaustive. It does, however, reflect the kinds of choices every mom is faced with. As you lay your heart and your life and your family before God, He will lead you to make the right choices. For He is the One who promises "I will instruct you and teach you in the way you should go; I will counsel you and watch over you" (Psalm 32:8 NIV). Indeed, the Lord will direct your steps, and "he will be [your] guide even to the end" (Proverbs 16:9; Psalm 48:14 NIV).

Choose to Put Your Personal Dreams on Hold

Put *your* dreams, your career and educational goals, the development of your hobbies and abilities on hold. You don't need to kill your dreams. Just keep them in the background while you live out your role of mom at warp speed. If a pocket of time comes along, then you can take a class or attend a special workshop and away you go, taking one step at a time.

Several chapters back I shared how I chose to drop the master's degree program and focus my attention on my home and my family. In that choice I was, in effect, determining to be the best mom and wife I could be...and those two points of concentration became a full-time commitment.

But as I slipped into the routine of mothering and got more organized at home, I became aware of certain times in the day when I could spend time reading and studying. So I enrolled in a Moody Bible Institute correspondence course.[1] I still remember how I would finish a course and eagerly wait for my grade. Then I would sign up for the next class in the series and nibble away. I also started memorizing Bible verses at those odd times during the day, such as when the girls were napping or while I watched them play on the swings and gym equipment at the park.

> *Life is not the result of dreams dreamed, but of choices made.*

In time, in a number of years, my dream came true. I completed every Bible course offered. No, I didn't get a degree. That's not what I wanted. But I got what I dreamed of—a working knowledge and understanding of the Bible, all accomplished in snatches of time here and there.

What are your dreams? Own them, write them down, pray about them...but manage them. As the wisdom of Ecclesiastes teaches us, "to everything there is a season, a time for every purpose under heaven" (Ecclesiastes 3:1). Several specifics are scattered throughout verses 2-8: "There is...a time to plant...a time to build up...a time to gain...a time to love." In other words, timing is important. We are to concentrate on doing the right things at the right time in our lives. "Earthly pursuits are good in their proper place and time, but unprofitable when pursued as the chief goal."[2] Everything in its own season!

Choose to Put First People First

Family is first. That's what Titus 2:3-5 teaches us. Here we read that the older women are to teach the younger women to #1—"love their husbands" and #2—"love their children." This is God's divine order. So choose to give the first people in your life the first fruits of your time, love, and energy.

When it comes to priority efforts, I can't help but think of Moses' mom (Jochebed) and Samuel's mom (Hannah). They knew—and practiced—their priorities. Each of these "moms after God's own heart" had only a handful of years—about three—to pour a lifetime of love and godly instruction into their little boys. And then Jochebed turned little Moses over to Pharaoh's daughter to be raised in Pharaoh's palace. And Hannah turned little Samuel over to be raised under the tutelage of the priest Eli. What if...they hadn't given their all to their little guys during the time they did have? What if...they hadn't gotten up every single morning and poured their all into eager hearts? What if...they hadn't been there? What if...they had been consumed with other pursuits? What if...they hadn't taken each day as a mom seriously? What if...?

But they were...and they did! And you and I—and all of mankind—are the better for it. These two boys grew to be men who served God mightily and helped change the world.

Choose to Be Mentored

Here's another bit of advice from Titus 2. Verses 3 and 4 say "the older women" are to "admonish the young women to love...their children." God's plan for us as Christian moms is that we be learning from those moms who have gone before us, who are taking their mommyhood seriously, who can show us the ropes, who can encourage us in our roles as moms.

One day, when I was reading through the galleys of Jim's book on the apostle Paul's mentoring ministry, I learned the history of the term "mentor." Legend has it that the man Mentor was the tutor of Telemachus, whose father Odysseus left home for almost a decade to fight in the Trojan War. Mentor, in essence, raised Telemachus and taught and trained him for life. Thus a mentor is one who tutors, teaches, and trains.

I've probably stated in most of my books that God gave me the gift of many mentors during the years when I was getting grounded in the Christian faith. Those wonderful women pointed me in a biblical direction, helped accelerate my growth in Christ, and provided models of what a godly woman, wife, and mom looks like. As one who's benefited from a mentor, my advice is choose to be mentored.

How? First, pray. Then look around for an "older woman," a mentor, to disciple you in your different roles, "mom" being one of them. Who seems friendly? Who takes an interest in you as a young mom? Who's got her mothering act together...somewhat, anyway? Pray again, and then approach her with your Number One question or problem at the moment. You can do this in a few minutes on the phone, you can talk with her briefly in the church lobby, or maybe it will work out for you to meet for a while, even if it's with your children and hers at the park or at a fast-food restaurant with a play area. Open yourself up and ask her for help. Seek advice. Then ask her the next question...and the next...and *viola!* you have a mentor!

Another way to be mentored is by joining a moms or MOPS (Moms of Preschoolers) group. MOPS International is a well-organized Christian association that has older mentors and mother-figures who assist young moms. One of my daughters is actively involved in one of these groups, and she constantly shares with me what she's learning. It's an important lifeline for her and the other moms.

Choose to Read Proverbs

I'm sure you've noticed that throughout this book I've often referred to the book of Proverbs. Proverbs is one of the wisdom books of the Bible, and it gives us wisdom for knowing how to deal with relationships, including relationships with our children. I was challenged as a new believer to read one chapter of the book of Proverbs each day. Over the years this practice has saturated my heart, soul, and mind with God's directions on how I should interact with people, my children included.

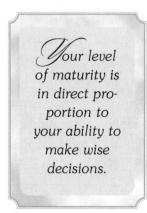

Your level of maturity is in direct proportion to your ability to make wise decisions.

For instance, are you looking for wisdom regarding the daily opportunities your kids give you to discipline and train them? Proverbs has the answers to your every quandary. For example, I found these principles that I call "The Three C's" when I needed to know how to treat certain common problems of dissension between siblings.

> **C**-asting lots—helps settle disputes
> (Proverbs 18:18)
>
> **C**-orrecting—helps reduce tension
> (Proverbs 29:17)
>
> **C**-asting out the instigator—helps restore
> peace (Proverbs 22:10)

Read Proverbs yourself. Receive its instruction, gain God's wisdom, and put it to work in your home. Then turn around and pass it on to the next generation. Help your children love and appreciate the book of Proverbs as much as you do. It will equip them with wisdom for life!

Choose to Study the Moms in the Bible

Oh, is this ever one of my passions! I have books and books on my library shelves about the women of the Bible. Reading about their lives as moms has given me encouragement since my girls were in diapers! These moms continue to teach me valuable lessons and principles as a mom—some in the positive and, unfortunately, some in the negative.

Reading about their lives brings us face-to-face with the great mothers of the faith—Eve, Sarah, Rebekah, Jochebed, Samson's mother, Naomi, Hannah, the Proverbs 31 mom, Elizabeth, and Mary. What an education to see how they handled the everyday trials and challenges all moms encounter! And what a treat to see how they loved their children—how they taught them, talked to them, told them about God, took care of them, trained them, talked to God about them, and tried their best! And what straightforward instruction—from God's Word to your heart!

As I prayed about how to end not only this section of the book, but the book itself, I reserved this "choice" for last—*Choose your attitude*. Why? Because it's something you can do right away. It's a little choice you can make in your heart right this minute. And I promise you, it's a little choice that reaps b-i-g blessings...daily and forever!

Being an unbelieving mom was a hard and hopeless time in my life. With two little babies only 13 months apart, I was Old Mother Hubbard—I was only 25, and I already had so many children that I didn't know what to do! And then, as a new Christian mom, I began to understand my role and accept my responsibility. I also learned that the Bible considers children to be "a heritage from the LORD" and "a reward" (Psalm 127:3), that to have children is to be blessed by God.

So I embraced God's exalted role of "mother." And I tackled my attitude. As one scholar advised, the language of the Bible is calling us as Christians "to change our attitudes and actions toward" our children and our mothering.[3] According to God's Word, I, as one of His moms, was to exhibit and live by—and live out—certain attitudes of heart.

What kind of mom does God want me—and you—to be? Answer: One who carries out her mothering with these attitudes of heart and in these ways:

Heartily—Whatever you do, including being a mom, do it heartily as to the Lord (Colossians 3:23).

Faithfully—Be faithful in all things, especially in your role of mom (1 Timothy 3:11).

Willingly—Do your work as a mom willingly, with both hands and your whole heart (Proverbs 31:15).

Excellently—Many moms do well, but seek to excel them all (Proverbs 31:29).

Joyfully—Rejoice always, no matter what your job as mom calls for (1 Thessalonians 5:16).

Prayerfully—Pray without ceasing while you're doing everything being a mom after God's own heart requires (1 Thessalonians 5:17).

Thankfully—In everything, especially in being a mom, give thanks, for this is the will of God in Christ Jesus for you (1 Thessalonians 5:18).

May you, my friend, be this mom—a mom after God's own heart...the mom you want to be.

From a Dad's Heart

It's been said of Billy Graham's mother that she was a simple dairy farmer's wife who never led a committee or a Bible study at church or made any outstanding public contributions. Her contribution at home, however, had eternal consequences. Billy's mother prayed reverently for 17 years until his salvation. Then she spent the next 50 years of her life praying for Billy and his ministry. Mrs. Graham chose to focus her attention on her home and family. Obviously this one choice reaped eternal dividends.

My mom also focused her attention on being the best wife and mom she could be. There were those wayward years when she may have been a little discouraged by my choices and conduct, but mom never gave up on me. And, by God's grace and mom's persistent prayers, I finally came around spiritually. Then she prayed and encouraged me until the day she died, even moving as a widow to live near me and my family so she could be of help with our family and with our ministry efforts. She was an excellent mom and grandmom, and her death left a real vacuum in our lives.

Choices are a funny thing. No one can make your choices for you. What you choose to focus your time and life on is ultimately between you and God. I know I speak for Elizabeth also when I urge you to seek God's wisdom and the counsel of your husband and of godly men and women as you make your choices about how you live out your role of being a mom.

As a dad looking at my family today and the role Elizabeth played in the lives of our daughters, I wonder how it would have been if she hadn't made the choice to focus on our children. What if...

> ...she hadn't been there during those preschool years when the majority of foundational learning takes place? If she hadn't been there to read Bible stories, correct bad habits, and personally ensure that our daughters' little minds were being filled with the things of God rather than the things of the world?

> ...she hadn't been there when, like so many dads who hold down 50-plus-hours-a-week jobs, my job called for long hours and nights or weekends away from home, when I was gone weeks

at a time on mission trips and at leadership conferences?

...she hadn't been there during those teen years when hormones and emotions were running wild? If she hadn't been there to send our kids off to school and be there at the door waiting for them with a sandwich and a Coke and a listening ear?

...she hadn't been there for them during those young adult years when decisions were being made as to career preparation and life-mates? If she hadn't been available to the girls anytime of the day or night when they just needed to talk?

...she hadn't been there when the girls started their own homes and the babies started arriving? If she hadn't been ready, willing, and able to jump on a plane each time a new grandchild was born and take care of both baby and mom until our daughters were able to resume normal activities? And even what if she hadn't been available to listen to the cries of a disheartened daughter after a miscarriage?

But Elizabeth was there, and she has been for more than 30 years. All of the precious moments represented were made possible partly because of the choices of one mom who focused her life and energies on two little girls who grew up to have seven little people of their own.

What choices are you making? And are there any moments you are missing because of some decisions you've made? It's not too late to change course. I'm not here to put a guilt trip on you. I know you love your children. And I know you want to be a good mom because you've made it to the last page of a book on being God's kind of mom. I also know you and your husband have goals that you've set together.

One day you and your husband will look back at the results of the choices you've made. What a blessing it will be to see that you sought God's wisdom as you made your decisions, that you were truly a mom after God's own heart! Congratulations on your desire to raise children after God's own heart and on your calling as a mom. It's a high and privileged one!

QUIET TIMES CALENDAR

Jan.	Feb.	Mar.	Apr.	May	June
1	1	1	1	1	1
2	2	2	2	2	2
3	3	3	3	3	3
4	4	4	4	4	4
5	5	5	5	5	5
6	6	6	6	6	6
7	7	7	7	7	7
8	8	8	8	8	8
9	9	9	9	9	9
10	10	10	10	10	10
11	11	11	11	11	11
12	12	12	12	12	12
13	13	13	13	13	13
14	14	14	14	14	14
15	15	15	15	15	15
16	16	16	16	16	16
17	17	17	17	17	17
18	18	18	18	18	18
19	19	19	19	19	19
20	20	20	20	20	20
21	21	21	21	21	21
22	22	22	22	22	22
23	23	23	23	23	23
24	24	24	24	24	24
25	25	25	25	25	25
26	26	26	26	26	26
27	27	27	27	27	27
28	28	28	28	28	28
29	29	29	29	29	29
30		30	30	30	30
31		31		31	

DATE BEGUN _____

July	Aug.	Sept.	Oct.	Nov.	Dec.
1	1	1	1	1	1
2	2	2	2	2	2
3	3	3	3	3	3
4	4	4	4	4	4
5	5	5	5	5	5
6	6	6	6	6	6
7	7	7	7	7	7
8	8	8	8	8	8
9	9	9	9	9	9
10	10	10	10	10	10
11	11	11	11	11	11
12	12	12	12	12	12
13	13	13	13	13	13
14	14	14	14	14	14
15	15	15	15	15	15
16	16	16	16	16	16
17	17	17	17	17	17
18	18	18	18	18	18
19	19	19	19	19	19
20	20	20	20	20	20
21	21	21	21	21	21
22	22	22	22	22	22
23	23	23	23	23	23
24	24	24	24	24	24
25	25	25	25	25	25
26	26	26	26	26	26
27	27	27	27	27	27
28	28	28	28	28	28
29	29	29	29	29	29
30	30	30	30	30	30
31	31		31		31

Notes

Focusing on the Heart

1. W.E. Vine, *Vine's Expository Dictionary of Old and New Testament Words* (Nashville: Thomas Nelson Publishers, 1997), p. 537.
2. William MacDonald, *Enjoying the Proverbs* (Kansas City, KS: Walterick Publishers, 1982), p. 31.
3. Vine, *Vine's Expository Dictionary,* p. 537.
4. Michael Kendrick and Daryl Lucas, *365 Life Lessons from Bible People* (Wheaton, IL: Tyndale House Publishers, Inc., 1996), p. 92.
5. Ivor Powell, *David: His Life and Times — A Biographical Commentary* (Grand Rapids, MI: Kregel Publications, 1990), p. 24.
6. Ibid., p. 27.
7. Charles F. Pfeiffer and Everett F. Harrison, *The Wycliffe Bible Commentary* (Chicago: Moody Press, 1990), p. 773.
8. John MacArthur, *The MacArthur Study Bible* (Nashville: Word Bibles, 1997), p. 1227.
9. Ibid., p. 1662.
10. Kendrick and Lucas, *365 Life Lessons,* p. 355.

1 — Take Time to Nurture Your Heart

1. See Elizabeth George, *A Woman's High Calling* (Eugene, OR: Harvest House Publishers, 2001), pp. 168-81.
2. Elizabeth George, *A Mom After God's Own Heart Growth and Study Guide* (Eugene, OR: Harvest House Publishers, 2005).
3. Charles F. Pfeiffer and Everett F. Harrison, *The Wycliffe Bible Commentary* (Chicago: Moody Press, 1990), p. 164.
4. Matthew Henry, *Matthew Henry's Commentary on the Whole Bible* (Peabody, MA: Hendrickson Publishers, 2003), p. 244.
5. *Life Application Study Bible* (Wheaton, IL: Tyndale House Publishers, Inc., 1996), p. 269.
6. *The One Year Bible* (Wheaton, IL: Tyndale House Publishers, Inc., 1986).

2 — Teach Your Children God's Word

1. "The Soul of a Child," in Eleanor Doan, *Speaker's Sourcebook* (Grand Rapids, MI: Zondervan Publishing House, 1988), p. 51.

2. Tedd Tripp, *Shepherding a Child's Heart* (Wapallopen, PA: Shepherd Press, 1995), pp. 29-32.

3. G.M. Mackie, *Bible Manners and Customs* (Old Tappan, NJ: Fleming H. Revell Company, n.d.), p. 158.

4. Information drawn from Matthew Henry, *Matthew Henry's Commentary on the Whole Bible*, (Peabody, MA: Hendrickson Publishers, 2003), p. 244.

5. Mackie, *Bible Manners and Customs,* p. 154.

6. E. Margaret Clarkson.

7. Mackie, *Bible Manners and Customs,* p. 159.

8. Curtis Vaughan, *The Word—The Bible from 26 Translations* (Gulfport, MS: Mathis Publishers, Inc., 1991), p. 339.

9. "The Heart of a Child," in Doan, *Speaker's Sourcebook,* p. 52.

3 — Talk to Your Children About God

1. See Proverbs 12:23-24, for example.

2. Richard W. DeHaan and Henry G. Bosch, *Our Daily Bread Favorites* (Grand Rapids, MI: Zondervan Publishing House, 1971), February 3.

3. George Barna survey results, *Transforming Children into Spiritual Champions* (Ventura, CA: Regal Books Gospel Light, 2003), p. 35.

4. Hans Finzel, *Help! I'm a Baby Boomer* (Wheaton, IL: Victor Books, 1989), p. 105.

5. Sid Buzzell, *The Leadership Bible* (Grand Rapids, MI: Zondervan Publishing House, 1998), p. 207.

4 — Tell Your Children About Jesus

1. George Barna survey results, *Transforming Children into Spiritual Champions* (Ventura, CA: Regal Books Gospel Light, 2003), p. 41.

2. Elgin S. Moyer, *Who Was Who in Church History* (New Canaan, CT: Keats Publishing, Inc.), 1974, p. 22.

3. Jerry Noble, cited in Albert M. Wells, Jr., *Inspiring Quotations—Contemporary & Classical* (Nashville: Thomas Nelson Publishers, 1988), p. 82.

4. Moyer, *Who Was Who,* p. 293.

5. Paul Lee Tan, *Encyclopedia of 7700 Illustrations* (Winona Lake, IN: BMH Books, 1979), p. 851.

5 — Train Your Children in God's Ways

1. Elizabeth George, *God's Wisdom for Little Girls: Virtues and Fun from Proverbs 31,* with paintings by Judy Luenebrink (Eugene, OR: Harvest House Publishers, 2000).

2. William MacDonald, *Enjoying the Proverbs,* quoting Jay Adams, *Competent to Counsel* (Grand Rapids, MI: Baker Book House, 1970), Walterick Publishers, P.O. Box 2216, Kansas City, KS 66110, 1982), p. 120.

3. See Proverbs 13:24; 23:13-14; 29:15,17.

4. Eleanor Doan, *Speaker's Sourcebook* (Grand Rapids, MI: Zondervan Publishing House, 1988), p. 48.

5. Benjamin R. DeJong, *Uncle Ben's Quotebook* (Grand Rapids, MI: Baker Book House, 1977), p. 142, no author's name given.

6. Heart to Heart Program cited in Doan, *Speaker's Sourcebook,* p. 49.

7. Horace Bushnell in Doan, *Speaker's Sourcebook,* p. 49.

8. The New American Bible and James Moffatt, A New Translation of the Bible, respectively, cited in Curtis Vaughan, *The Word—The Bible from 26 Translations* (Gulfport, MS: Mathis Publishers, Inc., 1991), p. 1221.
9. Robert Jamieson, A.R. Fausset, and David Brown, *Commentary on the Whole Bible* (Grand Rapids, MI: Zondervan Publishing House, 1971), p. 470.
10. Ralph Wardlaw, *Lectures on the Book of Proverbs*, vol. III (Minneapolis: Klock & Klock Christian Publishers, Inc., 1982 reprint), p. 38.
11. Jim George, *A Young Man After God's Own Heart* (Eugene OR: Harvest House Publishers, 2005), p. 86.
12. Bruce Barton, *Life Application Bible Commentary—Ephesians* (Wheaton, IL: Tyndale House Publishers, Inc., 1996), p. 122.
13. J. David Branon, as cited in Roy B. Zuck, *The Speaker's Quote Book* (Grand Rapids, MI: Kregel Publications, 1977), p. 51.
14. "Home Life" in Doan, *Speaker's Sourcebook*, p. 50.

6 — Take Care of Your Children

1. Pat Ennis and Lisa Tatlock, *Designing a Lifestyle that Pleases God* (Chicago: Moody Publishers, 2004), pp. 113-15.
2. Tiger's Milk® is a nutrition bar loaded with 18 vitamins and minerals and 11 grams of protein.
3. Curtis Vaughan, *The Word—The Bible from 26 Translations* ASV (Gulfport, MS: Mathis Publishers, Inc., 1991), p. 1246.
4. Alice Gray, Steve Stephens, John Van Diest, *Lists to Live By for Every Caring Family* (Sisters, OR: Multnomah Publishers, 2001), pp. 96 and 110.
5. Ibid., p. 19.
6. Elizabeth George, *Beautiful in God's Eyes—The Treasures of the Proverbs 31 Woman* (Eugene, OR: Harvest House Publishers, 1998).
7. See Proverbs 1:10-19; 5:1-11; 7:1-27.

7—Take Your Children to Church

1. "A Child's Ten Commandments to Parents," by Dr. Kevin Leman, from *Getting the Best Out of Your Kids* (Eugene, OR: Harvest House Publishers, 1992). Quoted in Alice Gray, Steve Stephens, John Van Diest, *Lists to Live By for Every Caring Family* (Sisters, OR: Multnomah Publishers, 2001), p. 130.
2. Robert Jamieson, A.R. Fausset, and David Brown, *Commentary on the Whole Bible* (Grand Rapids, MI: Zondervan Publishing House, 1971), p. 1429.
3. Drawn from Richard Mayhue, *Seeking God* (Fearn, Great Britain: Christian Focus Publications, 2000), p. 148.
4. Bruce B. Barton, *Life Application Bible Commentary—Mark* (Wheaton, IL: Tyndale House Publishers, Inc., 1994), p. 285.
5. George Barna survey results, *Transforming Children into Spiritual Champions* (Ventura, CA: Regal Books Gospel Light, 2003), p. 41.
6. Joe White, Jim Weidmann, *Spiritual Mentoring of Teens* (Wheaton, IL: Tyndale House Publishers, 2001), p. 49.
7. Paul Lee Tan, *Encyclopedia of 7700 Illustrations* (Winona Lake, IN: BMH Books, 1979), p. 844.
8. Mary Louise Kitsen, "Generations of Excuses," reprinted by permission.

8—Teach Your Children to Pray

1. Herbert Lockyer, *All the Prayers of the Bible* (Grand Rapids, MI: Zondervan Publishing House, 1973), p. 64.
2. *Matthew Henry's Commentary on the Whole Bible* (Hendrickson Publishers, Inc., 2003), p. 383.
3. D.L. Moody, *Thoughts from My Library* (Grand Rapids, MI: Baker Book House, 1979), p. 122.
4. "This I Carry with Me Always," *Christian Parenting Today*, May/June 1993, p. 23.
5. Stanley High, *Billy Graham* (New York: McGraw Hill, 1956), p. 106.
6. George Barna survey results, *Transforming Children into Spiritual Champions* (Ventura, CA: Regal Books, published from Gospel Light, 2003), p. 35.
7. For your teen girls, see Elizabeth George, *A Young Woman After God's Own Heart* and *A Young Woman's Call to Prayer* (Eugene, OR: Harvest House Publishers, 2003 and 2005). For your teen boys, see Jim George, *A Young Man After God's Own Heart* (Eugene, OR: Harvest House Publishers, 2005).
8. *The Prayers of Susanna Wesley*, ed. and arr. by W.L. Doughty (Grand Rapids, MI: Zondervan Publishing House, Clarion Classics, 1984), p. 46.
9. Arthur Bennett, ed., *The Valley of Vision* (Carlisle, PA: The Banner of Truth Trust, 1999).
10. Joe White and Jim Weidmann, *Spiritual Mentoring of Teens* (Wheaton, IL: Tyndale House Publishers, 2001), pp. 76, 35.

9—Try Your Best

1. Elisabeth Elliot, *The Shaping of a Christian Family* (Nashville, TN: Thomas Nelson Publishers, 1991), pp. 95.
2. Judith Warner, "Mommy Madness," *Newsweek, Inc.*, 2005, quoting from *Perfect Madness* (New York: Riverhead Books, 2005).
3. Elizabeth George, *Loving God with All Your Mind* (Eugene, OR: Harvest House Publishers, 1994/2005).
4. See especially Elizabeth George, *A Woman After God's Own Heart*® and *A Wife After God's Own Heart* (Eugene, OR: Harvest House Publishers, 1997 and 2004).
5. Judith Warner, "Mommy Madness," *Newsweek, Inc.*, 2005, February 21, 2005, www.msnbc.msn.com/id/6959880/site/newsweek, quoting from her book *Perfect Madness* (England: Riverhead Books, a division of Penguin Group (USA) Inc., 2005).

10—Talk to God About Your Children

1. John MacArthur, *The MacArthur Study Bible* (Nashville: Word Publishing, 1997), p. 877.

Making the Choices that Count

1. Moody Bible Institute Distance Learning, 820 North LaSalle Blvd., Chicago, IL 60610, 1-800-758-6352 or check out www.mdlc.moody.edu.
2. John MacArthur, *The MacArthur Study Bible* (Nashville, TN: Word Publishing, 1997), p. 929.
3. Gene A. Getz, *The Measure of a Woman* (Glendale, CA: Regal-Gospel Light Publications, 1977), p. 73.

Personal Notes

Personal Notes

Personal Notes

Personal Notes

_____

_____

_____

_____

_____

_____

_____

_____

_____

_____

_____

_____

_____

_____

_____

_____

_____

_____

_____

_____

Personal Notes

Personal Notes

If you've benefited from *A Mom After God's Own Heart,* you'll want the companion volume

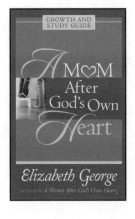

A *Mom After God's Own Heart*
Growth
and
Study Guide

This guide offers additional scriptures, thought-provoking questions, reflective studies, and personal and practical applications that will help you be the best mom you can be.

This growth and study guide is perfect for both personal and group use.

A Mom After God's Own Heart Growth and Study Guide is available at your local Christian bookstore or can be ordered from:

Elizabeth George
PO Box 2879
Belfair, WA 98528
Toll-free fax/phone: 1-800-542-4611
www.ElizabethGeorge.com
www.JimGeorge.com

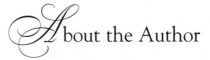

About the Author

Elizabeth George is a bestselling author and speaker whose passion is to teach the Bible in a way that changes women's lives. For information about Elizabeth's books or speaking ministry, to sign up for her mailings, or to share how God has used this book in your life, please write to Elizabeth at:

Elizabeth George
P.O. Box 2879
Belfair, WA 98528

Toll-free fax/phone: 1-800-542-4611
www.ElizabethGeorge.com

God Loves His Precious Children

Jim and Elizabeth George share the comfort of Psalm 23 with children in original prose. Engaging watercolor scenes and memorable rhymes bring the truths of each verse to life and invite young ones to gather God's promises along the way.

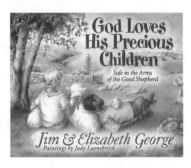

God's Wisdom for Little Girls

Sugar and spice and everything nice—that's what little girls are made of...and so much more! Best-selling author Elizabeth George draws from the wisdom of the book of Proverbs to encourage young girls to apply the positive traits and qualities illustrated in each verse.

Judy Luenebrink's charming illustrations complement the text, which emphasizes that there is more to being a girl than simply being sweet and nice. God desires for them to be helpful, confident, thoughtful, eager, prayerful, creative, cheerful, and kind—one of His little girls!

God's Wisdom for Little Boys

Share with the little boy in your life the gift of God's wisdom from Proverbs, and celebrate with him the character and traits of a godly man. As you read together fun rhymes that illustrate wisdom and strength, he will discover how special he is as a child of God.

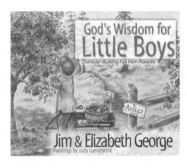

Judy Luenebrink's vibrant illustrations will capture the attention of little boys...and the adults who are reading to them.

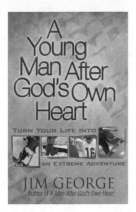

A Young Man After God's Own Heart

Jim George takes teenagers on a radical journey of faith. Through God's extreme wisdom and powerful insights from the life of warrior and leader King David, readers will discover biblical principles that blaze a trail to godly living. *A Young Man After God's Own Heart* helps guys grow into men who honor God in all they do. Great for Sunday school, youth group studies, and individual reading.

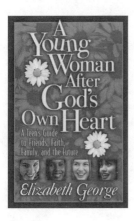

A Young Woman After God's Own Heart

This young woman's version of Elizabeth George's bestselling book *A Woman After God's Own Heart®* shares the intentions and blessings of God's heart with teen girls. On this journey they discover His priorities for their lives—including prayer, submission, faithfulness, and joy—and how to embrace those priorities in daily life.

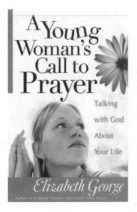

A Young Woman's Call to Prayer

From her own journey, the Bible, and the lives of others, Elizabeth reveals the explosive power and dynamic impact of prayer on everyday life. *A Young Woman's Call to Prayer* gives step-by-step guidance for experiencing an enthusiastic prayer life. Great for Sunday school, group studies, and individual reading.

A Woman After God's Own Heart® Study Series

Bible Studies for Busy Women

God wrote the Bible to change hearts and lives. Every study in this series is written with that in mind—and is especially focused on helping Christian women know how God desires for them to live."

—Elizabeth George

Sharing wisdom gleaned from more than 20 years as a women's Bible study teacher, Elizabeth has prepared insightful lessons that can be completed in 15 to 20 minutes per day. Each lesson includes thought-provoking questions, insights, Bible study tips, instructions for leading a discussion group, and a "heart response" section to make the Bible passage more personal.

Living with Passion and Purpose — LUKE — Elizabeth George — 0-7369-0816-1

Becoming a Woman of Beauty & Strength — ESTHER — Elizabeth George — 0-7369-0489-1

Putting On a Gentle & Quiet Spirit — 1 PETER — Elizabeth George — 0-7369-0290-2

Discovering the Treasures of a Godly Woman — PROVERBS 31 — Elizabeth George — 0-7369-0818-8

Nurturing a Heart of Humility — CHARACTER STUDIES MARY — Elizabeth George — 0-7369-0300-3

Walking in God's Promises — CHARACTER STUDIES SARAH — Elizabeth George — 0-7369-0301-1

Experiencing God's Peace — PHILIPPIANS — Elizabeth George — 0-7369-0289-9

Pursuing Godliness — 1 TIMOTHY — Elizabeth George — 0-7369-0665-7

Cultivating a Life of Character — JUDGES/RUTH — Elizabeth George — 0-7369-0498-0

Growing in Wisdom & Faith — JAMES — Elizabeth George — 0-7369-0490-5

HARVEST HOUSE PUBLISHERS
EUGENE, OREGON 97402
www.harvesthousepublishers.com

Books by Elizabeth George

- Beautiful in God's Eyes
- Encouraging Words for a Woman After God's Own Heart®
- God's Wisdom for a Woman's Life
- Life Management for Busy Women
- Loving God with All Your Mind
- A Mom After God's Own Heart
- Powerful Promises for Every Woman
- The Remarkable Women of the Bible
- A Wife After God's Own Heart
- A Woman After God's Own Heart®
- A Woman After God's Own Heart® Deluxe Edition
- A Woman After God's Own Heart® Prayer Journal
- A Woman's Call to Prayer
- A Woman's High Calling
- A Woman's Walk with God
- A Young Woman After God's Own Heart
- A Young Woman's Call to Prayer

Children's Books

- God's Wisdom for Little Girls

Study Guides

- Beautiful in God's Eyes Growth & Study Guide
- God's Wisdom for a Woman's Life Growth & Study Guide
- Life Management for Busy Women Growth & Study Guide
- Loving God with All Your Mind Growth & Study Guide
- A Mom After God's Own Heart Growth & Study Guide
- Powerful Promises for Every Woman Growth & Study Guide
- The Remarkable Women of the Bible Growth & Study Guide
- A Wife After God's Own Heart Growth & Study Guide
- A Woman After God's Own Heart® Growth & Study Guide
- A Woman's Call to Prayer Growth & Study Guide
- A Woman's High Calling Growth & Study Guide
- A Woman's Walk with God Growth & Study Guide

Books by Jim & Elizabeth George

- God Loves His Precious Children
- God's Wisdom for Little Boys
- Powerful Promises for Every Couple
- Powerful Promises for Every Couple Growth & Study Guide

Books by Jim George

- God's Man of Influence
- A Husband After God's Own Heart
- A Man After God's Own Heart
- The Remarkable Prayers of the Bible
- A Young Man After God's Own Heart

*This book
belongs to*

_____

*...a Woman After
God's Own Heart*

A Woman After God's Own Heart®

Elizabeth George

HARVEST HOUSE PUBLISHERS

EUGENE, OREGON

A WOMAN AFTER GOD'S OWN HEART is a registered trademark of The Hawkins Children's LLC. Harvest House Publishers, Inc., is the exclusive licensee of the federally registered trademark A WOMAN AFTER GOD'S OWN HEART.

A WOMAN AFTER GOD'S OWN HEART®

Copyright © 1997/2006 by Harvest House Publishers
Eugene, Oregon 97402
www.harvesthousepublishers.com

Library of Congress Cataloging-in-Publication Data
George, Elizabeth, 1944– . A woman after God's own heart / Elizabeth George.
    p. cm.
  ISBN-13: 978-0-7369-1883-1
  ISBN-10: 0-7369-1883-3

  1. Women—Prayer-books and devotions—English.   2. Christian women—Religious life.
  3. Women—Conduct of life. I. Title.
  BV4844.G43 1997 96–45436
  248.8'43—dc21

*To my cherished friends and daughters
Katherine George Zaengle and Courtney George Seitz,
who share my deep desire to become
women after God's own heart.*

Acknowledgment

As always, thank you to my dear husband, Jim George, M.Div., Th.M., for your able assistance, guidance, suggestions, and loving encouragement on this project.

Contents

Dear Seeker of God's Heart

God knows how deeply humbled I am each time someone like you writes to let me know how He has used His truths in *A Woman After God's Own Heart®* to positively impact you, your family, your home, and your love for Him. His truths are truly transforming (John 17:17)! And He also knows how blessed I am when someone like you brings a tattered and torn, dirt-darkened, tearstained, coffee-splattered, dog-eared, doodled-on-by-your-children book through a line for me to autograph. As I always say, "The best book is a used book!"

Well, my dear reading friend, at last—thanks to Harvest House Publishers—this wonderful updated and expanded edition of *A Woman After God's Own Heart®* is now available! Its debut was prompted by women like you who have heard me speak from the book or studied through my video Bible study of *A Woman After God's Own Heart*®.[1] These women asked about the additional insights I now share in person or on CD that reflect my growth and understanding of practicing God's priorities for the ten years that have passed since I wrote this book. This new edition is just for you...to read and reread, to carry with your Bible, to take along in your backpack (or diaper bag, as the case may be!), to study with friends, to leave on your nightstand as a refresher, and to bless and encourage others as a life-changing gift.

It's wonderful being a woman after God's own heart, isn't it! To know Him. To love Him. To enrich the lives of others. To follow Him...and to partake of the blessings He extends to us when we do. No woman's life could be more satisfying than the life enjoyed by a woman after His own heart, a woman whose heart's desire is to do God's will (Acts 13:22)! May God richly bless you and yours as you continue to follow after Him.

In His everlasting love,

Elizabeth George

A Word of Welcome

Imagine living life so that people thought of each of us—today and long after we're gone—as a woman after God's own heart!

Thousands of years after he walked this earth, we still think of King David—the faithful shepherd boy who slew Goliath, the warrior who mercifully spared King Saul's life on more than one occasion, the King who danced with joy as the Ark of the Covenant was returned to Jerusalem—as *a man after God's own heart* (1 Samuel 13:14 and Acts 13:22)!

Before you protest, "But I'm hardly in King David's category!" let me remind you that he was far from perfect. (For instance, does the name "Bathsheba" ring a bell?) Despite his tendency to forget to consult God, despite his cold-blooded arrangements to

murder Uriah so he could marry Bathsheba, and despite his less
than solid parenting, David has been given the title "man after
God's own heart." I find that very encouraging as I continue on
the path of being a woman after God's own heart.

I also find encouraging the fact that this path is, in the words
of Richard Foster, "the path of disciplined Grace."[1] He goes on
to explain:

> It is discipline, because there is work for us to do.
> It is Grace, because the life of God which we enter
> into is a gift which we can never earn....Discipline
> in and of itself does not make us righteous, it merely
> places us before God....The transformation...is
> God's work.[2]

Our transformation into being a woman after God's own
heart is indeed God's work. But what I offer here are the disciplines we can follow to place ourselves before God—disciplines
regarding our devotional life, our personal growth, our home,
our marriage and family, and our ministry—so that He can do
that work in our heart. You'll find practical insights about what it
means to follow God in every area of life, insights about nurturing an impassioned relationship with God, experiencing personal
growth, caring for your home, loving your husband, enjoying your
children, and giving to others. The journey is an exciting one,
and you'll find much joy along the way. So I welcome you to join
me as each of us seeks to be the woman God calls us...and will
empower us...to be, a woman after His own heart.

Part 1

The Pursuit
of God

1

A Heart
Devoted to God

But one thing is needed, and Mary has chosen that good part,
which will not be taken away from her.

LUKE 10:42

I had done it thousands of times before, but two days ago it
was different. I'm talking about the walk I take each day in the
dewy part of the morning. As I moved through my neighborhood I noticed a woman—probably in her late seventies—walking on the sidewalk by the park. She had an aluminum walker
and appeared to have suffered a stroke. She was also a little bent
over, a telltale sign of osteoporosis.

What made this outing different for me? Well, just three days
earlier we had buried my husband's mother. Lois was in her late
seventies when God called her home to be with Him…and Lois
had used an aluminum walker…and Lois had suffered from osteoporosis…and Lois too had experienced a slight stroke.

Still grieving over our recent loss, I was a little down even before

15

I spotted this woman who so reminded me of Lois. I had already used the few tissues I had taken with me. And my heart and mind were filled with thoughts like *What will we do for Thanksgiving? We always had Thanksgiving at Lois's. She always fixed the turkey, dressing, cranberry sauce, and homemade pies. What will a family gathering be like without her?* On and on my thoughts went. *She won't be in her regular seat at church Sunday....I no longer have any reason to take the freeway exit that leads to her house. Besides, it is no longer her house....Now who was praying for us? How will the loss of her prayer power affect all of us—Jim's ministry, my ministry, the girls' lives, this book?*

As I watched that dear, brave woman struggling to walk and remembered Lois's battle with cancer and pneumonia at the end of her life, I realized I was taking a hard look at reality. Every one of us has a body that will someday fail us—and that someday is not necessarily too far off.

I was also sharply reminded once again of how desperately I want my life—indeed each and every day of it, each and every minute of it—to count. Yet as I took in this scene and thought these thoughts, I was aware that my fiftieth birthday had come—and gone. My thirtieth wedding anniversary had done the same. And my two little babies had graduated from life at home to life in their own homes with husbands to love and babies of their own to consider. I was running out of time!

A Change of Heart

Now I don't want you to think this book is a "downer"! This is certainly not at all how I intended to begin a book about a woman after God's own heart. But these thoughts don't mark the end of my walk—or my story. Let me tell you what happened next.

As I pushed forward on my walk, I realized that I needed to push my thoughts forward too. I had been thinking earthly thoughts—human thoughts, physical thoughts, worldly thoughts—rather than thoughts of faith. My perspective was off! We as Christians are to walk by faith, not by sight (2 Corinthians 5:7), so I turned my mind and heart upward and began to adjust my perspective to match God's view of my life (and Lois's life and yours), His eternal view that encompasses our past and our future as well as our present.

Rushing to my rescue was one particular verse from the Bible. I had memorized it long ago and had since applied it to my life in many ways. The words were fresh in my mind because the pastor who had shared the platform with my husband, Jim (Lois's son and only child), at her memorial service had used it when speaking of her life. They were words Jesus had spoken of to Mary, the sister of Lazarus and Martha. He said, "But one thing is needed, and Mary has chosen that good part, which will not be taken away from her" (Luke 10:42).

As I thought on this word from God about one of His women—a woman Jesus was defending from criticism with this statement—I found myself looking straight into the core meaning of "a heart after God," and I was greatly comforted.

> *To be God's women, to love Him fervently with whole hearts, is our sole desire.*

First, I was comforted about Lois. Although her life with us was over, she had sought to make it count every day and for eternity. She had chosen the one thing, the necessary thing, each day for most of her life. She had chosen with her whole heart to seek to live her life for God. She loved God, worshiped God, walked with God, served God, and looked forward to being with Him in eternity. In spite of a painful cancer and being twice widowed, Lois knew true inner peace and joy as she nurtured a heart of devotion to God. I have no doubt that my mother-in-law's life had definitely counted for the kingdom.

I was also comforted about my own life. After all, God knows the desires of my heart—indeed, He has put them there (Psalm 37:4)! He knows the amount of daydreaming—and praying—I do about becoming the kind of woman He wants me to be. He also knows that while I am daydreaming I am frightfully aware that the years are drifting by and that there is less and less time left for becoming that woman. But God's peace became mine as I was reminded one more time that when, day by day, I choose the one thing necessary—which shall never be taken away from me—my life too makes a difference. God wants my heart—all of it—and my devotion. When I choose to give it to Him, when I choose to live totally for Him, He makes it count. He wants to be Number One in my life, the priority above all priorities!

And, dear friend and woman after God's heart, I am comforted for you too because I know you join me in yearning for the things of God. To be God's woman, to love Him fervently with a whole heart, is our sole desire. And whether you're pushing a stroller or a grocery cart or an aluminum walker, whether you're single, married, or a widow, whether your challenge is eight children or no children, whether life has you nursing children with measles, a husband with cancer, or your own osteoporosis, your life counts— and counts mightily—as you face its challenges with a heart full of devotion to God.

As I said earlier, I had not planned to open this book with thoughts like these. But because of the life Lois nurtured and chose each day to live, a tribute to her is a fitting beginning for a book about a woman after God's own heart. Lois showed me how important it is to choose to love God and follow after Him...with a whole heart…each day…as long as we live. Every day counts when we are devoted to God!

A Heart Devoted to God

A closer look at Mary, a woman who sat at Jesus' feet and received His praise, further opens up for us the meaning of a heart devoted to God. What did Mary do that moved our Savior to praise her?

Mary discerned the one thing needed—The events leading up to Jesus' words set the scene for us to look into Mary's heart (Luke 10:38-42). Jesus (probably accompanied by His disciples) arrived at the home of Mary's sister, Martha, for a meal. I'm sure it was a joyous and festive time. Imagine, God in flesh coming for dinner! He was total love, total care, total concern, and total wisdom. It would be heaven on earth to be in His presence— the presence of God.

But Martha, Mary's sister, didn't discern the miracle of God in the flesh. Consequently, she marred His visit by her behavior. She crossed over the line of graciously providing food and became overly involved in her hostessing. When Jesus opened His mouth to impart words of life—the Word of God spoken by God Himself—and Mary slipped out of the kitchen to sit quietly at His feet, Martha broke. She interrupted the Teacher, her guest, to say something to this effect—"Don't you care that I'm putting this meal together all by myself? Tell Mary to help me!" Martha failed to discern the priority and importance of time with God.

Mary, a woman after God's own heart, made the choice that indicated her heart's devotion: She knew it was important to cease her busyness, stop all activity, and set aside secondary things in order to focus wholly on the Lord. Unlike her sister, who was so busy doing things *for* the Lord that she failed to spend time *with* Him, Mary put worship at the top of her to-do list.

Mary chose the one thing needed—Because Mary was a woman after God's own heart, she was preoccupied with one thing at all times—Him! Yes, she too served. And she too tried to fulfill her God-given responsibilities. But there was one choice that Mary made that day in Bethany, a decision to do the one thing that mattered most: Mary chose to spend time worshiping God. She knew that nothing can take the place of time in God's presence. Indeed, time spent sitting at His feet fuels and focuses all acts of service. And, as her Master noted, time spent hearing and worshiping God can never be taken away, for it is time spent in eternal pursuits, time that earns permanent and everlasting dividends. Mary chose to spend that precious time with Him.

Yes, But How?

How can you and I become women devoted to God, women who love God deeply and live for Him daily? What can we do to follow Mary's example and begin making choices that tell the whole watching world that we are women after God's own heart, choices that position us so God can impassion our hearts toward Him?

1. *Choose God's ways at every opportunity*—Commit yourself to actively choose God and His ways—as Mary did—in your decisions, words, thoughts, and responses. *A Woman After God's Own Heart* is about living according to God's priorities, and we want the choices we make to reflect that God is our Ultimate Priority. After all, the word "priority" means "to prefer." We want to choose to prefer God's way in all things. And several guidelines

help. This is simple but, believe me, I know how easy it is to let our guard down.

Proverbs 3:6—"In all your ways acknowledge Him, and He shall direct your paths" could be the theme verse of this book—and of life! This well-loved verse describes a two-step partnership with God. Our part is to stop and acknowledge God along the way, and His part is to direct our paths. This means we are to consult with God regarding our decisions, thoughts, words spoken, or responses. Before we move ahead or merely react, we need to stop and pray first, "God, what would You have me do—or think or say—here?"

What exactly does Proverbs 3:6 look like in daily life? Let me share two examples. I wake up and the day begins. As I merrily go about the business of life, a crisis suddenly arises. The phone rings, and it's bad news or a decision needs to be made. I try to remember to mentally—and maybe even physically (as Mary did)—stop and check in with God. I pray, "God, what do You want me to do here?" I endeavor to simply pause in my mind and spirit and acknowledge God. That's my part of the partnership. It may take a split second or some minutes in prayer.

Or I'm again merrily going about my day—and I run into someone who says something that hurts me. Before I blurt something out (this is my goal anyway!), before I give an eye for an eye (or a word for a word), I try again to stop...pause...sit mentally in God's presence...and lift my thoughts to Him: "O.K., God, what do You want me to do here? What do You want me to say? How do You want me to act?" I even ask Him, "What expression do You want on my face as I listen to this person say these things?" I acknowledge God. That's my part.

And then God takes over and does His part—He directs my

paths. Often it's almost as if the next thought to enter my mind is from Him. Because I ask Him for direction and want to do things His way—not my way—He directs me. He instructs me and teaches me in the way I should go (Psalm 32:8). He guides me in what to do, how to act, and what to say. God is faithful to His promise: "Your ears shall hear a word behind you, saying, 'This is the way, walk in it'" (Isaiah 30:21).

The saying "good, better, best"—Perhaps as a child you heard your teacher at school say,

> Good, better, best,
> never let it rest,
> until your good is better,
> and your better best.

Well, I try to apply this saying in very practical ways to my own decision-making and choices. That's what Mary did. According to Jesus, she chose the *best* way. Here's just one way that doing so has helped me.

> *Choosing God and His ways deepens our devotion to Him.*

In Los Angeles people can spend a lot of time in the car, and I was no exception. There in the car—all alone—I had options about what I could think and do. For years I drove around with an easy-listening music station on the radio. That was a fairly good choice. However, after some thought, I decided a better choice for me would be to listen to classical music (a passion of mine). After thinking about my choice a little more, I decided an even better choice would be playing a CD of uplifting Christian music. Then I moved up the "better" scale again as I chose to listen to

sermon CDs instead—recordings of a man of God teaching the
Word of God to the people of God. Next, playing CDs of the
Bible seemed even better. Then one day I turned the whole audio
system off and landed on what for me was the best choice for my
car time—memorizing Scripture. Good to better to best!

When I was a new Christian, I heard a more spiritually mature
woman at church tell about a choice—a Mary kind of choice—
she made each day as soon as her husband left for work. She said
she could do almost anything she wanted—turn on the TV and
watch a soap opera or talk show, read the *Los Angeles Times*, or—
her choice—pick up her Bible and have her quiet time. Here was
a woman—a woman after God's own heart—paying close attention to what was good, better, and best, and striving to make the
best choices.

That, dear reader, is our challenge too. Choosing God and
His ways deepens our devotion to Him.

Standing in awe of God—A favorite passage of mine ends
with these words: "Charm is deceitful and beauty is passing,
but *a woman who fears the Lord,* she shall be praised" (Proverbs
31:30).

Author and Bible teacher Anne Ortlund expressed her own
awe of God: "In my heart I do have a fear....I long to grow more
godly with each passing day. Call it 'the fear of the Lord,' being
in awe of Him and scared to death of any sin that would mar my
life at this point."[1]

This same heart for God and fear of missing His best because
of faulty choices was shared by another woman I admire, Carole
Mayhall of the Christian discipleship organization The Navigators.
Twice I've heard Carole share at women's retreats, and both times
she said, "Daily I live with [one] fear—a healthy fear if there is

such a thing. [It is] that I will miss something God has for me in this life. And it is mind-expanding to contemplate all that He wants me to have. I don't want to be robbed of even one of God's riches by not taking time to let Him invade my life. By not listening to what He is telling me. By allowing the routine, pressing matters of my minutes to bankrupt me of time for the most exciting, most fulfilling relationship in life."[2]

Are you in awe of God and what He wants to do in you, for you, and through you?

2. *Commit yourself to God daily*—Our devotion to God is strengthened when we offer Him a fresh commitment each day. Every morning, in a heartfelt prayer either written or silent, start fresh with God by giving Him all that you are, all that you have... now...forever...and daily. Lay everything on God's altar in what one saint of old called the "surrendered life."[3] Give God your life, your body (such as it is), your health (or lack of it), your husband, each child (one by one), your home, your possessions. Nurture the habit of placing these blessings in God's loving hands to do with them what He will. After all, they are not ours—they are His! A daily prayer of commitment helps us to release what we think are our rights to these gifts. As the saying goes, "Hold all things lightly and nothing tightly." I also find these words from nineteenth-century devotional writer Andrew Murray helpful: "God is ready to assume full responsibility for the life wholly yielded to Him."[4]

So aim at some kind of commitment to God made daily. It can be as simple as this prayer, the first of F.B. Meyer's seven rules for living: "Make a daily, definite, audible consecration of yourself to God. Say it out loud: 'Lord, today I give myself anew to you.'"[5]

Perhaps the prayer of commitment I love best (and have written on the front page of my Bible) is that of Betty Scott Stam, a China Inland Mission worker. She and her husband were led through the streets of China to their execution by decapitation, while their baby lay behind in its crib. This was her daily prayer:

> Lord, I give up all my own plans and purposes, all my own desires and hopes, and accept Thy will for my life. I give myself, my time, my all, utterly to Thee to be Thine forever. Fill me and seal me with Thy Holy Spirit. Use me as Thou wilt, send me where Thou wilt, work out Thy whole will in my life at any cost, now and forever.[6]

In this case, the cost was high. This total commitment to God cost Betty Stam her ministry, her husband, her child, her life. But that kind of commitment is indeed our high calling as His children (Romans 8:17).

3. *Cultivate a hot heart*—I am especially challenged about the temperature of my own heart whenever I consider these words spoken by Jesus: "I know your works, that you are neither cold nor hot. I could wish you were cold or hot. So then, because you are lukewarm, and neither cold nor hot, I will vomit you out of My mouth" (Revelation 3:15-16). According to this Scripture, which heart condition do you think God considers the worst?

Think about these chilling facts: To be cold-hearted means to be decidedly below normal, to be unemotional, unaware, unconscious of God. Imagine...being unemotional about the things of God! And then there's the lukewarm heart. It's only moderately warm. It's indifferent! Imagine being indifferent toward God!

Hot—the third option—is where we want to be. That's having

> *We should be fiery and excited about God, and God will fuel our fire.*

a high temperature, characterized by violent activity, emotion, or passion. It's fiery and excited. Now that's the heart of someone committed to God!

Have you ever been in the presence of a person who is hot-hearted toward God? I have. Mike was asked to say grace at a potluck dinner. Well, when you have a hot heart for God you can never just say grace. Prostrate in his heart and soul, Mike began a prayer of heartfelt worship. His passion tumbled out of his mouth as he thanked God for His salvation, for the fact that he had been transferred from darkness into the kingdom of light, that he had been lost but was now found, blind but could now see. On and on Mike went until I, frankly, lost my appetite because I had found other meat—for the soul! Mike's hot heart moved me to forget about a mere hot meal for my stomach.

Our heart for God should be like a boiling pot. Our heart should be characterized by God-given and intense passion for our Lord. After all, when a teakettle is boiling on your stove, you know it. It sputters and steams. It actually hops up and down and jiggles from side to side, empowered by its violent heat. Hot to the touch, it shares the heat that is within. There is no way to ignore its fire. Likewise, we should be fiery and excited about God, and God will fuel our fire.

That's what I want for you—and for myself. I want Jesus' presence in our lives to make a difference. I want us to overflow with His goodness and praise. I want our lips to speak of the great things He has done for us (Luke 1:49), to tell of His wonders (Psalm 96:3). "Let the redeemed of the LORD say so" (Psalm 107:2)!

Heart Response

Oh, dear sister, how would you rate your heart condition? I pray that your heart belongs to Christ, that you have entered into an eternal relationship with God through His Son, Jesus. If this is true for you, thank Him for the wonderful privilege of being called a child of God!

However, if you are unsure about where you stand with God or if you know quite clearly you are living your life apart from God, purpose to make things right with Him. Spend time in prayer. Confess and deal with any sin. Invite Jesus to be your Savior, and by doing so, welcome Christ into your life and become a new creature in Him (2 Corinthians 5:17). Your prayer might go something like this:

> God, I want to be Your child, a true woman after Your heart—a woman who lives her life in You, through You, and for You. I acknowledge my sin and receive Your Son, Jesus Christ, into my needy heart, giving thanks that He died on the cross for my sins. Thank You for giving me Your strength so that I can follow after Your heart.

Go ahead. Turn your heart heavenward. Open up your heart. Invite Christ in. He will then make you a woman after His own heart!

Now you can begin—or begin anew!—to put yourself in a position where God can grow in you a heart of devotion. Every activity in this book is aimed at helping you place yourself before God so He can turn your heart toward Him. Our goal is to have no will but His will. Right now utter a prayer for more heat!

2

A Heart Abiding in God's Word

For [you] shall be like a tree planted by the waters,
which spreads out its roots by the river.
JEREMIAH 17:8

The Bible speaks of "a time to plant" (Ecclesiastes 3:2), and for my husband, Jim, that time came as a result of the massive 1994 earthquake we went through in Southern California. A part of the devastation we experienced at our home (only three miles from the quake's epicenter) was the loss of our block-wall fences.

After a year of waving to our neighbors only a few feet away, it was a blessing to have those fences back in place. But the new walls were so bleak. So naked. The old ones had been charming—seasoned by age, blanketed by climbing roses and ivy, serving as friendly arms that embraced our lawn, patio, house, and anyone who happened to be there enjoying the beauty. Its stark-but-hidden stone facade had functioned as an invisible support for far lovelier things—things alive and blooming that added fragrance, color, and ambiance to our yard. And now we were forced to start all over again. It was our time to plant.

So Jim planted...13 baby creeping figs whose job was to soften the harshness of the new walls. Twelve of those new figs dutifully shot out their magic fingers and began a friendly possession of the wall. One plant, however, slowly withered, shrank, and finally died.

Coming home from work on a Friday afternoon, Jim picked up a replacement plant at the nursery, changed clothes, got out our shovel, and bent over the dead vine, fully prepared to work at digging it out of the ground so he could put the new one in. But, much to his surprise, the shovel wasn't necessary. As he grasped the plant, it easily came out of the ground. There were no roots! Although the plant had enjoyed all the right conditions above ground, something was missing beneath the surface of the soil. It didn't have the root system vital for drawing the needed nourishment and moisture from the soil.

This garden scenario portrays a spiritual truth for you and me as God grows in us a heart of faith: We must nurture a root system! Roots make all the difference in the health of a plant, and their presence or absence ultimately becomes known to all. The plant either flourishes or fails, thrives or dies, blossoms or withers. The health of anything—whether a garden plant or a heart devoted to God—reflects what is going on (or not going on!) underground.

Drawing Life from God's Word

If God is going to be first in our hearts and the "Ultimate Priority" of our lives, we must develop a root system anchored deep in Him. Just like a plant with its roots hidden underground, you and I—out of public view and alone with God—are to draw from Him all that we need to live the abundant life He has promised His children (John 10:10). We must seek to live our lives near to God—indeed, hidden in Him! As we seek a deeper life in Christ, we do well to consider some facts about roots.

Roots are unseen—Like a creeping fig or any other plant, your spiritual roots are underground, invisible to others. I'm talking about your private life, your hidden life, the secret life you enjoy with God out of the public eye. An iceberg illustrates the importance of what is hidden.

When Jim and I were teaching in Alaska, a commercial fisherman took Jim out on his boat. Not only did Jeff show Jim eagles, seals, and whales, but Jeff also gingerly guided his boat around an iceberg. He explained to Jim that only one-seventh of an iceberg is visible above the surface, and any wise fisherman knows not to get too close because underneath spreads the other six-sevenths. What was visible to the eye—only a fraction of the huge, icy mass—was enough to evoke fear, awe, and respect in any sailor.

And that's what you and I want for our lives. We want what other people see of our lives—the public portion—to stir up this kind of awe and wonder. We want our strength in public to be explained by what goes on in private between us and God.

But it's so easy for you and me to get this all backwards. It's easy to think that what counts in the Christian life is the time spent in public with people, people, and more people. We seem to always be with people—people at work, people on campus, people in the

The impact of your ministry to people will be in direct proportion to the time you spend with God.

dorms, people from Bible studies, people we live with, people in discipleship settings or fellowship groups.

But the truth is that "the greater the proportion of your day—of your life—spent hidden in quiet, in reflection, in prayer, [in study,] in scheduling, in preparation, the greater will be the effectiveness, the impact, the power, of the part of your life that shows."[1] As I heard one Christian leader say, you cannot be *with* people all of the time and have a ministry *to* people. The impact of your ministry to people will be in direct proportion to the time you spend away from people and with God.

And our effectiveness for the Lord requires wise decisions regarding time. I carry in my Bible a quote that helps me make the kinds of choices that allow time for developing the underground life: "We [must] say 'no' not only to things which are wrong and sinful, but to things pleasant, profitable, and good which would hinder and clog our grand duties and our chief work."[2] (What are those "pleasant, profitable, and good things" for you?)

Our effectiveness for the Lord also requires solitude. In his little book *The Greatest Thing in the World*, Henry Drummond made this observation: "Talent develops itself in solitude; the talent of prayer, of faith, of meditation, of seeing the unseen."[3] So that our roots grow deep into Him, God calls us away from this world.

Roots are for taking in—What happens when you and I do slip away to be with God in study and prayer? We receive. We take in. We are nurtured and fed. We ensure our spiritual health and growth. When we spend time with Christ, He supplies us with strength and encourages us in the pursuit of His ways.

I call this time with God "the great exchange." Away from the world and hidden from public view, I exchange my weariness for His strength, my weakness for His power, my darkness for His light, my problems for His solutions, my burdens for

His freedom, my frustrations for His peace, my turmoil for His calm, my hopes for His promises, my afflictions for His balm of comfort, my questions for His answers, my confusion for His knowledge, my doubt for His assurance, my nothingness for His awesomeness, the temporal for the eternal, and the impossible for the possible.

I saw the reality of this great exchange at one of our church's annual women's retreats. My roommate and dear friend was in charge of this event, which was attended by approximately 500 women. Karen handled each challenge graciously and put her administrative genius to work with each crisis. But I noticed that as the starting time for each session neared and panic rose among the organizers who hoped things would go smoothly, Karen disappeared. As breathless, perspiring, frazzled women came running into our room asking, "Where's Karen? We've got a problem!" she was nowhere to be found.

On one of those mysterious occasions, I glimpsed Karen walking down the hotel hall with her retreat folder and burgundy Bible in hand. She had prepared well in advance for the approaching session. She had carefully gone over the plans, the schedule, and the announcements one last time. But she sensed a need for one more thing—quiet time with God alone. She needed to look at a few precious portions of His empowering Word and then place our event completely in His hands through prayer.

Later—after Karen reappeared from her time of taking in— I couldn't help but notice the sharp contrast between her and the others. As the anxiety of other women rose, Karen exhibited God's perfect peace. As they fretted, worried, and wondered, Karen knew all was and would be well. As others wilted under the pressure, Karen's strength—God's strength in Karen—shone with supernatural brilliance. Underground and away from the crowd, she had exchanged her needs for God's supply.

Roots are for storage—Roots serve as a reservoir of what we need. Jeremiah 17 tells us that the person who trusts in the Lord…

> shall be like a tree planted by the waters,
> which spreads out its roots by the river,
> and will not fear when heat comes;
> but its leaf will be green,
> and will not be anxious in the year of drought,
> nor will cease from yielding fruit (verse 8).

This trusting soul, whose roots are collecting life-giving water, will exhibit several qualities.

First, she will *not be afraid* of the scorching heat, even if the days turn into a long year of drought. Instead she will endure the heat with leaves of green. The reservoir she has stored up from God's Word will sustain her through the fiery trials, no matter how long they last.

She will also *bear fruit faithfully*. She will not cease to yield fruit even in times of drought. Because of stored-up nourishment from God Himself, she will be like a tree of life—producing in and sometimes even out of season (Psalm 1:3).

As you and I regularly draw needed refreshment from God's Word, He creates in us a reservoir of hope and strength in Him. Then, when times are rough, we won't be depleted. We won't dry up, disintegrate, or die. We won't run out of gas, collapse, exhaust, or give out. Instead we will simply reach down into our

Roots deep into God's truth are definitely needed as reserves when times are rough.

hidden reservoir of refreshment and draw out what we need right now from what God has given us. We will be able to go from "strength to strength" (Psalm 84:7).

This is exactly what happened to me during my mother-in-law's illness. Her hospitalization was a crisis that challenged my endurance. My husband—her only child—was overseas and literally unreachable. Because of the constant demands of this difficult season, I had no chance for formal quiet times. As I stood by Lois's bed, tending to her by the hour, I had no option but to reach down into my reservoir.

And what did I find stored up there? As evidence of God's marvelous grace, I found strength in many Scriptures I had memorized over the years. I gained spiritual energy from psalms read, studied, and prayed through in earlier (and quieter) times alone with God. As I tapped into God's power through prayer, I experienced His peace that passes all understanding guarding my heart (Philippians 4:7). And I was fortified by the example of my Savior and a host of men and women in the Bible who had also drawn what they needed from God's Word. Roots deep into God's truth are definitely needed as reserves when times are rough!

Roots are for support—Without a well-developed root system, we become top heavy—lots of leafy, heavy foliage appears above ground but nothing supports it from underneath. Without a network of strong roots, sooner or later we have to be staked up, tied up, propped up, straightened up—until the next wind comes along and we fall over again. But with firm, healthy roots, no wind can blow us down.

Yes, the support of a healthy root system is vital for standing strong in the Lord! I'm reminded of the process used in bygone days for growing the trees that became the main masts for military and merchant ships. The great shipbuilders first selected a tree located on the top of a high hill as a potential mast. Then they cut away all of the surrounding trees that would shield the chosen one from the force of the wind. As the years went by and the winds blew fiercely against the tree, the tree grew stronger until finally it was strong enough to be the foremast of a ship.[4] When we have a solid root system, we too can gain the strength needed for standing firm in spite of the pressures of life!

Yes, But How?

How does a woman draw near to God's heart? What can we do to put ourselves in a position where God can grow each of us into a woman of remarkable endurance?

1. *Develop the habit of drawing near to God*—Only through routine, regular exposure to God's Word can you and I draw out the nutrition needed to grow hearts of faith. I know firsthand how hard it is to develop the habit of drawing near to God and how easy it is to skip and miss. For some reason I tend to think I'll spend time with God later, I'll get around to it in a little while, or I'll miss just this one day—but catch up with God tomorrow.

I've learned, however, that my good intentions don't go very far. It's easy for me to start the day planning to have a devotional time a little later…after I've done a few things around the house, made some phone calls, tidied up the kitchen, started the dishwasher, made the bed, and picked up those clothes on the floor, and—oh, I almost forgot—wiped off the bathroom counter. Suddenly I'm off and running. Somehow I never get to time for the most important relationship in my life—my relationship with God! That's why I have to be firm with myself and aim for habitual, scheduled time with God whether I *feel* like it or not, whether it *seems* like the best use of my time or not. I must draw near to God.

Here's a question to think about: If someone asked you to describe the quiet time you had this morning, what would you say? This is exactly the question Dawson Trotman, founder of The Navigators ministry organization, asked men and women applying for missions work. He once spent five days interviewing candidates for overseas missionary service. He spent a half hour with each one, asking specifically about their devotional life. Sadly, only one person out of 29 interviewed said his devotional life was a constant in his life, a source of strength, guidance, and refreshment. As Trotman continued to probe into the lives of those men and women planning a lifetime of service for God, he found that since they had come to know the Lord, they had never had a consistent devotional life![5]

Developing the habit of drawing near to God definitely helps make our devotional life what we need it to be—and what God wants it to be! To help make this a reality, I've placed a "Quiet Times Calendar" at the back of this book just for you. As you use it, aim for consistency. Begin with even a brief time each day. Great lives are made up of many "little" disciplines. Begin the "little" discipline of meeting with the Lord daily and then filling in your Quiet Times Calendar. Just fill in the squares for each day that you have a quiet time. Remember that the goal is solid lines—like a thermometer, not a "Morse code" measurement (dot-dot-dash) or a "measles" measurement (here a dot, there a dot, everywhere a dot dot). I pray you'll be blessed like this dear woman was:

> I have been attempting to have daily quiet times
> for awhile now. This past week, however, I found

that having to actually record the days I had my
quiet time has encouraged me to be more faithful
with them. Instead of brushing it aside in the morning, I chose to have it, even if it couldn't be as long
as I hoped for.

2. *Design a personal time for drawing near to God*—As women
we're used to designing, planning, and scheduling the events of
life. We know how to pull off parties, projects at work, weddings,
and retreats. When it comes to planning, your quiet time should
be no different—especially considering its eternal value. Consider
what kind of quiet time would be ideal for you. What elements
would make it a quality time?

When? Keep in mind one of my mottos: *Something is better
than nothing.* The only "wrong" time for having your time alone
with God would be *no* time. So pick a time that matches your
lifestyle. Some moms of newborns have their time with the Lord
in the middle of the night when they are awakened by a crying
baby. Some working women have theirs during the lunch break—
in the car, in a restaurant, or at their desks. My dear mother-in-
law had hers at night in bed because pain made sleep difficult,
and God's Word helped her relax and rest. Another woman takes
her calendar in hand every Sunday afternoon, looks at the week's
events, and then makes an appointment with God at the time that
best fits each day. Hudson Taylor admitted to a friend that "the
sun has never risen upon China without finding me at prayer."[6]
How did he accomplish that? "To ensure a quiet time for uninterrupted prayer, he always rose very early in the morning before
daylight and, if nature demanded it, would continue his sleep after
his season of prayer."[7] When would be best for *you?* Once you
pinpoint the best time, you've taken an important first step!

Where? Right now my bed is my place, but for many years I used the breakfast table. Then, for some reason, I moved into the living room and took over the couch and coffee table. In the summer the patio is my spot. It doesn't matter where you meet the Lord—as long as you do it! I have friends who set up desks and counters as their place to be alone with God. Another woman converted an antique cupboard to meet her needs. A book I read suggested purchasing a door at the hardware store and laying it across two low file cabinets.[8] Another woman converted a hall closet into her "prayer closet." Do what you need to do to make a specific spot *your* place to meet with the Lord.

What aids? Gather some essentials—a good reading light, highlighters, pens, pencils, markers, sticky notes, 3" x 5" cards, legal pads for writing, a prayer notebook, and a box of tissues. You might add a hymnal to guide your singing or a CD player for Christian praise or teaching CDs. Maybe you need your memory verses, a journal, a Bible-reading schedule, a devotional book, or some reference books. Whatever you need, see that it's there.

Whatever it takes, fellow seeker after God's heart, do what you must to be alone with God so that He can fine-tune your heart to His. As one wise saint wrote, "Every believer may and must have his time when he is indeed himself alone with God. Oh, the thought to have God all alone to myself, and to know that God has me all alone to Himself!"[9]

3. *Dream of being a woman after God's heart!*—Motivation is key when it comes to nurturing a heart of devotion, and dreaming helps motivate us. As a wake-up call to the seriousness of daily life and to find fresh urgency about your walk with the Lord, *describe the woman you want to be spiritually in one year.* Let your answer put wings on your dreams.

> *God will take you as far as you want to go, as fast as you want to go.*

Do you realize that in one year you could attack a weak area in your Christian life and gain the victory? You could read through the entire Bible. You could be ready for the mission field. You could be mentored by an older woman—or mentor a younger one yourself (Titus 2:3-5). You could complete a counseling training curriculum or some training in evangelism. You could finish a one-year Bible school course. You could memorize xx verses from the Bible—you choose the number. (After his conversion, Dawson Trotman began to memorize one verse a day for the first three years of his Christian life—that's a thousand verses!)[10] You could read a dozen quality Christian books. Dream on—and do it!

Next, *describe the woman you want to be spiritually ten years from now.* Jot your present age in the margin here and write underneath it the age you will be in ten years. Imagine what those intervening ten years might hold, and you'll see that you will need God for the events of those years! You will need God to help you overcome areas of sin and grow spiritually. You will need Him to help you be a wife...or to be single...or when you become a widow. You will need God to help you be a mother—no matter what the ages of your children. You will need God if you are to be His kind of daughter, daughter-in-law, or mother-in-law. You will need God to help you successfully serve others. You will need God as you care for aging parents. You will need God as you move into old age yourself. And you will need God when you die.

Do you believe you can be this woman? With God's grace and in His strength you can! That's His role in your life. But there is also a place for your effort. As Scripture says, "[*You*] keep your heart with all diligence, for out of it spring the issues of life" (Proverbs 4:23).] You determine some elements of the heart. You decide what you will or will not do, whether you will or will not grow. You also decide the rate at which you will grow—the hit-and-miss rate, the measles rate (a sudden rash here and there), the 5-minute-a-day rate, or the 30-minute-a-day rate. You decide if you want to be a mushroom, which appears for a night and shrivels away at the first hint of wind or heat, or an oak tree, which lasts and lasts and lasts, becoming stronger and mightier with each passing year. As my husband continually challenged his students at The Master's Seminary in years past, "God will take you as far as you want to go, as fast as you want to go." So how far…and how fast…do you want to move toward becoming the woman of your dreams?

Heart Response

Well, here we are—women with hearts after God, dreaming of "more love to Thee, O Christ, more love to Thee!" Here we stand, staring at the very core of God's heart—God's own Word. Truly the treasures of God's Word are fathomless (Romans 11:33). His Word stands as His counsel forever, the thoughts of His heart to all generations (Psalm 33:11). By it we were born again (1 Peter 1:23), by it we grow (1 Peter 2:2), and by it we walk through life as it lights the path for our feet (Psalm 119:105). Surely drawing near to God's Word should be of utmost importance to us each day. What joy we discover when we grow to love it more than food for our bodies (Job 23:12).

At one time I cut out and kept an obituary of a composer who made himself work on his music at least 600 hours each year, keeping track in a diary of each day's progress.[11] He spent his entire life on something good, but something temporal, something with no eternal value. Now imagine what kind of transformation would occur in your heart if you spent time—or more time—drawing near to God through His Word—time spent on something of eternal, life-changing value! Won't you purpose in your heart to spend more time near to God's heart by spending more time in His Word?

3

A Heart Committed to Prayer

I will lift up my eyes to the hills—
from whence comes my help?
My help comes from the LORD.
PSALM 121:1-2

I remember one particularly special day of my life very clearly. It was my tenth spiritual birthday and a significant turning point for me. Having dropped my two daughters off at school and gotten my husband off to work, I sat at my old desk in the family room, alone in the house with only the sound of our wall clock ticking. Resting there before God and rejoicing in a decade of being His child, I thought back over those ten years. Although at times they'd been rough, God's great mercy, His wisdom in every circumstance, and His care in leading and keeping me were all very obvious.

I shuddered at the memories of how my life had been without Him. Overwhelmed by emotion and crying tears of joy, I lifted my heart in a time of thanksgiving to God. Still with a heart full of gratitude, I dabbed my eyes, took a deep breath, and prayed, "Lord, what do You see missing from my Christian life? What needs attention as I begin a new decade with You?" God seemed to respond immediately by calling to my mind an area of great personal struggle and failure—my prayer life.

Oh, I had tried praying. But each new effort lasted, at best, only a few days. I would set aside time for God, read my Bible, and then dutifully bow my head, only to mumble a few general words that basically added up to "God, please bless my family and me today." Certainly God intended prayer to be more than that—but I couldn't seem to do it.

But on that tenth spiritual birthday I reached for a small book of blank pages that my daughter Katherine had given me for Mother's Day four months earlier. It had sat unused on the coffee table because I hadn't quite known what to do with it. But suddenly I knew exactly how to put it to use. Full of resolve, conviction, and desire, I wrote these words—straight from my heart—on the first page: "I dedicate and purpose to spend the next ten years (Lord willing) developing a meaningful prayer life."

These are simple words, written and prayed from a simple desire within my heart. But that day those simple words and that little blank book began an exciting leg on my journey and adventure of following after God's own heart! My new commitment to prayer put into motion a complete makeover of my whole life— every part and person and pursuit in it.

When I decided to learn more about the awesome privilege of prayer, I fully expected drudgery and joyless labor. But as I moved ahead to develop a meaningful prayer life, I was surprised by the blessings that began to blossom in my heart. As a favorite hymn tells us, "Count your blessings, name them one by one." I want to name a few blessings of prayer now because they are blessings that you too can know as you cultivate a heart of prayer.

Blessing #1: A Deeper Relationship with God

Although I'd heard that prayer would deepen my relationship with God, I had never experienced it. But when I started to spend regular, daily, unhurried time in prayer—when I lingered in intimate communion with God—that deeper relationship was mine. When you and I commune in prayer with God, we grow spiritually in a multitude of ways.

Prayer increases faith—I now know firsthand that this is true. I saw it for myself when I followed some advice I once heard. When some parents asked Dr. Howard Hendricks of Dallas Theological Seminary how to teach their children about faith in God, he answered, "Have them keep a prayer list." And that is exactly what I did. Like a child, I wrote out a prayer list in my special book and began taking my concerns to God, my Father, each day. I was awed as, for the first time ever, I paid close attention to how He answered item after item.

Prayer provides a place to unload burdens—Problems and sorrows are facts of life (John 16:33), but I didn't know how to handle them apart from the verse of Scripture that instructed me to cast all my cares and burdens on God (1 Peter 5:7). So, armed with this advice, I rolled up my sleeves and went to work forwarding my concerns to God in prayer. Soon it became natural for me to start each day by giving all the cares of life to God in prayer, and I would rise up relieved, freed from many heavy weights. Author and fellow pray-er Corrie ten Boom offers a vivid image of this privilege:

As a camel kneels before his master to have him remove his burden, so kneel and let the Master take your burden.[1]

Prayer teaches us that God is always near—A verse that I recited thousands of times during the thousands of aftershocks following the 1994 Northridge earthquake was Psalm 46:1—"God is our refuge and strength, a *very present help* in trouble." God is always near, and the more I prayed, the more this truth struck home. I began to realize the fact of His omnipresence, the reality that He is always present with His people, including me and you! I found Oswald Chambers' words to be true: "The purpose of prayer is to reveal the presence of God equally present all the time in every condition."[2] Cultivating a heart of prayer is a sure way to experience God's presence.

Prayer trains us not to panic—Jesus taught His disciples that we ought always to pray and not to faint (Luke 18:1). Turning to God for every need during my regular daily prayer time ingrained in me the habit of prayer. Soon I was replacing my tendency to panic at the first hint of any problem with God's strength—and I'd make the switch on the spot through prayer!

A Prayer for Peace

Grant that it may not be in the power of any to rob me of the peace that results from a firm trust in Thee. Whenever crosses or troubles are met without, may all be well within.[3]

—Susanna Wesley

Prayer changes lives—You've probably heard the saying, "Prayer changes things." After attempting a more regular prayer life, I think we can also say, "Prayer changes *us!*" The men at The Master's Seminary, where my husband ministered, found this to be true as well. Every student is required to take a class on prayer, and the professor asks the men to pray for one hour a day for the duration of the semester. Is it any surprise to learn from the students' evaluations of their three years spent at seminary that, almost to a man, the prayer class truly changed their lives?

Blessing #2: Greater Purity

Yes, prayer changes lives, and one major change is greater purity. Becoming pure is a process of spiritual growth, and taking seriously the confession of sin during prayer time moves that process along, causing us to purge our life of practices that displease God. That's what happened to me when I began working on my prayer life.

For me, gossip was a serious struggle. Even though I knew God spoke specifically to women about not gossiping (1 Timothy 3:11 and Titus 2:3), I did it anyway. Convicted of my failure to follow God's guidelines and aware that my gossip didn't please God, I tried some practical remedies like taping little notes on the telephone (Is it true? Is it kind? Is it helpful?) and setting some self-imposed rules for my speech. I even prayed each day that I wouldn't gossip. And still I gossiped!

Real change began when I started not only to pray about gossip, but to confess it as an offense to God each time I did it. One day, about a month after I got serious about confession, I reached the height of my frustration. I was so sick of failing, sick of offending my Lord, and sick of confessing the sin of gossip every single day that I submitted myself to God for more radical surgery (Matthew 5:29-30). I asked Him to cut gossip out of my life. The Holy Spirit led me to that decision, guided that surgery, and has empowered the purification process. Let me quickly tell you that I've had my lapses, but still that day was a significant turning point for me. Purification—purging my life of a major sin (1 John 3:3)—took place, in part because I faced my sin regularly in prayer. Do you see the progression? Sin led to confession, which led to purging.

A Prayer for Purity

May I be incapable of rest or satisfaction of mind under a sense of Thy displeasure! Help me to clear accounts with thee....[4]

—Susanna Wesley

Blessing #3: Confidence in Making Decisions

How do you make decisions? I know how I used to make decisions before I learned to pray about them. Maybe you can relate. The phone would ring around nine in the morning. A woman would ask me to speak at her church, and, because I'd just eaten a scrambled egg and some toast, taken my thyroid pill, had a cup of coffee, and gone for a walk, I would be full of energy and blurt out, "Sure! When do you want me to come?" At four in the afternoon, the phone would ring again, another woman was calling with the same basic request, but, because it was the end

Make no decision without prayer.

of a long day and I was beat and ready to relax, I would answer this lady, "No way!" (My actual words were more gracious, but those were the words I was thinking.)

Why did I respond so differently? What criteria did I use for these decisions? In a word, *feelings.* While I was feeling full of fresh energy in the morning, my answer would be yes. In the late afternoon, when I was worn out, my answer would be no. My decisions were based on how I felt at the moment. I wasn't making spiritual decisions—I was making physical decisions.

This approach to decision-making changed as I began to write down in my special little book every decision I needed to make. I developed a motto for myself: *Make no decision without prayer.* Whatever option arose, I asked for time to pray about it first. The more important the decision, the more time I asked for. If there wasn't time for me to pray about it, I generally answered no because I wanted to be certain my decisions were actually God's choices for me. And I followed this approach for everything— invitations to showers, weddings, lunches, opportunities to minister, problems, ideas, crises, needs, dreams. I wrote down every decision I needed to make and took each one to God in prayer.

Imagine the difference this practice can make in a woman's life! The principle *make no decision without prayer* keeps me from rushing in and committing myself before I consult God. It guards me against people-pleasing (Galatians 1:10), and it ended my practice of making commitments and later calling to back out. Another benefit of praying first about my decisions is that my tendency to second-guess my commitments has stopped. As the events on my calendar approach, I feel no dread or fear or resentment. I don't wonder, "How did I get myself into this? What was I thinking when I said I'd do this? I wish I hadn't said yes." Instead I experience a solid confidence—confidence in *God*—and the excitement of anticipating what He will do at these events. A woman after God's own heart is a woman who will do *His* will (Acts 13:22)—not her own. The maxim *make no decision without prayer* has helped me do just that!

A Prayer for Direction

Forbid that I should venture on any business without first begging Thy direction and assistance.[5]

—Susanna Wesley

Blessing #4: Improved Relationships

Understandably prayer—specifically prayer for the people closest to us—strengthens our bonds with those dear people, but being a seeker of God's heart results in better relationships with people in general. How does this happen? These prayer principles, which I discovered as I began to pray regularly, help answer that question.

- *You cannot think about yourself and others at the same time*— As you and I settle our personal needs with God in private prayer, we can then rise up and focus all our attention outward—away from self and on to others.

- *You cannot hate the person you are praying for*—Jesus instructed us to pray for our enemies (Matthew 5:44), and God changes our hearts as we do so.

- *You cannot neglect the person you are praying for*—As we invest ourselves in prayer for other people, we find ourselves wonderfully involved in their lives.

An end to self-centeredness, the dissolution of ill will, and an end to neglect—these results of praying for someone will inevitably improve our relationship with him or her.

Blessing #5: Contentment

As the wife of a seminary student for ten years, I faced real challenges in the area of contentment, and a large source of frustration was our finances. While I lived in a tiny house with peeling paint and a living room ceiling about to cave in—and all Jim's income was designated for tuition, rent, and groceries—God dealt with me. I desperately needed His victory in the area of my heart's desires and dreams for our home and lives, and those needs pressed me to Him in prayer. Over and over again, day after day, I placed everything in God's hands, letting it be His job to meet those needs—and another prayer principle was born: *If He doesn't meet it, you didn't need it!* Through the years God has faithfully met the many needs of our family. We've experienced the reality of God's promise that no good thing will be withheld from those who walk uprightly (Psalm 84:11)—and you can too.

Blessing #6: God-Confidence

Dr. James Dobson wrote, "Believe it or not, low self-esteem was indicated as the most troubling problem by the majority of the women completing [his] questionnaire. More than 50 percent… marked this item above every other alternative on the list, and 80 percent placed it in the top five."[6] These women (and maybe you're one of them) could benefit from the tremendous *God-*confidence I began to enjoy as I kept cultivating a heart of prayer. And it's even better than self-confidence and self-esteem.

God-confidence comes as the Holy Spirit works in us. As we pray and when we make choices that honor God, the Holy Spirit fills us with His power for ministry. When we are filled with God's goodness, we are confidently and effectively able to share His love and joy. As women of prayer open to the transforming touch of the Holy Spirit, we will find His divine life in us overflowing into the lives of others.

> *There isn't time or space to list the many blessings that can be ours as we pray!*

Also, as a result of practicing the principle *make no decision without prayer,* we experience a divine assurance with every step we take. As the events we've prayed about and committed to arrive, we can enjoy the settled assurance that they are God's will, and we can therefore enter into them with delight, anticipation, and courage. We can truly serve the Lord with gladness (Psalm 100:2), not glumness. We can delight to do God's will (Psalm 40:8) instead of dreading it.

Blessing #7: The Ministry of Prayer

When I read Edith Schaeffer's book *Common Sense Christian Living,* I came across a concept that changed my life. While talking about prayer, Mrs. Schaeffer focused on the mind-boggling fact that prayer makes a difference in history. She wrote, "Interceding for other people makes a difference in the history of other people's lives."[7] Looking at the life of the apostle Paul, she noted that he always asked others to pray for him because he expected "a difference to take place...in answer to prayer. Paul expect[ed] history to be different because intercession [was] taken seriously as an important task."[8]

This mature understanding of prayer encouraged me in two distinct ways. First, I came to grips with the power of prayer to change lives. I knew from experience that prayer had changed my life, but…the lives of others? That idea was new to me. It seemed impossible, but Mrs. Schaeffer assured me that even I, a young Christian, could have a role in the mysterious ways of God. She helped me believe that my infant prayers could make a difference in history!

The second revelation was recognizing prayer as a ministry, which was an important realization for me. At the time I was a mother with two little ones at home, and I felt left out at church. I struggled because I couldn't attend all the wonderful women's studies and events, even though I knew my place at that time was at home. Coming face-to-face with the fact that prayer is a ministry ended my feelings of uselessness and ineffectiveness. The blank-paged book Katherine gave to me was key to the beginning of my prayer ministry. I used that book to jot down the names of our staff at church, the missionaries we knew, and the requests shared by others. My heart took flight as I joined God in the vital ministry of prayer!

There isn't time or space to list the many blessings that can be yours and mine as we pray. I've only shared a very few! But I know that as you bow your knees and heart before God and begin cultivating a heart of prayer, you will taste and know that the Lord is good (Psalm 34:8).

Yes, But How?

How can we cultivate a heart of prayer and enjoy the blessings that accompany a life of committed and devoted prayer? Here are some quick thoughts.

- Start a prayer log to record requests and responses as you travel your own personal journey of prayer.

- Set aside some time each day to linger with the Lord in

prayer and remember that *something is better than nothing.* Begin small—and watch for the mighty effects!

- Pray always (Ephesians 6:18) and in all places, enjoying God's presence with you wherever you go (Joshua 1:9).
- Pray faithfully for others—including your enemies (Matthew 5:44).
- Take seriously the powerful privilege of the ministry of prayer.

Heart Response

First things first! Of course you and I want our relationship with God to have the reigning position in our hearts. I know that, like me, you want to walk so closely with Him that His fragrance permeates all of your life and refreshes all who cross your path. This happens when you meet with God in prayer, prostrate in soul and humble in heart.

So, dear praying friend, no matter where we are—at home or in another country, in the car or in the shower, in a wheelchair or in the hospital, sitting alone or in a room with thousands of people—you and I can be in tune with God through prayer. We can also lift countless others toward heaven and boldly ask our omnipotent God to make a difference in their lives. I pray you will take this powerful privilege—and responsibility!—seriously.

Now think about this: Do you think praying—even for just five minutes a day—could change your life? It can! Lingering in God's presence through prayer will increase your faith in Him, provide a place for you to unload your burdens, remind you that God is always near, and help you not to panic. It is one way God has provided for us to commune with Him. And when you accept His invitation to commune with Him, He will transform your heart and change your life.

4

A Heart That Obeys

I have found David…
a man after My own heart,
who will do all My will.
ACTS 13:22

Watching my daughters grow into responsible women has been a constant delight to me as a mother. Now that they've become adults and ventured out on their own, I hope and pray that I've given them enough of the basics to build their lives on—the basics of faith in Christ, the basics of homemaking, and the basics of cooking. One night, though, I wasn't so sure.

For several years Katherine enjoyed the fun and fellowship of sharing an apartment with some young women from our church. Part of the adventure was cooking for the group on her assigned nights. But when she began to date her Paul (who is now her husband), the two of them spent many an evening at our home "hanging out" with Jim and me. On one of those nights Katherine decided to dig out a smudged old recipe—a long-time family favorite—and bake some brownies to top off our evening. Because

I don't normally make them for just Jim and me, we could hardly wait for those brownies to cool down enough to eat them with tall glasses of cold milk!

> The heart God delights in is compliant, cooperative, and responsive to Him and His commands.

Finally we each had a huge, warm brownie to bite into—but after one taste we knew we wouldn't be taking a second bite. Something was missing. Not wanting to hurt Katherine's feelings, we took turns mumbling something somewhat kind like, "Hmmm, these taste different..." or "Hmmm, they sure do *smell* good..." and "Oh, Kath, thanks for making us brownies." Finally I asked her if she might have left anything out. With all of the gusto in the world, she cheerfully volunteered, "Oh yes, I left out the salt! At the apartment I've been learning to cook without salt. Salt's bad for us." Those brownies had to be thrown out because a single missing ingredient—a little teaspoon of salt—kept them from being edible.

Just as a batch of brownies requires several ingredients to become what we intend it to be, several ingredients are key to us becoming women after God's own heart. We've already talked about devotion to God, devotion to His Word, and devotion to prayer. But one more ingredient—as important as salt in brownies—goes into making you and me women after God's own heart, and that is obedience. The heart God delights in is a heart that is compliant, cooperative, and responsive to Him and His commands—a heart that obeys.

Two Kinds of Hearts

The title for this book—*A Woman After God's Own Heart*—is drawn from God's description of King David. God testified,

"I have found David…a man after My own heart, who will do all My will" (Acts 13:22). These words were spoken in startling contrast to the character of the reigning king of Israel, Saul.

Here's a little background information. Speaking on behalf of God, the prophet Samuel rebuked Saul for failing to obey God's specific instructions (1 Samuel 13). Again and again, as reported in 1 Samuel, Saul overstepped his bounds, the ones God set for him. On several occasions he specifically disobeyed God. Although he was very careful to offer prescribed sacrifices to God, Saul failed to offer God the ultimate sacrifice—obedience from a heart wholly devoted to Him (1 Samuel 15:22). Clearly Saul was not responsive to God or His laws.

Finally, after one extremely serious act of disobedience, God sent Samuel to Saul with a twofold message: "Your kingdom shall not continue" and "The LORD has sought for Himself a man after His own heart" (1 Samuel 13:14). God was communicating something along this order—"Saul, you're through as king. I've put up with your rebellious, unresponsive heart long enough, and now I've found just the right man to serve me. This man who will take your place is a man with a responsive heart, a man with a heart of obedience, a man who will follow all my commands, fulfill all my desires, and do all my will."

Here we witness two very different kinds of hearts—the heart of David and the heart of Saul.

- In his heart, David was willing to obey, but Saul was satisfied with merely external acts of sacrifice.
- David served God. Saul served himself and did things his way.
- David was concerned with following God's will, but Saul cared solely for his own will.

- David's heart was centered on God, and Saul's was centered on Saul.

- Even though David didn't always obey God, he had what mattered over the long haul—a heart after God. In sharp contrast, Saul's devotion to God was impulsive and sporadic.

- Although David was well-known for his physical prowess and might as a warrior, he was humbly dependent upon God, trusting in Him and repeatedly acknowledging, "The LORD is the strength of my life" (Psalm 27:1). Saul, on the other hand, was proud. He relied on his own skill, his own wisdom and judgment, and his arm of flesh.

God gave both of these kings opportunities to lead Israel, but in the end they walked down different paths—Saul away from God and David toward Him. Saul's heart was unresponsive to God's will, while David's was devoted to obedience. They were like two different musicians, one who sits down at a piano and plunks on it, here a little, there a little (almost everyone can play "chopsticks") and the other who sits for hours at a time, a disciplined, faithful, and dedicated student. The first creates immature, irregular, discordant sounds that fade away, while the other learns, grows, excels, and lifts the hearts and souls of others as he fine tunes himself to the Almighty. Saul's song—his walk with the Lord—was impulsive, transitory, and undeveloped. But David, the sweet psalmist of Israel, offered up to God the purest melodies of devoted love and committed obedience. Truly, his was a heart after God!

Yes, But How?

How can we follow after David in our devotion to God? What

can we do so that God can grow in us hearts committed to obedience? A heart committed to doing God's will is an important ingredient when it comes to living out our love for God.

God calls us to take care of our hearts. As I noted earlier, God tells us to "keep your heart with all diligence, for out of it spring the issues of life" (Proverbs 4:23). As we walk this path of life, God says we are to ponder the path of our feet (verse 26) and look straight ahead, not side to side (verse 25). Rather than turning to the right or to the left (verse 27), we are to follow ways that are established by God (verse 26). The key, God says, to living a life of obedience—a life that stays on His path—is the heart. If we keep our hearts, if we diligently attend to them and guard them, then all of the issues, the actions, the "ongoings and the out-goings" of life will be handled God's way.[1] A heart responsive to God and His ways leads to a life of obedience—and these proven guidelines can help us stay on God's path.

Concentrate on doing what is right—When God looked into David's heart, He saw what He wants to see in us—a heart that will do His will. A wholehearted love for God looks to Him through His Word and prayer, always watching and waiting, ever ready to do what He says, prepared to act on His expressed desires. Such a heart—tender and teachable—will concentrate on doing what is right.

> *Let God lead you on His path so you can be sure you're doing the right thing.*

But what about those situations where you're not sure what is right? In your heart you want to do the right thing, but you're just not sure what that right thing is. First, don't do anything until you know what is right. Ask God for guidance. Take time to pray, to think, to search the Scriptures, and to ask advice from someone more seasoned in Christ. If a person is asking you to do something you are unsure of, simply say, "I'm going to have to give this some thought and prayer. I'll let you know later." Do nothing until you know what the right thing is.

Besides, consider the following Scriptures. We are told, "In all your ways acknowledge Him, and He shall direct your paths" (Proverbs 3:6). We also know that "if any of you lacks wisdom, let him ask of God…and it will be given to him" (James 1:5). Also, act on the truth of James 4:17—"To him who knows to do good [to do the right thing] and does not do it, to him it is sin." Look to God and pray, "I don't want to sin so I have to know what the right thing, the good thing, is. Please, what is the right thing?" Let God lead you on His path so you can be sure you are doing the right thing. The bottom line? When in doubt, don't (Romans 14:23). Or, put another way, when in doubt, it's out!

Cease doing what is wrong—The split second you think or do anything contrary to God's heart, stop immediately! (Such action is key to training your heart to be responsive to God.) Just put the skids on the activity. If it's gossip, stop. If it's an unworthy thought, stop (Philippians 4:8). If there's a spark of anger in your heart, stop before you act on it. If you've spoken an unedifying word, stop before you speak another. If you've said yes to something but you're not at peace about that decision, stop. Or if you get into a situation that turns out to be sinful or something you didn't plan on, stop and get out!

Everyone has experiences like these. They happen every day. And how you respond reveals what's at the core of your heart. Ceasing an activity or thought process before sin progresses any further turns your heart right back around toward God and puts you back on His path. So call on the Lord. He will give you strength…whatever the temptation, whatever the dangerous path (Hebrews 2:18).

Confess any wrong—Because Christ covered our sins by His blood through His death, you and I are forgiven. We may not *feel* forgiven—but you and I only need to *know* that we are. But we still keep sinning. So when I've done something contrary to God's Word, I've learned to acknowledge in my heart, "This is wrong. This is sin! I can't do this!" After all, "if we say that we have no sin, we deceive ourselves, and the truth is not in us" (1 John 1:8). So I call sin "sin," and by doing so I train my heart to be more responsive to God's convicting Spirit.

When you and I confess our sins like that, God "is faithful and just to forgive us our sins and to cleanse us from all unrighteousness" (1 John 1:9)—and the sooner we confess, the better! And as you confess your sin, be sure you're also forsaking it. Proverbs 28:13 warns, "He who covers his sins will not prosper, but whoever confesses *and* forsakes them will have mercy." Don't be like the farmer who said, "I want to confess that I stole some hay from my neighbor." When the clergyman asked, "How much did you steal?" the farmer declared, "I stole half a load, but make it a whole load. I'm going back to get the other half tonight!"

Clear up things with others—Confession makes things right with God, but if we've hurt another person, we need to clear things up with that person too. When it is appropriate, we need to admit our wrongful behavior to the person involved…something I had to do the first morning I sang in our church choir. A sweet woman reached out to me, smiled, and asked, "Hi! Are you one of the new guys?" For whatever reason, I snapped, "No, but I'm one of the new *girls*." As I spoke those words, I was immediately convicted, but we were filing in to sing, to worship! I limped through all those moving (and convicting!) hymns about our precious Jesus. Finally I got back into the choir room and apologized. I waited until the woman I had been so mean to got there and then said, "I really have a smart mouth, don't I? I'm sorry I responded to your kindness with such a smart remark. Will you please forgive me?"

Continue on as soon as possible—Our enemy Satan delights when our failure to obey God keeps us from serving Him. You and I can all too easily wallow in the fact that we've failed God and then allow our emotions to keep us from going on and following after Him. Oh, we know we are forgiven. And we've stopped the behavior, acknowledged and confessed our sin, forsaken our thoughts or actions, and cleared up the situation. But we still say to ourselves, "I can't believe I did that, said that, thought that, acted like that. How could I have done that? I'm unworthy. I am totally unfit to serve God."

When that's the case, we need to turn to another truth from God's Word and let it lift us up, dust us off, refresh us, and set us back on His path. Speaking divine directions to us through His Spirit, God encourages us—those of us who have confessed our disobedience and been forgiven—to be "forgetting those things which are behind and reaching forward to those things which are ahead...[and pressing] toward the goal for the prize of the upward call of God in Christ Jesus" (Philippians 3:13-14). Once we've acknowledged and dealt with our failure to follow God wholeheartedly, once we've addressed our acts of disobedience, you and I are to forget those things from the past and go on. Oh, we are to remember the lessons learned, but we are also to train our hearts to obey by obeying this command from God to go on.

Heart Response

Now, dear follower of God, we've come to the end of the first section of this book. And what we've learned about our hearts will help us determine to follow the path God lays out for us in the chapters to follow. We're preparing to examine other aspects of our busy and complicated daily life in the pages ahead, but before we step away from focusing on our relationship with God, you (and I) need to take a serious look at our own hearts.

Obedience is a foundational stepping-stone on the path of God's will—the path you'll be following as a woman after His heart. Sure footing here will prepare you to respond later to what God has to say. So right now consider whether your heart is totally in God's hands. Have you yielded your will to Him? When God looks into your heart, does He easily see your willingness to obey Him?

In Saul's day, God declared that He is looking for a heart that will obey Him, that will do all His will. Do those words describe your heart? Is God's desire your desire? Does your heart follow hard after God (Psalm 63:8), close to Him, on His heels, literally clinging to Him?[2]

Can you pinpoint any behavior in your life that calls for a heart response of confession and a change of location onto the path of obedience? If so, stop right now, acknowledge that area of disobedience, confess that sin, choose to forsake that behavior, and then step right back onto God's path of beauty, peace, and joy. As you desire all that God desires, love all that He loves, and humble yourself under His mighty hand (1 Peter 5:6), then your heart will indeed be a heart after God. What a blessed thought!

Part 2

The Pursuit
of God's Priorities

5

A Heart
That Serves

I will make him a helper.
GENESIS 2:18

It was a bright autumn day at the University of Oklahoma. As I hurried toward my first class after lunch, I noticed him again. He was smiling as he came my way. Every Monday, Wednesday, and Friday our paths crossed as he too rushed to class. His name—Jim George—was unknown to me at the time, but he looked extremely nice, he was cute, and I loved his smile! Well, evidently he noticed me too because soon a mutual friend set up a blind date for us.

That was in November 1964. On Valentine's Day we were engaged, and our wedding took place the first weekend school was out, June 1, 1965. That was more than 40 years ago—and I wish I could say, "That was 40-plus wonderful, blissful, happy years ago," but I can't. You see, Jim and I began our marriage without God, and that meant rough times. From the beginning we fumbled, we argued, and we let each other down. Because we didn't find fulfillment in our marriage, we poured our lives into causes, friends, hobbies, and intellectual pursuits. Having two children also didn't fill the emptiness we each felt. Our married life droned on for eight frustrating years until, by an act of God's grace, we became a Christian family, a family centered on Jesus Christ as the head, a family with the Bible to guide us.

Giving our lives to Jesus Christ made a tremendous difference inside our hearts, but how would Christ change our marriage? We each had been given new life in Christ, but what were we going to do about the tension in our marriage and therefore in our home?

I had much to learn about being a woman, a wife, a mother who pleased God, and thankfully—soon after naming Jesus as my Lord and Savior—I had in my hands a calendar for reading through the Bible. On January 1, 1974, I began to follow that schedule, and as I read I did something that I recommend you do too. I marked every passage that spoke to me as a woman with a pink highlighter.

Well, God went to work on my makeover that very day. On January 1, my first day of reading, I came across the first aspect of my job assignment as a Christian wife—I was to serve Jim, to help him. I marked these words in Genesis 2:18 in pink:

> It is not good that man should be alone;
> I will make him a helper comparable to him.

Called to Serve

To begin our discussion we must realize that a woman after God's own heart is a woman who carefully cultivates a servant spirit, whether she is married or not. She desires to follow in the steps of Jesus, who "did not come to be served, but to serve" (Matthew 20:28). Such following calls for lifelong attention to the heart attitude of serving.

And if you are a married woman, that attitude and service starts at home with your family. And more specifically, with your husband. God has designed the wife to be her husband's helper. So the first step on my journey of a thousand miles to becoming God's kind of wife was beginning to understand that *I am on assignment from God to help my husband.*

Exactly what is this "helper" from Genesis 2:18, I wondered. Borrowing a few of Jim's Bible-study books, I learned that a helper is one who shares man's responsibilities, responds to his nature with understanding and love, and wholeheartedly cooperates with him in working out the plan of God.[1] Anne Ortlund talks about becoming a team with your husband, pointing out that being a team eliminates any sense of competition between spouses. Writing about this partnership of marriage, she describes a wife being solidly behind and supportive of her husband. She declares, "I have no desire to run parallel to Ray, sprinting down the track in competition. I want to be behind him, encouraging him."[2]

> *A servant spirit helps me be more like Christ as I esteem others—especially my husband—as better than myself and commit myself to service.*

I can honestly say that I became a better wife—and a better Christian—when I became a better helper. Realizing *I am on assignment from God to help my husband* opened my eyes. According to God's plan, I was not to compete with Jim or impede his progress. Instead, I am to be solidly behind him and supportive of him—helping him.

Because my husband was a leader in our church, I read many

books about leaders' wives, hoping to learn from them more about how to support and encourage Jim. Reading about the wife of former President Dwight D. Eisenhower, gave me further insight into the attitude of a helper. Julie Nixon Eisenhower explained, "Mamie had seen her role as one of emotional support for her husband….She had no interest in promoting herself. Most of all, she was the woman behind the man, the woman who proudly proclaimed, 'Ike was my career.'"[3]

As God impressed on my heart the importance of a servant spirit, especially in my role as a helper to my husband, I wrote out a prayer of commitment. As I did, I stepped back a few paces to ensure that, in my own heart, Jim was clearly in front and I was definitely stationed behind him to help. On that day—and in that prayer to God—I began a life of serving Jim that has continued for more than three decades. Oh, I have many things to do! What woman and wife doesn't? But my primary purpose and role each day is to help Jim, to share his responsibilities, to respond to his nature, and to wholeheartedly cooperate with him in God's plan for our life together.

This mind-set, this servant spirit, helps me be more like Christ as I esteem others—especially my husband—as better than myself (Philippians 2:3) and commit myself to service.

Yes, But How?

How can we develop a heart committed to service, a heart intent on emulating Christ in service to another person? What can a wife do so that God can grow in her a heart committed to helping her husband? Consider these suggestions.

Make a commitment to help your husband—I had to ask myself, Would I or wouldn't I try to become a helper? Would I or wouldn't

I follow God's plan for me to help my husband? The decision was mine. And it's yours too. And when you do decide to do it God's way, you might want to write your own prayer of commitment to God like I did. It was a lifesaver—and a cheerleader—when my energy and understanding fell short. Let your words reflect your decision to help your husband, to be a team with him, and to make helping him the priority focus of your every day.

Focus on your husband—God wants us wives to focus our energy and efforts on our husbands. Each of us is to focus on *his* tasks, *his* goals, *his* responsibilities. I know firsthand this can be an area of struggle because our sin nature cries out, "Me first!" But God wants us to say, "You first!" when it comes to our husbands. So periodically ask yourself about your marriage, "Who's Number One?"

One practical way I try to help Jim by focusing on him and his responsibilities is by asking him two questions every day:

"What can I do for you today?"

"What can I do to help you make better use of your time today?"

You may worry (as I did initially) about what major, time-consuming demands your husband might make. But I have to tell you the first time I asked Jim these questions all he wanted was a button sewn on his favorite sports coat. That's all! And it was no problem for me to whip out a needle and thread and make Jim my Number One human priority by sewing on a little button.

Sometimes, though, the requests are larger. For instance, I remember a week of "larger" demands as Jim prepared to go to Germany for five months with his Army Reserve unit. His days were full of physicals…while I ran to the safe deposit box for wills, birth certificates, and our marriage license. He had dental visits and blood typing…while I looked up mortgage records, worked on his passport, and set up an email account. He was also fixing up the house and organizing his job before he left the country—and all this as one of my book deadlines rapidly approached.

But even when I don't like how the day unfolds or the answers Jim gives to my two questions (I now know his answers can change the pattern of my entire day!), I do want Jim to be my highest human priority. And I want him to know he is. After all, that's my assignment from God—to ease my husband's life by helping him.

And even if there is no husband in your life today, you can nurture a heart of Christlike service as you focus on helping and serving other people. Whether you are married or not, serving the people in your life is part of God's will for you. It pleases Him when you follow His will, benefits the lives of those you serve, and shows Christ to the world.

Ask of your actions, Will this help or hinder my husband?— That simple question can be a good lens through which to look at how we act in our marriages. Let me give you a simple example. Your husband's boss asks him to go on a business trip, and you pout and punish him because he has to go. Does that help your husband or hinder him?

When my husband became a full-time seminary student *and* a full-time staff member at church *and* traveled extensively with our missions pastor, I read every book I could find about Mrs. Ruth Graham, wife of evangelist Billy Graham. Because her famous husband was absent from home almost ten months a year, I learned much from her about being alone. Listen to this wise statement from her: "We have to learn to make the least of all that goes and the most of all that comes."[4] This encouragement from a fellow helper made me a better helper to Jim as he prepared for each trip (even a five-month trip to Germany!) and decreased my urge to pout and punish.

Here's another example. Your husband has told you the state of the budget, but you want something right away and are pushing to get it. I know that situation well from experience. We had lived in our home (the one with the peeling paint and the sagging ceiling!) for more than a decade, and it was finally time to do some remodeling. I was ecstatic. To me, a fireplace had been the one thing missing in our charming little house all these years, and this was our opportunity to install one. But Jim sat down and clearly showed me there wasn't enough money in our loan to add a fireplace.

But oh how I wanted that fireplace. So I said things like, "Wouldn't this be a great evening for a fire in a fireplace…if we had one?" and "Just think…if we had a fireplace, we could put some logs on and have dinner in front of a warm fire!"

> *Is your heart committed to service—specifically to serve and help your husband?*

But then I asked the question, "Elizabeth, are you helping or hindering?" And I knew the answer immediately (and so do you)! One day God helped me realize I was nagging, and I committed before the Lord not to mention a fireplace to Jim again…ever. I wrote out that commitment in yet another prayer to God, and—thanks to God's grace—I *never* talked about a fireplace again.

And another example. Your husband thinks your family should move so he can better provide for the family, and you either don't want to move or you firmly declare, "Not there!" As a pastor, my husband counseled a couple in this situation. The husband was a truck driver who wanted to change careers because of the wear and tear it put on their marriage (the reason they had come for counseling in the first place). A terrific job opportunity finally opened up for him half a state away where they could afford to purchase a home and begin their family. Sharon, however, didn't want to move. She loved her job and was next in line for a significant promotion at work. But realizing God's plan that she help her husband—who was trying his best to provide *financially* through a better job and *spiritually* through a better situation for their marriage—enabled her to help, and not hinder, his leadership. They made the move—and oh, what an abundance of blessings God had waiting for this precious couple in their new hometown.

And one more example. Your husband wants to have a daily time reading the Bible together as a family, but you don't want to…or you don't want to study what he has chosen…or you never quite get up early enough to have breakfast ready in time to allow for family devotions. In most families the wife is usually responsible for the morning schedule at home. And because she controls the schedule, she has the ability to make a family worship time happen—or not happen. If her heart is committed to service, she has the power to help her husband accomplish this goal and others.

Is yours a heart committed to service, specifically to serving and helping your husband? What an abundance of blessings God has waiting for *you* when yours is such a heart!

Heart Response

Helping. It's a simple and noble assignment—and it reaps rich rewards. Living out God's assignment certainly benefits our husbands and anyone else we serve, but we benefit as well as we learn to serve as Christ did. Being a servant is a sign of Christian maturity. It is the true mark of Christ (Philippians 2:7), who served to the point of death (Matthew 20:28). So how do you measure up as a helper? In your marriage, do you see yourself as a team player, free of any competitive actions, thoughts, or desires? Is bettering your husband's life your primary concern? Is helping your husband the main focus of your energy? Have you committed your heart to following God's plan for you, His plan that you help and not hinder your husband? As you and I promote the well being of our husbands—and of the multitude of other people God has placed in our lives—our service glorifies God.

6

A Heart That Follows

Wives, submit to your own husbands.
EPHESIANS 5:22

Having started down the road toward becoming my husband's helper, I kept reading my Bible. As I did so, I discovered more to my role of wife, and I saw other qualities I needed if I were to be the kind of wife God wants me to be. In fact, the number of times my pink marker hit the pages showed me I had a lot of work to do. The next big item I noticed was *I am on assignment from God to follow my husband's leadership.*

As a new Christian, I found what the Bible refers to as "submission" to my husband and following his leadership to be a foreign concept. Therefore I had to do some research. When I did, I learned that in the Bible "submission" (*hupotasso*) is primarily a military term meaning to rank oneself under someone else. This heart attitude is lived out by leaving things to the judgment of another person and yielding or deferring to the opinion or authority of someone else.[1]

As I said, the concept was new and I felt my heart hesitating. But I kept studying (and praying to be a woman—and wife— after God's own heart), and the Bible helped flesh out the heart attitude that God desires in His women. Here's what I found.

"Be Submissive One to Another"

First, I discovered the fact that the Christian lifestyle—for men as well as women—is one of submission. You and I are called to be "submitting to one another" (Ephesians 5:21). God's desire for us—married or single, young or old, male or female— is to honor, serve, and subject ourselves to one another. We as Christians are to...

- "submit...to everyone who works and labors with us" (1 Corinthians 16:16).
- be "submitting to one another in the fear of God" (Ephesians 5:21).
- "obey those who rule over you, and be submissive" (Hebrews 13:17).
- "submit to God" (James 4:7).
- "submit yourselves to every ordinance of man for the Lord's sake, whether to the king as supreme, or to governors...for this is the will of God" (1 Peter 2:13-15).
- "be submissive to your masters [employers]" (1 Peter 2:18).
- "all of you be submissive to one another" (1 Peter 5:5).

It's clear that we reflect Christ's character as we move away from selfishness and, acting out of honor for other people, defer to them. A heart willing to follow and submit, dedicated to honoring and yielding to others, is to be the heart of God's people, His church, and His women.

And that includes wives to husbands—"Wives, submit to your own husbands" (Ephesians 5:22 and Colossians 3:18). When it comes to marriage, God arranged for the sake of order that the husband lead and the wife follow. For marriages to run smoothly, God has said, "The head of every man is Christ, the head of woman is man, and the head of Christ is God" (1 Corinthians 11:3).

Now don't be alarmed. The husband's headship doesn't mean we wives can't offer wise input (Proverbs 31:26), enter into a discussion, or ask questions for clarification during the decision-making process. But the husband's headship does mean that he is responsible for the final decision. Author Elisabeth Elliot describes her father's headship in her childhood home. She writes, "'Head of the house' did not mean that our father barked out orders, threw his weight around, and demanded submission from his wife. It simply meant that he was the one finally responsible."[2]

> *God, the perfect Artist, designed marriage to be beautiful, natural, and functional by giving it a single head, the husband.*

In the end, the husband is accountable to God for his leadership decisions, and we are accountable to God for how we follow that leadership. Our husbands answer to God for leading, and we answer to Him for following. Now I ask you, which responsibility would you rather have?

God's instruction that the man lead and the woman follow results in *beauty* as well as order. I remember as a child seeing the stuffed "head" of a goat in a museum—only it had two heads. It was abnormal, grotesque, a freak attraction, an oddity—and so is a marriage with two heads. But God, the perfect Artist, designed marriage to be beautiful, natural, and functional by giving it a single head, the husband. Thank You, Lord, that marriage is Your work of art.

The Privilege of Choice

Another translation—and yet another pink passage—showed me that I am responsible for whether or not I submit. It said, "Wives, submit [or subject] *yourselves* unto your own husbands, as unto the Lord" (Ephesians 5:22 kjv).

That means submission is a wife's choice. She decides whether or not to follow her husband. No one can do it for her, and no one can make her do it. Her husband can't make her submit and follow, her church can't make her, her pastor can't make her, and neither can a counselor. She must decide to choose to defer to her husband and follow his leadership.

I gasped—and grew as a Christian wife—when I read about four women just like you and me who were meeting each week to study the Bible. One week they happened upon 1 Corinthians 11:3, a verse about the headship of the husband in marriage. This is the verse we just considered that tells us, "The head of every man is Christ, the head of woman is man, and the head of Christ is God." Coming face to face with God's plan called them to make some decisions, some choices.

> The leader for that evening read [the verse] aloud, paused, and read it again...Every one of those women—they all knew it—was the head in her marriage...
>
> Someone said weakly, "Does St. Paul say anything else about [headship and submission]?" An index

was consulted, and the other Pauline statements (Colossians 3:18; Ephesians 5:22ff.; 1 Timothy 2:11ff.) were read out. There was some discussion. Finally the leader said, "Well, girls—what do we do?" Someone else said, "We've *got* to do it."...

Then came the miracle. In less than a year the four women, with amazement and delight, were telling each other and every other woman they knew what had happened. The husbands, all four, had quietly taken over...and, with no exceptions, every one of the women felt her marriage had come to a new depth of happiness—a joy—that it had never had before. A *rightness*.

Seeing this astonishing thing that not one of them had thought possible...the four wives one day realized an astonishing further truth: they realized that their husbands had never demanded and would never have demanded the headship; it could only be a free gift from wife to husband.[3]

Are you giving the gift of headship? Are you experiencing the rightness that comes from a decision to follow God's plan for marriage? Are you using your privilege of choice to follow God... and your husband?

An Important Distinction

The "who" of submission for a wife is clear in Ephesians 5:22— "Wives, submit to your *own husbands*," not to other people we admire and respect. And this is an important distinction.

A Christian woman, married to a man who was not a believer, came to me for some counsel. Sue wanted to quit her job and attend Bible college for four years in preparation for entering full-time Christian work. After telling me her heart's longings, I asked her, "Well, Sue, what does your husband say about this?" She quickly answered, "Oh, he doesn't want me to do it."

"Why, Sue," I exclaimed, "God has spoken!" You see, God's plan for marriage is that each wife honor and follow her husband. When Sue talked about her dream with her pastor and her Christian employer, both of them told her to go ahead with her plans. She was all too ready to honor the guidance of others. But the Bible is clear. We are to submit to our own husbands.

Believe me, I know that sometimes we're tempted to dismiss God's plan. We say or think things like, "My husband isn't walking with God, so I don't have to submit to him" or "My husband isn't a Christian, so I don't have to submit to him." The apostle Peter wrote the following words to help women in those exact situations, women with unbelieving and/or disobedient husbands: "Wives, likewise, be submissive to your own husbands, that even if some do not obey the word, they, without a word [from their wives], may be won by the conduct of their wives" (1 Peter 3:1). In other words, our submission to our husbands preaches a lovelier and more powerful sermon than our mouths ever could. Conduct counts!

It's important to mention here the one exception to following your husband's advice, and that is if he asks you to violate some teaching from God's Word. If he's asking you to do something illegal or immoral, go to a trusted pastor or counselor and follow the advice you receive there.

Looking Up Helps

Ephesians 5:22 also gives us the "how" of submission—"Wives, submit [or subject] to your own husbands, *as to the Lord.*"As soon as I stopped thinking about following Jim and started looking up and thinking about following the Lord, my struggle to submit slowly began to abate. I sort of mentally set Jim to one side, and that left me staring straight into the Lord's face. Suddenly following Jim became much simpler—and easier. It had nothing to do with Jim and everything to do with the Lord. As a familiar Scripture says, "Whatever you do [and I added in my heart and mind the words "including following my husband!"], do it heartily, *as to the Lord* and not to men" (Colossians 3:23). So if you're struggling, look up, dear one. Remind yourself it's *Him* (the Lord), not him (your husband)!

Something to Think About

Here's something else to think about. What is the scope of our submission to our husbands? On what matters, decisions, and situations are we to submit? How would you answer these questions after reading this scripture? "Let the wives be [subject] to their own husbands in *everything*" (Ephesians 5:24). So whenever I'm tempted to say "Yes, but…" or "But what if…" I try to remember those two little words—"in everything." Those two words cover large and small issues alike. Case in point…

After the massive rumblings of the 1994 California earthquake, Jim and I went together to select lamps to replace those that had broken. We were delighted to find an affordable Tiffany glass table lamp. But when we got our lamp home, my heart sank as I opened the box and saw the faded, washed-out colors. They were nothing like those on the model. The pastel greens and pinks would never do in our forest-green library. But Jim thought it looked okay and said there was no reason to take it back. It was definitely not easy, but I said nothing, regarding this as another opportunity to submit to my own husband…as to the Lord…in everything…and without a word.

Granted, the lamp is a small thing, but such small things are a good place to start submitting "in everything." We'll get to some larger things later, but at this point ask God to give you His grace the next time a small thing comes your way.

But wait! That's not the end of my story. Here's what happened next. One day I smelled something burning, followed my nose, and found smoke rising out of that new lamp, caused by an electrical shortage in its wiring. Racing to unplug it from the wall, I noticed that the glass panels were completely blackened from the smoke and the current. The end of the story? We took the lamp back, got a full refund, and purchased another lamp…with the rich colors I had wanted in the first place. Jim was honored, I grew in grace, and God supplied another lamp. I hope and pray that, in time, you have many such wonderful stories about God's grace and His enablement of your choices to follow and honor your husband.

A Life of Faith

Do you know the main reason why we wives hesitate to follow our husband's leadership? God says it's *fear*. We are afraid of what will happen if our husbands do things their way instead of our way…or another way. Clearly, underneath God's call to us to submit lies a much deeper, more fundamental call to live a life of faith in God. "The holy women" of the Bible "who *trusted in God* also adorned themselves, being submissive to their own husbands," and we can follow in their steps if we "do good and are *not afraid with any terror*" (1 Peter 3:5-6).

Faith is the opposite of fear (Mark 4:40), but how does faith fit with following a husband's leadership? It is by faith that you and

I believe God works in our lives directly through our husbands. It is by faith in our sovereign God that we trust that God knows our husbands' decisions and the end results of those decisions, and trusting that God redeems, if not guides, those decisions. And so it is by faith in God that our fear is dispelled and we gain the strength to submit. Why not ask God, as the disciples did, to increase your faith (Luke 17:5)?

The Root…The Motive for Submission

Perhaps the Scripture that reached deepest into my heart as God's call to submission was taking root in my heart was this one—"Admonish the young women to…[be] obedient to their own husbands, *that the word of God may not be blasphemed*" (Titus 2:4-5), meaning discredited or dishonored. As I pondered this verse, the idea of following my husband's leadership suddenly leaped into the heavenly realm, rising far above all my earthly, petty, selfish, and fleshly excuses for not wanting to let Jim lead.

Once again it became clear to me that following Jim had nothing to do with him and everything to do with *Him*—with God! God has instituted it, commanded it, and given me the faith in Him to be able to obey His Word—and He is honored when I do. My respect and deference to my husband testifies to all who are watching that God's Word and His way are right. That makes God's call to nurture hearts that follow our husbands a high calling indeed.

Yes, But How?

How does a wife follow her husband? Here are some steps I have taken.

Dedicate your heart to honoring your husband—Change requires a decision, and that's definitely the case with submission. You and I have to decide to follow our husbands, make up our minds to practice (or work on!) it, and dedicate our hearts to honoring God and our husbands in this way.

Remember to respect—Develop the basic heart attitude of respect. Doing so helps us in the practice of following. God states, "Let the wife see that she *respects* her husband" (Ephesians 5:33). God isn't telling us to *feel* respect, but to *show* respect, to act with respect. A good way to measure our respect for our husbands is to answer the question, *Am I treating my husband as I would treat Christ?*

You reveal your respect for your husband in little daily acts. Do you, for instance, ask your husband to do something—or do you tell him? Do you stop, look, and listen to him when he's talking? Do you speak about him with respect to your children, your parents, and others?

Respond to your husband's words and actions positively—Ooooh, submission came hard for me! So when I first became a believer in Christ, I had much to learn from God and the lovely women I met at my church. Old ways die hard. I would buck, snort, kick, and fight (at least in my spirit!) with Jim about everything—which lane he should drive in, whether or not we got donuts on the way to church on Sunday morning, his method of disciplining the children versus mine, how he should handle his ministry. On and on our struggles went. I knew what Scripture said. In fact, I'd even memorized the passages we've been considering. But I still struggled. For me the breakthrough came with developing a positive response. I trained—yes, trained—myself to respond positively to anything and everything my husband said or did. And the training was a two-phase process.

Phase One: Say nothing!—Have you ever been in the presence of a woman who doesn't respect her husband? She nags at him, picks on him, and disagrees with him in public. She corrects him, battling with him over every little thing ("No, Harry, it wasn't eight years ago. It was seven years ago"). Or she cuts him off, interrupts, or, worse, finishes his sentences for him.

Clearly, saying nothing is a great improvement over that kind of behavior. Saying nothing is also a giant step toward learning submission. All we have to do to give a positive response is keep our mouths closed and say nothing. It took me some time, but I finally realized that my mouth doesn't always have to be moving. I don't always have to express my opinions—especially after Jim made a decision. Why speak thoughts I'll later regret?

Phase Two: Respond with a single positive word—After I was beginning to master saying nothing in Phase One, I graduated to Phase Two and started to respond with one positive word. I chose the word "Sure!" (and that's with an exclamation mark behind it and melody in my voice). And I began to use this positive response and say, "Sure!" on the small things.

My dear friend Dixie also chose the word, "Sure!" and let me tell you something that happened in her family as a result. Dixie's husband loved to go to Sam's Club, a crowded and noisy discount warehouse. Many times he would announce after dinner, "Hey, let's all go to Sam's Club!" Well, Dixie—with three

> *Once you've begun to respond positively to the small things, you'll quickly find it easier to respond positively to larger issues.*

children, one of them a baby at the time—could have presented a watertight case against dragging the entire family out to Sam's Club on a school night after dark—but she didn't. She also never challenged Doug's leadership in front of her little family. Instead she just smiled, responded "Sure!" and got everyone into the car for another trip to Sam's Club.

Some years later as, one by one, Dixie's family members shared around the Thanksgiving dinner table about their favorite thing to do as a family, all three of her grownup children said, "Going to Sam's Club as a family!" Family unity, fun, and memories came because of Dixie's sweet heart—and word ("Sure!")—of submission.

Once you've begun to respond positively to the small things, you'll quickly find it becoming easier and even natural to respond positively to larger and larger issues—like car purchases, job changes, and household moves. I amazed myself one morning at 5:30 when the phone rang. Jim was calling from Singapore where he was traveling with our missions pastor. He didn't say, "Hello, how are you? How are the children? I miss you so much, I love you so much, and I can't wait to see you." No, instead he blurted, "Hey, how would you like to move to Singapore and minister?" And out of my mouth blooped "Sure!" followed by "Where is it?"

Maybe it was the early hour, or my loneliness for Jim, or the surprise...or maybe it was because in the preceding ten years I had grown in the area of following my husband. Whatever the reason, my training in responding positively paid off. God gave me the grace to say "Sure!" (And yes, we did go to Singapore and lived there for a year. It was a wonderful experience for our middle-school-aged daughters as well as for Jim and me. The four of us loved it so much we wanted to spend the rest of our lives there!)

Ask of each word, act, and attitude, "Am I bending or bucking?"— Whenever tension wells up in your heart and you're resisting or questioning your husband's direction, ask, "Am I bending or bucking?" Your answer will point to the problem. Enough said.

Heart Response

Oh, dear one, don't let this look at God's guidelines for marriage be a cold exercise. We are talking primarily about a *heart* response! Your husband is your life mate. Whatever he is like, he is God's good and perfect gift to you, part of God's plan for your personal fulfillment and, more important, for your spiritual development. Your Christian character becomes evident each and every time you choose from your heart to bend, to yield, to honor, to submit, to follow your husband. It's one way that you, as a woman after God's own heart, honor God.

And what if you have a difficult husband? What if there are issues where you aren't sure what to do? By all means, take advantage of the wise people in your church—a pastor or counselor, a more seasoned and experienced person, or a more spiritually mature woman (as in Titus 2:3-5).

And what if you have no husband? God gives each of us, His children, a multitude of opportunities every day to develop a heart that considers others. Out of honor for God, you can give preference to other people in your life (Romans 12:10). Your dedication to honoring people honors God and brings beauty to your life that reflects your heart after God.

7

A Heart That Loves

Part 1

*Admonish the young women
to love their husbands.*
TITUS 2:4

As I read along toward the end of the New Testament, little did I know that God had saved until last His most exciting insight about being a wife! In the tiny book of Titus, I discovered that *I am to hold my husband first in my heart after God.* That's the clear implication of God's instruction to the older women in the church who are to teach the younger women how to be women after God's heart. The first thing listed for married women to learn and practice is to love their husbands (Titus 2:3-4).

Heartfelt Yet Practical Love

When I looked at Titus 2:4 in my Bible, I thought, "Well, of course I love my husband!" But just to be sure about God's meaning, I made another trip to Jim's bookshelf. What I found on that blessed trip revealed another aspect of my job assignment from God. Let me explain.

God loves (*agapeo*) you and me unconditionally, regardless of our shortcomings, and certainly we wives are to love our husbands with that kind of unconditional love. But when God instructs us to "love" our husbands in Titus 2:4, the word is *phileo,* meaning *friendship* love—a love that cherishes, enjoys, and *likes* our husbands! Each of us is to value our husband and build a friendship with him.[1] We should see our husband as our best friend and want to be with him more than with any other person.

Yes, But How?

How can a wife nurture a heart of love, a heart prepared to support her husband in practical ways "until death us do part"?

Decide to make your husband your Number One human relationship—Our relationship with our husband is meant to be more important than the relationships we enjoy with our parents, friends, a good neighbor, a brother or sister, a best friend, and even our children—and the way we use our time should reflect that ranking.

I learned a lot about this kind of decision while reading a book written by a mother and her married daughter, Jill Briscoe and Judy Golz. Right before her daughter was married, Jill sat her down and told her that once she was married, she couldn't come running home and she was no longer to be dependent on her parents for anything.

Then the daughter wrote: "When [Greg and I] were first married, I almost automatically reached for the telephone whenever I had a certain problem or very good news to share. Usually before I finished dialing your number, Mom, I realized what I was doing, and I made sure Greg knew about it first before calling you."

Judy also asked her mother, "Do you remember the time Greg and I had a newly married tiff and I called you in tears? The first thing you said to me was, 'Judy, does Greg know you are calling me?'"[2]

I say, "Bravo!" to this mother who voluntarily stepped out of a Number One relationship with her daughter and showed her the way to make her husband her new Number One human relationship! After all, God said that we are to "leave and cleave"—to leave our parents and cleave to our mate (Genesis 2:24). When parents are overly involved in a child's marriage, problems can arise.

In *Building a Great Marriage*, author Anne Ortlund suggests that couples consider signing an agreement that spells out the status between marriage partners

> *Your husband is to be Number One in your life (after God)—and he needs to know it. And everyone else needs to know it too.*

and parents. She suggests the wording might go something like this: "I am no longer accountable to obey my parents. I am freed from that authority, to be bound, joyfully and securely, to my mate."[3] A pastor I know includes vows for the parents during the wedding ceremony: They basically vow to *stay out* of the new couple's marriage!

Whenever I counsel a young married woman, I enthusiastically encourage her to talk to her mother and mother-in-law about recipes, skills, crafts, interests, the Bible, and spiritual growth. But I am emphatic when I say not to talk to either woman about her husband. (And that works the other way, too. Mothers and mothers-in-law shouldn't be discussing their husbands with their daughters and daughters-in-law.)

To make your husband Number One will take some work as you deal with drop-in parents, learn not to plan things with either set of parents (or anyone else for that matter) without asking Mr. Number One first, and handle expectations ("Of course you'll be spending Christmas with us?…Or coming over every Sunday?… Or calling every day?"). Your husband is to be Number One in your life (after God)—and he needs to know it. And everyone else needs to know it too.

Begin to choose your husband over all other human relationships—Again, this includes your children. Two psychologists stated, "The point at which many marriages jump the track is in *over*-investing in children and *under*-investing in the marriage."[4] I read this true-life story to myself often.

"It's Too Late Now"

Today's letter will have a somber tone. I'm about to tell you a sad story…of a woman who put her children ahead of her husband….

These last two years he's been especially lonesome. Reason? His wife has literally latched onto their youngest daughter. She's one of those hang-on-to-your-children-for-dear-life mothers [and] this year when the last one enrolled at the university, she came unglued…. Now the lady is turning to her husband, hoping….

When was the last time they were close? He simply can't remember, and he can't forget the bitterness. All those years in second place he'd made a life of his own. Had to…. Not right. Of course it isn't. But…all these years his wife has been talking *to* him, *at* him, seldom *with* him…. Think of the fun they could be having now if they had developed a friendship.

I know too many men who, when their children came, turned down a lonesome road. And when you've gone too long single file, it's hard coming back to double. So much has happened alone it just seems easier to say, "It's too late now."…

You're wise to keep checking priorities…. You *can* be both mother and wife. But the wise woman remembers she will begin *and* end as a wife.[5]

Ask of your lifestyle, "Am I spoiling my husband rotten?"—This is what loving your husband is really all about—spoiling him rotten. And here are nine tried-and-true ways to groom yourself in the fine art of showering your husband with friendship love.

1. Pray for Your Husband Daily

The apostle James observed, "The effective, fervent prayer of a righteous man avails much" (James 5:16). Certainly the same is true of the prayers of a righteous wife for her husband. To pray for your husband efficiently and regularly, create a page for him in your journal. Write his name at the top, and then list the aspects of his life you want to faithfully hold up to God—his relationship with God, his spiritual growth both at home and in the church, any projects or deadlines on the job, his schedule for each day, his spiritual gifts, and his ministry involvement.

> *As you invest your time, your heart, and your life in prayer for your husband, you'll find arguments decreasing and mellowing.*

If your husband is not a Christian, your primary prayer project is to beseech God to touch your dear one's life with His saving grace. Let the truth of God's Word be the substance of your prayers, truths like God is "not willing that any should perish" (2 Peter 3:9) and God "desires all men to be saved and to come to the knowledge of the truth" (1 Timothy 2:4). God's role is to save your husband. Your role is to pray fervently as you continue to love and serve him (1 Peter 3:1-6).

As you invest your time, your heart, and your life in prayer for your husband, you'll wake up one day and find arguments decreasing and a mellowing—even a warming—in your heart toward your husband. Truly, *it's impossible to hate or neglect a person you are praying for!*

Furthermore, Jesus teaches, "Where your treasure is [in this case, the treasure of your time and effort invested in prayer], there your heart will be also" (Matthew 6:21). Focusing on your husband in prayer will help you focus on him in your heart, your thoughts, and your actions. You'll also be surprised at the fruit born in your own life from this prayer—the fruit of understanding, cheerfulness, patience, helpfulness, and calmness. You'll realize that while you were praying for your husband, God changed *your* heart!

2. Plan for Your Husband Daily

It's a fact. Nothing just happens—including a great marriage! As much as you and I might desire to be wives who lovingly support their husbands, such loving support comes only with planning. As the Bible states, "Forethought and diligence are sure of profit" (Proverbs 21:5).[6] Here are some plans that will help you show your husband—and the watching world—that he is your highest human priority.

Plan special deeds of kindness—Each morning I ask God, "What is something I can do for Jim today that would help him, cheer him up, make him feel special, lighten his load?" Answers to that question include sewing on that missing button, running an errand for him, doing something on his "fix-it" list, even replacing old, worn-out socks with new ones. Let God be your guide.

Plan special dinners—This means dinners *he* likes. Take a lesson from Louise, a friend of mine who wrote from her new home in Oklahoma where her husband has his roots:

> One day I was cleaning out my recipe file at the kitchen table, putting all of my recipes into two piles—one to keep and one to throw away. Earl walked in and sat down at the table with me, picked up the pile closest to him and started sorting through them.
>
> "Oh, honey, I love this one!…And here's one of my favorites you haven't made in a long time…. Oh, I remember the night you made this one…. Hmmm, I wondered what happened to this one!" On and on Earl went.
>
> Elizabeth, he was going through the pile I was throwing out! I had made a decision to stop serving beef to my family. But now I've refiled all those "meat and potato" recipes and scheduled one night a week for the beef dishes.

Plan special times alone—And these times definitely have to be planned. In order to have special times alone with each other when the children were young, I scrimped and saved on our grocery budget so Jim and I could hire a babysitter each week for two hours. On our date we walked across the street to McDonald's, ordered two coffees (with unlimited refills), and, for a little more than a dollar, talked to our hearts content for two whole hours.

As the children grew older and their activities outside the home increased, Jim and I made a policy to *take advantage of any and all time alone.* It was easy to let special opportunities slip by unused, so we actively watched for chances to make our time alone a celebration of love.

While our children were growing up, Jim and I also planned a getaway for the two of us every three months—a practice we continue even with our empty nest. Those trips called for much research, saving, and planning (we traded babysitting with friends), but those priceless times were definitely worth the effort. We'd return 24 hours later refreshed and with a renewed commitment to each other and to our marriage.

Plan special dinners alone—Again, planning is key, and my neighbor Terri was a great model of this. Every Thursday she did "hot dog night" for her three boys. All week long she built up hot-dog night until the boys could hardly wait to eat them on Thursday—at 4:30! After devouring their yummy meal, they didn't even notice when they were whisked into the bathtub at 5:30. By 6:30 a story had been read, prayers said, and lights were out. Then out came Terri's linen tablecloth and napkins, two place settings of china, her sterling, and her crystal. She dropped a log into the fireplace and made a fire as a casserole emerged from the oven. Candles were lit, the lights turned down, and—voila!—a special dinner for two.

Plan an early bedtime for children—Plan to have your young children in bed early each night so that you'll have some quality time with your husband without competition from the kids.

An early bedtime is a practical way of choosing your husband's company over the distractions and interruptions of little ones. If you're avoiding these precious, cozy times alone with your husband, ask yourself why—and then remedy the situation.

Plan to go to bed at the same time—I know a night owl can be married to an early bird, but if it's at all possible, adjust your schedule to your husband's. Doing so will help make you a team, give you greater opportunities to help him get off to work each morning, keep the family on a schedule, and nurture physical love in your marriage. Again, planning is key.

As I said at the beginning of the chapter, we should see our husbands as our best friends, and we should work on building friendships with them. That work takes planning, but the rewards are definitely worth the effort as they flow out of a heart that loves.

Recently a wife told me that because her husband worked until almost midnight each evening, she was always asleep in bed when he arrived home from work. After all, she had her own job to rest up for. Well, she made the decision to set her alarm clock to go off in time for her to be slightly awake and "up" physically and mentally when her husband arrived home. She shared that when she announced her decision to her guy, she could see both joy and relief in his face and eyes. He couldn't believe it! And he was so happy. And, bonus of bonuses, it wasn't even a week before he asked her if she would share in couple devotions with him, something she had wanted for years.

You may not get this kind of response (and remember, you don't do things for your husband to *get* anything). But you will get an opportunity to be a couple, to visit, to prepare your husband a snack, and, if nothing else, to welcome him home with a smile and a hug.

Heart Pause

Why not pause and pray for your husband—your Number One friend—right now? Thank God for the love He has placed in your heart for your husband and ask for God's help in sharing it with your husband. After you say amen, do something special for your husband today that sends a message of friendship from your heart to his.

And then prepare your heart to discover in the next chapter even more ways to lavish love on him.

8

A Heart That Loves

Part 2

*Admonish the young women
to love their husbands.*
TITUS 2:4

What can you and I do to show our husbands affectionate, indulgent, friendship love? I promised you nine suggestions, and here are the rest of them. Whisper a prayer for your husband as you consider these ways to show him you care.

3. Prepare for Your Husband Daily

Preparing for your husband's homecoming each day shows him that he's a priority and communicates your heart of love.

Prepare the house—Take a few minutes before your husband is due home to pick up. Have the children help by putting away their toys. The goal is not perfection, but instead an impression of order and neatness. Many of my friends light scented candles, cut and arrange fresh flowers from the garden, turn on relaxing music, start a fire, and even pop something into the oven so their guys arrive home to a variety of sensations, which together communicate, "I'm glad you're home."

Obviously the opportunity for this step of preparation will come easier for a wife who's at home during part of the day or for a stay-at-home wife and mom. But even a working wife with a heart for her husband can think twice about how the house looks when she leaves it. After all, it's the first thing both she and her husband will see when they arrive home. It's amazing how much order can be achieved in five minutes by a woman working at full speed.

Prepare your appearance—If company were coming, you'd do a little something to freshen up, wouldn't you? Well, your husband—your Number One human priority—is far more important than company, so he should get the most special treatment of all. Run a comb through your hair, freshen your makeup, and change your clothes so he's not seeing the same old jogging outfit you had on when he left in the morning. Put on a bright color, a little lipstick, and a squirt of perfume (perfume rejoices the heart—Proverbs 27:9). After all, the most important person in your life is about to walk through the door.

Prepare the children too. In her classic book *What Is a Family?* Edith Schaeffer points out: "People so easily get annoyed with straggly looking children. It is good…to face the fact that the whole family will treat each other differently if they are dressed for the occasion, whatever that occasion may be."[1] Dirty faces, runny noses, hair hanging in the face don't make the best "Welcome Home!" Committee.

Prepare your greeting—You probably know approximately when your husband will get home from work each day. So warm his welcome as you wait and watch for him. If it's dark, for instance, turn on the porch light. In our home I watched out the front window until I saw Jim drive up. Then, prompted by my "Daddy's home!" the girls headed out the door with me to greet him.

Also be sure to plan your words of greeting. Your greeting will be more fruitful if you do. A good man ponders what to say (Proverbs 15:28), and "a good word makes [the heart] glad" (Proverbs 12:25). The moment of your husband's homecoming is not the time to ask, "Where have you been? Why are you so late? Why didn't you call? Did you pick up the milk?" It's also not the time to start listing the trials of your day. So ask God to give you just the right words—words that are positive and welcoming, words that focus on your husband and his frame of mind rather than yours. What you first say when your husband arrives home can set the tone for the entire evening.

Prepare the children to greet their father too. Be sure the TV is off. Give younger children a snack if it helps eliminate whining and grumpiness while they wait for Daddy—and for dinner. Learn from a darling cartoon I have of a mother and her two children standing in the family room with a checklist. Mom announces, "Your dad will be home any minute, let's go over the list: TV remote, check; comfy pillows, check; dinner, check; loyal canine companion, check; doting family, check!" How's your family doing in the doting department?

You can imagine my joyous surprise when Jim and I were visiting with one of my daughters and it was getting close to time for Dad to arrive home. It was dark, and it was late. But my daughter went into the living room, pushed the Off button on the TV, announced to her young children that Dad was only a few minutes away and she wanted everyone to give him a big greeting.

Furthermore she didn't want to hear the TV…or any bickering for the rest of the evening, that this was their dad's special time at home with his family. We *all* had a grand dinner and evening.

Set the table—Have dinner as close to ready as possible. Even if you haven't started the meal, a set table is the promise of what is to come.

"The king is in the castle!"—Countries with monarchs fly the royal flag over the palace when the king is in residence, and the hurry and scurry of servants' feet can be heard throughout the castle during his stay. Adopting this attitude and this approach (have your kids join you!) will help you pamper and love your king when he arrives home.

"The party!"—In an interview before Anne Bancroft's death, Hollywood couple Mel Brooks and Anne Bancroft discussed their then 40-year marriage. Anne specifically described her husband's homecoming. Each evening she would sit in her favorite chair and wait, listening for the sound of her husband's car, the crunch of its tires on the gravel driveway, the silencing of the engine, the slam of the car door, and the jingle of keys as he slipped one into the door lock. As the dead bolt slid open, she would grab the arms of her chair with both hands and think, "Oh boy! The party is about to begin!"

Now you and I aren't married to Mel Brooks, but we can both work on this kind of heart attitude. Like Anne, we can rejoice that the best part of the day has arrived—when our husband gets home and the party is about to begin!

Clear out all visitors—End your visiting well in advance of your husband's homecoming. He doesn't need to arrive home to a noisy houseful of moms and kids. After all, he's the king.

Stay off the phone—You're sure to hurt someone's feelings if you're on the phone when your husband walks through the door after work—either his feelings as you grimace and try to communicate with faces, sign language, and a weak wave or the feelings of the person on the other end of the phone line when you abruptly announce, "Oops, I have to go! My husband's home" and hang up. You know when your husband usually gets home, so set a cutoff time for making and receiving phone calls from friends.

As wives with a heart full of love for God and for the special husband He has given each of us, you and I are privileged to be able to prepare for his arrival home and to lavish our love on him. Do pour out God's love, which is poured out in your heart (Romans 5:5), when your husband walks through the door of his home. As Martin Luther said, "Let the wife make her husband glad to come home." Be sure he's not treated and greeted as the man who wrote the following words was!

The Homecoming

You know, when I get home after work, the only one who acts as if she cares at all is my little dog. She really is glad to see me and lets me know it.... I always come in the backdoor because Doris is in the kitchen about then.... But she always looks up from whatever she is doing with the most startled look, and says, "Oh, are you home already?"...Somehow she makes me feel like I've done the wrong thing just by getting home. I used to try and say hello to the kids, but I don't do that anymore. Seems I would get in between them and the TV set at just the wrong minute....So, now I just pick up little Suzy, my dog, stick her under my arm and go out in the yard. I act like I don't care, and maybe I shouldn't really—but I do. It gives me the feeling that all I am hanging around there for is just to pay the bills and keep the place up. You know, I believe that if the bills were taken care of and nothing broke, I bet I could be gone a whole week and nobody would even notice it.[2]

I know full well that in many marriages the wife arrives home after her husband, and maybe that's true for you. If so, what can you do to prepare for your husband?

Prepare all the way home—Put on some fresh lipstick and comb your hair. Use the trip home to plan those uplifting words of greeting—and then share them with a smile, a hug, and a kiss, of course! Plan to sit and snuggle a few minutes, if possible, and debrief the day's events. Have something in mind for dinner (or in the Crock Pot!), something simple and low-stress that will leave you more energy for your husband. Become an expert on quick, appealing meals. Even though you're tired, you can light candles, start a fire, and maybe even hum and laugh.

Pray all the way home—Prayer is the most important preparation of the heart. In prayer leave behind the events and people of your day and turn your heart toward home and your precious husband. Pray for your greeting, your words, your mealtime, your evening. Ask God for physical strength and energy. Relinquish any hopes and expectations of receiving help from your husband. If you get it, praise God—and your husband—profusely, but enter into your evening ready to give and expecting nothing in return (Luke 6:35). Reaffirm to God that your beloved husband is Number One, and ask for His joy in serving him.

4. Please Your Husband

If your husband is the king of the castle, you will surely delight in pleasing him. And pleasing him means paying careful attention to his wants, his likes, and his dislikes—and this takes a little doing.

What are your husband's likes? What are you doing in response to them?

My friend Gail is married to a sports nut so—after years of arguments over his habit of watching sports on TV every Saturday—she decided to join her husband in his particular "like." Gail purchased two Los Angeles Dodger T-shirts and baseball caps. As the game time neared on the next Saturday, she spread a red-and-white checked tablecloth on the floor in front of the TV, passed out the T-shirts and caps, and served a meal of foot-long Dodger dogs. Both of them had a ball at the ol' ball game!

Suzy, another friend of mine, had an even greater challenge when it came to pleasing her husband. Gary, a firefighter for the Los Angeles Fire Department, "liked" a farmer's breakfast of bacon, eggs, hash browns, and toast before he went to his job. So Suzy got up at 4:00 to fix him the breakfast he needed before he left for work at 5:00.

My Jim "likes" the salt and pepper shakers on the table. Monica's husband "likes" to read the paper in the morning before leaving for work. When Elaine's husband comes home to relax, he "dislikes" seeing toys strewn around the family room. Kathy's spouse "dislikes" the top of the refrigerator being dirty—something only he can see. What are your husband's likes and dislikes? And what are you doing in response to those?

5. Protect Your Time with Your Husband

You make your husband your Number One human priority when you protect your time with him instead of treating him as a built-in babysitter and darting out the door to shop when he gets home.

One wife and mother put it this way:

> This past week I made a small change in my weekly routine in order to put my husband as a priority. Generally I do my weekly grocery shopping in the evening, while my husband watches our two-year-old son. I've done this ever since my son became old enough to grab things in the basket. I felt that by shopping in the evening, I wouldn't have to look out for things rocketing from the basket and being squished and shaken. I could also be a whole lot quicker if I went by myself, thus conserving my time. Last week, though, I realized this probably wasn't the best use of my husband's time or of our evening, so I went shopping during the day. It didn't take that much longer, and my husband seemed to appreciate it.

Consider the following as a general principle, no matter how many decades you've been married: *If my husband is at home, I am at home.* My friend Debbie had to choose between time with her husband and time at our women's Bible study when his day off fell on the same day. Tom was understanding and supportive.

He said, "Go ahead, I'll make Wednesday morning my time to mow the lawn each week." So Debbie prayed...and chose time with Tom. Choosing to nurture her Number One human relationship, she has never attended Wednesday morning Bible study. Instead she goes to the Bible study offered on Wednesday night, when the entire family is at church for their various activities and commitments.

Being at home with your husband in the evenings is important too. It's easy to fill up your evenings with good things and miss out on enjoying the best thing—time with your man. One woman said she didn't know where her husband was every night. Then one night she stayed home—and there he was![3]

Ruth Graham is a wife who knows the value of protecting time with her husband. After a visit with Ruth at her home, an interviewer reported: "Everything is geared to Billy when he is in Montreat [their home]. Ruth refuses to have a firm schedule when Billy is there....The daily routine [is] carefully designed around her husband...."[4] A neighbor of the Grahams wrote, "Because Ruth is out of circulation when Billy comes home, her friends call him 'The Plague.'"[5] How's that for a goal?

6. Physically Love Your Husband

Read 1 Corinthians 7:3-5. A fundamental principle for marriage is "rendering affection" to one's mate. The Song of Solomon is a book of the Bible that details physical love in marriage. Proverbs 5:19 says our husbands are to be drunk with our sexual love.

I remember hearing God's view of physical love taught at a seminar I attended when I was a new Christian. I was so impressed (and convicted) I went straight home and announced to Jim that I was available to him physically at any and all times for the rest of our lives together! That may have been a slight overreaction, but I wanted to act on God's Word—and Jim got the message.

7. Positively Respond to Your Husband

We've discussed picking a positive word of response—a word or phrase like "Sure!" "Fine!" "No problem!" "Okeydokey!" "All right!" "Great!" "You bet!" "Anything for you, darling!" and "Cool!" (Notice the exclamation marks?) Imagine the lack of tension in a home where the husband's thoughts, decisions, and words are greeted so sweetly instead of met with resistance, negativism, or a lecture.

My simple but positive response meant no power struggle, no hurt feelings, no bitter words, no raised voices—and a much better start to our day.

Your immediate and gracious answer creates a nonthreatening atmosphere for communication and for asking questions—questions like "When would we consider doing that?" "How would we pay for something like that?" "What would this mean to the children?" and "Is there any other information we need?" Think of your response as being like a sandwich you're making. The first slice of bread—your initial response—is a positive, "Sure!" The items in between the bread (the meat, lettuce, tomatoes, etc.) are questions you ask for clarification, questions like those I just mentioned. The final slice of bread—your response of submission—is another positive "Sure!" Let me tell you about a sandwich I once made.

Early one morning while I was drying my hair with a blower, Jim asked if I could help him find something. My first (and fleshly) thought was "Can't you hear? I'm drying my hair!" A less selfish option—and a better one—was to yell above the noise of the blower, "Sure! I'll be right there as soon as I finish drying my hair." But God gave me the wisdom and grace to do the least selfish—and best—thing. I said, "Sure!" (the first slice of bread) as I turned off the blower. Then I asked my husband (here's the stuff between the two pieces of bread), "Do you need me to do that right now or is there time to finish drying my hair?" Even though I asked the question, I was ready to do whatever Jim said (the second slice of bread, the slice of submission). I stopped to communicate with Jim, indicating my willingness to serve. He had no problem with me finishing my hair, but the point was my readiness and desire to respond to him. My simple but positive response meant no power struggle, no hurt feelings, no bitter words, no raised voices—and a much better start to our day.

And just a note here. Sometimes the stuff between the two pieces of bread—the information gathering, processing, and discussing—can take time. It can require more than one conversation, even days or weeks as the two of you communicate. But the point is, you are more likely to be *able* to communicate when you are more positive to your husband's thoughts, dreams, and ideas.

8. Praise Your Husband

I have very few "nevers" in my life, but one primary "never" is never speak critically or negatively about my husband to anyone. I try instead to practice the wise advice a dear and godly saint at our church gave me in my wife-formative years. Loretta smiled and sweetly cooed to the group of younger wives I was in, "Ladies, never pass up an opportunity to bless your husband in public." (And, I would add, don't forget to bless him to his face as well!)

If you catch yourself speaking critically about your husband, quickly shut your mouth and do these three things:

- Search your heart. "Hatred stirs up strife, but love covers all sins" (Proverbs 10:12). Something is out of sync in your heart because "a heart of love draws a curtain of secrecy over the faults and failures of others....Love does not gossip."[6]

- Seek a solution. If some serious area in your husband's life needs attention, follow a better path than putting him down. Instead, devote yourself to prayer and, if you need to speak up, do so after much preparation and with gracious, edifying, sweet speech (Ephesians 4:29; Proverbs 16:21-24). You may also need to speak to a counselor, but remember that your time with a counselor is not for venting about your husband, but for getting help for *yourself* so you can properly deal with the problem.

- Set a goal. Make a resolution not to speak destructively about your husband but to bless him at every opportunity.

Blessing your husband in public—and in private—is one way to sow seeds of love for him in your heart.

9. Pray Always

We have come full circle. We began with prayer, and we end with prayer. A woman after God's own heart is a woman who prays. When does prayer make a difference? Try praying at these times.

- Before you speak in the morning
- Any time he is home
- Before he returns home
- Throughout the evening

- On the way to answer the phone (it could be him)
- When you are arriving home and he is already there

Take every opportunity throughout the day to ask God to enable you to be the kind of loving and supportive wife He wants you to be.

Heart Response

Surely the most important relationship in a married woman's life deserves her most focused attention. This chapter and the previous one have offered practical ideas from the Bible, books, my life, the experiences of other wives, and even the input from some husbands. To summarize, a wife who loves her husband is a wife who prays, plans, prepares, pleases, protects, physically loves, positively responds—and then prays some more. Put this whole list to work and you'll communicate "I love you" more powerfully than words alone can. And remember that a heart that loves is a heart that plans. So put on your thinking cap and begin the work of showing your husband the love that is in your heart!

9
A Heart That Values Being a Mother

Do not forsake your mother's teaching.
PROVERBS 1:8 NIV

"There is no greater place of ministry, position, or power than that of a mother."[1] I'm glad I didn't read these words when I first became a Christian. God had not yet taught me the truth of this statement, and I might have totally dismissed it. When Christ became the heart and soul of our home, I had two preschoolers, ages one-and-a-half and two-and-a-half. Katherine and Courtney were cute, but they had never been trained or disciplined. We had our moments of fun and shared some good times, but our home was generally filled with tension as I tried to coax and cajole and threaten them into acceptable behavior.

Even with my girls at such tender ages, I was absent from the home. Enrolled in a master's degree program in marriage and family counseling, I focused my time, my energy, and the effort of my heart on pursuing a counseling license to help *other* families—while I neglected my own. Farming out the children for long days spent with a variety of babysitters and different daycare centers, we had only to endure each miserable evening and weekend. The possibility of motherhood being a ministry or a place of great position and power was completely foreign to me.

But God—our ever-faithful God—opened my eyes and turned my thoughts about mothering around to His wise and perfect ways. When I first became a Christian, I sat in on a women's Bible study one night a week. There I began hearing things I had never heard before—comments about the "privilege" of being a mother, the awesome "responsibility" of raising children for God, and the "role" of the mother in training and discipling her little ones.

With the teacher continually pointing us to the Bible, I once again put that pink marker to the pages of Scripture, highlighting in my own Bible what spoke to me—this time as a mother. Studying these rosy highlightings, I discovered four passions that reflect a heart that values being a mother. We'll discuss two in this chapter and two in the next.

A Passion for Teaching God's Word

A woman after God's own heart is first and foremost a woman who has in her own heart a deep and abiding passion for God's Word. And her children—not the children at her church, not the women at her church, not her friends, her neighbors, or anyone else—are to receive the firstfruits of this burning personal passion. The Bible speaks at least twice of "the law" or teaching of the mother (Proverbs 1:8; 6:20), indicating that you and I as mothers are *on assignment from God to teach His Word to our children.* We as moms can do many things for our children, but teaching God's Word must be our passion. Why? Because God's Word (the Hebrew word *tora,* which means the divine law, the Word of God, the Bible) has value for salvation and value for eternity.

God uses His Word to draw people to Himself. The apostle Paul teaches that "faith comes by hearing, and hearing by *the word of God*" (Romans 10:17) and that "*the Holy Scriptures… are able to make you wise for salvation* through faith which is in Christ Jesus" (2 Timothy 3:15). Furthermore, God's Word never

> *We must have a passion for God's Word before we can share it with our children.*

returns to Him without first accomplishing His divine purposes (Isaiah 55:11). In light of this saving power of God's Word, we must place His Holy Scripture first on the list of things our children must know—and first in our own hearts! And it's obvious we must first have a passion for God's Word before we can share that passion with our children.

A Passion for Teaching God's Wisdom

Closely related to our call to teach God's Word to our children is our call to teach them His wisdom. In fact, the second meaning of the Hebrew word *tora* is wisdom. This definition encompasses principles, counsel, traditions, models of praise, guidelines for decision-making, and godly practices based on the Bible. Used in this sense, *tora* refers to practical and scriptural wisdom for daily life.

In Proverbs 31:1-9, we catch a glimpse of a mom who valued being a mother and treasured both her son and God's wisdom. In this chapter, her son King Lemuel records "the utterance which *his mother taught him*" (verse 1). Imagine the intimacy of the scene suggested here as a young prince perhaps sat at his mother's knee, absorbing—maybe even writing down—the words of wisdom his mother shared with him. He remembered her wisdom for the rest of his life, used it to guide his reign as king, and then passed it on at the end of the book of Proverbs. From her heart—to his heart—to your heart and mine!

Whenever I think of the calling to teach practical wisdom to my children, I think of salt. According to the Bible, my speech is to be "seasoned with salt" (Colossians 4:6), and this wonderful mothering verse gives me—and you—instruction, permission, responsibility, and encouragement to salt our children continually with God's wisdom. Out of our mouths at every opportunity must come salt—God's truth, words from the Bible, applications of the Bible's teachings, and references to God's presence with us and His sovereign power in the world.

In Deuteronomy 6:6-7, God says this to parents: "These words which I command you today shall be in your heart. You shall teach them diligently to your children, and shall *talk* of them when you sit in your house, when you walk by the way, when you lie down, and when you rise up." First a mother and father fill their own hearts with God's Word (verse 6) and then they deliberately and diligently teach their children at every opportunity each day presents (verse 7).

We need to talk about God to our children whether it's the "in" thing or not.

When I discovered that I was on assignment from God to teach Katherine and Courtney God's Word and His wisdom—to season and preserve their lives with the salt of His truth—I had to train myself to be on tiptoe, ready and waiting for the opportunities that came as we sat and walked and drove through each day. I made the *decision* to be that ever-waiting, ever-watching mom, prepared to teach my daughters about God through the course of our everyday life.

I was helped along in my decision when I read that even the great evangelist Billy Graham had to choose to speak about the Lord. He realized he needed to create opportunities to share God's truth. So in the early days of his ministry and fame, he made a *decision* to mention the Lord every time he gave an autograph. He made a *decision* to turn every interview toward the gospel message. Writing to his wife Ruth, Billy reported, "I have decided in businessmen's luncheons to go all out for the Gospel. I am not going to give a talk on world events or give them sweet little lullabies."[2]

As mothers who want to raise children after God's own heart, we make a decision to "go all out for the Gospel" and relate every tiny thing to God. We need to talk about God with our children whether it's the "in" thing or not. After all, people talk about what is important to them, and when you and I talk about God, we communicate that God is supremely important to us. And let me remind you that you'll have more opportunities to talk about God's ways (and you'll be better heard!) if the TV is off—and that requires another decision.

Also, be aware that the practical wisdom of God is taught in two ways. The first is what we've been discussing, that we teach by our words, by our *talk*. But we also teach by our *walk*—by the way we live our lives. Our walk encompasses all that we do and say and all that we don't do and don't say. Our children are watching, and we are constantly teaching our children something, either positive or negative.

How's your walk? What are your children seeing about God in you? What are you teaching your children?

Yes, But How?

How does a mother who treasures her children, prizes God's Word, and values His wisdom go about teaching truth to her children?

Make some serious decisions—Discovering my mandate to teach the Bible to my daughters made me realize I needed to make several important decisions. Would I impart the Word of God to my two girls? Would I make time in our busy daily schedule for Bible teaching? And would I speak of the Lord continually? I knew that answering yes to these questions was dependent on yet another important decision—Would I reach over and turn off the TV (here we go again!) and pick up the Bible or a Bible storybook instead?

Whatever age the children are—16 days or 16 years—we must be teaching them about God and His Word in our homes. That privilege and responsibility is clearly part of our calling as women and moms after God's own heart. That kind of teaching needs to be part of the home we are building for God (Proverbs 14:1), a home that honors our Lord. Furthermore, this kind of teaching is exactly what our children need—whether they think so or not. You and I both know that we mothers give our children what they need, not what they want.

Recognize your role of teacher—Reading more about how Billy and Ruth Graham raised their children deepened my passion to impart God's Word to my own. When asked her opinions on her role as mother and homemaker, Ruth replied, "To me, it's the nicest, most rewarding job in the world, second in importance to none, not even preaching." Then she added, "Maybe it is preaching!"[3] Can you see your role of mother as that of preaching, of instructing and imparting biblical truth at every opportunity?

Consider these examples—As mothers on assignment from God, you and I cannot underestimate the urgency of planting His truth in our children's (or grandchildren's) hearts and minds early in life. What if the noble mothers of the Bible had missed their opportunities to sow the seeds of loving God in the hearts of their children?

- Jochebed had baby Moses with her for probably only three brief years before he went to live in Pharaoh's pagan household (Exodus 2). Yet this woman, who valued her role as a mother and was passionate about God and His truth, imparted enough of that truth to Moses in those few short years to help equip him to make serious choices for God later in life (Hebrews 11:24-29).

- Hannah faced a similar challenge. Like Jochebed, she only had her little Samuel for about the same three years before she delivered him at the doorstep of the house of the Lord to be raised by someone else (1 Samuel 1–2). And, like Jochebed, she taught her son enough of God's law to help equip him to become a powerful prophet, priest, and leader of God's people in the decades to follow.

- God chose Mary to raise His Son, Jesus, and she undoubtedly took seriously her assignment from God and daily poured God's rich truth into His little heart. Of course God chose the right home and the right mother for His precious Son, and by age 12 Jesus was amazing the teachers and scholars in the temple at Jerusalem with His knowledge. He was already going about His Father's business (Luke 2:46-49).

Are you sowing seeds of God's love and His truth in the hearts of your children? It's never too early or even too late to start—and something is better than nothing. So set a pattern, be sincere, and be consistent.

Memorize Scripture and read the Bible together—The biography of Corrie ten Boom, author, evangelist, and prisoner of the Germans during World War II, provides a more contemporary example of how a parent can pour God's Word into his children's hearts. Early in life, Corrie's father instilled in his family the importance of memorizing the Scriptures, and he saw that they learned Bible passages after their mother died. This memorization served his children well as they suffered and, with the exception of Corrie, eventually died for their faith. Corrie's storehouse of Scripture helped her survive the Nazi concentration camps. Her father told Corrie, "Girl, don't forget that every word you know by heart is a precious tool that [God] can use through you."[4] God's Word did indeed arm Corrie ten Boom and help her endure the pain and torment of the concentration camp. God also used His Word, hidden away in her heart, as a mighty instrument of evangelism right there in the camp as Corrie offered salvation, hope, and comfort to other suffering prisoners.

As important as memorizing Scripture is, we can't overlook the value of daily Bible reading. In addition to assisting his children in memorizing God's Word, Corrie's father read one chapter of the Old Testament to his family every morning after breakfast and one chapter of the New Testament every evening after dinner.

The parents of Elisabeth Elliot also took seriously their job of teaching God's truth to their children. Mrs. Elliot, whose first husband was savagely murdered on the mission field and whose second husband died after a long battle with cancer, testified to the value of her early training. She wrote, "In times of deep distress I have been sustained by the words of hymns learned in family prayers....Bible reading followed the hymn singing. My father believed in reading...*regularly* (twice a day aloud to us)."[5]

Missionary John Stam, martyred in China because of his faith, described daily life in his childhood home this way: "Three times every day, when the table was set for meals, Bibles were placed ready, one for each person. Before the food was served, prayer was offered, and then a chapter was read, each person taking part.... In that way, the Bible took first place in the daily intercourse of parents and children. It was the foundation, the common meeting-ground, the test and arbiter of all their thinking. It held and satisfied their hearts."[6]

Are you catching the vision—and passion—for God's assignment to pour His Word into the hearts of your children? The assignment never ends! When Elisabeth Elliot's husband Jim was killed, her mother wrote her a letter containing Scripture verse after Scripture verse. Even when Elisabeth was grown, raised, married, and a mother herself, her mother continued to pour God's Word into her heart.[7]

Follow the model of other mothers—God has allowed me to know a special family in which every member has a passion for His Word. When her first baby arrived, the mother decided to recite the Scriptures she was memorizing to her little ones each night as she tucked them into bed. One of her college-age daughters exclaimed to me, "Mrs. George, I don't even know how I learned so much Scripture by heart. I guess I've just heard my mother say it over my bed so often that I picked it up!"

This mother, who both valued being a mother and treasured God's Word, recited lengthy passages and even entire psalms and books of the Bible to her children at bedtime. When her son was playing basketball in

> *As mothers, you and I have countless, daily opportunities in our homes to plant God's Word deeply in the minds and souls of our children. We just need to take advantage of those opportunities.*

college, he made it a practice to go into the gymnasium before each game, lie down on a bleacher, and recite Romans 6 through 8 to calm his nerves and focus his heart on God. This son's fiancée told me that on her holiday visits to his home, this godly mother also tucked *her* into bed, reciting Scripture and praying with her—at age 22—as she made the rounds to all of her adult children's rooms. Another daughter, following in her mother's footsteps, told me how she and her husband returned home for Christmas and gave her mom the gift of a flawlessly memorized recitation of the book of 1 Peter. Her mother wept!

As mothers, you and I have countless, daily opportunities in our homes to plant God's Word deeply in the minds and souls of our children. We just need to take advantage of those opportunities. And we have the blessed privilege of tending their hearts and bringing them up in the training and admonition of the Lord (Ephesians 6:4). But first we must comprehend that the little (and once-little-and-now-big) hearts God has placed in our care as children and grandchildren are treasures indeed. Then we must nurture a heart of passion for His Word so that our passion will overflow into the lives of those we love.

Heart Response

As mothers, we cannot impart what we do not possess, so it is vital that you and I nurture a fierce passion for God's Word and wisdom in our own hearts. Do you treasure His truth, laying it up in your own heart (Psalm 119:11)? Do you spend time each day pouring it into your heart and mind—and into the hearts and minds of your children? Are you committed to giving God's Word a reigning position in your home and family life? What steps are you taking to ensure a regular time for teaching, reading, studying, discussing, memorizing, and even reciting the Bible?

10

A Heart That Prays Faithfully

What, my son?...And what, son of my vows?
PROVERBS 31:2

"Aim at nothing and you'll hit it every time." This saying fit my mothering like a glove before I found direction in God's Word. Up to that point I did nothing in our home to train my children. But once I found guidance, I moved ahead full steam. I took seriously my newly discovered and God-given "license to preach," and soon we as a family were poring over God's Word—and pouring it into our hearts. We picked verses to memorize together. Katherine and Courtney began having their own "quiet time" in addition to family devotions. And we all loved the wonderful Bible stories we shared at various times during the day. It was uplifting to center our home and our talk on God.

But my pink marker had another stop to make, this time at Proverbs 31:2—"What, my son? And what, son of my womb? And what, son of my vows?" These were the words of a mother, so they might have a message for me—but I couldn't begin to imagine what that might be. (What do *you* think this verse means?) In the end, this verse proved to be the most challenging aspect of my assignment from God, and the challenge continues to this day.

Well, I exhausted Jim's books and made a few trips to the seminary library before I began to understand the truth hidden in the verse and the message it had for me as a mother. I finally saw that this verse presents two more passions as it outlines my job assignment as a mom. First, this verse tells me that *I am on assignment from God to pray for my children.*

A Passion for Prayer

Proverbs 31:2 reveals a mother's anxious care for her child's good. He is the son of her vows, meaning a son she asked God for in prayer and dedicated to God (like Samuel in 1 Samuel 1). "Son of *my* vows" also suggests that her child was the object of *her* daily vows and prayers,[1] "a child of many prayers."[2] As one commentator noted, "Motherly training and dedication [provide]...the first imparting of religious instruction, the solemn dedication of her child to the service of God, [and] repeated and earnest prayer on his behalf. Her child is not only her offspring; he is 'the son of her vows,' the one on whom she has expended her most fervent piety."[3]

> *Each morning I asked God during my prayer time to touch my girls' hearts and open them to Jesus.*

How lovely is this image of a mother who thinks, loves, acts, speaks, and prays with a large and passionate heart! In her godliness she asks God for a child, dedicates that child to God, and then teaches him the ways of the Lord we discussed in the previous chapter.

But this mother's passion for God and for training her son in His ways doesn't stop with mere verbal instruction to the child. No, she also speaks *to God* on behalf of the child. The desires of her mother-heart go deeper and higher than basic teaching and training. She is a mother who prays, who expends her greatest efforts to nurture a righteous walk with her God *so that* she may effectively pray for her child. As a woman after God's own heart, she is vigilant about her own walk with God, dealing with sin in her own life (we're back to our first priority!) in preparation for entering God's holy presence and interceding for her beloved child.

Let me share how I began to live out God's daily (and lifelong) assignment of walking with Him and praying to Him. As a Christian mother (and like you, I'm sure), I desperately wanted my children to embrace the Savior I love. My highest aspiration was for Katherine and Courtney to become Christians—but that was something I couldn't make happen. Only God can do that. So I had no place to go but to God with this heartfelt desire for my girls.

Each morning when I woke up, I knew I would be asking God during my prayer time to touch my girls' hearts and open them to Jesus. I also knew that God's Word says, "If I regard iniquity in my heart, the Lord will not hear" (Psalm 66:18). I didn't want my sin and shortcomings to keep God from hearing my request for my daughters. No sin was worth its momentary pleasure when laid beside the eternal salvation of my children. I wanted something far greater than the brief pleasure that comes with speaking my mind, giving in to anger, and a multitude of other sins that might feel good for the moment. I wanted two souls for God!

Such is the mind-set of the godly mother of Proverbs 31:2 when she speaks of her child as "the son of her vows." And such is the mind-set you and I need to have regarding our own children.

We must be committed to nurturing and maintaining a godly life because a soul—the soul of each child—is involved. We gladly strive for a righteous walk—a righteous life—*so that* we can pray more effectively for our children!

Another thing I wanted for each of my daughters was a Christian husband, if they married. Again, because I couldn't choose for them, I once more turned to God with my fervent request. And rightly so. After all, my role was to be a mother who endeavored to walk with God, a mother who prayed fervently for her daughters to know God, to follow Him, and to be blessed with Christian husbands.

I'm sure these next statements are obvious, but I'll say them anyway. First, I did not pray for Katherine and Courtney every day—but my deep desire for their spiritual development was there every day (and still is). I carried my daughters with me in my heart every minute of every day, and I still do—along with their husbands and children.

Second, I have never walked through a day without sinning in some way. But because of my daughters and my desires for their walk with God (and my own walk with God, or course), I made the effort (and still do). I fought the battle against sin (and still do). I tried (and still try) to walk in a righteous way, according to God's standard and not the world's or my own. I took seriously (and still do) God's commands to put away sinful behaviors and to put on those that please Him and reflect Christ. All of these endeavors helped prepare me to pray on my children's behalf. And, besides training our children in God's Word and His ways (we'll get to that next), praying is all you and I can do!

Yes, But How?

How does a woman after God's heart foster a love for and a

commitment to praying for her children? How can you and I move toward fulfilling God's assignment to pray for our sons and daughters, grandsons and granddaughters?

Learn from godly and praying mothers and grandmothers—Real life examples will encourage you and model for you the role of prayers.

- Soon after his conversion, Billy Graham's mother set aside a period every day to pray solely for Billy and the calling she believed was his. She continued those prayers, never missing a day, for seven years until Billy was well on his way as a preacher and evangelist. His mother then based her prayers on 2 Timothy 2:15, asking that what he preached would meet with God's approval.[4]

- Leroy Eims of The Navigators' staff had a godly friend whose mother has prayed one hour each day for him since he was born.

- Jeanne Hendricks, wife of Dallas Theological Seminary professor Howard Hendricks, spent a season in intense prayer for one of her children. During his late adolescence, her son went through what Jeanne called a "blackout" period. He was unenthusiastic, moody, and depressed, communicating only with single-syllable responses. "This was one of the most traumatic times of my life," Jeanne admits. "He was so far from the Lord and from us. I felt like the devil himself was out to get my child. I prayed as I never had before."[5] I was present at a women's retreat where Mrs. Hendricks shared that during the half year when this situation continued, she covenanted with God to give up her noon meal. As she fasted each day, she prayed for her son for one hour until God broke through to him.

- Dr. and Mrs. James Dobson fast and pray for their children one day a week.

- Harry Ironside, former pastor of Moody Memorial Church in Chicago, had a mother who "never ceased to pray for his salvation. Throughout his life Harry would recall the substance of her pleas to God for him: 'Father, save my boy early. Keep him from ever desiring anything else than to live for Thee....O Father, make him willing to be kicked and cuffed, to suffer shame or anything else for Jesus' sake.'"[6]

Which model will you start following this week?

Ask God for His insights for your children—As you read about the remarkable mothers in the Bible and all their children accomplished for God, you can catch a glimpse of how God might work through your children. One of God's chosen mothers was Hannah, whose son, Samuel, began ministering for the Lord at a young age and later led God's people as prophet and priest (1 Samuel 3:1). The lovely and humble Elizabeth (Luke 1:60) helped nurture in her young son a love for God, and later his ministry as John the Baptist stirred people's passions when he preached and prepared the way of the Lord Jesus (Luke 3:4). And we never fail to be moved by Mary, the young woman who found favor with God (Luke 1:30) and was blessed among women (verse 28) to teach, train, and love her child, God's Son, our Lord Jesus Christ!

A Passion for Godly Training

As important as it is to *pray* for our children—for salvation and for Christian mates—we must not stop with prayer. We must also model a life dedicated to the Lord and train our children to follow His ways. Many times a woman starts off well—she gets married, wants a baby, prays for a baby, has a baby, and goes through a ceremony at church where she dedicates the baby to God. But then something happens—the baby becomes a reason for missing church.

Nancy, a young mother in my church, called me with a typical dilemma. It seemed that every time she put her baby into the church nursery he caught a cold. She knew the baby needed to be at church, she needed to be at church, and the family needed to be worshiping together, so she wondered what she could do. As we talked, she came up with a solution. She would take her baby into the church service and sit in the back row. If (or when!) the baby got fussy, Nancy would move out to the foyer where she could hear the message over an intercom system. If the baby still didn't calm down, she would walk around the church patio with her baby in the stroller. Nancy was so relieved that the entire family could go to church together again.

Another mom, married to one of our pastors, has sat in the foyer of her church through the baby and toddler stages of their three children. Each one of them

> *Our decision to take our children to church communicates to them—from birth on—the importance of worship and fellowship.*

has spent countless hours of pleasure at church crawling and climbing up and down the stairs leading to the church offices while Heidi listened to the sermons over the intercom. Those children have never known what it's like to *not* be at church on Sunday mornings.

Now this is not a lecture on rules about going to church, but I will say that attending worship faithfully instills an important habit in our children's lives and something into their hearts that nothing else can give them. Our decision to take our children to church communicates to them—from birth on—the importance of worship and fellowship in a corporate body (Hebrews 10:25). And this decision reaps untold dividends. For starters, your children will never know an option for Sunday.

Another reason to get your little (and big) ones to church is Sunday school. The teachers not only faithfully teach God's truth, but they also support at church what you are doing and teaching your children at home. These classes echo and therefore strengthen your messages about values, conduct, character, friendships, goals, and salvation through Christ—messages relevant to the important decisions children make as they grow up. Finally, whether you dedicated your children to God in your heart and prayers or in an official church ceremony, Sunday school is a practical way for you to live out that commitment.

Talk about church with eager anticipation all week long.

But getting there isn't easy. Believe me, I know! However, in most families the wife and mother (that's you and me!) is the key to getting the family to church on Sunday mornings. And what can you and I do to get our family off to church with more pleasure and less hassle? First of all, talk about church with eager anticipation all week long. Let your children see you looking forward to going to church. Also, begin preparations for Sunday on Saturday. Lay out the special church clothes for the next morning. Be sure baths are taken and hair is washed the night before and start preparing Sunday breakfast and lunch. One more thing—an early Saturday bedtime makes Sunday morning go more smoothly.

Another way we train our children in God's ways is to take

them—whatever their ages—to church for *maximum,* not just minimal, exposure to His people and their activities. Attend both church and church classes—and don't miss night church, if your church has an evening service. On Wednesday nights (or some other weeknight), many churches usually have something for children, youth groups for the junior high and high school students, and perhaps even activities for all ages. Getting your children involved is vital to training them up to know and serve God.

Granted, each opportunity in itself may not seem to offer much, but added up over a lifetime this frequent and regular exposure to God's Word and His people makes a powerful statement about our priorities and whom we serve. Getting our children to church for more than just the courtesy worship service visit (although even that can be a major accomplishment) is an essential part of training them in godliness.

When our two girls were growing up, we constantly reminded them that their priorities were family first, church second, and school third. Whenever there was a school event we told them, "That sounds like fun and maybe you can go, but if a special opportunity comes up for our family, or if a church activity conflicts with that school event, we're going to do that instead." Of course we attended a ton of school activities. And, of course, we encouraged our girls to bring their school friends to church activities. But Jim and I tried to apply "good, better, best" to our family activities, putting family first by taking them to church.

And of course getting them there meant driving! What mother isn't constantly driving her child to school, T-ball, basketball, football, soccer, swimming, ballet, gymnastics, shopping outings, and friends' homes (to name just some of the popular destinations)? We did most of the above, plus I added to all that activity by taking the girls to church too, to their youth group activities, and the homes of other church families—and it was wild…and wonderful!

On many Friday nights Jim and I would drop the girls off at the skating rink or bowling alley for an evening of activity with their church group and go to bed with the alarm clock set for midnight to wake us up in time to pick them up. Or, when the youth group had an all-night event at the church, we set the alarm for 6:30 (on a Saturday morning!) so we could pick them up at 7:00 when they were finished. These were definite sacrifices. And yes, it certainly would have been easier on us for the girls to stay home. But for us the end results (wholesome activities, safety, fun, exposure to God's Word, getting to know godly youth leaders and dedicated Christian kids, hearing the gospel, and getting to know Christ) far outweighed the inconveniences.

Heart Response

You and I will never know on this side of heaven all that our prayers accomplish on behalf of our children. Truly, the effectual, fervent prayer of a righteous mother avails much with God (James 5:16)! It is God's job to work in our children's hearts, but it is our job to make God's standards the standards of our own hearts and then to walk by those standards. Can you think of any area of your life that does not measure up to God's criteria? Where you are failing to follow Him? Once again, that's what this book is all about—becoming a woman after God's own heart. I hope and pray—for myself as well as for you—that we come to treasure God's Word, His wisdom, and His ways so that we can go boldly before His throne for our children's good (Hebrews 4:16)!

Also, the Bible tells us to examine ourselves. You and I need to do that often to, first, live a life that pleases God and, second, fuel our passion for godly training. God's kind of training takes time and dedication, and sometimes the passion needed for the long haul wanes. Ask your own heart, Am I committed to getting my children to church so they can be exposed to truth, no matter what it costs me? And am I committed to getting them there for maximum exposure to God, His truth, and His people—regardless of the personal sacrifice involved? Can you look ahead and envision the impact your faithful and regular decisions to train your children in godliness will have on them? It's never too late to shore up any weak areas in your heart or in your parenting. It all starts with you—and your heart after God! But thankfully it doesn't stop there. God is your willing and able partner as you raise your children to know Him and love Him and serve Him.

11

A Heart Overflowing with Motherly Affection

Part 1

Admonish the young women...
to love their children.

TITUS 2:4

As soon as I read God's instructions for Christian mothering, which we've been looking at, I began trying to follow them in our home. Chaos slowly became order, disobedience was being replaced by obedience, and structure began to emerge as we worked on keeping a daily schedule. But instead of feeling maternal, I felt like a drill sergeant, enforcer, and police officer all rolled into one. *Is this what a godly mother is?* I wondered. I knew in my heart that something was missing.

How I thank God that He showed me what that something was as I continued reading my Bible, eagerly searching for more verses on mothering. I found God's answer in Titus 2:4. There I read that mothers are "to love their children." On the surface, this statement may not seem revolutionary, but when I (once again) borrowed my husband's books and dug into these four words, I found relief and freedom. I discovered that mothers are to be affectionate. They are to treat their children lovingly. In short, they are to be children-lovers.[1]

One more bit of information helped transform me from drill sergeant to a mother whose heart was overflowing with motherly affection. As we learned earlier when we discussed loving our husbands, the Greek language has several words for *love*. *Agapeo* is the kind of love God has for us as His children. He loves us in spite of our sin; He loves us unconditionally; and He loves us regardless and no matter what. And certainly we mothers are to extend this kind of godly love to our children.

> I began to treasure Katherine and Courtney. They became people I wanted to be with, people I had fun with and played with, people whom God wanted to be my highest human priority after Jim.

But *phileo* is the word God chose to convey mother-love here in Titus 2:4. *Phileo* love is affectionate love, a love that cherishes its object. It is friendship love, a love that enjoys children, a love that *likes* them! God calls parents to build the family on a foundation of biblical teaching, instruction, and discipline. The home gains a heart, however, when parents not only *love* their children but *like* them as well.

Our home certainly changed when I discovered God's call to enjoy my children. Oh, the praying and the training continued, but I let the party begin. God worked in my heart and changed me as I sought to follow His Word. I noticed that as I poured my life into the training and discipline and instruction God commanded, I began to treasure Katherine and Courtney. I saw my children as more than my duty. They became people I wanted to be with, people I had fun with and played with, people whom God wanted to be my highest human priority after Jim. Let me share some ideas for putting this kind of love into practice, the ten marks of motherly affection I strove to show for my two children…and now my seven grandchildren.

1. A Heart That Prays

The greatest gift of love you and I can give our children is to pray for them. For decades, I've believed the message of this anonymous poem I received as a new Christian:

> Some have had kings in their lineage,
> Some to whom honor was paid.
> Not blest of my ancestors—but,
> I have a mother who prays.
>
> I have a mother who prays for me
> And pleads with the Lord every day for me.
> Oh what a difference it makes for me—
> I have a mother who prays.
>
> Some have worldly success
> And trust in riches they've made—
> This is my surest asset,
> I have a mother who prays.
>
> My mother's prayers cannot save me,
> Only mine can avail;
> But mother introduced me to Someone—
> Someone who never could fail.

> Oh yes…I have a mother who prays for me
> And pleads with the Lord every day for me.
> O what a difference it makes for me—
> I have a mother who prays.
>
> —AUTHOR UNKNOWN

Beginning each day by praying for your children benefits them in countless ways even as it draws them deeper into your heart.

2. A Heart That Provides

A heart overflowing with motherly affection lovingly and graciously provides the necessities of life for her precious family— nourishing food, clean clothing, and a safe home. Although we may not get too excited about running our homes on a schedule or cooking another meal or doing another load of laundry, a heart filled with motherly affection does just that. It puts self aside and loves the people in her home by caring for their physical needs. To fail to do so on a regular basis is neglect. (Neglect is defined by the U.S. Court system as *the deliberate failure to meet the physical…needs of a child*.)[2]

Many mothers wonder why their children act up, talk back, are grumpy, and require so much discipline. Maybe it's because Mom isn't providing the basics of nutritious, scheduled meals, clean bodies, clean clothes, and adequate sleep and rest.

3. A Heart That Is Happy

When our children (and our husbands!) can count on us to be happy, home life and family relationships take a leap toward heaven. Whether the alarm has just gone off in the morning, or you're picking the children up from school, or they're walking in the door after their own activities, they need to know that you will be happy. I decided to work on the habit of happiness when I read Psalm 113:9 (another verse I marked in pink): "He [makes] the barren woman to keep house, and to be a *joyful* mother of children."[3]

So I began to pray—a lot! I would pray when I heard my girls' first little waking up sounds and walked toward their rooms. In later years I prayed as I went to pick them up from school. I wanted them to see that I was excited about being with them after they had been gone all day at school. (As Elisabeth Elliot

> As mothers, we are the Number One influence in our children's lives.

said at a seminar I attended, "You create the atmosphere of the home with your attitudes." I kept that in mind!)

I also learned to "light up" after reading this personal account written by a son about his father.

Something about my father attracted me like a magnet. When school was out, many times I would rush to his hardware store instead of going out with my friends. What drew me to my father? Why did I prefer a visit with him over some of my favorite activities? As soon as I set foot in his store, it seemed as if his whole personality lit up. His eyes sparkled, his smile gleamed, and his facial expressions immediately conveyed how glad he was to see me. I almost expected him to announce, "Look, everybody, my son is here." I loved it. Although I didn't realize it at the time, those tremendously powerful nonverbal expressions were the magnets that drew me to him. Ninety-three percent of our communication is nonverbal....Whenever you see [your child],

"light up" with enthusiasm, especially in your facial
expressions and tone of voice. That light comes from
the inner knowledge that he's valuable.[4]

As mothers, you and I are the Number One influence in our
children's lives. We have the privilege of "lighting up" when we see
them and sharing with them the happiness that is in our hearts.
And that happiness is wonderfully contagious.

4. A Heart That Gives

The Bible is full of exhortations for Christians to be about the
business of giving. As we've seen several times already, that's how
our Savior lived. Mark reports, "For even the Son of Man did not
come to be served, but to serve, and to give His life a ransom for
many" (Mark 10:45). Here are a few principles that can help us
be mothers who give, mothers who serve—and who do so with
affection, warmth, and energy.

Give because it is your role—Because of who God is, a woman
after His heart is a woman who gives. As Christians we are to give,
as wives we are to give, as mothers we are to give, as singles we are
to give, as members of a church body we are to give. That's our
role, our assignment from God, as His children. We give the smile,
the cheerful greeting, the hug, the compliment, the encouragement, the praise, the meal, the time, the listening ear, the ride…
and the list goes on and on.

As Edith Schaeffer points out in every chapter of *What Is
a Family?*[5] *someone* has to create family memories and under-
take the wondrous task of having the family become a work of
art. Someone has to be the nest maker and interior decorator.
Someone has to take time to pray and plan surprises. Someone
must see the family as worth fighting for, worth calling a career,
worth the hard work of training a child in godliness, worth the

relentless tasks involved in running a home. On and on Mrs. Schaeffer writes, showing the reader that this "someone" is the wife, the mom, and the homemaker and that, as such, she must embrace a life of being the giver. That's our role as mothers.

Give generously—Take heed of these two sowing and reaping passages from the New Testament (only the pronouns are changed!): "She who sows sparingly will also reap sparingly, and she who sows bountifully will also reap bountifully" (2 Corinthians 9:6) and "Whatever a [mother] sows, that she will also reap" (Galatians 6:7). As I considered the principle of sowing and reaping, I realized that, in a general way, what I put into my children on a daily basis—seeds of patience or impatience, faith in God or lack of faith, kindness or selfishness—would be what I might gain back in years to come.

Give expecting nothing in return—Even as we consider the principle of sowing and reaping, we must remember that mothers are to have no ulterior or selfish motives when it comes to giving. We serve and take care of our children simply because God says to. Just as we do for our husbands, we give to our children expecting nothing in return. We don't give motherly love in order to receive praise, thanks, recognition, or good behavior. (Those things may never come.) No, we give our love in a myriad of practical forms simply because God expects that of mothers. There are no other options, no conditions, no exceptions, and no fine print when it comes to God's clear command that we are to love our children (Titus 2:4).

5. A Heart of Fun

Living in your home should be an absolute ball for every family member. To make that true in my home, I worked on developing and using a sense of humor. I learned to smile and laugh—a lot.

I checked out silly riddle books from the library every week, and my girls and I laughed and rolled on the floor as we read them.

Most of all, I began to freely use the words "I love." I used that phrase to point out the good of every aspect of our lives: "I love Saturdays…the Lord's Day…Wednesday nights at church… having your friends over…our evening dinners together…our family devotions…praying with you…praying for you…going for a walk with you…sitting around and listening to music together. I love everything—and especially I love you!" I still say "I love you" to Katherine and Courtney—now grown and married and moms themselves—(and Jim, too, of course) every time I see them, or tell them goodbye, or talk to them on the phone.

> *Let the meal be a time for physical refreshment and pleasant fellowship.*

Also, to have a happy home, be sure to make mealtime fun. We can learn a lesson from how and when our resurrected Lord spoke to Peter, the disciple who had three times denied knowing Him. Rather than confronting Peter before or during the meal, Jesus *waited until after* the meal. He let the meal be a time for physical refreshment and pleasant fellowship (John 21:15). Are we doing the same in our homes?

Heart Pause

We're halfway through the ten marks of motherly affection. Are you catching a vision for God's plan for your relationships with your children and for how to lavish love on them? As God's mothers, we pray, provide, and play. Pause now and ask God to fill your heart with more love for your children—with love that prays for and takes care of our children, a love that teaches and trains, and a love that laughs and plays.

12

A Heart Overflowing with Motherly Affection

Part 2

Admonish the young women…
to love their children.

TITUS 2:4

God's assignment to mothers can sound overwhelming if we don't remember that through His Word, in His power, and by His grace He fully provides all that we need to do what He commands. What a privilege to care for the children He blesses us with and to raise them for His purposes! Now for a few more marks of motherly affection.

6. A Heart That Celebrates

Another principle I took to heart from God's Word is the "extra mile" principle. Our Lord teaches, "Whoever compels you to go one mile, go with him two" (Matthew 5:41). Let's face it,

145

we *have* to be mothers, and we *have* to do the duties. That's the first mile of our job assignment from God. So...why not go the extra mile and make everything you do special? Why not turn the mundane into a celebration?

Take, for instance, the evening meal. We *have* to have dinner—so why not make it special? Simply light a candle, find a flower or some interesting greenery in the yard, use seasonal decorations, change tablecloths and placemats, or use special dishes. My daughters loved the few odds and ends of a stoneware pattern with rose clusters and gold edges that I picked up at a garage sale. My friend Judy purchased a red plate with gold lettering around the edge reading, "You are special today." Whenever she senses that someone in her family is down or going through tough times, she prepares her "Red Plate Special," setting the hurting member's place at the table with that bright plate.

Or you can eat in special places—and I don't mean a restaurant! Use your patio. Pack a picnic. Eat cross-legged on the floor in a different room. Be creative not only about where you eat but also about what you eat when. Serve a "backwards dinner" and start with dessert. Or number the different parts of the meal, have each person draw a number, and then serve dinner in the order the numbers were drawn! Or make dinner a treasure hunt with clues leading to each item on the menu—some hidden inside the house and some outside. You can go the extra mile toward fun and celebration with very little effort.

And why not make your church day the most special day of the week? Ruth Graham "made Sunday the best day of the week. There was always some kind of shared activity or outing in the afternoon and the children were given treats....It was the Lord's day, a day to rejoice and be grateful."[1] Do whatever you need to do to go the extra mile and celebrate being Christians.

Finally, if someone is sick, bring out the "sick tray" and serve meals on it with a flower, a candle, a few stickers, and special dishes. And don't forget to put the "sick bell" by the person's bed. Let your patient ring it anytime for anything! The mundane tasks of daily life—the first mile—are great opportunities for celebrating the extra mile.

7. A Heart That Gives Preferential Treatment

Titus 2:4 teaches us that our husbands and children are to take priority over all other human relationships and responsibilities. That's why I developed this principle to guide the motherly affection of my heart: *Don't give away to others what you have not first given away at home.* And let me tell you how this principle was born.

Late one afternoon I was hurrying my two little girls into the car so we could deliver a meal to "Mrs. X" who had just had a baby. All day long I'd labored on the meal for this woman who needed the help of people in the church, a woman I didn't even know. I had baked a pink, juicy ham, created a pressed Jell-O salad in a pretty mold, steamed brightly colored vegetables, and topped it all off with my most special dessert. As we started out the front door, Katherine and Courtney wanted to know who the food was for. I lowered the beautifully arranged tray to their level and took advantage of this opportunity to teach them about Christian giving. I explained, "Mrs. X has had a baby, and we're taking dinner to her family so she can rest after being in the hospital."

That sounded good until my own children asked, "What are we having for dinner?" When I

> *Is there a difference in the tone of your voice you reserve for your friends and the one you use with your family?*

said that we were having macaroni and cheese with hot dogs (again!), I was sharply convicted of my wrong priorities. I had put someone else, Mrs. X, ahead of my own family. I had gone *many* extra miles to make the meal I was taking to someone I had never met, but I was throwing together something quick and easy for my own husband and children. In short, I was giving something to someone else that I had not first given to the people closest to me!

Since that moment, I have made the same meal for those at home—people light years more precious to me than anyone else ever will be—that I make when I do a good deed. And when I take a dish to a potluck, I make two of them. When I take a dessert for some gathering, I take it with two or three pieces missing—pieces left behind for my VIPs.

This principle—*Don't give away to others what you have not first given away at home*—applies to far more than just food. We talk to people on the phone, for instance, but we don't talk to our own children. We listen to other people, but we don't listen to our children. We spend time with other people, but we don't with our children. We give smiles and joy to others, but don't always share these with our children.

One mother asked, "Have you ever noticed a difference in the tone of voice you reserve for your friends and the one you use with your family? It's so easy to give our best to comparative strangers and toss our families the leftovers." She then went on to report, "One young mother of eight children came into the family room and found all her children bickering. She gently admonished them, 'Children, don't you know the Bible says we should be kind to one another?' Her oldest, who was nine, looked thoughtfully around the room and replied, 'But, Mommy, there's nobody here but the family!'"[2]

8. A Heart That Is Focused

When I read Jesus' words that "no one can serve two masters" (Matthew 6:24), another mothering axiom was born: *Beware of double booking.* By "double booking," I mean trying to focus on our children and other people at the same time. Here's an example of double booking.

Once I was counseling a mother on the phone about the rocky relationship she had with her teenage daughter. We had talked well over 20 minutes when I heard her say, "Oh, hello, honey." When I asked, "Is someone there?" this mother said coolly, "Oh, it's only my daughter." It was 3:30 in the afternoon. This daughter—this *"only my daughter"*—had left in the dark at 7:00 that morning. The mother hadn't seen her daughter for more than eight hours, and all her daughter got was, "Oh, hello, honey"— a clear case of double booking. This mom had clearly double booked by being on the phone with me (this time I was Mrs. X!) when she knew her daughter—the one she was having problems with—was about to come home. She sent a message to both of us that, at that moment, I was more important than her God-given daughter.

Now let me tell you about another mother whom my friend

> *She was not about to lose one second of her precious time with her daughter by having us there.*

Beverly and I both admired as a Christian, a wife, and a mother. When we called to schedule a get-together, she invited us to a lovely lunch that we enjoyed in her breakfast room. From our table inside, however, we could see another table outside on her patio—a table set with linen placemats, starched linen napkins, freshly cut flowers in a vase, two sterling silver spoons, two crystal plates, and two crystal goblets for ice water. That lovely table had been set in honor of *her* teenage daughter's much-anticipated arrival home from school. This thoughtful, loving mom had two more desserts in long-stemmed crystal glasses waiting in the refrigerator—and she did something like this *every* day! (On those days when she had to be gone when her daughter came home, she left a love note on a set table and a special treat in the refrigerator.)

At 2:30, this wise mother—a mother who understood her priorities and watched the time—began to shoo the two of us out the door because someone more special was coming! She graciously said, "Well, I'm sorry we have to end this, but I'm expecting my daughter home in 15 minutes, and that's our special time." She was not about to lose one second of her precious time with her daughter by double booking and having us there. She had given us the gift of time—rich, life-changing time for Beverly and me—but our hostess truly lived out her priorities. She knew where to focus her efforts. (When we left, I barely had time to rush home and throw some placemats and granola bars on the table before Katherine and Courtney came home in the car pool. But I also knew all future welcome home snack times would be a *little* more special.)

9. A Heart That Is Present

Our presence in the home is important. No dollar amount can ever be put on the value of our presence at home after school, in the evening, at night, and on weekends and holidays. No Tupperware party, crystal party, or plant party with the girlfriends can compare to sharing dinner with your family, helping your kids get ready for bed, tucking them in, reading to them, praying with them, and kissing them good night. *Nothing* can compare!

When I was invited to participate in a certain ministry opportunity, I asked my daughters their thoughts on my involvement. I wanted them to *know* they held the premiere place in my heart and were more important to me than other people or activities. Then, having received my husband's okay and my children's blessing, I accepted the ministry opportunity, knowing all was well at home. I had my family's full support. They wanted me to minister and were at home praying for me. Only once in 25 years of mothering did one daughter (a sixth grader at the time) say, "I wish you didn't have to go." We had just arrived back from the mission field, were settling back into a school routine, and I had thrown myself back into church activities. Well, that's all she had to say to let me know I was needed at home. I had overestimated her stability and underestimated the time it would take to adjust our way back into our culture.

10. A Heart That Is Quiet

Remember how we learned not to talk about our husbands? That same principle applies to the children too. The Proverbs 31 mother offers us a lesson about quietness. We learn that "she opens her mouth with wisdom, and on her tongue is the law of kindness" (verse 26). Words from this lovely mother's lips are marked by wisdom and kindness, and neither of these qualities promote talking about her children in a negative way. After all, "love covers all sins" (Proverbs 10:12). A loving mother whose heart is quiet never broadcasts any harmful or critical information, not anything general and nothing specific, about her children. A friend of mine communicated volumes about her home life (and her heart) every time she warned younger moms in quite general terms, "Just you wait. Having teenagers is awful!"

How I thank God for Betty, a sharp contrast to my friend. Betty never failed to speak positively and enthusiastically about her child-raising years. She would ask me, "How old are the girls now?" When I answered, "Nine and ten," she exclaimed, "Oh, I remember when my boys were nine and ten. Those are wonderful years!" Years later when my answer to her same question was "thirteen and fourteen," Betty again cried out, "Oh, I remember when my boys were thirteen and fourteen. Those were wonderful years!" No matter what age Katherine and Courtney were, Betty saw them as wonderful years. Oh, I'm sure she encountered the usual challenges, but Betty was a mother whose heart was filled with motherly affection for her boys, whose home was filled with fun, whose heart was positive about God's job assignment for her—and whose lips were respectfully quiet about any difficulties.

God's solution for the challenges we face raising children (the children He gave us and the challenges He knows we face as we train them up) is the "older women" of Titus 2:3. So I encourage you to develop a relationship with an "older woman" like Betty who can help and encourage you. Talk to her—and to God— about mothering. Ask her and the Lord your questions about how to fulfill that awesome responsibility and blessed privilege with a heart of affection for her children.

Heart Response

We've come on quite a journey through Scripture as we've learned about being God's kind of mom. How blessed we are to pray for our dear children. What a challenge to train them in God's ways. And what a delight to set the tone in the home—a tone of love and laughter and fun. Is yours a heart filled with motherly affection? Do you cherish your children—and do they know you do? Do you enjoy your family and look forward to spending time with them? Being the kind of mother who pleases God calls for prayer. After all, He is the one who makes our hearts joyful, generous, giving, happy, and quiet. He enables us to focus on and live out our priorities. And He provides what we need to go the extra mile and mother our children the way He wants us to. The job assignment isn't easy, but we can do all these things through Christ who strengthens us (Philippians 4:13)!

13

A Heart That Makes a House a Home

The wise woman builds her house.
PROVERBS 14:1

One evening at bedtime, right before I turned off my light, I read this lovely description of a home written by Peter Marshall, former chaplain of the United States Senate. Maybe it will open your eyes and touch your heart as it did mine.

> I was privileged, in the spring, to visit in a home that was to me—and I am sure to the occupants—a little bit of Heaven. There was beauty there. There was a keen appreciation of the finer things of life, and an atmosphere in which it was impossible to keep from thinking of God.
>
> The room was bright and white and clean, as well as cozy. There were many windows. Flowers were blooming in pots and vases, adding their

fragrance and beauty. Books lined one wall—good
books—inspiring and instructive—good books—
good friends. Three bird cages hung in the bright-
ness and color of this beautiful sanctuary, and the
songsters voiced their appreciation by singing as if
their little throats would burst.

Nature's music, nature's beauty—nature's peace....
It seemed to me a kind of Paradise that had wandered
down, an enchanted oasis—home.[1]

What hit me—aside from the beauty of this image—was the
realization that my home (and yours) can be a little bit of heaven,
a kind of paradise, to my dear family and to all who enter its
sanctuary. As I fell asleep that night, I dreamed about making
my house a home in which it was impossible to keep from thinking of God.

But when reality set in the next morning with the squawk of
my alarm clock, I knew dream time was over. It was time to go to
work if I was going to make my dream come true. *But how?* was
the urgent question on my mind. And once again God's perfect
Word came to my rescue with His answers.

The Business of Building

Proverbs 14:1 reads, "The wise woman builds her house."
Needing building instructions for making my house a home, I
took this verse apart, starting with the positive aspect of building. "To build" means, literally, to make and to set up a house[2]—
and this verse refers not only to the structure and upkeep of the
home, but also to the family itself. You see, a home is not only a
place—it's also people! One insightful scholar explains the verse
this way:

Although the Hebrew word for "house" and "home" is the same, "home" is the preferred word here. A house is not always a home and this verse does not speak of house construction, masonry, or carpentry but of home building; the knitting together of family and the day-by-day routine of creating a happy and comfortable place for a family to live.[3]

And who is responsible for the quality of life in that place where the family lives? The woman! She sets the mood and maintains the atmosphere inside the home. In fact, this proverb teaches that if the woman is wise, she diligently and purposefully creates that atmosphere. She doesn't just hope it will happen.

Creating the atmosphere—Creating the atmosphere of a home is very much like using your thermostat to regulate the temperature inside your house. You decide on an ideal temperature for your family and set the dial to a comfortable level. Then the thermostat takes over and goes to work maintaining the desired temperature. If the house starts to get hot, the thermostat automatically turns on cold air to cool it off. If cold air moves in, the thermostat receives the signal and gets busy warming up the house.

> *God gives us the heart, the wisdom, and the words to create a healthy atmosphere.*

Well, I've discovered that in my home *I* am the thermostat. I want the atmosphere inside our house to be warm, cheerful, loving, positive, and constructive. So I try to go to God's Word each morning and pray, giving Him the opportunity to set the temperature of my heart to match His. Then I go to work to maintain the comfort in my home. If things start to get hot (hot words, hot tempers, hot emotions), I set about to bring in cooling, soothing words ("a soft answer turns away wrath"—Proverbs 15:1) and words of peace ("the fruit of righteousness is sown in peace by those who make peace"—James 3:18).

Likewise, if things start to cool off (cold hearts, cold feet, cold shoulders), I go to work giving a good word that makes hearts glad (Proverbs 12:25), remembering that "a merry heart makes a cheerful countenance" (Proverbs 15:13) and that "he who is of a merry heart has a continual feast" (Proverbs 15:15). Such times are a challenge, but as I seek to live God's way and look to Him for the grace to do so, He gives me the heart, the wisdom, and the words to create a healthy atmosphere. He will do the same for you as you build the atmosphere of your home.

Building a refuge—As the center of family life, the home ministers to our family far more than we might imagine. I remember a time my husband made this fact very clear. He'd had "one of those days" that had stretched him to his absolute limit. A seminary student at the time, Jim had left the church parking lot at 5:00 in the morning to attend classes and deliver his senior sermon. After his commute back to the church through downtown Los Angeles traffic, he had officiated at a funeral and graveside service for a woman who, having no one to help bury her husband, had called the church the day Jim was "pastor of the day." All of this was topped off with a late meeting at church.

What a blessing if every member of your family and mine knows home is the one place on earth where everything will be all right.

I had the porch light on and was watching out the kitchen window as I waited—and waited up—for Jim. When he finally got to the front door, he didn't walk in—he sort of slumped in.

On the way in, my exhausted husband sighed, "Oh, Liz, all day long I kept telling myself, 'If I can just get home, everything will be all right.'"

"If I can just get home, everything will be all right." What a blessing it would be if every member of your family and mine knew that there is one place on earth where everything will be all right! Home would truly be a wonderful haven and refuge for them, a "hospital," as Edith Schaeffer says.[4] And what a worthwhile goal for us—to build the kind of home which strengthens and renews each family member. Mrs. Dwight Eisenhower had that goal for her famous husband and president of the United States. She wanted to build a "home [where] he belonged to her world, a world of lighthearted family life where there were no pressures."[5] Imagine such a refuge!

Our children as well as our husbands benefit from our building efforts. One counselor reported that "a secure home life tends to reduce frustration and uneasiness in a child's life, and it gives them the ability to cope with pressures more effectively."[6] And that's only one advantage that we give our children when we go about the business of building a home.

What is true about the importance of a home in life is also true as the end of life nears. When terminal cancer forced Bible scholar and author Dr. Francis Schaeffer to leave his beloved L'Abri in Switzerland and live in America where he could receive the best treatment, his wife's first concern was to establish a home. When she was asked, "Why a 'home'?" Edith said she would answer that "home is important to a person to help him or her get well, as well as being important for family times together if someone is dying. In either case, beauty and familiar surroundings have an effect on the physical, psychological, and even spiritual state."[7] What a worthwhile building project—making our home a refuge for our family. Even the word "refuge" brings a calmness to heart and soul.

Avoiding the negatives—"Every wise woman builds her house," Proverbs 14:1 begins, but the second half is just as important— "the foolish [woman] pulls it down with [her] hands." To pull down a home means to break or destroy it, to beat or break it down—to ruin it.[8] How can a woman pull down her own home? How can she be a one-woman demolition machine? My own experience offers two answers to that question.

First, a woman can cause great damage actively—by working destruction. What, for instance, does anger out of control do? It throws, it slams, it tears, and it rips. It also breaks things as well as rules. As if *doing* these destructive deeds weren't bad enough, anger out of control also *speaks words* that break, destroy, ruin, and kill.

Molly Wesley, the wife of Methodism's founder John Wesley, must have been a woman who pulled down her home. Her husband wrote her a letter listing ten major complaints including "stealing from his bureau, his inability to invite friends in for tea, her making him feel like a prisoner in his own house, his having to give an account to [her] of everywhere he went, showing his private papers and letters without his permission, her use of fishwife's language against the servants, and her malicious slander."[9] These are sure ways to pull down a home!

The second way to ruin a home is passive—by simply failing to work. We can slowly erode the foundation of our home by our laziness, by simply "never getting around to it" (whatever "it" may be), by neglect, by forgetting to pay a bill…or two, by successfully putting things off, by not spending enough time at home. Then there's the problem of too much—too much TV, too much reading, too much shopping, too much time with friends, too much time spent on the phone or internet.

I know that your heart is intent on following after God's heart and His ways. That's why you're reading this book. So I am certain you want to make your house into a home. Having that heart desire is an important step. Making a house a home is indeed a matter of the heart.

Yes, But How?

How does a woman who desires in her heart to make a house a home carry out the building process? What can we do to be used by God to create the kind of place He has in mind for our families?

Understand that wisdom builds—The wise woman is aware that she's on assignment from God and knows that building a home is a lifelong endeavor. The teaching of the Bible is clear, and so is the sharp contrast between the wise woman and the foolish woman. Wisdom builds—and builds and builds—avoiding any attitude or act that doesn't build. And this kind of building effort is wise whether you're building a home for yourself or for a husband and children. Let me explain.

When my two daughters were growing up—when they were preschoolers and when they were career women living at home and every step in between—they were building their own room, which was their "little house." I used a 3" x 5" card system for work chores, with a set for me and a set for each of them. When I cleaned the house, Katherine and Courtney each cleaned their room. While I dusted, they dusted—and on and on their cards went, matching mine task for task. They each had their own dirty clothes basket and, from the time they could climb up on their

Tommie Tippie, dump in soap, and turn the dials on the washing machine (all of which kids love to do!), they have washed their own clothes, folded them, and put them in their drawers.

(A brief postscript—and praise. Today housework is no problem for either of my daughters. They've done it for years. They've developed the necessary skills. In fact, at one time the newlywed Courtney even earned extra money as her Proverbs 31 contribution to the income by cleaning the homes of others.)

Even if you share a room or an apartment, you still have your "house," your part of the place, to build. I talked with one ingenious mother of four little girls who share one bedroom. Each girl had her own bunk, shelves, and drawers to take care of. LaTonya also used masking tape to divide the floor space into four squares, making each daughter responsible for one square of the play area.

As I regularly reminded my daughters—and myself—"What you are at home is what you are!" We are either about the business of building the home, its atmosphere and its order, or we are pulling it down through destructive attitudes and neglect. How we take care of the place, the people, the checkbook(!), the clothes, etc., is very telling. Wisdom builds. Are we building?

Decide to begin building—It's never too late to begin—or begin again—to build your house, to create an enchanted oasis called "home." Only our enemy Satan would want us to think otherwise. We can begin at any time—even today.

> *Make a positive decision to do your work in the home willingly.*

A student in my "Woman After God's Own Heart" class wrote on her homework paper, "As I heard God's Word—and read it for myself in my Bible—I was so convicted I wanted to start right away to build my home. Putting God's principles to work in my home made an instant difference, so much so that my husband said last night, 'Gee, Kate, I'm glad you went to hear Elizabeth George!' " (I could only grin and give praise to God for what I had learned!)

Begin by making a positive decision (or by recommitting yourself) to do your work in the home "willingly" (Proverbs 31:13) and "heartily" (Colossians 3:23). The attitude of your heart is key. And don't forget to make another decision. Decide to immediately stop any destructive habits that are pulling down and destroying the little bit of heaven you are trying to build for others...and to the glory of God.

Each day, do one thing to build your home—I began to "each day do one thing to build my home" after reading an article I clipped out of the *Los Angeles Times* entitled "10 Good Reasons to Make the Bed." I confess I was a remedial case, and—you guessed it—I started making the bed each day because Reason #1 said, "Since the bed is the biggest item in the room, making the bed renders the whole room 80% better."[10]

Look around your home (or apartment or room or half a room), inside and out. Make a list of the things that need to be added, repaired, set up, etc., so that your area is more of a refuge. Then do just one item on your list each day—or even one each week.

You may also want to deal with one attitude that—if improved, if transformed by God—would enhance the atmosphere of the home. I used my own prayer notebook, for instance, to go to work on my nagging. After reading that it takes 21 days to eliminate a bad habit and form a new one, I thought, "Hey, I could do that with nagging!" Well, let me quickly tell you that it has taken much longer (decades longer!) than three weeks to lick this major problem area. But let me also tell you that every day and every effort does make a positive difference in my home, my family's heaven on earth.

Heart Response

In this single verse God gives us wisdom for a lifetime—"The wise woman builds her house, but the foolish pulls it down with her hands" (Proverbs 14:1). Search your heart and your home. As you consider these two women, which one is most like you? Where are you placing your focus and investing your energy? Look beneath the cleaning and cooking…to your heart.

Again, this book is all about taking God's wisdom and ways to heart, and I know you want what He wants. Respond to Him now by affirming that "the word of the LORD is right…the counsel of the LORD stands forever, the plans of His heart to all generations" (Psalm 33:4,11). God—who made us and knows us best—wants us to make a house a home, and He will help us do that.

14

A Heart That Watches Over the Home

She watches over the ways of her household.
PROVERBS 31:27

One of my most appalling memories from the days before I became a Christian is neglecting my household as, hour after hour, I sat curled up on our couch reading—and reading—and reading—anything and everything. Reading was a passion for me, something of far greater importance to me than a mere hobby or interest. And as I read, little Katherine and Courtney—wearing only diapers—roamed around the house unsupervised and untrained.

But thankfully, the minute Christ came into our home, He began to do His transforming work! I started attending a Bible study for young married women at my church on Wednesday nights. There, the powerful truth of God's Word turned my marriage upside down. (I should say right side up!). And there I studied *The Happy Home Handbook*,[1] which would turn my heart and home around.

Once I was in the Bible study, I used the corner of my couch for doing my weekly lesson (instead of reading for hours on end). One lesson had the (at least for me) utterly strange title "Why Work?" There I sat—my house ignored, my husband and children neglected—sifting through my new Bible to look up the Scripture references about work and why God thought work was so important. Soon I grabbed my pink marker to highlight another guideline God has given me as one of His homemakers.

Watching and Working

That guideline was tucked into that eye-opening description of the Proverbs 31 woman. The verse simply said, "She watches over the ways of her household, and does not eat the bread of idleness" (verse 27). Reading these 16 words, I suddenly knew that my couch days were over, but I performed one last act there. I reached for several of Jim's Bible reference books to find out what this "watching" meant.

I learned that as it is used here, "to watch" means "to hedge about" as with thorns, much like a mother bird or animal might do to protect her young. The verb expresses the active guarding, protecting, saving, and attending to something precious. This kind of watching involves observation and preservation. A woman who watches over the ways of her household is a woman who watches over her precious home.[2] Here was another aspect of my God-given goal, and I realized *I am on assignment from God to watch over my home and the people in it.*

To better understand the significance of the word *watch,* consider its use in Psalm 5:3—"My voice You shall hear in the morning, O Lord; in the morning I will direct it to You, and I will look up." "To look up" is the same Hebrew word as *watch.* The psalmist carefully prays to God in the morning and then becomes a lookout, keeping watch, being on the lookout, expecting his prayer to be answered.[3]

And there's more! *Watch* is used throughout the Bible to describe people who were posted to report the first sign of God's answers to prayer.[4] At the top of Mount Carmel, for instance, the prophet Elijah threw himself on the ground and began to pray. No rain had fallen for three-and-a-half years, and he began to beseech God for rain. As Elijah prayed, he had his servant run and look at the horizon for rain clouds, a sign that God was answering his prayer. Elijah prayed for rain seven times, and the servant looked out for the rain seven times—until there was an answer from God (1 Kings 18:41-44).

When you and I pray and as we watch over our homes, we must do so with the fervency and earnestness of an Elijah. This prophet and others like him spent their lives waiting, watching for God to fulfill the promises they'd spoken on His behalf. We are to be just as fervent as we make our houses homes and care for the people in them. Then we will be able to see and celebrate when God does His part—the answering, the blessing, the changing!

Looking Over the Functions of the Home

So what are some of the specific things you and I are to watch over in our homes? Maybe your list is like mine. In my home, I am the one who watches over safety, health, cleanliness, and security. (Whenever I'm gone, I leave instructions on the refrigerator door reminding Jim—and Katherine and Courtney, too, when they were older and living at home—to lock the doors at night because that's my job when I'm home.) And then there is the money—recording, saving, supervising, giving, spending, and stretching it.

> *What a great way to be a helper for your husband as you antici-pate, perceive, and act on needs in the home. Before your husband even* thinks *of some-thing, you have taken care of it!*

I also take care of clothing needs and maintenance, the appliance warranties and service contracts, and the food planning and preparation. As the one who does the grocery shopping and stocks the pantry and refrigera-tor, I watch over the nutrition, the selection, and the types of foods and beverages available in the house. I also oversee the calendar, keeping an eye open to upcoming events and trying to anticipate future needs. And all the while I intently watch over the attitudes and unexpressed needs of each family member.

Eighteenth-century preacher Jonathan Edwards was blessed to have a wife who watched over his home. He trusted every-thing to Sarah's care with complete confidence, and one partic-ular example shows what a true watcher is. One day Jonathan Edwards looked up from his stacks of books and studies and asked Sarah, "Isn't it about time for the hay to be cut?" Because she was a watcher and a worker, because she stood guard over what was precious, she was able to reply, "It's been in the barn for two weeks."[5]

What a blessing you can be to your family as you watch, as you keep a lookout over the various functions of the home. And what a great way to be a helper for your husband as you antici-pate, perceive, and act on needs in the home. Before your husband even *thinks* of something, you have taken care of it!

Yes, But How?

How can we place ourselves before God so He can grow in us

hearts that effectively watch over our precious homes? Here are some steps you can take as God cultivates such a heart in you.

Step 1: Understand that this role as helper and guard is God's plan for you—As Proverbs 31:10-31 illustrates, a woman after God's own heart—married or not—watches over the ways of her household and refuses to eat the bread of idleness (Proverbs 31:27). When I realized that these instructions were from God—and not from my mother or my husband or the woman teaching my class—I was hit hard by the truth, which is what I needed. And as I thought about all that is involved in first building the home and then watching over a household, I was shocked at the huge responsibility God has given me at home.

Furthermore, God calls me (and you) to be a "virtuous" woman (Proverbs 31:10), adding yet another challenge to our role in the home. The word *virtuous* means moral strength, strength of character. But a second meaning emphasizes physical ability and physical prowess. And Proverbs 31 is all about a virtuous woman in both senses of the word. This portrait reveals her strength of character and moral excellence as well as her strength of body—her industriousness, energy, work, skill, and accomplishments—as she watched over her precious household and refused to eat the bread of idleness.

As I looked at this excellent woman in all her splendor, I realized I had played up the moral aspect of virtue and downplayed the work part. Yet doing the work of watching is part of God's perfect plan for me—and you—as He grows us into women of excellence. Once we understand that, we are pointed in the right direction.

Step 2: Begin watching over your home (versus eating the bread of idleness)—When I learned about "watching," I realized that, at best, I was *glancing* over my house. My efforts were certainly nothing like what God describes in Proverbs 31. So I made some real—and difficult—decisions about watching (the positive) and about not eating the bread of idleness (the negative).

In a moment, I'll share some helpful time-management principles, but now I'll tell you about the *one* that governs all of my waking hours, all of my life—"In all labor there is profit" (Proverbs 14:23). This bit of wisdom has helped me become more of a watcher and less of an idler. Here's how I put it to work.

> God's Word has worked for me, helping me tune my heart to His will and His ways. God is faithful and will do the same for you.

Throughout the day, I tell myself, "Elizabeth, there is profit in all labor. It's great to keep the work in nice, neat piles labeled A-tasks, B-tasks, and C-tasks, but if you just keep moving, it'll all get done." So I keep moving all day long. I have lists and a general schedule (which can even include a break or a nap), but other than my quiet time (remember, our pursuit of God must come first), I'm busy doing something all day long.

Even when Katherine and Courtney were young, I set about to ingrain this principle in them so they wouldn't have the same struggles I had. So, for instance, they didn't watch TV unless they were doing something. That means that if they were watching TV, they were also busy organizing their school notebooks, covering books, cleaning out drawers, baking chocolate chip cookies, painting fingernails. On and on their TV activities went because there is profit in all labor.

While they were doing their busywork in front of the TV, so was I. I would go through my recipes, plan the menus for the upcoming week, read articles and clip coupons out of the newspaper, scan magazine articles, and sometimes paint my fingernails too.

One result of this training in busyness is that, to this day, none of us derives much pleasure from TV. We can all take it or leave it. We're unable to simply plop down and become engrossed in a television program. Put differently, we don't know how to eat the bread of idleness. To us, it tastes bad. And we do know how to get a lot of work done.

As this example shows, God's principles were His solutions to my disorganization and inefficiency in my home. I had to do a complete 180-degree turn. But I'm on the way (and so are my daughters as they watch over their homes and are now training their seven little ones), thanks to the instructions one woman after God's own heart found in the Bible. God's Word has worked for me, helping me tune my heart to His will and His ways. God is faithful and will do the same for you.

Step 3: Eliminate idleness—I'm not sure where Jim picked up the following list of "time robbers," but he passed it on to me, and I want to pass it on to you. Use it first to help you identify time robbers in your daily life and then to help you buy back time for watching and working in your precious home. Here are the major time robbers:

- Procrastination
- Inadequate personal planning and scheduling
- Interruptions by people without appointments (This includes interruptions by way of the telephone. And please note, your children are *not* interruptions—they are your greatest work and the best investment of your time!)

- Failure to delegate
- Poor use of the telephone
- Reading junk mail
- Lack of concern for good time management
- Unclear priorities

Which robber will you corral this week as you become a more alert, better watcher over your home?

Heart Response

Oh, my dear sister and friend, we must pray for eyes to see the vision God has for our precious home and for hearts to understand how important what happens in our home is to Him. May our goal be that our houses be made into homes that show forth God's desires for the beauty and purpose of those structures.

Do you see God's ideal for your home life? Do you see the value of every meal prepared, every rug vacuumed, every piece of furniture dusted, every floor mopped, every load of laundry washed, folded, and ironed? Is it your heart's desire to pay the price of watching and working?

Take inventory of your own heart attitude toward that precious place you call home. Are you praying—and then watching for the glory of God's answers? My friend Ginger recently started praying for her home. Hear what she reports:

Every morning when I have my quiet time I go through the whole house and pray for each room. For the kitchen I pray that everything made there will show my love for my family. (All my recipes have long since been revised so the fruit of the Spirit is added in—a pinch of love, a handful of patience, etc.) I pray that each room will be filled with God's love and protection. This way I have a new outlook on housework. It is no longer work. I am even able to sing while I clean the bathroom!

Ask God to perform open-heart surgery in you. Ask Him to open it up and fill it with His desires for your home and the strength and passion to fulfill those desires.

15

A Heart That Creates Order from Chaos

I will therefore that the younger women...
guide the house.
1 TIMOTHY 5:14 (KJV)

I had heard about time management and organization but never paid much attention. Standing in the supermarket checkout line, I'd invariably see some magazine promising that an article inside would end my time-management problems once and for all. And, as a voracious reader, I spent a lot of time in bookstores, and there I would find whole rows of books on time management and organization. But for a long time I had zero motivation in this area.

Responsibility and Accountability

What finally did motivate me wasn't a magazine article or a book or a teacher or even my husband's pleas. It was God's Word! Continuing to read through my Bible using my pink marker to

175

highlight those verses with special meaning to me as a woman, I found a verse that worked its way into my unorganized heart. There was no way I could miss the word "guide" as I read, "I will therefore that the younger women...guide the house" (1 Timothy 5:14 KJV). Other versions of the Bible read "preside over a home or be mistress of the house."[1] Either way, the message was clear.

Furthermore, the why of this statement was clear. Here's the situation Timothy faced: The young widows of Timothy's church were "idle, wandering about from house to house, and not only idle but also gossips and busybodies, saying things which they ought not" (1 Timothy 5:13). Their loose, undisciplined behavior led those outside the church to think and speak poorly of Christianity (verse 14). Obviously, having a home to manage would contribute positively to these women's lives by, at the very least, eliminating the opportunity for these negative behaviors.

God was speaking to me! I was certainly idle and guilty of a few of the other bad behaviors mentioned in this passage. Clearly I needed to take action and make some changes. But first, to be sure I was headed in the right direction, I wanted to get a handle on the meaning of *guide*.

> *Every day we are called to manage what God has given us, what He has provided through our husbands' efforts and our own.*

To "guide a house" means to be the head of or to rule a family, to guide the home. The one who manages a house is the goodman of the house, the householder.[2]

Yet this management has built-in accountability, describing as it does the work of a steward or a servant. The woman who manages her house is *not* the head of the home (her husband is if she is married, and God is if she is not). Instead, she is the householder, the home manager.

Many of Jesus' parables offer us insight into this kind of management. In these stories that teach a lesson about God's kingdom, Jesus generally describes a landowner who, taking a leave of absence, delegates the work and the goods of the house to his householder and manager. The most familiar of these is the parable of the talents (see Matthew 25:14-30). When the owner returned from a long journey, he called all his servants together so they could give an account of the work they did while he was gone.

Whether we realize it or not, this parable reflects what you and I do in the home. Every day we are called to manage what God has given us, what He has provided through our husbands' efforts and our own. What a blessing it is to us when we serve Him well in this capacity. And what a blessing we are to our family when we properly manage the house. In fact, Martin Luther wrote, "The greatest blessing...is to have a wife to whom you may entrust your affairs."[3] That's what being a home manager is all about!

Yes, But How?

How does a woman who wants what God wants, a woman who wants to know order instead of chaos, a woman after God's own heart, manage her home? Let me tell you how I began to manage our home.

First, understand that home management is God's best for us— God isn't asking His women to *like* being a home manager (although that comes with time as we reap the multitude of blessings that result from better home management). And God isn't asking us to *feel like* managing our home. He is simply calling us to do it. Home management is His plan, His way. It's His good and acceptable and perfect will for us (Romans 12:2). It's His "best" for us. Remember the saying that helps me make decisions? "Good, better, best, never let it rest, until your good is better and your better best." Choosing to manage our homes is choosing God's best for us.

Second, decide to take home management seriously—Why? Because God uses the management of the home as a training ground for our usefulness in the church. How well you and I maintain our personal relationship with God, how devotedly we love our husbands and our children, and how effectively we manage the home indicates how well we would manage a ministry. It's true that what we are at home is what we are!

> *If we manage our homes effectively, we will have time to be involved in church ministry.*

If, for instance, I do a poor job at home, I'll do a poor job in the church. If I take shortcuts at home, I'll do the same in ministry. If I'm a sloppy manager at home, I'll be a sloppy manager at church. Such poor habits become a lifestyle.

But the opposite is also true. If I am organized in the home, I'll probably be organized in my church ministries. If I am a good steward of the responsibilities of the home, I'll probably be a good steward of the responsibilities of ministry outside the home. Jesus said, "He who is faithful in what is least is faithful also in much; and he who is unjust in what is least is unjust also in much" (Luke 16:10).

I realized that—as much as I wanted to—I couldn't run out the front door of my home, leaving it in a shambles, and go over to the church to do the work of ministry. I came to understand that God has charged me with the stewardship of managing my home, and He uses this primary area of ministry to train me for managing other areas of ministry. At home, as I try to live according to God's instructions to me, instructions I find in His written Word, I develop faithfulness and learn to follow through. At home I became a faithful steward (1 Corinthians 4:2), which prepared me for other areas of faithful stewardship.

Once I have shown myself to be a faithful manager at home, I am more free to run out the door and do the work of ministry outside my home. And the same applies to going to a job. All is well at home. Everything is somewhat under control. The people are cared for, and the place is cared for. My management responsibilities on the domestic front are fulfilled.

And let me be clear: I'm not talking about years and decades spent at home waiting for the children to grow up and leave so we have less at home to manage. That option wouldn't teach our children much about the importance of being a contributing member of the body of Christ, the church. But if we manage our homes effectively (and you'll find more about this in the final section of this book), we will have time to be involved in church ministry in some capacity.

On a daily basis, management of the home happens—and happened—for me when I have a schedule. At certain times I plan to do housework. I always reserve time for cultivating my relationship with Jim and, in the past (and to a great extent even today although they live thousands of miles away), with Katherine and Courtney. Although I was not able to be involved in all the ministries I'd like to, I was always involved in *something* at church. The point is, order emerges out of chaos when we schedule what's important.

Third, live as though you will be accountable for the condition of your home and the use of your time…because you will!—In fact, when our husbands (or anyone else) walk in the door and look around the house, we have just revealed what we've been doing in response to God's call to us to manage the home. What do people see when they enter your house? Do they find calm—or chaos? Peace—or panic? Palace—or pigpen? Evidence of preparation—or procrastination?

Now think for a moment about the feeling you get when you enter a hotel room. What greets you? Order. Quiet. Cleanliness. You can still see the vacuum tracks in the carpet. The bed is made (and remember it occupies 80 percent of the visual space in a room!). The last sheet of toilet paper has been folded to a point. No TV or stereo blares. Order reigns. Someone has done the work of effective management, and his or her efforts make the room a sanctuary.

> *How would the Lord— and your family—rate your service, your meals, and your management?*

I well remember the day Jim and I checked out of just such a place. We had been staying in a hotel for six days while Jim was processed at the Army Headquarters in Los Alamitos, California, for five months of active duty. Although Jim was in the ministry, he had been a pharmacy officer in the U.S. Army Reserves since college. This was our first time for activation and deployment in over 30 years… and off he went via military aircraft to Fort Benning, Georgia, and then on to Wuerzburg, Germany, for five months.

Anyway, Los Alamitos was too far from our home for Jim to commute back and forth for the six days. Hence, the hotel stay. And the entire time we were there, I had that feeling of order despite the fact it was a time of great chaos for our family.

When we checked out of the hotel, the hotel clerk gave me a

card to fill out, rating the facilities and the service we had received during our stay. It was a pleasure to give a top rating on every count. We had been well taken care of. The hotel staff met our needs as they took care of our room and our food, even giving me a 30 percent discount on meals!

As I filled out that evaluation card, I wondered how the Lord—and my family—would rate my service, my meals, and my management. With the Lord's grace and with management skills I've learned and practiced over the years, I'm doing better every day. God's ways work!

Twelve Tips for Time Management

When Jim was a seminary student, I went with him to the campus every Friday and spent the entire day in the library. I found the time-management section and systematically read each book in it, jotting down principles from all of them. So now, as we consider time management and organization in the home, I want to share with you my top 12 time-management principles, the ones that made the greatest difference in my home by helping me know order in chaos.

1. *Plan in detail*—Have a planner and write everything down in it. I've found that the more you plan, the better you manage and the more you achieve. Also, the more detailed your plans are, the better. Try planning twice a day—last thing in the evening and first thing in the morning. (More about this in chapter 22!)

2. *Deal with today*—All God asks of you and me is to handle and manage today, only today. Jesus said, "Do not worry about tomorrow, for tomorrow will worry about its own things. Sufficient for the day is its own trouble" (Matthew 6:34). God also says,

"*This* is the day the LORD has made; we will rejoice and be glad in *it*" (Psalm 118:24). Saint Augustine paraphrased Psalm 90:12, "Number every day as your last day."

Each day is important in and of itself:

- What you are today is what you are becoming.
- You are today what you have been becoming.
- Every day is a little life, and our whole life is but a day repeated.

3. *Value each minute*—Know how long it will take you to complete each task in your home. Are you facing a 2-minute task or a 20-minute one? Then decide if the task is the best use of the time. And how much is a minute worth? It's priceless or worthless—depending on how you use it.

4. *Keep moving*—Remember the principle of momentum: "A body at rest [human or otherwise] tends to remain at rest, and a body in motion tends to remain in motion." Use this law of physics to your advantage. Tell yourself, "Just one more thing…just five more minutes." Keep moving and you can cross one more thing off your "to do" list!

5. *Develop a routine*—Or, as the experts say, try "horizontal" planning. "Trying to do the same thing at the same time each day conserves and generates energy. It conserves energy by cutting down on indecision. You perform menial tasks by rote. It generates energy through habit—the habit of expecting to make phone calls, plan the meals, read the paper, attend a class, or go to a meeting—at a particular time."[4] Try to put as many tasks as possible into a routine.

6. *Exercise and diet*—Studies show that exercise increases

metabolism, creates energy, causes you to sleep better, and produces pleasure hormones that contribute to positive attitudes, joy in life, and a general lust for life. Also, don't be spooked by the word "diet." The word simply means "a way of life." So develop a dietary "way of life" that gives you the energy and health you need to accomplish God's best.

7. *Ask the "half the time" question*—"If my life depended upon doing this task in half the time I have allotted, what shortcuts would I take?" Then take them.

8. *Use a timer for everything*—Whatever the task, use your timer. (I'm using one right this minute, and its ticking is pushing me forward.) Setting the timer for "just five minutes" can get you started. Setting the timer for "I'll quit in five minutes" can keep you going. Also, when you set the timer, try to beat the clock. After all, as Parkinson's Law says, "Work expands to fill the time allowed for its completion." The timer helps you allow less time. And there's something extremely motivating about hearing your life tick away!

9. *Do the worst first*—What is the worst task on your to-do list? Do it first and you'll keep that heavy cloud of dread from hanging over you all day long. Use your timer to help you get started. And once that worst is done, your attitude will be greatly improved, and you'll have more energy for the tasks that remain.

10. *Read daily on time management*—Just five minutes a day will help motivate you. If you don't have a good time-management book, start by reading over these 12 principles every day.

11. *Say no*—Make your schedule. Let it be Plan A. Then

follow your plan by saying no to yourself and to others. Move to Plan B only if God is moving you to Plan B.

12. *Begin the night before*—Look what you can do the night before!

> Plan the next day
> Plan the next day's meals
> Select, lay out, and prepare clothes
> Clean up the kitchen
> Run the dishwasher
> Set the table for the next meal
> Tidy up the house
> Prepare lunches and meals
> Defrost meat
> Sort the wash and get a load going in the
>   washer
> Put things you need to take with you by the
>   door

Little steps like these can bring great results when it comes to time management and being organized at home. I've also noticed that these little steps snowball. Once you get started, you'll find energy and enthusiasm to keep moving.

Heart Response

Before we leave the subject of order in the home, let's take a look at the heart of the home—which is your heart! What is your attitude toward your home and your housework? Is your heart in tune with God's? Are you desiring what He desires for the management and guidance of your home? Do you want to be the home manager God wants you to be? Do you acknowledge that responsibilities at home grow greater character... that managing your home enhances the lives of those you live with...and that a well-organized home makes for far better service to the Lord and His people? Ask God to help you move toward better management—and don't wory: Slowly but surely counts.

16

A Heart That Weaves a Tapestry of Beauty

Admonish the young women…
to be homemakers.
TITUS 2:4-5

As God's women, you and I are blessed with the God-given assignment to weave a tapestry of beauty in our homes. One devotional writer of old saw the noble role as "making home first of all a center of attraction by its order and cleanliness and comfort; then by its harmonies of peace and love, so that no discordant notes may mar the music of its joy; and then by…securing the safety of economy and the honor of a wife who 'weaves' all into beauty and order at home."[1]

This is exactly what a woman after God's own heart would gladly spend her life trying to achieve! But, as always, we must first adapt His *attitude* in our hearts if we are to *act* in ways that glorify Him.

Beauty from Busyness

As I continued searching God's Word, He whet my appetite for His kind of home and the beauty that comes when we serve Him there. I found a gold mine—and used my pink marker a lot—in the small book of Titus. In Titus 2:3-5 I found yet another vision for my efforts at home in these words: "Admonish the young women to be…home-makers" (verse 5).

> To successfully make the home of my dreams and God's call a reality, I have to be there, working and weaving on it every day.

I don't know about you, but I had an aversion to that word *homemakers*—until I discovered what God had in mind. Before that, it sounded like dull labor and mundane chores. But looking once again at Jim's study books, I learned that to be a homemaker means to be a stayer-at-home, to be domestically inclined, a good housekeeper, and a keeper at home.[2] Another source emphasized that a woman's primary sphere of activity and contribution is the home,[3] and still another concluded that we are to be active in or busy with household duties.[4] The commentary that most moved my heart said that I am simply to be a "home lover."[5]

Any woman who carries in her mind and heart the thought "Home sweet home!" qualifies as a home lover. That term definitely portrays a fitting *attitude* in response to the call of Titus 2:4-5, but weaving a tapestry of beauty in our homes also calls for *action*. To successfully make the home of my dreams and God's call a reality, I have to be there, working and weaving on it every day. I have to plan the picture and select the colors, threads, and textures. I have to know what I want the finished tapestry to look like. And I have to pay attention to details along the way.

This project called "home" takes effort and time each day.

The effort and the activity—the time, the work, the care, and the mental and physical muscle—combine to make a home beautiful. Such beauty comes when I am active at home, busy responding to the call and challenge and joy of weaving a tapestry there.

Yes, But How?

How does a woman who wholeheartedly wants to weave a tapestry of beauty in her home begin?

Understand the beauty and blessings of God's will for you—God is teaching us His will when He calls us to be homemakers. And I figure that if God calls me to serve at home, to be on top of things, and to see that my good housekeeping chores get done, then I want to do just that. So I resolved (and you may want to do the same) to be at home more often.

Now, *by faith,* I stay at home more often than I might naturally choose, keeping and caring for and loving my home, trusting God to bless my obedience. Oh, I'm not home all the time, but I am there much more than I was. And there are many blessings. For starters, when I'm home, I'm spending less money… because I'm not shopping. I'm also eating fewer calories because somehow, when I'm out, I usually end up eating out. And I'm saving the time and gas money it takes to go somewhere in the car. The ultimate bonus, though—and God knew this would be the case—has been the sense of well being I've experienced. I can see that all is well at home, that everything is under control (at least generally anyway!). The priceless reality of well being has come simply because I have chosen to spend a little more time at home.

Hear what happened when one dear woman in my "Women

After God's Own Heart" class made that same choice. She wrote:

> In the past, each new day would present many choices of who I would visit, where I would go, or what I would do! When my husband came home, he'd be lucky to find the bed made, much less something even defrosted for dinner. I really did not enjoy being home, as I am a people person and even put friends above my family.
>
> I am very happy to say that God has completely turned my life and priorities around as a result of my discovering *His* plan for my days. I now roll out of bed and make the bed immediately, and I'm learning to establish chores to do each day to keep my house in order. I plan my menus two weeks in advance and now have dinner cooking before my husband comes in the door.
>
> What a joy it has become to choose my husband, children, and home before other things, and it brings *real* satisfaction and contentment I've never known before.

Isn't this a beautiful picture—and a beautiful tapestry?

Understand that homemaking can be learned—Sadly, effective housekeeping isn't one of the many spiritual blessings we receive immediately and automatically when we become Christians. (Eternal life, the Holy Spirit dwelling within us, forgiveness for our sin, to name a few, are.) But the how-to's of homemaking can be learned, and Scripture says in Titus 2:3-5 that older women in the faith are to assist and teach younger women these how-to's.

This concept gave me so much hope, because—as I've tried to tell you—I was certainly clueless about making our house a home. So I began to look around for one of these Titus 2-type older women, someone who had her act together at home. Well, thank the Lord, I didn't have to look very far—her husband was our Sunday school teacher!

Meet Jane! Jane is an amazing woman, clearly a woman after God's own heart. Although we were the same age, she seemed to possess the wisdom of a woman a quarter of a century older than me. As I watched her, I saw character that spoke of her carefully nurtured relationship with God. When I saw Jane with her husband, I saw a woman who helped, followed, respected, and loved her husband. And her two preschool-age boys were obedient, polite, and definitely under control.

Well, Jim helped me find the courage to call Jane and ask to meet with her. She was absolutely delighted (I could hear it in her voice). And do you know where she wanted to meet? In her home where—like its mistress—everything was clean, neat, efficient, tidy, and in order. (Notice that I didn't say "a large, gorgeous showplace.")

I praise the Lord that Jane spent that time with me because she gave me the initial direction and nudge for me to tackle weaving my own tapestry. We first talked at length about her devotional life. Besides telling me exactly what she studied and how she did it, she showed me where she studied and let me peek at her prayer book.

Then we talked about marriage. She suggested a list of books to read and, again, shared with me *exactly* how she tried to love and serve her husband. The same with her sons. Jane made me privy to her personal and biblical principles for discipline, training, instruction, and love in the home.

Finally we got to the matter of the home itself, and I really got a bonus. Jane took me on a tour of her little house, opening cupboards, drawers, closets, and doors. I was speechless: The insides of her house didn't look like the insides of mine. And don't get me wrong. Jane wasn't bragging or boasting. She was *teaching* (that's what the Bible says older women are to do for younger ones). She was showing me a system that worked for her. She showed me how she kept her home neat in a minimum of time.

I can still hear Jane instructing me in her kitchen. She stooped down to the lower cabinet cupboards and opened the doors. There were the dishes. She explained, "My principle is 'a place for everything and everything in its place.' And right here is the place for the dishes and napkins. It's right next to the dishwasher so when my sons unload the dishwasher they can put them right here on their own level. Then, when it's time for them to set the table, they can easily get to the dishes and napkins."

You can't put a price on a lesson like that! I got it all, I heard it all, and I *saw* it all. Those few hours with Jane were definitely life changing!

Meet Beverly! I had another friend who taught me how to clean my house. It all began with a ministry call. I was organizing a planning meeting for our women's committee at church, and Beverly said, "Don't plan it for Friday because that's the day I clean my house!" She sounded so excited about her housekeeping plans that I asked if I could come over some Friday and watch her clean.

She said "Sure!" So we set a date and I went to Beverly's house…on a Friday morning. Well, while I was there I got another invaluable lesson. Beverly started on the worst first—her bath-rooms. I saw exactly how she cleaned them, the products she used to clean them with, and her assortment of brushes, scrub sponges, scrapers, and cloths. Then she showed me how she cleaned each room—in a circle, starting just to the left of the door and moving item by item around the room. She was done in minutes!

I also remember reading about discipleship groups in another book by Anne Ortlund, which met (guess where?) in her home. At the first meeting, Anne shared, she takes the group through her home and tells them, "Well, this is my house. This is me. You are welcome to look in any drawer or cupboard or room or closet or book. What you find there will be me. The real me."[6]

Be home more often—My dear husband Jim unknowingly made a major contribution to the beauty of our home. As a young mom with two little ones and a home to maintain, I began to whine and complain to Jim, "I don't know what's wrong—I just can't seem to get anything done." Well, Jim—an expert on time manage-ment and a man with the spiritual gift of administration—was the wrong person to sound off to.

First he told me to get my calendar (a novel idea!). Then, once I had it spread out on the kitchen table, he said, "Now, Liz, which day do you need to do something out of the house?" Well, of course I said Wednesday. That's the day of our women's Bible study at church, and I defi-nitely wanted—and desperately needed—to be there.

Then Jim stated, "OK, Wednesday is your day out. I want you to try to do all your errands and running around and

> *I am so thankful that my wise Jim helped me structure my life so I could be busy at home, using my time and energy to weave some-thing beautiful, some-thing of eternal value.*

visiting with friends on Wednesday, and be at home the rest of the week."

Although he didn't actually say it, I was grounded. But oh, how many times since then have I thanked Jim—and God—for that guidance. His simple piece of advice changed my life and helped turn our home into a tapestry of beauty. To this day, and throughout the decades, whether my house was full of kids or an empty nest, I still aim at leaving the house for errands or visiting or ministry purposes no more than once during the week.

Only later did I find a proverb that spoke of the value of Jim's advice—"Wisdom is in the sight of him who has understanding, but the eyes of a fool are on the ends of the earth" (Proverbs 17:24). In other words, wisdom sees the thing straight in front of us, the thing between our own two feet—and that is our home. The wise woman realizes the value of being home. But the foolish woman (which is what I was) is always looking "out there" (in the mall, in the outlet stores, in a friend's home, etc.) for fulfillment, excitement, activity, and meaning. I am so thankful that my wise Jim helped me structure my life so I could be busy at home, using my time and energy to weave something beautiful, something of eternal value. Even today, I still follow this weekly plan of one day out because it worked so well for me.

I want to quickly say that I too have known a variety of lifestyles. I've been a full-time executive secretary, a full-time teacher, a night-school teacher, a stay-at-home mom, a part-time teacher, and a part-time bookkeeper in my home.

Now I work full-time-plus helping manage all that is involved in our expanding multigenerational family and the ministry my husband and I enjoy…plus Jim and I travel regularly to speak… and we both try to write every day. My days begin early and last long into the night because I have not only my "work" to do, but am still hard at work letting God use me to weave His beauty into the tapestry of our home. You see, whatever my "work" is, my husband, children, grandchildren, and home will always be a higher priority and more important to me. My work, my ministry, is further down the list of God's priorities for me. (More on this later.) Near the top, right behind the *people* in my life—my husband, my children, and my grandchildren—is taking care of the *place* of home, being a home lover, a homemaker.

After all, no one is responsible for managing the George home (the people as well as the place) except me. So I've said no to many things I really like to do so that I can have the time at home to keep working on my tapestry of beauty. For instance, I rarely go out to lunch. I shop by mail or online, if at all. I've given up long, extended visits on the phone. I've even had to whittle my reading down to what is essential. All these changes (and others) came when I decided to spend more time at home and on my home.

I told you I was a voracious reader, and one clever book on home management contained a chapter title that caused me to chuckle—"This Little Piggy Stayed Home!" Doesn't that say it all? I watched the two authors of this book, the "side-tracked sisters," interviewed on NBC's *The Today Show* about the principles in their best-selling book. The main principle is "Never leave the house before you've done all the...duties for the day." There's no way to keep from having an orderly home if you follow this advice. But it does require one thing—you'll have to spend some time at home to get the daily work done!

Organize your outings—It took me a while, but I soon realized that I couldn't, for instance, just run to the cleaners. Instead, I understood for the first time that I needed to stop by the cleaners when I was running all my other errands. I developed an "on the way" routine that covered all my errands—the carpool *and* the cleaners *and* the post office *and* the bank *and* the grocery store *and* any other necessary stops.

> *If you have a job outside the home, consider these two ways to be better organized so you can spend more time at home. First, run errands on the way to and from work. And second, use your lunch hour!*

One morning while I was at the cleaners, I saw the ultimate example of this "on the way" practice. A Volkswagen bug pulled up (in the fire lane!) and the woman driving it jumped out of the car without even turning off the engine. She grabbed her dirty clothes, dashed in, and threw them on the counter while the clerk ran to get her cleaned ones. Out she ran (literally), off to the next stop on her list. Now picture this: She was wearing a business suit and her errand running shoes—her tennis shoes—and her hair was in hot rollers! It was 8:15 in the morning, and this woman was running her errands "on the way" to work.

Perhaps like that woman, I've read many insightful books specifically for working women. Their main piece of advice has to do with the use of discretionary time—time that is considered to belong to the employee to use any way she likes. Discretionary time includes the lunch hour. You see, a working woman can either spend her lunch hour visiting or gossiping and listening to empty talk and complaints, or she can spend it (as the books suggest) going to the post office, grocery shopping for nonperishables, making important phone calls, or doing a multitude of other things that make it possible for her to *go home* the second work is over.

If you have a job outside the home, consider these two ways to be better organized so you can spend more time at home. First, run errands on the way to and from work. And second, use your lunch hour. You'll be more content when you arrive home, and therefore more able to be the kind of homemaker you and God want you to be.

Heart Response

Now, dear fellow weaver, take God's teaching to heart. Do you cherish your home? Is it "home sweet home" to you? When you are away from it, do you yearn for it? Is your heart truly centered in your home? Are the place and the people there more important to you than anyone or anything else?

When I responded to God's call to homemaking and to questions like these so many years ago, I wrote out an "I will" list about my home sweet home. (Earlier I had gone through the book of Psalms, writing out every "I will" uttered by the psalmist, which I thought was a good exercise for doing business with God.) I called my covenant with God "The Heart of a Homemaker." You'll notice that it touches on much of what you've read so far.

1. I will get up before my family in order to prepare myself spiritually and physically.
2. I will prepare breakfast for my family and sit with them while they eat.
3. I will work diligently to send every member of my family off in a good mood.
4. I will consult my husband every day to see if there is anything special he wants me to do for him.
5. I will keep a neat and orderly home.
6. I will respond positively.

7. I will seek to meet my husband's needs.

8. I will put my husband before my children.

9. I will personally meet and greet each family member as he or she returns home.

10. I will be predictably happy.

11. I will prepare special, good food for my family.

12. I will make dinner a special time.

13. I will grow daily in the areas of the Lord, marriage, family, and homemaking.

Is yours the heart of a homemaker? For help, ask God for His transforming touch. As He empowers you to obey, He will give you joy at the task to which He calls you and enhance the beauty of the tapestry you are weaving.

17

A Heart Strengthened by Spiritual Growth

Grow in the grace and knowledge
of our Lord and Savior Jesus Christ.
2 PETER 3:18

As I'm sure you can tell, the book of Proverbs is a delight to me. I love God's refreshing wisdom, and I love the woman pictured at the end of the book, the Proverbs 31 woman (verses 10-31). Whenever I read those verses, this excellent woman reminds me of a watch. From the outside, we see her hands moving. We witness all the activity of those 22 verses, her busyness as she lives out her assignments from God as wife, mother, and homemaker. But

> *I have learned what keeps us fresh and excited and motivated in our godly pursuits—and this is spiritual growth.*

there's something inside, something deep within her heart, that makes her tick, moving her along, energizing her efforts, and motivating her activity.

You and I need that same God-given something inside to empower our actions as women after His heart. As we go about fulfilling God's assignment to us as women—whether we're married or not, whether we're moms or not—there has to be a *Mover* inside our heart or we won't become women after God's own heart. If there's nothing inside, without God's Spirit inside, we won't be able to keep on keeping on. We won't be able to find the strength to faithfully carry out God's Word and His will. We won't be able to finish the path we've started out on.

Well, I have learned what keeps us fresh and excited and motivated in our godly pursuits—and that is spiritual growth. Our spiritual growth in Jesus Christ—growing to be more like Him strengthens our hearts, fills them, and empowers us to obey His commands.

Spiritual Growth Begins in Jesus Christ

You and I have two options for how we live. We can live our lives with Jesus Christ or without Him. It's a clear-cut black/white, either/or situation. The Bible says, "This is the testimony: that God has given us eternal life, and this life is in His Son. He who has the Son has life; he who does not have the Son of God does not have life" (1 John 5:11-12). As this Scripture tells us, there is *no* life without Jesus Christ!

That's the frightening condition I lived in for 28 years. I grew up in a wonderful home with loving parents who were faithful to take me to church and expose me to God's truth both there and daily at home. But several key pieces were missing from my spiritual understanding. One of those pieces was accurate knowledge of who Jesus Christ is. I loved Him and believed that He was the Son of God, but it never clicked that being the *Son of God* meant He *was* God. Only by eventually reading a book filled with clear teaching from the Scriptures did I grow to understand that Jesus Christ was God in flesh, living on earth, and dying on a cross to save sinners like me and give us eternal life.

The second missing piece was a biblical understanding of sin. I'm still amazed when I think about all those years I truly loved God, loved Jesus, loved the Bible, believed in the Holy Spirit and the miracles of the Bible, and even prayed. I was a "good" person (I didn't steal or murder), and I thought that was all that mattered. I had no knowledge of the fact of personal sin—that "*all* have sinned and fall short of the glory of God" (Romans 3:23 NIV). And since I didn't sin—the logic went—I didn't need a savior!

I've told you a little about my early life—that Jim and I began our marriage without God, that I was venturing down a path that led me away from my husband and children. One day, standing in the middle of the kitchen with little Katherine hanging on one leg and littler Courtney on the other, I raised my fists to the ceiling and yelled, "There has *got* to be more to life than this!" Hearing this cry of desperation, God began to move me toward Him and a complete knowledge of Him, His Son, *and* my sin. When He was done with me, I realized at last that *I needed a Savior!* And what did I find in Jesus, my Savior?

A new beginning—When you and I come to a saving knowledge of Jesus Christ, we are given a new beginning, a fresh start, forgiveness for the past, wisdom for handling life, and power for doing what's right. The apostle Paul explains it like this: "If anyone is in Christ, he is a new creation; old things have passed away; behold, all things have become new" (2 Corinthians 5:17).

God's love and acceptance—Whenever I am down, discouraged, doubting, depressed, defeated, or dismayed (someone once quipped that all these "D" words are from the Devil!), I stop and remind myself, "No matter what has happened, no matter what life looks like, no matter what you're feeling, you are accepted in the Beloved—and nothing else matters!" Indeed, God has "made us *accepted* in the Beloved" (Ephesians 1:6)!

God's power in the Holy Spirit—Can you imagine having the power of God at work in your life? When Christ is your Savior, that's what happens. God empowers you through His Holy Spirit to do good, to effect change in your life, to make your life fulfilling and meaningful, to help others, and to minister for Christ. Jesus said, "You shall receive *power* when the Holy Spirit has come upon you" (Acts 1:8).

God's total sufficiency—No matter what the problem, the hurdle, the struggle, the suffering you face, God promises, "My grace is sufficient for you" (2 Corinthians 12:9). Whether you're dealing with temptation, a difficult marriage, problems with the children, needs in the home, personal challenges, loneliness, demands at work, health issues, a stretching ministry, or any other difficult situation, God promises, "My grace is sufficient for you."

Spiritual Growth Involves the Pursuit of Knowledge

In addition to being our Savior, Jesus is our model for how to live a life that pleases God. When we look at His life, we see that "Jesus increased in wisdom" (Luke 2:52). One proverb (a constant challenge to me) reflects the importance of such growth stating, "The heart of him who has understanding seeks knowledge, but the mouth of fools feeds on foolishness" (Proverbs 15:14). Put another way, an intelligent person purposefully seeks knowledge, but fools nibble randomly, vacantly chewing on words and ideas that have no value, no flavor, and no nutrition.

What are you and I feeding our minds? Are we heeding this biblical warning about the danger of "garbage in, garbage out"? May we *purposefully* seek knowledge and guard against spending precious time on things that have no value. One way I guard my mind is by following the advice of a special woman, advice that has provided help for living a godward life as well as fodder for teaching, books, study materials, and ministry. She told me, "Elizabeth, you've got to have five fat files!"

Create five fat files—You're probably as puzzled as I was when I heard her say these words, so let me explain. But even before I do, take the first step and purchase or round up five manila file folders.

Aim at expertise—Next, select five areas you'd like to become an expert in and label a file for each of them. A word of caution: choose areas from the spiritual realm. Remember the proverb? You don't want to feed on pursuits that have no value. Instead choose topics of eternal value. To help you determine those five areas, answer the questions, "What do you want to be known for?" and "What topics do you want your name associated with?"

Personal spiritual growth is all about preparation for ministry. It's about filling yourself up first so that you have something to give.

I have a friend, for instance, whose name many people associate with prayer. Whenever we needed someone at church to teach on prayer, lead a day of prayer for our women, or open a meeting with worship prayer, everyone automatically thinks of her. For more than 20 years, she has been studying what the Bible teaches about prayer, looking closely at the men and women of the Bible who prayed, reading about prayer, and praying. Prayer is definitely one of her areas of expertise, one of her five fat files. Another friend is known for her knowledge of the Bible. Whenever the women at church needed someone to lead a survey of the Bible or give an overview of the prophets, we would call on Betty. Still another friend speaks to church groups about time management. These three women have become experts.

Through the years, I've compiled a list of the fat files that the students in my "Woman After God's Own Heart" class kept. I now share some of the topics to stimulate your thinking. They range from the practical—hospitality, health, child-raising, home-making, Bible-study methods—to the theological—attributes of God, faith, fruit of the Spirit. They include areas for minis-try—biblical counseling, teaching, serving, women's ministry—as well as areas of character—the devotional life, heroes of the faith, love, virtues of godliness. They center around lifestyles—single-ness, parenting, organization, widowhood, the pastor's home—and zero in on the personal—holiness, self-control, submission, contentment. Wouldn't you love to sit in on the classes these women may teach in ten years—or read the books they may even-tually write? After all, such personal spiritual growth is all about preparation for ministry. It's about filling yourself up first so that you have something to give in ministry!

Fill the files—Now start putting information into your files. They'll get fat as you follow the exhortation to "read everything on [your] subject...articles, books, specialized magazines, and news clippings...attend seminars...teach on the subject(s)... spend time with those who are the best in these areas, picking their brains....seek and sharpen your expertise."[1]

Most importantly, read your Bible to see firsthand what God says about your areas of interest. After all, His thoughts are the primary knowledge you want. I even code my Bible. You know by now that pink highlights passages of interest to women, and you're probably not surprised to learn that one of my five fat files is "Women." Besides marking those passages in pink, I've put a "W" in the margin beside them. Anything in my Bible that relates to women, wives, mothers, homemakers, or women of the Bible has a "W" beside it. I did the same thing with "T" for teaching, "TM" for time management, etc. Once you pick your areas and set up your code, I guarantee you'll be so excited and motivated that you'll wake up *before* the alarm clock rings eager to open God's Word, pen in hand, to look for His wisdom about the areas where you want wisdom!

And as you continue your quest for knowledge about five spiritual topics, remember that you are working on this personal growth in order to minister to others. I made a fresh commitment regarding eternal matters because I was so sobered by Jim's mother's memorial service. As I told you earlier, Lois exemplified the saying,

> Only one life, 'twill soon be past,
> only what's done for Christ will last.

Each morning Lois filled her mind with the things of God, and then she spent the rest of that day allowing that fullness to fill others in ministry. We are saved to serve (2 Timothy 1:9), and serving requires that we be full of things eternal, things worth sharing. Our fullness becomes the overflow that is our ministry. It's what we have to give and pass on to others. As a dear mentor constantly drilled into me, "Nothing going in equals nothing going out!"

Spiritual Growth Includes Stewardship of Your Body

You may have been hoping this subject wouldn't come up, but we're told in the Bible that how we manage our body affects our ministry and the quality of our lives. The apostle Paul put it this way: "I discipline my body and bring it into subjection, lest, when I have preached to others, I myself should become disqualified" (1 Corinthians 9:27).

The goal in the physical realm is discipline, the self-control that is a gift of God's grace (Galatians 5:23). His Spirit in us gives us strength to resist temptation, to control our appetite rather than allowing it to control us, and to train our body into obedience.

Every time I ask a woman who is enjoying an energetic life and ministry how she does it, I cringe a bit as she says the two predictable words—*diet* and *exercise*. If the goal is a quality of life filled with quality days of serving the Lord, attention to the body is key!

Spiritual Growth Means Becoming Like Jesus

As Jesus grew up, He increased not only in wisdom (the mind) and stature (the body), but He also increased in favor with God (Luke 2:52). Oh to be like Jesus! How can you and I grow in this direction?

Increase in knowledge—As we've seen, Jesus is our model. God desires for us to follow in His footsteps and grow in the knowledge of God (Colossians 1:10) as well as in the grace and knowledge of our Lord and Savior Jesus Christ (2 Peter 3:18). Like Paul's prayer for the church in Philippi, our prayer for ourselves should be that our "love may abound still more and more in knowledge and all discernment" (Philippians 1:9). And we should be doing something with all that knowledge, for we are to be *doers* of the word, not hearers only (James 1:22)!

Have a plan—Increasing in knowledge is a lot like getting the evening meal on the table. You have to have a plan. When it comes to making dinner, you know that you have to do certain things at certain times if your family is to sit down at a designated time in the evening and eat. Likewise, when it comes to increasing your knowledge of God, you have to do a certain thing (sit down) in a certain place (your place) with certain items (pen, paper, reading schedule, study guide, whatever you need) at a specific time (your time). When you do, you'll enjoy a feast from God and His Word!

Do something—So develop a plan, remembering (once again) that *something is better than nothing*. The important thing is to do something. Keep a record of your time with God for your own encouragement and accountability. I remember picking up my record one day, thinking, "It's only been a few days, Lord," and discovering it had actually been two weeks since I had done "something"! Don't be like I was. Have a plan to do something… and follow your plan.

Spiritual Growth Blesses Others

As Jesus grew, He also "increased…in favor with God and

men" (Luke 2:52). Try these three ways to improve your relationships with people.

Mind your mind—It's unavoidable. Your actions will reveal your attitude toward people. That's the message of yet another proverb: "For as he thinks in his heart, so is he" (Proverbs 23:7). Thoughts that are critical, negative, harmful, and jealous not only go against God's Word (Philippians 4:8), but they spawn actions that are critical, negative, harmful, and jealous. So train yourself to think loving, positive, sweet thoughts when it comes to other people.

Mind your mouth—Our relationships with people are enhanced when we follow in the steps of the Proverbs 31 woman who "opens her mouth with wisdom, and on her tongue is the law of kindness" (Proverbs 31:26). If her thoughts weren't wise or kind, her mouth was shut!

Mind your manners—The Number One way to be pleasing to God and approved by man is to be the servant of all. Our servant assignment from God is to give honor and preference to one another (Romans 12:10). Regarding others as more important than yourself gives you the mind and manner of Christ (Philippians 2:4-5).

You and I are to focus away from self and outward to others. We are to become other-oriented. To do this, as mundane as it sounds, we have to train ourselves to, for instance, stop talking about ourselves (and our children) and instead ask about the other person. We may also have to learn some good manners because love has good manners (1 Corinthians 13:5).

I love what Anne Ortlund says. First she writes, "There are two kinds of personalities in this world, and you are one of the two.

People can tell which, as soon as you walk into a room: your attitude says either 'Here I am' or 'There you are.'" Then she illustrates the latter by describing "a Hawaiian woman who strings a number of leis early each Sunday morning, not for anyone in particular! Then she comes to church praying, 'Lord, who needs my leis today? A newcomer? Someone discouraged? Lead me to the right people.'"[2]

Are you a "There you are" person, looking around for how you can encourage someone with God's love? He can make it happen as you let Him grow you into a woman after His heart.

Heart Response

How joyous! As Christian women, you and I are filled with all spiritual blessings (Ephesians 1:3). We are filled with the goodness of God (Galatians 5:22-23) and the Spirit of God (Galatians 4:6). We are also gifted for ministry (1 Corinthians 12:7-11; Romans 12:6-8). Now that we have been filled, God wants us to share those blessings with others, to invest our lives in other hearts, to give away His blessings, to pass them on. That, dear friend, is why you and I must be about the business of spiritual growth.

Because spiritual growth is grounded in Jesus Christ and empowered by His Spirit, I must ask you, "Is Jesus your Savior? Does He live in your heart?" After all, His presence is what makes you a woman after God's heart! Do you enjoy the assurance of eternal life? God has promised that "as many as received Him, to them He gave the right to become children of God, even to those who believe in His name" (John 1:12) and that "whoever believes in Him should not perish but have everlasting life" (John 3:16).

As a member of the family of God, you've also been given the mind of Christ (1 Corinthians 2:16). Are you purposefully filling your mind with knowledge from God's Word, knowledge you can give away to others? Does your body belong to God, to be groomed, cared for, and disciplined for maximum usefulness and His glory? And are you nurturing love for others—thinking, speaking, and acting toward them as Christ would?

God calls you to love Him, first and foremost, with all your heart, soul, strength, and mind (Luke 10:27) and to allow that rich love you enjoy in Him to overflow into your family, into your neighbors, into the lives of others (Luke 10:27). That's why a heart strengthened by spiritual growth in Him is so very important.

18

A Heart Enriched by Joy in the Lord

Be filled with all the fullness of God.
EPHESIANS 3:19

One Sunday morning I stopped on the church patio to talk to a long-time acquaintance. For the 30 years I attended that church, Sharon helped women like me grow in the things of the Lord and live out His priorities. Sharon has been a faithful Titus 2:3 older woman and mentor—a blessing to many.

As we talked that morning, she seemed electric—lit up, sparks flying, flowing and sizzling with live juice. Everything about Sharon that day evidenced both the vital life she lives in the Savior and her wholehearted pursuit of continued growth in Him. I can still picture her broad, brilliant smile and her eyes bright with inner energy. Uncontainably excited, she involuntarily punctuated her message with gestures and waves.

What was she so excited about? Well, Sharon was looking forward to hearing a very special speaker the next day. She could hardly wait, and judging by her exhilaration, I bet she didn't sleep that night! Her words tumbled out as she explained that she had already attended a weekend workshop led by this scholar and that it had been the most exciting weekend of her life, the most stimulating thing she'd ever done. This teacher had taken Sharon to new depths in God's Word, in her understanding of His ways, and in her ministry. As she talked, I knew I was in the presence of a woman who was growing in both the knowledge and love of her Lord. No wonder she was so happy and excited! No wonder she had so much to give to others! No wonder I felt blessed by her ministry of refreshment.

Everyone who gets close to these women receives something from the fullness of their lives. My deepest desire and prayer for you is that you will be this kind of woman.

Another woman like Sharon at this same church was a reader. I never saw her without a book resting on top of the Bible she always carries. Every time we spoke, she would ask, "Oh Elizabeth, have you read this book? It's a must!" And off we would go into a wonderful discussion of her latest find and why that particular book was so important to us as Christians. I was blessed by her ministry of refreshment too.

I hope you get a sense of how stimulating these women are and how they spurred me on in my own spiritual growth. These two women after God's own heart are alive and growing. There's an infectiousness about their lives and hearts that never fails to challenge and motivate me. It is impossible for me to leave their presence unchanged. The joy they gained from their growth in the Lord shines forth, and everyone who gets close to these women receives something from the fullness of their lives.

Even more than hoping you get a sense of women like these, I hope that God has placed some of these women in your life. But my deepest desire and prayer for you (and for myself too!) is that you will *be* this kind of woman. As God grows you into a woman after His heart, you will never lack for His joy or a fulfilling ministry for His kingdom!

In the preceding chapter, we began to plan for a life of spiritual growth that would lead to ministry to others. After all, as my mentor shared repeatedly with me, when nothing is coming in, nothing can go out. If, then, you and I are to have an effective ministry to others, we must first be filled. What can you do to be filled with all the fullness of God so that He can use you in ministry? Here are a few suggestions.

Spiritual Growth Is Aided by Discipleship

God's ideal plan for us as His women—and another aspect of His job assignment for us—is that we teach other women the "good things" we've been learning, that we mentor or disciple them, that we pass on all that God has taught us (Titus 2:3-4).

The word *discipleship* can call to mind a variety of scenarios. Most often we equate discipleship with one-on-one, weekly meetings with another woman for years on end. That would be wonderful, but for most people that is neither a reality nor even a possibility. We can, however, choose from some enriching alternatives if we really want to grow.

Classes are ours for the taking. Churches in every town offer Bible studies and Bible classes. Correspondence courses are also available.[1] All you and I have to do is enroll, do the work, and let God grow us.

Books offer another avenue for growth and help you develop skills for ministering to women. Like this book, most of my books (see the list in the back of this book) contain study questions or have companion growth and study guides available for personal study, growth, and discipleship.

Counsel from fellow Christians is also a valid form of discipleship. If you're having a problem, ask a trusted and godly person—and you'll receive God's perspective and the prayer support you need. Even if you're unable to attend any classes or meet with a mentor right now, you can always ask for counsel.

Interviewing other Christian women is one of my favorite means of growth and discipleship. When God sent a godly, older woman to my church, I took one look at her busy life and saw clearly that she would never be able to commit to a series of discipleship sessions with me. So I made a list of all the questions I wanted to ask her and set up an appointment. We met just that one time, but those two precious hours she gave me were life changing! Much of my philosophy of ministry and many of the things I teach (including my five fat files) are a direct result of that one blessed time in her presence, drinking in her wisdom.

Observation is another biblical means of growth. After all, "the hearing ear and the seeing eye, the LORD has made them both" (Proverbs 20:12). So make sure you are watching, watching, watching! It's a great way to learn. In fact, Bible teacher Carole Mayhall says one way to learn how to love and demonstrate respect and support your husband is to watch other women. When it comes to admiring your husband, for instance, "keep a list of how other women show admiration for their husbands."[2]

Watch, learn, write down what you learn, and then try those new behaviors yourself.

Reading plays an important role in spiritual growth. Of course, the primary book to read is your Bible. There you'll find God's direct teaching. Beyond God's Word, read the books of the women I've been mentioning throughout this book and others like them who have put into print for us their mentoring programs, their counsel, and their observations. When we read such books, we are discipled.

If you're not quite convinced, consider these thoughts about the value of reading:

- Mrs. Billy Graham told her daughters, "Keep reading and you'll be educated."[3]

- Don't forget to focus your reading on the areas of your five fat files! "The most important key to reading effectiveness can be summed up in one word—selectivity."[4]

- "Don't read at random—only what relates to your total life goals."[5]

- "One characteristic common to every effective person is that they are avid readers."[6]

- "Reading is the best way to gain knowledge…. [But] only 5% of the people living in the U.S. will either buy or read a book this year."[7]

If you're thinking, "But I don't have *time* to read! How could I with all these job assignments from God?" or "Wait a minute—books cost money!" a wise first step would be a sober evaluation of how you're living your life. It's easy to think you don't have time to read, but the simple act of carrying a book everywhere you go gets many books read. I used to set my timer and read for just five minutes a day. That approach also gets many books read.

As for the money, it's also easy to think you can't afford books. An option for many people is checking out books from your church library. But you may have the funds to build a library without knowing it. Did you know that the average household spends more than $50 a month (some even up to $200 a month!) for cable television service? How about spending the amount you spend for cable TV on edifying Christian books that stimulate spiritual growth? Have a book budget that matches your cable fees. Those TV programs will become less enjoyable next to life-giving books that enrich your spiritual growth.

Spiritual Growth Is Aided by Goals

I'm in the midst of preparing a Saturday seminar about setting and reaching goals. Needless to say, I am thrilled to be talking about something that helps guide me every day! I can't imagine a day (or a life) without goals. Goals give me a target. As I rise each morning and take aim at my day, the arrow I shoot may wobble and weave, but at least it's in flight and headed some-where. The arrow may miss the bull's eye, falling a little short or sometimes even quite wide of the goal, but at least it was going—*I* was going—somewhere. Just as goals help us in the day to day, goals are definitely an aid when it comes to our spiritual growth. Here's how.

Goals provide focus—It's definitely true that if you aim at noth-ing, you'll hit it every time. So when I was a mom with preschool-ers, I aimed at something—reading one book a year. I asked myself, "If I could read only one book this year, what would it be?" I picked Edith Schaeffer's book *What Is a Family?* Reading that one book when our children were young helped me determine the road I wanted our family to head down. I read it in bits and pieces, remembering that *something is better than nothing*. I set a goal—and reached it. And that one book I set out to read went straight into my heart—and my life. It was so powerful and helpful that I chose to read it again…and again. As time— and years—went by, my list of books grew to include a variety of other titles centered around my own personal five fat files, all of which have contributed to my personal and spiritual growth and to my ministry to others.

Goals provide an opportunity for specific measurement—Setting goals that are specific helps you move forward in the direction you want to go. So when it comes to making goals for yourself, stay away from the vague. For example, the goal "to be a godly woman" or "to walk with God" is honorable but hard to measure. It's far better to be specific. Answer the question "What does a godly woman *do?*" and let your answer give you specific and measurable behaviors (i.e., Bible study, prayer time). Write down steps you can actually take toward those behaviors (baby steps count!) and mark them off as you accomplish them. I'm often asked about my writing, including questions like "How do you do it?" and "What must I do to write a book?" My answer is always the same. I have a goal to write five pages each day. Now that's specific. There's nothing vague about that.

Goals provide encouragement—When a week, or month, or year is over, do you ever wonder, "Wow, what did I do? Where did it go?" I know I used to mourn the end of each year, wondering what I had to show for the passage of time, for a *whole* year. But as I began to write down specific, measurable goals and keep track of my progress in my planner, I could see firsthand the growth that had taken place, the number of books that had been read, the variety of classes and seminars taken, the audiences I had shared God's truths with, the books written, the number of family reunions and birthdays celebrated and babies added to our expanding family, even the pounds lost and a year's worth of efforts at physical fitness. Believe me, as you keep track daily of your efforts and God's grace, you will be able to celebrate the progress made, and give God thanks.

Spiritual Growth Depends on Choices

Once you've settled on some specific goals, you'll have to continually make the right choices if you are to reach those goals. What kinds of choices?

Choices based on priorities—To reach the goals you set for your spiritual growth, you'll have to choose between working on a Bible course, taking a theology class, reading a book, meeting with a mentor...or another luncheon outing, shopping (again) in the mall, watching still more TV, attending another church social, or working on a craft. Filling yourself up with spiritual things so that growth occurs and your life is a river of refreshment to many requires many tough choices.

Choices based on goals—Once you've decided to spend time on your spiritual growth, you still have to choose which project—and your five fat files can guide you. You'll also want to consider your spiritual gifts. These two guides will help you aim at the best choice.

Spiritual Growth Requires Time

God will honor the time we commit to learning more about

Him, the time we find, redeem, save, allow, and schedule for our spiritual growth. An image from Scripture (an image I love) encourages me here. The prophet Isaiah wrote, "Those who wait on the LORD shall...mount up with wings like eagles" (Isaiah 40:31). The time we spend in solitude with our Bible and our prayer list, our secret life spent with our heavenly Father, is time spent waiting upon the Lord. Then, in the fullness of time, in God's perfect timing, there is the mounting up, the taking flight like that eagle. We are able to soar because we've been with the Lord—as the lives of many heroes of the Bible illustrate.

- Moses was the adopted son of Pharaoh's daughter and, as such, experienced every known privilege for 40 years. But then God took him into the desert to be a shepherd, a nobody, for the next 40 years of his life (Exodus 3:1). After those 40 years of God preparing him, Moses burst on the scene with signs, wonders, miracles, and faithful service to God (Exodus 3–14).

- Potiphar was the captain of the guard for Pharaoh, and Joseph served ten years as master of Potiphar's household (Genesis 39). But one day Joseph found himself in prison, a nobody, forgotten as the days and months rolled by. Then, after two or three years, which God used to prepare him for leadership, Joseph burst on the scene, helped save his people, and served as second in command over the entire known world (Genesis 41).

- John the Baptist was another of God's nobodies. For 30 years he lived in the wilderness, wearing animal skins and eating locusts and wild honey (Matthew 3:4; Luke 1:80). After those 30 years of preparation, John burst on the scene preaching like no man ever had, preaching so powerfully

that his listeners thought he was the Messiah (Luke 3:15)!
John's ministry lasted no longer than one brief year, yet it
demanded lengthy spiritual preparation.

- Paul was a terrible somebody who persecuted Christians.
But then one day he was dramatically converted from
Christian-hater to Christian—and he disappeared into the
Arabian desert for three years (Galatians 1:17-18). After
those three years, during which God prepared him for an
amazing and far-reaching ministry, Paul burst on the scene,
preaching, teaching, and working signs and miracles.

- And then there is Jesus. As God in flesh, He was never a
nobody. But He too put in His time in obscurity, away
from the crowds, involved in the mundane. According to
God's plan, Jesus spent time as a child in Galilee with a
family, time inside a carpenter's workshop, and time in
the wilderness for 40 days of prayer and fasting (Matthew
4:1-11). And then one day Jesus burst on the scene exhib-
iting the power and glory of God in action! But after 30
years of preparation, His earthly ministry lasted for only
three short years.

God's perspective on time is different from ours, and we may
question His use of time. We may be tempted to think that quiet,
hidden time with Him doesn't count—that it doesn't show, it
doesn't matter, and no one cares. After all, nobody sees it. There's
no glory, no splash, no attention given to those weeks, months,
years of waiting on God. No one sees us read and study God's
empowering Word. No one is present to watch us memorize and
meditate on God's life-changing truths. God alone sees us on
bended knee in the heart-wrenching work of prayer, work He
uses to prepare us for ministry.

But then, just like the heroes of the Bible and just like our Savior Himself, one day we are prepared. When the timing is right, when the opportunity for ministry presents itself, we too mount up with wings like an eagle—ready to do God's work! We are then privileged to live out the saying that success

> *Treat yourself to a private retreat and wait on the Lord. Let God prepare you to mount up with wings like an eagle so that you one day burst on the scene in vital ministry to His people!*

comes when preparation meets opportunity. God is responsible for presenting the opportunities—in His time, place, and manner—but we are responsible for cooperating with His efforts to prepare us.

And that preparation happens when we spend time alone with our Lord. Good comes out of that time. In fact, for good reason, solitude has been called "the school of genius." It's also true that "most of the world's progress has come out of...loneliness."[8] So clear your calendar. Set aside time to place yourself before God so He can bring about spiritual growth in you. Treat yourself to a private retreat and wait on the Lord. Let God prepare you to mount up with wings like an eagle so that you one day burst on the scene in vital ministry to His people!

Spiritual Growth Results in Ministry

The importance of your spiritual growth—the main point of this section—is summed up in the statement, *You cannot give away what you do not possess.* Involvement in ministry requires that you be a full vessel—as my friend Karen (another Karen!) will show you.

As a mother with two little boys at home, Karen desired to

be a full vessel. So she began waiting on the Lord. She set up her five fat files and began to read and read and read(!) on one of her selected files, *the spiritual development of children.*

Soon Karen's older son went off to kindergarten for three hours a day. At the end of the year, when the teacher was setting up "graduation" exercises, she asked Karen to give a message on imparting spiritual truth to your children. With that invitation, a prepared Karen burst on the scene—and had a hundred people hear what she had learned.

Because Karen had faithfully waited on the Lord and put herself in a position where He could fill her and grow her, she possessed something she could give away. Everywhere she went, her lips and life spoke of the fullness that was being gained in private. She was so enriched and excited about what she was learning that it spilled out of her heart. Because the springs of her heart were being fed from an underground source, she had an excitement that refreshed others, and a natural overflow and ministry resulted.

And I'm sure you're a lot like Karen. As a woman after God's own heart, you undoubtedly want to know God and His Word. You want to make the choices He would have you make. You also desire God's power and imprint to clearly be on your life. Your heart beats with His out of concern for others. And you want to spend your life trying to live out God's purpose for you. That's what Karen longed for, so she set about filling herself up.

Spiritual Growth: Experiencing the Joy of the Lord

In your mind, picture a real woman you admire and then describe her as I described Sharon at the beginning of this chapter.

Most likely, the woman you admire is stimulating, challenging, energetic, and joyful. She is growing and fresh, excited and exciting, learning and willing to share what she is learning. She motivates you, and you love to be in her presence. She has nothing to fear, and you never hear her sigh or see signs that she's bored. For her, life is never dull!

Such a woman—and I hope you know at least one—is probably involved in and committed to spiritual growth. She has spent time with God and been filled by Him, so when she's in public, she can't help but share her love for Jesus. She can't help but share the joy of knowing Him and walking with Him. He has filled her heart to overflowing, enabling her to offer a ministry of refreshment to other people. As you watch these Proverbs 31 women dip into the reservoir created by their time of preparation with God and as you listen to their enthusiasm for life and for the Lord, you must admit that you are in the presence of a woman who truly knows His joy. That's where real joy comes from—time spent alone with the Lord as He enriches you and prepares you for the ministry of helping others.

Heart Response

You are blessed indeed if you know one of these joyful, enriched women who have responded to God's call on their lives. You will be even more blessed if you accept the invitation to do likewise. So take a moment and wait upon the Lord as you consider these questions:

- Exactly how am I spending my precious God-given time and energy? Am I wasting it on choices that have no heavenly value or am I making the good, better, and best choices?

- Do I acknowledge the value—the necessity—of time spent in preparation?

- Is allowing God to prepare me for ministry even a goal of mine? Or am I letting time—and life—slip away unused, uninvested in eternity?

God has done His part—He has saved you (2 Timothy 1:9), given you eternal life (1 John 5:11), blessed you with all spiritual blessings (Ephesians 1:3), gifted you for spiritual ministry (1 Corinthians 12:11), and prepared a place for you in heaven (John 14:2). And now He calls you to do your part—to catch His vision, to set aside time, to make growth in Him a goal, to spend time and energy so that He can prepare you for ministry, and to trust Him to provide you with opportunities to minister to and enrich His people out of the overflow of your own joy-filled and enriched life.

A Heart That Shows It Cares

Be steadfast, immovable,
always abounding in the work of the Lord,
knowing that your labor is not in vain in the Lord.
1 CORINTHIANS 15:58

When my daughter Courtney returned from her honeymoon, Jim and Katherine and I had exactly one week to help her pack and say goodbye as she and her Paul put their wedding gifts on a sea freighter and flew to the island of Kauai where Paul was a teacher. Hawaii is a long way from Los Angeles, and having a family member that far away was a real adjustment for Jim and Katherine and me. "Oh, well," all of us on the mainland thought, "we'll just *have* to visit them!" So Jim and I, along with Katherine and her husband, Paul, started planning a trip to Hawaii. (Yes, each of my daughters married a Paul!)

Five months later we flew to Maui for a long-awaited reunion. The four of us met Paul and Courtney and began a wonderful

Thanksgiving holiday together as a family. One of our sightseeing ventures took us on the famous Road to Hana where the Maui highway ends. Yes, we suffered our share of lightheadedness and car sickness as the road snaked around and around for 30 miles (and five hours!), but at the end of the road was a breathtaking view of the Seven Sacred Pools.

These seven pools had been formed in the rocks and lava beds by rain rushing down the mountainsides toward the Pacific Ocean. Originating high above in altitudes unseen because of the ever-present rain clouds, the fresh water fell to the ground. First it filled the highest pool. When that top pool was full, the still falling rain caused its contents to overflow and cascade into another pool down the mountain. As soon as that second pool filled up, it too overflowed...into another one further down the slope...and another...and another...until the last and final pool poured its contents into the immensity of God's sea.

Reflecting on God's Plan

As I stood with my family looking at (and photographing) this wondrous handiwork of God, I thought of the life you and I are seeking to live as God's women. These seven pools illustrate for us the fullness we can enjoy—and the far-reaching impact we can have—as we live according to God's plan.

Picture again that top pool, high on that mountain, veiled in a cloudy mist, hidden from the sight of others. Like that pool, you and I enjoy our hidden life with God, the private life we nurture in Him. Unseen by others, you and I are filled by God's Spirit as we dwell in His presence and drink from His Word. In that holy mist He replenishes our dry souls until we are filled with His goodness. Then that fullness overflows down into the next pool, the hearts of the people nearest and dearest to us— our husbands.

Then it happens again. Still high on the mountain, we share with our husbands from the fullness of our relationship with God, tending and nurturing that most important human relationship and developing the qualities that God desires in us wives. God grows in us a servant spirit and a heart filled with love that evidence themselves with that man. Soon this crystal pool of love swells until it cascades into the hearts of our children.

Yes, the hearts of our children are the next pool our love and energy are to fill. If God gives us children, He entrusts them to our care, to be loved and taught and trained and filled with the knowledge of Him. All that God has filled us with and all the blessings that spring from a love-filled, Christ-centered marriage overflow to refresh and supply the tender hearts of our dear children.

> *When we are faithful to follow after God's heart—when we tend and nurture each aspect of life as He instructs—the ministry He uses us in can have an impact beyond measure.*

The bounteous richness of our relationships with God, husband, and children then splashes into the next pool, filling our home with God's love and the beauty of family. The springs of God's love and care feed the spiritual life, family life, love life there in our refuge. Soon, too, this pool is filled to overflowing....

And then the waters rush down to the next level of need, satisfying our soul's desires. That rapidly filling lagoon is where dreams are dreamed, where we get a glimpse of what God wants you and me to do for Him and His people. Here we feel passionately that we want our lives to count. Here we desire to serve others according to God's purpose for us. Having been filled from the pools higher up the mountain, now we plunge in. We submerge ourselves in this fresh pool of knowledge, discipline, and training until, sure enough, the water level rises to the brink and surges beyond its limits, pouring forth into God's limitless ocean of ministry and service that builds His people up.

From our vantage point, as we reflect on how God might use us, we are silenced, awestruck. Now we understand! His ways are wise, and His ways work. When we are faithful to follow after God's heart—when we tend and nurture each aspect of life as He instructs—the ministry He uses us in can have an impact beyond measure.

Again, my heart sister, can you see it? Those seven pools show us how God can use our lives most effectively for His kingdom. God wants us to first touch those closest to us, but He can also use us to touch the multitudes. Having addressed the importance of spiritual growth, now I want us to look at how the water in that pool spills out into God's ocean of ministry. Let's consider some ways every Christian woman can influence the lives of others—countless others—for eternity. There is nothing listed here that you and I cannot do with God's help.

Learn to Reach Out

Again and again Jesus tells us to give—to give to everyone (Luke 6:30); to give hoping for nothing in return (verse 35); to give in the generous way God, who is kind to the unthankful and evil, gives (verse 35); and to care for others by giving (verse 38). You and I can learn to give in this way, to overflow with care for all others. Here are a few ideas.

Your presence and sometimes a single touch are worth a thousand words—When it comes to reaching out, remember this principle of ministry: Your very presence is a source of comfort. You may not have the exact words to say or the perfect Scripture to share.

But in many if not most situations, your touch can bring comfort far greater than words.

Be a giver—Just as you and I learned with our husbands and children, we can give the smile, the greeting, the warm question, the touch, the hug, and the name (always use the person's name!).

Be bold—Be bold and give to the people God places in your path. If, however, you find yourself avoiding a certain person, ask God to show you why. Sin in our hearts—hearts meant to overflow with care for others—keeps us from being confident in our relationships. So find out what is going on—or not going on—in your heart that's hindering your ministry. Then go a step further and decide what you will say the next time you see that person. Actively search for him or her and *give* the warm, friendly greeting you planned. With a heart clean before God, you should have nothing to hide, nothing to withhold. Learn to reach out to the people you meet up with every day.

Become a generous soul—Don't just give, but give liberally, cheerfully, bountifully, hilariously, extra, above and beyond (2 Corinthians 9:6-7)! "The generous soul will be made rich," Proverbs 11:25 informs us. But becoming that "generous soul" can be a process, and I've been in process for decades.

My husband, Jim, is this wonderfully generous soul who gives everything away. He's given away our cars, our groceries, our money, our savings, his suits, and our home to be used by others when we are away. I'm learning to be more generous, and one important lesson came when a couple from our home church showed me what it's like to be on the receiving end of such generosity. While we were missionaries in Singapore, they came for a visit. As we shopped the streets and harbor of that world-port city, Billie bought two of everything—and then gave the second of each (batik clothes, Christmas ornaments, china) to me when she left! What a joy to me—and what a privilege that you and I can give that kind of joy to others by giving generously.

It's been by God's blessing, but over the decades I've grown in this grace of giving. I remember growing to the point of conviction over my lack of generosity that I made "Giving" a category on my daily prayer list. In other words, I went after this Christlike character quality and trait God calls us to. I began to regularly ask God, "Who can I give to today? Who, Lord, is in need? How can I bless others with what You have blessed me with?" Yes, financial giving was part of what I was acting on. But I'm not just referring to money. No, our giving reaches into every part of our soul and our possessions. You and I have groceries in the pantry, clothes or baby items someone else could use, books that can encourage and edify others. We just need hearts that are open and generous.

Now, can you imagine how shocked I was when Jim and I were interviewed together on a Valentine's Day radio program where Jim was asked what he admired most about me...and he replied, "Elizabeth's generous heart. She is a very giving person." By God's grace and transforming power, *He* had worked that miracle in my heart...and He can do the same in yours.

Determine to withhold nothing—Proverbs 3:27 exhorts us, "Do not withhold good from those to whom it is due, when it is in the power of your hand to do so." What are some of the good things "in the power of your hand"? Praise, encouragement, thanks, a greeting, kindness, good deeds, and a note of appreciation are a few of the good things we hold. And you and I *choose* whether or not we will share these blessings.

I am encouraged each time I remember the first Bible lesson I ever taught. Our former pastor's wife hesitated and then made her way up the aisle afterwards. Struggling inside, she finally said, "I've been asking the Lord if I should say anything to you because I don't want this to go to your head or puff you up—but you are a good teacher!" Believe me, I will rarely suffer from overconfidence! My tendency is toward the other end of the scale, toward inadequacy, inferiority, and inability. But this esteemed woman chose not to withhold the good—those words of encouragement—when it was in the power of her hand (and heart) to give it. Let's make that same choice!

Learn to Look Out

I love the tender heart of the shepherd Jesus describes in Luke 15. When one of his 100 sheep was missing, he left the 99 and went looking for the one that was lost (verses 3-6). God cares for you and me this way, and He wants us to care for others this way too. Here are some tips for getting started.

Develop a "generous eye"—Solomon said, "He who has a generous eye will be blessed, for he gives of his bread to the poor" (Proverbs 22:9). I like to think of a generous eye as being like the eyes of God, which "run to and fro throughout the whole earth" (2 Chronicles 16:9). When I go into public places, I intentionally look for wounded sheep—and, believe me, they are there. I've found women in the ladies' room crying, sitting on the church patio weeping, standing behind our prayer room door sobbing. One night during church I sat beside a woman who cried for one-and-a-half hours! I could hardly wait for my pastor to finish praying so I could ask her, "Can I do *anything* to help you? Can I pray with you? Can I get you something? Would you like to talk?" People all around us need a tender word—or more. (Do you see why you and I must be developing and overcoming selfish tendencies? That way we can give to others.)

Be direct—Whenever you see a person in need, be direct. Walk straight up to the wounded sheep and see what she needs and what you can do. Don't hope someone else comes along. Don't run looking for the pastor. God has allowed *you* to find this person in need. Now allow *your* heart to overflow with care.

Go to Give

Missionary and martyr Jim Elliot once said, "Wherever you are, be all there. Live to the hilt every situation you believe to be the will of God."[1] I keep these words in mind whenever I attend any church or ministry event, and I go expecting God to use me. Here's an overview of my approach—and I encourage you to make it yours.

Be all there—Before I go to an event, I pray that I will go to give—to reach out, to look out, to be direct, to withhold nothing. Then, as I go, I put my thought life on guard. While I'm at Bible study, I don't want to be thinking about what I'm going to fix for dinner that night. During my pastor's message, I don't want to be planning my week. I don't want to be concerned about what happened before I got there or what will happen after the event. I want to be all there.

Live to the hilt!—Not only do I want to be all there, but I want to also live each moment to the hilt. And I like the advice of Anne Ortlund, a wife of a pastor. She encourages women to be "hanger-arounders."[2] As long as you're there, as long as you've given an evening or a morning to an event or Bible study or worship service, give totally. Try to reach out to as many sheep as you can. Minister to as many people as you can in as many ways as you can.

Divide and conquer—Agree with your closest girlfriends, mother, or daughter *not* to sit together, walk together, share coffee time together, or visit. Instead share the commitment to divide and conquer. Remember, you came to give! Your family and closest friends have greater access to your life, plenty of one-on-one time with you in private, so why should they also have all your public time? They can talk to you later. One friend and I have made a pact that when we find ourselves gravitating toward each other, one of us will announce, "Come on! Let's go touch some sheep!"

And one more word about going to give. You'll find yourself doing a lot of receiving—you'll find yourself quite blessed—as you let God use you in this way!

Develop Your Prayer Life

Have you noticed how again and again in this book we come back to prayer? A woman after God's own heart is a woman who prays. Her heart naturally overflows in prayer as well as care. And since praying for people is a powerful way to care for them, you and I should want to join with God in a ministry of prayer, a ministry that makes a huge difference in people's lives. Learn—as I have—from J. Sidlow Baxter's story about how he developed his prayer life.

> I found that there was an area of me that did not want to pray...[and] there was a part of me that did. The part that didn't was the emotions, and the part that did was the intellect and the will....

[So] I said to my will: "Will, are you ready for prayer?" And Will said, "Here I am, I'm ready." So I said, "Come on, Will, we will go."

So Will and I set off to pray. But the minute we turned our footsteps to go and pray all my emotions began to talk: "We're not coming, we're not coming, we're not coming." And I said to Will, "Will, can you stick it?" And Will said, "Yes, if you can." So Will and I, we dragged off those wretched emotions and we went to pray, and stayed an hour in prayer.

If you had asked me afterwards, Did you have a good time, do you think I could have said yes? A good time? No, it was a fight all the way.

What I would have done without the companionship of Will, I don't know. In the middle of the most earnest intercessions I suddenly found one of the principal emotions way out on the golf course, playing golf. And I had to run to the golf course and say, "Come back."…It was exhausting, but we did it.

The next morning came. I looked at my watch and it was time. I said to Will, "Come on, Will, it's time for prayer." And all the emotions began to pull the other way and I said, "Will, can you stick it?" And Will said, "Yes, in fact I think I'm stronger after the struggle yesterday morning." So Will and I went in again.

The same thing happened. Rebellious, tumultuous, uncooperative emotions. If you had asked me, "Have you had a good time?" I would have had to tell you with tears, "No, the heavens were like brass. It was a job to concentrate. I had an awful time with the emotions."

This went on for about two-and-a-half weeks. But Will

and I stuck it out. Then one morning during that third week I looked at my watch and I said, "Will, it's time for prayer. Are you ready?" And Will said, "Yes, I'm ready."

And just as we were going in I heard one of my chief emotions say to the others, "Come on, fellows, there's no use wearing ourselves out: they'll go on whatever we do."…

Suddenly one day [weeks later] while Will and I were pressing our case at the throne of the heavenly glory, one of the chief emotions shouted "Hallelujah!" and all the other emotions suddenly shouted, "Amen!" For the first time [all of me was involved] in the exercise of prayer.[3]

Prayer isn't easy! It's definitely a discipline, but it's also a ministry that flows from a full heart. Three decisions can help you place yourself before God so He can fill your heart with concern for others.

Determine a time—Just as Mr. Baxter looked at his watch and said, "It is time," we too ensure that the ministry of prayer takes place by establishing a set time for it. Schedule a time, turn off the phone, leave other things undone, and sit or kneel down… and pray.

> *By setting a time, determining a place, and having a plan, nothing and no one will be forgotten. Everything and everyone will be covered when you pray.*

Determine a place—Choose a location that is quiet, where you can be alone to "press *your* case at the throne of the heavenly glory."

Determine a plan—Use a notebook to help you organize

your ministry of prayer. In my notebook, I first list everyone I want to pray for. Then I decide how often I want (or time and urgency allows) to pray for each one. Some are daily (including my "enemies"—Luke 6:27-28), but most are weekly. Finally I assign a specific day to each category. I also keep a page for "special requests" and another for extended family members. Create as many pages and categories as you need to pray for the people God has placed in your life to care for.[4]

By setting a time, determining a place, and having a plan, nothing and no one will be forgotten. Everything and everyone will be covered when you pray. These practical steps enable us to fulfill God's desire that we be "praying always...with all perseverance and supplication for all the saints" (Ephesians 6:18).

Heart Response

Do you feel the mist on your face as you let God fill you? Are you aware of how full your heart is, the heart after God He has been growing in you while you read 19 chapters of this book? And do you sense how its overflow is tumbling and splashing into a sea of love for the people around you? It is a glorious experience to be filled to overflowing with the love of God and then to be used by Him!

I hope too that your heart is at rest and that you've found your deepest fulfillment in seeing how God extends His love to so many through you. First His love flows to those people closest to your heart, those people at home. Then His love moves on through you to invigorate and refresh countless others. As this happens, your gracious and generous God miraculously refills you, replacing and multiplying all that you selflessly give away to others.

As you consider this process, I pray that you are encouraged. Once you've tasted the blissful joy born of personal sacrifice (if you haven't already), I pray that your heart is filled with deep spiritual satisfaction and contentment. May you know beyond all doubt that your labor for the Lord is never in vain (1 Corinthians 15:58). And may you never grow weary of doing good, "for in due season [you] shall reap if [you] do not lose heart" (Galatians 6:9)! Ask God to give you a greater desire to serve Him and others. Go to Him for wisdom as you choose where and how to minister. And be sure you always make the time to fill your own heart so that you have something to give to others. Finally, look to God to give you strength for His work and a broader vision of the eternal value of serving Him and His people.

20

A Heart That Encourages

A good word makes [the heart] glad.
PROVERBS 12:25

Sitting in our Sunday school class, I listened and took notes as Jim continued his series on the "one anothers" in the New Testament. He was teaching about the ministries each of us Christians is to have to our fellow members of Christ's church. This particular Sunday Jim spoke on edifying one another—encouraging them, building them up, contributing positively to their lives, and benefiting them in some way.

Summarizing the lesson with a point of application, Jim challenged our class. He exhorted, "With every encounter, make it your aim that people are better off for having been in your presence. Try in every encounter to give something to the other person." I have never forgotten these words. What a great—and simple—way to positively influence the lives of other people. Everyone needs edification and encouragement, and we are free to offer that when we have hearts filled by God. Here are some hints for encouraging God's people.

Take Time to Be Filled

If you take time to sit at Jesus' feet and be filled by God's Spirit as you study the written Word, if you focus on overcoming internal obstacles to doing God's work, you will never lack for ministry. God's fullness in you will naturally overflow into the lives of others. I think immediately of two women who increased their ministry potential when they overcame their shyness.

Evangelist Corrie ten Boom had a problem with shyness. Determined to overcome it, she enrolled in a Dale Carnegie course so she could learn to talk to people. If she could talk to people, then she could witness to them about Jesus Christ. Developing herself in this way led to greater ministry.

You have more to give to your neighbor if you regularly place yourself before God and let Him grow you, strengthen you, transform you!

Mrs. Howard Hendricks is a pastor's wife who had a problem with shyness. Like Corrie ten Boom, Jeanne enrolled in a Dale Carnegie course and also a Toastmasters for Women to learn how to talk with people individually and in groups. Twice I've attended women's retreats where Mrs. Hendricks was the retreat speaker—speaking each time to more than 500 women. Developing herself led to more capable ministry.

Ministry and service to others is stimulated when we take the time to develop our skills and overcome our weaknesses— and that makes sense. After all, how much can a teacher teach, a counselor counsel, an administrator administrate? Only as far as each has grown! And each of us grows, each of us finds power and knowledge for overcoming personal weaknesses and for more effective ministry in Jesus Christ. And Jesus Himself said, " 'You shall love the LORD your God with all your heart, with all your soul, with all your strength, and with all your mind,' and 'your neighbor as yourself' " (Luke 10:27). You have more to give to your neighbor if you regularly place yourself before God and let Him grow you, strengthen you, transform you!

Memorize Scriptures of Encouragement

Do you remember when we discussed "salting" our children with truths from the Bible? Well, children are not the only people in your life who need salt! You can have the ministry of salting—the ministry of encouragement—with everyone you meet. If you "let your speech always be with grace, seasoned with salt" (Colossians 4:6), you will never fail to better the lives of those you encounter. Your life and lips will offer refreshing encouragement to all who cross your path. Like our Messiah, you will be able to "speak a word in season to him who is weary" (Isaiah 50:4).

> *If you are faithful to commit to memory selected gems from God's Word, you'll suddenly find them adding real substance to your conversations.*

But, as we've seen before, we can't give away what we do not possess. So it's good to memorize some pertinent words of encouragement from the Bible to share with people in need. Knowing Scripture gives you "a word in season," something timely and appropriate to the situation.

Think of the Scripture passages you memorize as a surgeon's instruments. The last things I saw before I slipped into unconsciousness before my own surgery several years ago were two trays of such instruments, one on the surgeon's right and one on his left. I remember thinking, "Look at all those instruments! All sizes! All shapes! All kinds! And so many of them! Whatever he needs is right there—ready for any and every purpose!"

That's what the Scriptures you've memorized become in the hands of God—instruments ready for any and every purpose. Whatever the need (in your own life as well as in the lives of those you talk with), every verse you know by heart is available, sharp, and ready for God to use to encourage a weary soul.

If you are faithful to commit to memory selected gems from God's Word, you'll suddenly find them adding real substance to your conversations. This is another natural overflow from a full heart—in this case, a heart filled to overflowing with God's Word. You'll find the content of the notes you write and the telephone calls you make taking on added depth. Your visits with others will become more meaningful as you share God's powerful truths and promises. In fact, because your heart is full of Scripture, you'll no longer be satisfied with meaningless, trivial conversations. Sharing God's Word will take your talks with others to deeper levels.

In case you're thinking, "But I can't memorize Scripture! I've tried, and it just won't work for me," I was recently in a friend's home whose pet parrot sang "The Star-Spangled Banner" in its entirety for me. As I stood there amazed at what I was hearing, I thought, *Well, if a parrot can learn "The Star-Spangled Banner," we human beings can all learn to memorize Scripture!* Think of the time it took for a bird to learn the melody and tune of such a complicated song. Surely you can learn a verse or two from God's Word. If you do, your filled heart will be a source of encouragement to many!

Make Phone Calls to Encourage

We are told in the Bible that "anxiety in the heart of man causes depression, but a good word makes it glad" (Proverbs 12:25), and you probably know that truth from experience. An easy way to encourage and make a heart glad is to reach out and touch someone by phone. I'm not talking about calling long lists of people or even making lengthy calls. A simple, quick call can do much to gladden the heart of the recipient.

I usually make these sunshine calls at about 5:30 in the afternoon. When my girls were at home, I would say to each one, "I have to make three phone calls. They won't take long, but I want to know if there's anything you need before I get on the phone." Speaking to Katherine and Courtney first conveyed to them their priority position in my heart over everyone else (including those I was calling). It also gave me the chance to take care of any of their needs before I got on the phone and to remind them that I wouldn't be available to them for a few minutes.

(And guess what? Today these years later, my two daughters are at the top of my list for making phone calls of encouragement. With seven little ones between them I know they need a good word now and then—even often! I know a familiar voice from someone who loves them can make their day...which is always busy and packed. I pray before I dial to be positive, energetic, uplifting. I pray to build them up, compliment them, remind them of their strengths, let them know how proud I am of them... and always express my respect for what good wives and moms they are. When they answer, the first thing I ask is, "Is this a good time to talk or would you like me to call you back?" And if they don't answer the phone, I leave a cheerful message that I'm thinking about them and will call again soon. In other words, I don't ask them to call me back. I've witnessed how hectic it can get in their homes, and they don't need one more thing—like "Return Mom's phone call" on their "to do" lists. My girls now live thousands of miles away on the east coast, but when they lived nearby I would also always ask, "How can I help you today? What needs to be done that I can do for you?"

Anyway, back to phoning others....When I call others, I say something like "I know you're about to eat—and so are we—but I haven't seen you lately, and I just had to give you a quick call and make sure you're all right." If there is a difficulty, I make an appointment to call back at a time when we can have a more lengthy and meaningful conversation. You and I can also reach out in this way to people recovering from illnesses or dealing with a crisis. The telephone offers us a very effective way to encourage others, and it takes very little effort. Most important to that ministry is a heart that cares!

When Jim pastored the senior citizens at our former church, I found that making phone calls was a simple way to encourage those in our class who were absent on Sundays. If they were ill or out of town they were thrilled that someone noticed, missed them, and checked up on them. My special friend Patty blesses me in the same way, leaving encouraging words on my answering machine when we haven't seen each other for a while. It always makes me smile to hear her message and know *someone* out there cares.

I use the internet too—24/7—as a tool for encouragement. How easy it is to sit down for a few seconds and dash off a few sentences to bolster a missionary on the other side of the world, a friend who has moved away, those in ministry at my church, a hurting woman....and, of course, my daughters.

Who can you share a smile with by phone or online?

Write Notes of Encouragement

Writing notes—again, by mail or email—to those who need encouragement is another way to share a good word that makes the heart glad (Proverbs 12:25). Again, when it came to the seniors Jim and I were shepherding, I would pray and ask God, "What can I—a young wife and mother—possibly give these saints? They have walked with You so long. They know You so well."

God was faithful to answer that plea from my heart. He showed me that I could write them encouraging notes. So when I took attendance each Sunday morning, I began noting who was absent, who was traveling, and who was ill. Later that afternoon at home, while the children napped and Jim and I relaxed, I wrote each of the missing sheep a note of encouragement. I just wanted to convey to them that we cared and were concerned as well as available—and that we looked forward to seeing them again soon.

The people I admire most in this area of note writing are those who set aside certain time slots in their day or week for the express purpose of writing notes and letters. It *is* a ministry! And if you're thinking again, "Oh, no! I'm already so busy. How can I add one more thing?" consider my simple approach. As I face a blank piece of notepaper, I tell myself, "Come on, Elizabeth, just three sentences!" Whether I'm writing to the sick, the bereaved, those in leadership, or a recent hostess, telling myself "Just three sentences!" gets me going.

> Sentence #1 conveys I miss you, I appreciate you, or I'm thinking of you.
>
> Sentence #2 lets readers know they are special to me and why.
>
> And sentence #3 says I'm praying for them and includes the verse I'm praying for them.

As you sit in bed or on a couch with your feet propped up, you can give this kind of encouragement to others out of your heart filled by God's love—and the recipients will be very blessed!

These days I try to carry with me a folder that contains the correspondence I need to answer, the names of those I need to thank in some way, and a liberal supply of notecards, envelopes, postcards, and stamps. I also carry my laptop computer, so that wherever I am—on a plane, in a hotel, waiting in an airport, relaxing at a conference center, waiting for my husband in the car, or sitting in the library, a coffee shop, or a pew at church a few minutes early—I can encourage others with a note. And so can you—in just three sentences!

Encourage Others Through Three Spiritual Gifts

When I read *Balancing the Christian Life* by theologian Charles Caldwell Ryrie, I discovered three more ministries that you and I—and all Christians—can have. In fact, as Dr. Ryrie pointed out, these three ministries are not only specific spiritual gifts, but they are commanded of all Christians. Dr. Ryrie describes them as "three of the [spiritual] gifts...probably all Christians could have and use if they would. They are ministering, giving, and showing mercy (Romans 12:7-8)."[1] Hear how Dr. Ryrie defines them:

> *Serving* is sometimes called help or ministering. "It is the basic ability to help other people, and there is no reason why every Christian cannot have and use this gift."
>
> *Mercy* is next. "Showing mercy is akin to the gift of ministering and involves succoring those who are sick or afflicted. 'Pure religion and undefiled before

God and the Father is this, to visit the fatherless and widows in their affliction' (James 1:27)."

Giving is another ministry you and I could—and should—be involved in. "Giving is the ability to distribute one's own money to others, and it is to be done with simplicity which means with no thought of return or gain for oneself in any way."[2]

Serving, mercy, and giving—each is a specific spiritual gift, but each is also commanded of us as Christians. *And* each was carried out and modeled for us by our dear Savior, in whose steps we are to follow. So commit now to kindle your efforts to serve, show mercy, and give—and thus fulfill the law of God and encourage His people.

Live Your Priorities

By living out your priorities you will teach and disciple many women—without saying a word. The best way to teach priorities to others is to model those priorities. After all—and this is another principle for us women after God's own heart—*one picture is worth a thousand words.* As we've discussed, God has given us such a picture in Proverbs 31:11-31. Here He paints a portrait of a woman living out her priorities. And have you ever noticed that none of her *words* are recorded? No, only her *works* survive.

By God's grace and in His power, you can encourage others just as this "wonder"ful woman encourages you. Simply concentrate on being who God wants you to be and doing what He wants you to do. Concentrate on mastering your priorities. Don't worry about organizing your thoughts, preparing a lesson, and getting up in front of a group. Just walk among the women at your church and in your neighborhood *doing* with all your heart what you are supposed to do.

Every Christian woman needs models and examples—and I am no different. I remember being a new Christian and going to church, looking for models. I carefully watched other Christian women. I observed how they behaved in church and even what they wore. Did they speak up in mixed groups? Did they pray out loud? I noted how they treated their husbands, how they showed respect, how they behaved as a couple in public. I also watched the moms with their children, noticing how they disciplined, the tone of voice they used when they spoke to their children, and even the expressions on their faces as they looked at their little ones. Nothing slipped by me because I knew I needed help!

> *Being what God wants you to be—being a woman after God's own heart—is a powerful ministry.*

As an experienced observer of other women, I know that *everything you do and don't do teaches*. Gossip may seem like a little thing, but when you don't gossip, you teach other women the beauty of obedience. When you say, "I'll have to ask my husband about that," you show other wives how to make their husbands a priority. When you plan your day around your children's schedules, you model for other moms respect and consideration for their children.

If you are in a phase of life that doesn't allow you to formally teach or lead or participate in a women's ministry, you're still teaching! Think about it this way—perhaps your very absence from those functions is teaching something about your priorities. Maybe some of the people who are in attendance shouldn't be there either.

Remember the quote I shared earlier? The wisdom goes like this: "We [must] say 'no' not only to things which are wrong and sinful, but to things pleasant, profitable, and good which would hinder and clog our grand duties and our chief work."[3] By now you are probably understanding more fully what your grand duties and chief work as a Christian woman, wife, mother, home manager, and worker in the church are. By now you know more clearly what God says is most important. Being what God wants you to be—being a woman after God's own heart—is a powerful ministry. Others can simply watch you and be encouraged in their own quest to follow God.

Heart Response

When you and I made our way through the section about our spiritual growth, we stretched ourselves. We set goals. We decided to do the work that growth requires. Our aim was to let God fill us up and prepare us for future ministry and service to others. Acknowledging that this would be hard but rewarding work, we forged ahead, increasing our knowledge and honing our skills.

Now consider the simplicity and ease of the ministries we've considered here!

✓ Writing a note
✓ Making a few phone calls
✓ Speaking words of grace
✓ Modeling God's priorities

Ministry is always a matter of the heart. If your heart is filled with a watchful concern for God's people, you will be privileged to refresh many souls in need of encouragement.

These are next to effortless. Each one, however, requires a heart filled with God's love and with sensitivity for others. Ministry is always a matter of the heart. *If* your heart is filled with a watchful concern for God's people, you will be privileged to refresh many souls in need of encouragement just like a rain cloud delivers much-needed moisture to a parched earth. I hope and pray your heart response to God will be to take the few moments these ministries call for and use them to share God's love with others.

Part 3

The Practice of God's Priorities

21

A Heart That Seeks First Things First

Early will I seek You.
PSALM 63:1

Step back with me for a moment to the Seven Sacred Pools mentioned in chapter 19. Remember how they illustrate the beauty of God's plan for our life as women after His heart. Like those sparkling pools, the unfolding of God's plan starts on the mountaintop. From there the view of life is breathtaking and sobering. Our vision of God and of His plan for us moves our hearts—His design is so pure, so right, so uncluttered, and it makes sense! Having seen the beauty of the vision, we now have to go forward and *do* God's will. So we take a deep breath and brace ourselves. But how do we get started? Where do we begin? The woman who wrote this poem after coming to the peak where you and I now stand may express what you're feeling.

> So much material,
> So much to learn,
> So much to change,
> An overwhelming concern.

"Something is better than nothing,"
We are told.
And, again, wisdom and understanding
Are better than gold.

Where do I begin? I'm not even thin!
I move one step forward—two back,
I find my priorities all out of whack.
I *want* to be on the right track.

Pray for me, I need it so,
For I've got a long way to go.
Many things are obvious today,
The answer to this dilemma—PRAY![1]

If these words could be yours, take heart! We haven't yet come to the end. God has more guidelines for *how* to live out His will. Furthermore, God makes His will known as we read His Word, pray, and seek counsel. And He always enables us to do His will. God's grace is always sufficient to the task (2 Corinthians 12:9-10)! In fact, He has already given you everything you need to live your life in full godliness (2 Peter 1:3), and you can do all things—you can be a woman after His heart—through the strength of Jesus (Philippians 4:13). Take heart as we look at some how-to's.

A Word About Priorities

Because our lives are complex and demanding, we need a plan if we are to live by God's priorities and obey His call to us. God's order for priorities makes the day-to-day, moment-by-moment decisions easier and simpler. I can tell you wholeheartedly that the life-management system presented in this book works. It has brought order to my cluttered life and enabled me to see more clearly when the storms of life start to rage. God's unchangeable Word has given me sure guidance when the tyranny of the urgent beats on my door, trying to shove aside the very few *really* important tasks in my life—my grand duties and my chief works of:

- Loving God and following after Him with a whole heart,
- Loving, helping, and serving my husband,
- Loving and teaching my two daughters and their families,
- Loving and caring for my home in order to provide a quality life for my family,
- Developing myself so that I have something to give to others, and
- Loving and serving God's people.

Practicing these priorities calls us to wear many hats, and we must wear all of them—but we can only wear one at a time! Knowing what your priorities are—and choosing to wear the right hat at the right time—keeps you fully focused on the most important thing at hand at any given minute.

Remember, too, that these priorities are offered to you to help you make decisions about how to spend your time and energy. They are offered not as rigid guidelines, but to help you gain greater control over your life. This list of priorities and the discussion of them is meant to give you knowledge, skills, and motivation as you follow after God. So as you strive to live according to God's priorities, don't forget the principle of flexibility. Just as Jesus stopped and ministered to the bleeding woman on His way to raise Jairus' dead daughter (Luke 8:41-56), we need to be flexible, evaluating along the way—with each new event, crisis, or person—what the *real* priority is for that moment.

A Word About Choices

You've heard me say it many times, and here I go again! "The choices we make are key to the priorities we practice." From the first pages of this book, we've been trying to choose good over evil, better over good, and best over better. The importance of such choices cannot be overestimated or overemphasized. As we've all heard, if you want to know what you'll be like in the future, just look at the choices you are making today. As now, so then! It's something of a riddle.

> *Our choices, which reflect our priorities, will help us fulfill God's design for our lives.*

And so are these two thoughts: "What you are today (based on the choices you're making) is what you are becoming" and "You are today what you have been becoming (based on the choices you've already made)." Our choices, which reflect our priorities, will help us fulfill God's design for our lives. Getting everything done—or deciding what doesn't need to be done—is a matter of choice. Whether you are dealing with the next five minutes, the next hour, tomorrow, or forever, the choices you make make all the difference in the world!

A Word About Others

Have you noticed that we haven't yet gotten to some areas of life? I haven't mentioned parents, brothers, sisters, or extended family. And we haven't discussed jobs or careers, friends, neighbors, hobbies, pastimes, social life, or a myriad of other ingredients that make up your full and unique life. All these elements need to

be addressed and managed as we live a life that pleases God—
and all of them are to be enjoyed!
As the Bible says, "God...gives
us richly all things to enjoy"
(1 Timothy 6:17).

To adequately discuss the
long list of other people and
other ventures God has put into
your life would require another

> *God will reveal your priorities when you pray, search the Scriptures, and seek wise counsel.*

book. So for now, simply add those "other" categories to the end
of the list of the six priorities you've just looked at because those
six don't change. Each of these six aspects, these six roles we play,
is specifically addressed in the Bible. We've been looking at *God's*
plan, *God's* priorities, *God's* assignments. Our life situation may
change, but God's Word never changes. As the psalmist proclaims,
"The counsel of the LORD stands forever, the plans of His heart
to all generations" (Psalm 33:11)!

So I will leave it to you to prioritize the remaining areas of
your life. God will reveal the order to you when you pray, search
the Scriptures, and seek wise counsel. He will show you how to
be a woman after His heart in every detail of your life!

A Word About Waiting

It's impossible to read the book of Proverbs and not get the
message that *wisdom waits*. As a general principle for practicing
your priorities, know that it is safer to wait and do nothing than
to rush in and do the wrong thing. One of the many proverbs
that expresses this biblical truth says, "He sins who hastens with
his feet" (Proverbs 19:2).

Let me share how we applied this *wisdom waits* principle in
our home one hot summer day. The phone rang, and the call was

for my daughter Katherine from a friend I had neither met nor ever heard of. This teenage girl was inviting my daughter to go to the beach right away. Her message was, "We're leaving right now, and we'll pick you up in 15 minutes!"

Well, Katherine didn't go to the beach that day. Why? First of all, our day was already planned ("Plan A is always best" is one of my mottoes), and it didn't include her going to the beach. Also, Jim and I had not met this group of friends (Who was driving? Would boys be going?). This plan was definitely something we could say no to. And we could—and did—wait for a planned beach outing later on.

A friend of mine also had an opportunity to wait. Her mother-in-law was demanding a written letter of apology regarding a very difficult situation—and she wanted it *right now! It had to go out in today's mail so she could have it tomorrow or else!* My friend sent the letter—a week later. Why? Because she wanted to pray, have her heart right, share with her husband, seek counsel, and then have someone read the letter to help her word it so that it would truly accomplish God's purposes, which were indeed better served by waiting.

I myself had an opportunity to practice the *wisdom waits* principle when a breathless salesman called. "I'm calling from right around the corner," he said. "We're in your neighborhood today—and today only. This is the chance of a lifetime. We can clean all your carpets *right now* for only xxx dollars, *but it has to be right now!*" I didn't take him up on this deal. Why? Because, again, I'd already made plans for the day and they didn't include moving all our furniture and having all the carpets cleaned. They didn't include that kind of chaos. (We like to plan our chaos!) Also, I hadn't discussed having the carpets cleaned with my husband. Although it sounded like a bargain price to me, I'm not so sure

Jim would have thought that was the *best* use of that amount of money "*right now!*" Good, maybe, but best? Not so sure.

As that carpet cleaning offer illustrates, the telephone gives us a chance to practice the *wisdom waits* principle. It's always ringing, demanding our attention and presenting opportunities to get off our Plan A track. But you and I don't have to give those opportunities attention *right now!* Instead, we simply have to decide who's in control. Choosing to wait rather than acting impulsively is one way to gain or stay in control. A quote I've written in my prayer notebook reminds me that "very few things in life call for an instantaneous decision on your part....Keep your cool.... Make delay your first strategy for avoiding [chaos and crisis].... A good rule of thumb to remember is that most things seem more important in the present than they actually are."[2] Wisdom waits. Will you?

Some Women Who Adjusted Their Priorities

One evening as I was reading (my "I'm going to read for just five minutes" time), I was struck by an account of a woman who seriously wanted to be God's kind of woman. Her name was Irene, and she was a Bible teacher much in demand. Her husband, Mike, however, was a nominal Christian who went to church but didn't get any more involved than that. Irene's priority list looked like this:

- God
- Teaching women's Bible studies
- Family

One day the Lord spoke to Irene through a verse in Ephesians: "Wives be subject—be submissive and adapt yourselves—to your own husband as (a service) to the Lord" (5:22).[3] When she saw this familiar verse in a different translation, Irene realized that serving her husband was a ministry, a service to the Lord. She began to seriously evaluate her life and her priorities.

Did she really love Mike? Did she put him first? She was everything to the Christian community she served, but not everything to Mike.

Irene dropped her outside activities and began to spend more time with Mike. When the church asked her to teach, she declined. When a friend asked her to lead a home Bible study, she refused. She stayed home with Mike. She watched TV with him, jogged with him, played cribbage, and made love to him. Irene dropped out of the picture as far as a visible Christian ministry was concerned. It was painful.

The subsequent two years were like "walking in a dark valley." Mike continued as a so-so Christian. Then in the middle of the third year, something stirred in Mike. He began to lead devotions and to do some teaching. His commitment to Christ solidified, and God began to develop him into a Christian leader. Irene realized that if she had remained in the limelight, Mike would have been too threatened to venture out. Today, at Mike's insistence, they teach together a class for couples. They have new priorities:

- God
- Each other
- Teaching Bible studies[4]

Irene took the significant step and reordered her priorities. Do you need to do the same? If so, please do it!

In another true story, a woman named Pat told of her ministry to inner-city kids. After a planning session for a theatrical production aimed at keeping the kids off the streets that summer, Pat dashed home at noon to see how her kids were doing.

As she arrived at the house, a police car pulled up behind her. Sitting in the backseat were her eight- and nine-year-old sons—frightened to death. While she was gone, the two boys had taken some matches from her kitchen and gone to a vacant lot to light firecrackers. The lot had caught fire, and the boys were apprehended by the neighbors.

It suddenly became obvious to Pat which kids she should be trying to keep off the streets that summer. She called the inner-city office and resigned![5]

Pat reordered her priorities. Again, do you need to do the same? And again, if so, please do it now!

Heart Response

It sure is easy for priorities to get "out of whack," as my poet friend said! And making the choices to get back on track can sure be tough. But Irene and Pat are like you and me—wanting to do all God's will—and therefore willing to make the right choices even though they're the hard choices.

Is God speaking to you right now about how you are living your life? Is time with Him the first thing you seek each new day? David cried out to God in the wilderness:

> O God, You are my God;
> Early will I seek You;
> My soul thirsts for You;
> My flesh longs for You
> In a dry and thirsty land
> Where there is no water
> (Psalm 63:1).

Without a regular time with God, your Ultimate Priority, your life will be a dry and barren wilderness, and everything and everyone in it—including you—will suffer.

Continue now to move through the list of our priorities and evaluate how you're doing. Are you neglecting any of your priority people—your husband or your children? Is your home blossoming into a haven of rest, refreshment, beauty, and order for you and your loved ones? Are you using the firstfruits of your free time to be filled spiritually so that you can serve God and His people? And, finally, when you are with other people, are they refreshed by you, receiving out of the overflowing refreshment you find in the Lord? Put simply, are you seeking first things first—every day?

22

Following After God's Heart

My soul follows close behind You.
PSALM 63:8

If you and I are meeting for the first time in this book, you haven't yet visited my friend Judy's garden. In *Loving God with All Your Mind*,[1] I described the planning and planting Judy did. Now, these years later, I wish you could see her lovely and serene country garden. Judy has added much for her visitors to ooh and aah over. One of those additions is the arbor that her white iceberg roses have claimed as their own.

Whenever I stand on Judy's porch, my eye travels first to that sweet arbor, a quaint reminder of times gone by. The urge to stroll down the pressed gravel path that passes through its magical opening is irresistible. A delight to the senses, this gracious rose arbor provides gentle fragrance, cool shade, and refreshing beauty—and I'm never alone as I approach. Birds, butterflies, and

> *When you and I take seriously our assignments from God, He blesses our obedience, and the resulting growth is astounding.*

the neighbor's cat are also drawn there. All creatures—great and small—love Judy's rose arbor.

Needless to say, something this lovely is certainly no accident, and it didn't happen instantaneously. Much time and attention went into creating this lovely garden retreat, and the time and effort continue. Judy works hard tending her arbor, first faithfully feeding and tilling and watering the ground in the cool, early-morning stillness. Then, retrieving her sharpened shears from the storage shed, Judy begins the painstaking routine of cutting away unruly growth, pruning off unnecessary shoots, and removing dead blossoms. Performing this surgery—removing anything that would hinder the formation and development of her roses—is a crucial task. The meticulous training still remains to be done, and Judy does this by tacking down and wiring her roses, interweaving the loose branches and blooms, carefully directing and redirecting their growth. People enjoy a place of great beauty because of Judy's labor of love.

And, dear friend and follower after God's heart, people enjoy the beauty in our lives, our families, and our homes when we work in the same diligent and deliberate way Judy does. When you and I take seriously our assignments from God, He blesses our obedience, and the resulting growth is astounding. Oh, there are pleasant tasks and bright moments, but there is also plain old hard work—work that may be unexciting but gives birth to God's blessings.

As we end this book committed to following hard and close after God (as David did in Psalm 63:8) and doing His will (Acts

13:22), let's consider what we can do to nurture, prune, and train our hearts so that we can enjoy the lovely fruit God intends His people to know when they honor Him. What can we do to place ourselves before God so that we can know His beauty and serenity in our hearts and under our roofs?

Plan Your Day

Making God's plan for our lives a reality calls for planning on our part. The first challenge we face is gaining control of one day—today. We must tackle the day at hand, and—as I mentioned before—I find it helpful to consider each day's agenda at least twice.

First, the night before, when you climb into your wonderful, welcoming bed, take your planner with you (or a 3" x 5" card, or a "to do" list, or a legal pad—whatever). As you sit there relaxing, list in chronological order the concrete events of the next day—any appointments, meetings, or classes, the carpool, school and work schedules, and breakfast, lunch, and dinner. Whisper a prayer to God asking Him to guide and bless the next day— His day—and then turn off the light. You'll find that these few minutes can reduce the number of surprises in the morning— surprises like, "Oops, I forgot you needed a lunch!" "Now where is that dry cleaning?" "I can't believe I didn't cancel that dental appointment!" and "Oh no, it's trash day, and I forgot again!"

In the morning, welcome the day with the psalmist's words of praise—"This is the day the LORD has made; we will rejoice and be glad in it" (Psalm 118:24). Then take out a sheet of paper and get ready to create a plan for practicing God's priorities throughout the day. (I use an 8½" x 11" sheet of paper folded in half lengthwise.) Begin by praying.

Pray Over Your Plans and Priorities

What exactly should you pray about? Let me share some ideas by describing how I create a plan for practicing God's priorities.

God—First I write the word "God" on one side of my folded paper, and pray, "Lord, what can I do today to live out the fact that You are the Ultimate Priority of my life?"

As I pray, God usually leads me to list certain actions like pray, read His Word, memorize Scripture, walk with Him, be aware that He is present with me minute by minute. I write it all down.

Husband—Next I write the word "Jim." Again I go to the Lord for help, asking, "God, what can I do today to let Jim know he is my most important human priority?" (And if you're not married, move on down the list.)

At that point, for instance, God reminds me that I can choose to be "up" when Jim arrives home at the end of the day and to stay "up" throughout the evening. I can choose to be physically available to him. I can make plans for a special date night on Friday when the children are busy with their activities. And of course I can sew on that button!

Children—Now it's time to pray, "Lord, what can I do today for Katherine and Courtney to let them know that, after Jim, they are more important than all the other people in my life? What can I do to communicate to each one individually how special she is to me? How can I show each of them my love?" (Again, if you don't have children, move on down the list.)

Many times the answers to this question are "sweet speech," "kindness," "a servant spirit," and "no nagging." Just write down the answers and ideas. For instance, when my girls were toddlers, I scheduled specific times during each day to set aside all other activities and have a special time of playing or reading with them.

Other ideas that came to me as I prayed about my girls included, as they grew older, selecting a special card for each of them and writing a love note, or picking up some fresh bagels as I came home from Bible study, or preparing a favorite snack for them after school, or surprising them by picking them up after school for a cola instead of having them come home in the carpool.

Now that my girls are married, I make plans to communicate daily with each through email and to send them good books as little surprise gifts to help them build their own homes and encourage them in their personal growth and interests. Truly, the loving and praying and planning never cease. And then there are the grandchildren! Well, you get the picture.

Home—Everyone lives somewhere, including you, married or not. So land here and start praying because this one's for everyone. As I shared earlier, praying about homemaking lifts it out of the physical realm and transports it into the spiritual. So I pray, "Lord, what can I do today regarding my home? What can I do today to make our home a little bit of heaven, our own home sweet home?"

Something like "be faithful in daily cleaning tasks" will appear on my home list. "Finish fully" appears almost daily because it's a character quality and discipline I'm working on right now—especially in the evenings after dinner when I'm tired. I also write down special projects like "pull out dead summer flowers to make way for fresh autumn ones" and "research a remodel."

Self—I lay my life before God and pray, "Lord, what can I do today to grow spiritually? In what specific ways can I prepare for future ministry?"

Always the word *read* appears. "Exercise" and "food selection" show up often. Completing a Bible lesson, typing out quotations from books I've read, and getting to bed on time are other items. This is truly and by necessity a diverse list that suggests the wide-ranging activities and interests of life.

Ministry—"And, Lord," I continue praying, "what can I do today to serve and minister to Your people?" This is always the longest list as I write down people to call, friends and missionaries to write, lessons to plan, organizing, researching, writing, purchasing name tags, preparing food for church events or the ill, visiting the hospital. Opportunities for ministry are always all around us!

Because this list is so long, I go one step further. I ask God to help me prioritize it by praying, "God, if I could only do one of these labors of love today, which one would You want it to be? And if I could do two?"

Other activities—As I've continually said, this book focuses on our top priorities, those God-given assignments found in His Word. But I know (and certainly God does too) there are other facets to life. That's why I think of living out our priorities as being somewhat like an oil painting. The artist includes the elements of a painting—background, composition, subjects, style. The Impressionists, however, discovered that dotting an entire completed canvas with spots of another color added sparkle to the picture.

The same is true of our lives. We must follow all the rules and guidelines—as set forth by God in the Bible—so that our lives will contain all the elements necessary for beauty. But God, "who gives us richly all things to enjoy" (1 Timothy 6:17), blesses us with dots of color—with people, events, interests, desires, personalities, and challenges that add a unique sparkle.

In this category, then, I list shopping for Christmas, browsing in a library or bookstore, getting together with a friend, planning another trip to visit one of my daughters, replacing a pair of shoes. Again, this list goes on and on—its items are important, but not urgent.

Schedule Your Plans and Priorities

Now I have my list, and I can carry this handy piece of paper around all day, or put it on the refrigerator door, or lay it on the kitchen counter, or tape it onto my computer monitor. But items on the list only represent dreams and desires and convictions until we put them into practice. And scheduling helps us do just that. So at this point I put the other side of my paper to use. It becomes my schedule for practicing my priorities for the day. This is Round 2 in praying over and planning my day—a day I desire to live after God's heart.

I begin praying again, "Okay, God, *when* will I have my devotions? *When* will I meet with You in our special place?" I then write "devotions" in a specific time slot on my schedule. "And *when* will I sew on that button for Jim...and plan our Friday date?" I jot these down for precise times as well. "And *when* will I get those blueberry bagels for my blueberry girl?...Do those daily good housekeeping chores?...Read and exercise—even for five

> *If you follow these steps of planning, praying, and scheduling, you soon discover how comforting it is to get up from your time of prayer with a clear plan for your day.*

minutes!" I ask the Lord when to do all those things He and I both want done, and I write them all into my schedule for certain times during the day.

When my time of prayer and scheduling is over, I hold in my hand a master plan for the day—a plan that reflects my priorities, a plan that enables me to be the woman after God's own heart that I desire to be. Wisdom always has a plan (Proverbs 21:5).

If you follow these steps of planning, praying, and scheduling, you'll soon discover how comforting it is to get up from your time of prayer with a clear plan for your day. That plan is most effective when it comes as a result of much care and prayer—when it comes as a result of committing your day and its activities to God for His glory, when it comes from seeking God for guidance on the good, the better, and the best. Having made this kind of commitment and having done this seeking, determine to stick to your plan—God's plan.

Practice Your Priorities

Each day presents many opportunities and challenges to practice our priorities. One way to simplify your moment-by-moment decision-making might be to assign your priorities these numbers:

#1 — God

#2 — Your husband

#3 — Your children

#4 — Your home

#5 — Your spiritual growth

#6 — Your ministry activities

#7 — Other activities

Let me show you how this works.

- Your children (#3) have just arrived home from school, and you're praying and snacking and talking together about the day. The phone rings. It's not your husband (#2), which means it is either a ministry (#6), a friend (#7), or a salesperson. The decision is simple. You don't leave the #3 priority to tend to the #6 or #7 (or even lower) priority. Be sweet and be kind…but be firm and be brief. Make arrangements for a call back. Quickly ask the salesperson to remove your name and number from his or her call list. Don't lose this important time with your children!

- Your neighbor (#6—a ministry) knocks on the door and interrupts your time with your children (#3). What are you going to do? Again, I learned to be sweet and be kind… but be firm and be brief. Reschedule a visit for a time when the children are settled or busy with homework. Edith Schaeffer suggests you say something like this:

  > "I will see you later; right now I am having a half hour (or an hour) with Naomi." You should use the name of the [child]. When you say, "I am talking to Debby [your child]," you are stating to yourself as well as to the person, "This is a human being I have an important appointment with." Your child is a person…and children need to grow up knowing they are important to you, that their lives are valuable to you.[2]

- Your husband (#2) is home and the house is quiet as you share a few rare minutes together—and the phone rings. It's a woman needing counsel (#6), a friend who wants to chat (#7), or another salesman. The decision is straight-forward, and you know it already. Be sweet and be kind... but be firm and be brief. Reschedule the visit for a time your husband (#2) is not at home.

These actions may sound harsh and heartless—like Judy cutting and training her roses on her arbor—but making these choices to live your priorities enables God to make your life a work of beauty. It's hard to make these choices and, yes, it can hurt, but they are necessary if our lives are to be what you and I—and God—desire them to be.

But take note. This planning—as important as it is—goes out the window in a true emergency. When Jim's mother was hospitalized, for instance, *all* activity ceased as Katherine and her husband, Paul, and I came alongside her. You can defi-nitely regard a true need like this as God's new plan for your day...or three days. But our goal is to be discreet (Titus 2:5)—meaning women who are thinking things through and show-ing good judgment.

A woman of discretion thinks through her choices and the messages they deliver to her husband, her children, her neighbor. A woman of discretion thinks a situation through and consid-ers all possible consequences, both good and bad. She weighs everything and—after some time spent praying, waiting on God, seeking His wisdom, and getting godly counsel—makes the right decision. You and I can do the same as we follow after God's heart!

Acquire God's Perspective on Your Day

As I prayerfully prioritize the activities of my day, God grants me a glimpse of His will for all the days of my life and that day in particular. This prioritizing also gives me a passion for what I am trying to achieve with my life efforts.

That passion has also been fueled by the following comments I first heard at a women's retreat when I was a young wife, the mom of two preschoolers, and about to enter the "Age 31" group (see below). Since the day I first heard these statements, they have motivated me to follow after God's plan for my life with all my heart, soul, mind, and strength. I want to pass these women's statements on to you in hopes that they will help fuel your passion and vision for God and His calling to you. But first let me set the stage.

A reporter interviewed four women and asked each of them what she thought about "the golden years," that period in life "after middle age traditionally characterized by wisdom, contentment, and useful leisure." Hear their thoughts—and fears.

> *Age 31:* "Golden years? I have so much to do before then that I doubt I'll ever have them. I have to help my husband succeed. I want to raise our children decently to get them ready for a very tough world. And, of course, I want time for me, to find myself, to be my own person."

> *Age 44:* "Only 20 years to go! I just hope we make it. If we can just get the kids through college and on their own, if we can just keep my husband's blood pressure under control and see me sanely through menopause....I'm just hoping we get there."

> *Age 53:* "Doubtful. Sometimes I think our golden years will never come. My parents are still alive and need constant attention. Our daughter was divorced

last year and lives with us again. Of course, she had a baby. And of course my husband and I feel responsible both for her and our grandson."

Age 63: "We're supposed to be on the brink, aren't we? Well, we're not. I'll be frank. We thought we were saving enough to live comfortably ever after, but we haven't. Inflation has eaten it up. Now my husband talks about deferring his retirement. If he does, so will I. We're keeping a house much too big for us. We're both unhappy about the way things have turned out."

Sobering comments, aren't they? As you and I stand looking down the corridor of time, life can appear so hopeless, so pointless, so futile. But now for God's vision, a godly perspective! It comes from a dear friend to whom I sent a copy of what you've just read. Here's her inspiring response:

Oh, Elizabeth—to treat each day as if it and it *alone* was our "golden day"—then what a beautiful string of golden days becoming golden years we would have to give back again to our Lord!

Imagine being a woman who treats each day as if it and it alone is her golden day! Now *that's* a woman after God's own heart. When I thought about this, I said, "That's it! Treating each day as if it and it alone is our golden day is the *how* of practicing priorities, and it's also the *why*—the motivation and the perspective we need—for practicing them."

Practice, Practice, Practice

That's what I want for you and me. I want us to approach each day as our golden day! To switch metaphors, I want your life and mine to be like a string of pearls, strung with day after day of precious days.

If you desire a good life, focus on having one good day, one quality day—today. After all, as someone has observed, "Every day is a little life, and our whole

> *Every day is God's gift of a fresh, unspoiled opportunity to live according to His priorities.*

life is but a single day repeated." So keep that focus on having a good day today and, at day's end, slip that single pearl onto your strand. The pearls on your strand will add up to a good life!

But what if yours was a day of failures? A day of merely trying to survive? A day of taking shortcuts? A day of neglecting things you wanted to focus on? We all have those days. But thanks be to God who enables us to forget the day that is done, to reach forward the next morning, and to press on toward the goal—the pearl—again and again and again (Philippians 3:13-14)! In His power and by His grace, we keep following after God's heart—no matter what.

After all, every morning He gives you a fresh new day, His gift of a fresh, unspoiled opportunity to live according to His priorities. Furthermore, by exercising the privilege of confession and because of Jesus' forgiveness, you have a clean start with the dawn. God's mercies are new every morning, and His faithfulness is great (Lamentations 3:22-23)! So every morning remember that your goal is simple. You want to have just one good day of living your priorities. Then keep focused on following God's plan for your life for just this one day. For just one day, try putting first things first.

When such a focused day is done, you'll probably be tired as you drop into bed. I know I am! But you'll also know an unmatchable peace in your heart. A peace that comes from resting in the Lord and doing things His way. A peace that comes from knowing that because you lived out God's priorities for you, all is well under your roof.

Why this peace? Because you sought the Lord and followed close after Him the whole day! The people in your life were loved and served out of the overflow of your full heart. Your home was cared for—and God's beauty and order reigned there in the refuge you created. You took care of yourself and grew as God stretched you in preparation for serving Him. And you did serve—anyone and everyone who crossed your path. You reached out, looked out, gave out, and lived out God's priorities for a woman after His heart.

And then there were the other things—perhaps your dear parents, needy souls at your place of employment, special friends,

So at the end of your day, your heart is satisfied and content. You have done the giving, the living, the following, and the loving. In return, God satisfied your longing heart and filled your hungry soul with his goodness.

time with a hurting neighbor, crafts to be made for giving away at the appropriate time. On and on your golden day went as you looked to God for His guidance, wisdom, and strength, as you loved Him by faithfully obeying Him, and as you leaned on Him during the challenges and trials of the day.

It was indeed a full day—but oh, what a rich one. And yes, your body is tired—but oh, what a satisfying tiredness. And, yes, it may not look like you've done much (there's no big splash, no headline news, nothing to tell anyone about)—but oh, the depth of the fullness you sense in your heart as God whispers to you, "Well done!"

As you finally stretch out in bed, wearily pull up the covers, and sink your head into the waiting pillow, you can know you have slipped another pearl onto your strand. This costly pearl is the most magnificent prize awaiting a woman after God's own heart. The reward for living life God's way is immeasurably, unspeakably, and indescribably wonderful. I'm struggling to find the words.

So at the end of your day, your heart is satisfied and content. You have done the giving, the living, the following, and the loving. In return, God satisfied your longing heart and filled your hungry soul with His goodness (Psalm 107:9). The peace you sense is the satisfaction that comes from gladly being spent in doing God's will, from being a woman after God's own heart—for just one day.

Now…let that one day—that one step—encourage you to string your *daily* pearls into a *lifetime* of living as a woman after God's own heart!

Part 4

In Praise
of God's Priorities

23

The Legacy of A Woman After God's Own Heart

For David,
after he had served his own generation
by the will of God, fell asleep.
ACTS 13:36

In the first few pages of this book I asked you to carefully consider David's usefulness to God as reported in Acts 13:22: "[God] raised up for them David as king, to whom also He gave testimony and said, 'I have found David the son of Jesse, a man after My own heart, who will do My will.'" Even with all of his faults, David had a heart for God—he desired to do God's will.

And now, dear heart sister, you and I have come full circle in our study of David's heart for God and our own full hearts. The apostle Paul's account of David's life began with an evaluation of

David's heart, and it ends with the results of his heart's commitment—David "served his own generation by the will of God"
(Acts 13:36).

David's last will and testament is that his life had an impact.
He served his own generation by the will of God. Why...and
how? Because David chose to submit his heart and service to
God's will, not his own.

Ten Years Later...

It's been much more than ten years since I began teaching this
material about becoming a woman after God's own heart. In this
book...and when given the opportunity to speak on this topic...
I have attempted to give you a glimpse into some of my own
personal struggles as I desired and sought to become a woman
after God's own heart, a woman who desires to do God's will.
It certainly hasn't been easy. Sometimes I take one step forward
and then quickly fall two steps back.

But energized and encouraged by the grace of God and
propelled by my heart's desire to love God through obedience, I
continued to move forward, be it ever so slowly. You see, I wanted
(and still want) to serve my "own generation"—especially my
husband and children, and now seven new members of a new
generation! I wanted (and still want) my family to have the best
I could be and the best I could give. And I wanted (and still do)
to do it God's way—by following God's will, God's plan.

In the decade since I initially wrote this book, I have had great
positive feedback from women like you who have read this book,
or heard me speak on some portion of it, or participated in one
of the "A Woman After God's Own Heart" video classes. So now
I want to take these final few pages and share my own reflections
on the past decade and also some reflections from others.

Reflections from a Woman After God's Own Heart

During these past ten-plus years, my life has changed dramatically. Our daughters met and married their wonderful husbands, had their babies, and their families have moved to the far ends of the United States (we live on the West Coast and they now live on the East Coast). On the other end of our lives, I lost both of my parents, and Jim lost his mother, his last living parent. Jim retired from The Master's Seminary to write and speak full time (which means he and I are not only busier than ever, but we are together 24/7!).

Believe me, nothing has slowed down. No, we moved quickly from the fast lane right into warp speed! We now have our daughters and sons-in-law and seven grandchildren, to whom we are fiercely committed. Plus both of us are writing daily as well as speaking on a regular basis while still growing in the Lord.

But even with all of these changes—and through them all—the priorities I write about in this book have been my guiding beacon. And, praise God, He has sustained me and enabled me to stay on target—to love Him first and passionately, to be the best wife and mom and grandmom I can possibly be, to continue growing in my knowledge of God, and to serve Him and His people. How can this be? Certainly it is to the praise of God's all-sufficient grace. And also partly it is because I have attempted with my whole heart (I hope and pray!) to practice and order my life by the priorities I talk about in this book—priorities I learned from God's manual for all of life, the Bible. I desired (and still do) and prayed (and still do) to have a heart that obeyed each and every time a new or difficult challenge came along. And, praise God again, I have witnessed and experienced His blessings!

How I would love to say I passed each test with flying colors!

But sadly, at times I slipped up. (I have my share of sad or bad memories.) But God, who knows all, knew my heart. He knew that I dearly wanted to follow Him, and His grace was definitely substantial, adequate, and enough—totally sufficient!

As I have reviewed this book and made the important updates and revisions, I have to say that these principles truly worked in my life…and still do. Through the decades and seasons of Christian growth and marriage and family and change, I have repeatedly revisited the priorities I wrote about in this book. And I have to report, I am convinced more than ever, that if I, or you, will follow God's priorities for us, our lives, as well as the lives of our loved ones and the lives of others who watch us or who are mentored by us, will be forever positively impacted. And on top of that, miracles of miracles, God will be honored and glorified (Titus 2:5)!

Reflections from Other Women After God's Own Heart

As Jim and I travel, I have the opportunity to meet and interact with thousands of wonderful Christian women. I also hear from thousands of others through mail and email. I am not one who saves letters and email, although I do try to answer each woman. (And during the process of revisiting this book, I wished I had saved both the communication from women and my responses to them!) What I wish to do here is share with you a composite of what so many have written. Perhaps you'll find your own heart response here.

Wives of many years—This band of married-for-many-years women has discovered and testified that "it's never too late to begin practicing your priorities." It's never too late to begin to follow God's commands and live out your assignment from God as a loving and supportive wife.

Let me give you one little story...

> At a woman's conference, I was sitting at the autographing table and a young woman and her mother came through the line to have me sign their well-worn copies of *A Woman After God's Own Heart*®. The daughter playfully poked her mom with her elbow and said, "Go ahead, Mom. Tell Mrs. George what happened." And so Mom shared!
>
> It seems that after the daughter and her mom began reading this book, the mom (married, lo, almost 40 years!) began practicing some of the principles I lay out in the "husband section." Her husband was in the process of retiring and took advantage of an exit physical exam provided by his company. Well, several weeks after the exam he asked his wife, "Honey, am I dying?"
>
> Stunned, she asked, "Why, no, not that I know of? Why? Why would you ask such a thing?"
>
> Her husband explained, "Well, I haven't heard anything from the doctor, and I thought maybe he had called you with bad news—to let you know I was dying—and that's why you have been so nice to me."

One absolutely marvelous thing about this true story is that this wife (even at "retirement" age!) was beginning to practice what she was reading and learning from God's Word—and her husband had noticed!

Another good thing is that it clearly demonstrates that it's never too late in your marriage to begin to practice God's priorities as a wife, even if you have been married 40 years.

Newlyweds—There's no way to count the number of times I've heard this comment: "I wish I'd had this book 20 years ago when I first got married!" This is one of the most often verbalized reflections of those who are married and have read this book.

And I am always quick to add, "Me too!"

Many newlyweds have also been spared from learning about marriage the hard way or later in their marriages because some caring women gave them this book as bridal shower gifts or wedding gifts. Furthermore, young marrieds have learned and responded to these biblical principles because some wise women gave them copies and used them as mentoring or counseling tools. You know newlyweds...they have very little money. And these dear ones probably would not have bought the book on their own.

And too because stars were in their eyes and fantasies filled their hearts, these brides probably didn't have a clue as to what marriage is really all about. They had no hint as to their roles and responsibilities as Christian women, let alone as wives! But I praise God that they read the book, followed the biblical principles, and then communicated with me to share their excitement and appreciation for the information. How I applaud their tender hearts that were sensitive to God's ways!

Single gals—On many occasions I have had single women write or introduce themselves at a conference who commented that upon reading the book, they were struck by how little of it actually applied to wives and moms only. They were prepared to feel left out and overlooked. But because they went ahead and read the book, they were delighted to discover that of the six priorities addressed in this book, only two apply directly to wives and moms. Refreshingly, the remainder of the book applied to and addressed *all* Christian women. The book wrapped its arms around them and drew them in. There was plenty of meat for them to chew on.

If you are single, I want to say to you that even the chapters dealing with marriage and family can be tremendously powerful and helpful tools as you mentor or counsel or teach others. If your heart and ears are open, you'll have countless opportunities as you sense or hear the distress of other friends, co-workers, even strangers, who are married women and moms with problems. And all you have to do is open your mouth and share with them what the Bible says about their situations. You may even want to open your pocketbooks and bless them with their very own copies of these life-changing, marriage-saving, family-preserving principles.

And who knows, maybe something from one or both of these sections on marriage and family might be of help to you as you pursue a life of godly character.

Working wives—When I originally began teaching these principles, less than 50 percent of Christian women worked outside their homes. Now that figure is closer to 70 percent. What has been the reaction of these working wives and moms?

Well, it has been overwhelmingly positive! This group of woman has been greatly encouraged as they gain greater insights into their real and most meaningful assignments in life—those of wife, mom, and homemaker. Yes, they work at "outside" jobs, but they now understand God's priorities and are embracing them as their own. They may have jobs and do those jobs heartily unto the Lord. But each woman now has a better understanding of what her real job is—practicing her God-given priorities.

And no, it isn't easy. Yet these working wives now know and recognize that essentially they have two full-time jobs, the first and most important one at home with their families, and the other at the office, the store, the schoolroom, or the hospital.

Stay-at-home wives—The letters and comments have been overwhelmingly positive from the group of ladies who stay at home. They have written with words of appreciation for the help given in this book that enables them to prioritize their busy and active homes and families. They testify that before they read *A Woman After God's Own Heart*®, they were busy doing many things—too many things—and many of the wrong things. Yes, they were at home, but their priorities were all in the wrong place...or "all out of whack" as the poem in chapter 21 puts it! The principles from the Bible shared in this book helped them reorient to God's priorities and bear good fruit... and better fruit...and the best fruit.

Concerned women—As I said, my Jim retired from teaching and administrating and began writing. His first book project came as a result of the mountains of letters and numerous comments from many wives who were reading my book *A Woman After God's Own Heart*®. Because they were now understanding their priorities and reaping the blessings from practicing them, they wanted to know if there was anything for their husband about his priorities. Jim's first book was appropriately entitled *A Man After God's Own Heart*.[1]

Then came requests from concerned wives and moms for something just for their marriages (not only for themselves, but also for their husbands). And there were cries for help from moms for more on loving and raising their children…and for their husbands as dads. Next came specific inquiries—"Do you have anything for my teen daughter…or son…or for my little ones?" Due to the need and desire for help, a groundswell was created by women who want to be women and wives and moms who follow after God. In time, and by God's grace, both Jim and I have written books that address these requests for information. (See our book list at the back of this book.)

What a joy it is for Jim and me to go to our mailbox daily and learn how women and men and teens and little ones are beginning to understand and live out God's wisdom and plan as they read these additional books. Just think of the marriages and families and children who are benefiting as they seek to live out God's plan! They, by the will of God, are serving their own generation as they follow after God's own heart.

24

The Legacy of Your Heart

*Be diligent to present yourself approved to God,
a worker who does not need to be ashamed....*
2 TIMOTHY 2:15

Reflection Time for You, a Woman After God's Own Heart

I hope you benefited from what I shared about other readers of this book in the last chapter. And now, having said all of that about those who have discovered God's design and begun to implement some or all of the principles we have talked about throughout this book, where might you start?

First of all, I am assuming you are responding positively to what I have written. At least (I hope and pray!) you didn't throw your book across the room when you hit any sensitive points. I am believing, since you made it to the end and to this final chapter, that you are ready to "go for it"…and have been doing so for 24 chapters! You are probably implementing many of the principles we have discussed so far. Well done! Please continue your journey to become a woman truly after God's own heart.

As the scripture at the beginning of the previous chapter bore witness, "David, after he had served his own generation by the will of God, fell asleep." Now, don't you desire to be a woman who serves her generation, whether that's the people at home—your husband, sons and daughters, grandsons and granddaughters… or parents or in-laws—or in your neighborhood or apartment building, or at church, or out in the workplace?

Here, dear friend and heart sister, are a few keys that have helped me in my desire to become—and keep on becoming— a woman after God's own heart. I pray they will encourage and help you as well.

Becoming a Woman After God's Own Heart

Key #1: Obey God's commands

I'm sure you agree that obedience to God and His commands is the primary key to the Christian life. As God told King Saul through the prophet Samuel, "To obey is better than sacrifice" (1 Samuel 15:22). You see, God doesn't want your outward obedience to be a ritual. Oh no, He wants your heart! He wants you to respond in obedience to His Word as He speaks directly to your situation. Your greatest impact will come as you "serve your generation by the will of God"—which means choosing to do things God's way, not your own way.

Obedience is not always easy. In fact, it's usually very difficult. Why? Because your (and my) human flesh wants to do things its way. There is a battle going on in your heart between doing what you should do and doing what you want to do.

How do you deal with this battle in your heart?

Key #2: Walk in the Spirit

You manage the battle in your heart by following this next key as you seek to "walk in the Spirit" (Galatians 5:16). When you "walk in the Spirit...you shall not fulfill the lust of the flesh." Looking to God for His help and obeying this one command will do away with the works of the flesh, which destroy lives, marriages, families, and homes (verses 19-21). As you ask for help from God and walk with Him according to His ways, you reap instead "the fruit of the Spirit," which is "love, joy, peace, longsuffering, kindness, goodness, faithfulness, gentleness, self-control" (verses 22-23). Imagine the heart, the life—and the marriage, family, and home!—where such fruit abounds.

My reading friend, you get started down this fruitful path by acknowledging to God that you want to follow Him. Go ahead and tell God if you don't quite understand how it's all going to work or work out. But also ask Him for the grace and strength to trust Him, to walk by faith. You'll notice a change right away in your walk!

Key #3: Pray regularly

I've already referred to prayer, but as you well know from reading this book, the role of prayer is so very important to fulfilling God's will for your life. It's vital! Prayer acknowledges your dependence on God. Prayer opens your heart to knowing and fulfilling God's will. Prayer gives you the assurance and confidence that, as you carry out God's priorities, He will give you the strength to see it through to the end. Dear one, if you want to serve your generation as a woman after God's own heart, then prayer must become an all-important part of your life.

Key #4: Adopt a long-range view

It took David a lifetime to fulfill God's will and serve his generation. And, beloved, it has taken me more than 20 years to come to the place in my life where I'm beginning to understand what it means to serve my generation. You've taken a good number of days or weeks to read and digest this book. Many of the concepts might have been foreign or difficult for you to understand and begin to implement. Please understand that something this important—as important as doing God's will and living out His priorities—will take a long time to complete. Indeed, it will take a lifetime. It's not something you can start and finish in a few days, weeks, months, or years. No, it is a long-range, life-long, wholehearted assignment from God. But be encouraged! This lifestyle is lived—and built—by following after God just one day at a time...and another day...and another day. So each day focus on the tasks and people in front of you.

Key #5: Accept your roles

This may seem somewhat similar to Key #4, except this key requires that you take on the task of being a woman after God's own heart in a personal way. It's one thing to have a goal, but it's quite another thing to actually accept the challenge, develop a strategy to press for the goal, make the sacrifices, pay the price to move forward, and blessing of blessings, to realize some part of it. This is where resolve and desire come in. Do you really believe God is asking you to serve your generation...and to serve according to His will? It seems so obvious, but until you accept your assignment as coming from God Himself, you will have difficulty taking it seriously. We simply cannot play around with taking such a high calling lightly. The lives and well-being of others are at stake…are at risk!

Never give up.

Key #6: Ask, "Who am I, and what is it I do?"

Each of God's women is at a different season in life. And for each, that season is also changing. I don't know where life finds you today. And I've shared a little about my present life challenges. But perhaps you are single…or married—with or without children who are younger or older, or somewhere in between. You may be older or younger in age. Whatever your (and my) age and stage, you must be constantly asking yourself, "Who am I?" Hopefully by now you will always answer this question with "I am a woman after God's own heart!"

And the second question you must constantly ask is, "What is it I do?" I'm sure you sense by now that the answer to this question will constantly change. And with each change, you make the necessary adjustments. As you daily seek with all your heart to follow God's laid-out plans and priorities for you, to walk by His Spirit, and to pray faithfully, He will help you make the choices that guide you into His path for each stage and age of your life. You will then forever be His woman, a woman after His very own heart.

Quiet Times Calendar

Jan.	Feb.	Mar.	Apr.	May	June
1	1	1	1	1	1
2	2	2	2	2	2
3	3	3	3	3	3
4	4	4	4	4	4
5	5	5	5	5	5
6	6	6	6	6	6
7	7	7	7	7	7
8	8	8	8	8	8
9	9	9	9	9	9
10	10	10	10	10	10
11	11	11	11	11	11
12	12	12	12	12	12
13	13	13	13	13	13
14	14	14	14	14	14
15	15	15	15	15	15
16	16	16	16	16	16
17	17	17	17	17	17
18	18	18	18	18	18
19	19	19	19	19	19
20	20	20	20	20	20
21	21	21	21	21	21
22	22	22	22	22	22
23	23	23	23	23	23
24	24	24	24	24	24
25	25	25	25	25	25
26	26	26	26	26	26
27	27	27	27	27	27
28	28	28	28	28	28
29	29	29	29	29	29
30		30	30	30	30
31		31		31	

Date Begun _____

July	Aug.	Sept.	Oct.	Nov.	Dec.
1	1	1	1	1	1
2	2	2	2	2	2
3	3	3	3	3	3
4	4	4	4	4	4
5	5	5	5	5	5
6	6	6	6	6	6
7	7	7	7	7	7
8	8	8	8	8	8
9	9	9	9	9	9
10	10	10	10	10	10
11	11	11	11	11	11
12	12	12	12	12	12
13	13	13	13	13	13
14	14	14	14	14	14
15	15	15	15	15	15
16	16	16	16	16	16
17	17	17	17	17	17
18	18	18	18	18	18
19	19	19	19	19	19
20	20	20	20	20	20
21	21	21	21	21	21
22	22	22	22	22	22
23	23	23	23	23	23
24	24	24	24	24	24
25	25	25	25	25	25
26	26	26	26	26	26
27	27	27	27	27	27
28	28	28	28	28	28
29	29	29	29	29	29
30	30	30	30	30	30
31	31		31		31

Dear Seeker

1. To order or learn more about the 10-session "A Woman After God's Own Heart Video Bible Study" taught by Elizabeth George, visit www.ElizabethGeorge.com or call 1-800-542-4611.

A Word of Welcome

1. Richard Foster, "And We Can Live by It: Discipline," *Decision Magazine,* September 1982, p. 11.
2. Ibid.

Chapter 1—A Heart Devoted to God

1. Ray and Anne Ortlund, *The Best Half of Life* (Glendale, CA: Regal Books, 1976), p. 88.
2. Carole Mayhall, *From the Heart of a Woman* (Colorado Springs: NavPress, 1976), pp. 10-11.
3. Oswald J. Smith, *The Man God Uses* (London: Marshall, Morgan & Scott, 1925), pp. 52-57.
4. Andrew Murray, on a bookmark.
5. Quoted in Ortlund and Ortlund, *The Best Half of Life,* pp. 24-25.
6. Betty Scott Stam, source unknown.

Chapter 2—A Heart Abiding in God's Word

1. Ray and Anne Ortlund, *The Best Half of Life* (Glendale, CA: Regal Books, 1976), p. 79.
2. C.A. Stoddards, source unknown.
3. Henry Drummond, *The Greatest Thing in the World* (Old Tappan, NJ: Fleming H. Revell Company, 1977), p. 42.
4. Jim Downing, *Meditation, The Bible Tells You How* (Colorado Springs: NavPress, 1976), pp. 15-16.
5. Robert D. Foster, *The Navigator* (Colorado Springs: NavPress, 1983), pp. 110-11.
6. Quoted in J.C. Pollock, *Hudson Taylor and Maria* (Grand Rapids, MI: Zondervan, 1975), p. 169.
7. Ibid., p. 169.
8. Anne Ortlund, *The Disciplines of the Beautiful Woman* (Waco, TX: Word, Inc., 1977), p. 103.
9. Mrs. Charles E. Cowman, *Streams in the Desert—Vol. 1* (Grand Rapids, MI: Zondervan, 1965), p. 330.
10. Cited in Foster, *The Navigator,* pp. 64-65.
11. Obituary of William Schuman, *Los Angeles Times,* February 17, 1992.

Chapter 3—A Heart Committed to Prayer

1. Corrie ten Boom, *Don't Wrestle, Just Nestle* (Old Tappan, NJ: Revell, 1978), p. 79.
2. Oswald Chambers, *Christian Disciplines* (Grand Rapids, MI: Discovery House Publishers, 1995), p. 117.
3. Clarion Classics, *The Prayers of Suzanna Wesley* (Grand Rapids, MI: Zondervan Publishing House, 1984), p. 51.
4. Ibid., p. 49.

5. Ibid., p. 54.
6. James Dobson, *What Wives Wish Their Husbands Knew About Women* (Wheaton, IL: Tyndale House Publishers, Inc., 1977), p. 22.
7. Edith Schaeffer, *Common Sense Christian Living* (Nashville: Thomas Nelson Publishers, 1983), pp. 212-15.
8. Ibid.

Chapter 4—A Heart That Obeys
1. Curtis Vaughan, ed., *The Old Testament Books of Poetry from 26 Translations* (Grand Rapids, MI: Zondervan Bible Publishers, 1973), pp. 478-79.
2. Ibid., p. 277.

Chapter 5—A Heart That Serves
1. Charles F. Pfeiffer and Everett F. Harrison, eds., *The Wycliffe Bible Commentary* (Chicago: Moody Press, 1973), p. 5.
2. Ray and Anne Ortlund, *The Best Half of Life* (Glendale, CA: Regal Books, 1976), p. 97.
3. Julie Nixon Eisenhower, *Special People* (New York: Ballantine Books, 1977), p. 199.
4. Quoted in Ibid., p. 80.

Chapter 6—A Heart That Follows
1. *Webster's New Collegiate Dictionary* (Springfield, MA: G. & C. Merriam Co., Publishers, 1961), s.v. submission.
2. Elisabeth Elliot, *The Shaping of a Christian Family* (Nashville: Thomas Nelson Publishers, 1992), p. 75.
3. Sheldon Vanauken, *Under the Mercy* (San Francisco: Ignatius Press, 1985), pp. 194-95.

Chapter 7—A Heart That Loves—Part 1
1. Gene Getz, *The Measure of a Woman* (Glendale, CA: Gospel Light Publications, 1977), pp. 75-76.
2. Jill Briscoe and Judy Golz, *Space to Breathe, Room to Grow* (Wheaton, IL: Victor Books, 1985), pp. 184-87.
3. Anne Ortlund, *Building a Great Marriage* (Old Tappan, NJ: Fleming H. Revell Company, 1984), p. 146.
4. Howard and Charlotte Clinebell, quoted in ibid., p. 170.
5. Charlie Shedd, *Talk to Me* (Old Tappan, NJ: Fleming H. Revell Company, 1976), pp. 65-66.
6. Curtis Vaughan, ed., *The Old Testament Books of Poetry from 26 Translations* (Grand Rapids, MI: Zondervan Bible Publishers, 1973), p. 572.

Chapter 8—A Heart That Loves—Part 2
1. Edith Schaeffer, *What Is a Family?* (Old Tappan, NJ: Fleming H. Revell Company, 1975), p. 87.
2. Jack and Carole Mayhall, *Marriage Takes More Than Love* (Colorado Springs: NavPress, 1978), p. 154, quoting Kay K. Arvin, *One Plus One Equals One* (Nashville: Broadman Press, 1969), pp. 37-38.
3. Anne Ortlund, *Building a Great Marriage* (Old Tappan, NJ: Fleming H. Revell Company, 1984), p. 157.
4. Julie Nixon Eisenhower, *Special People* (New York: Ballantine Books, 1977), pp. 52-53.
5. Betty Frist, *My Neighbors, The Billy Grahams* (Nashville: Broadman Press, 1983), p. 31.
6. William MacDonald, *Enjoying the Proverbs* (Kansas City, KS: Walterick Publishers, 1982), p. 56.

Chapter 9—A Heart That Values Being a Mother
1. Phil Whisenhunt, *Good News Broadcaster*, May 1971, p. 20.
2. Stanley High, *Billy Graham* (New York: McGraw Hill, 1956), p. 28.

3. Quoted in High, *Billy Graham,* p. 126.

4. Carole C. Carlson, *Corrie ten Boom: Her Life, Her Faith* (Old Tappan, NJ: Fleming H. Revell Company, 1983), p. 33.

5. Elisabeth Elliot, *The Shaping of a Christian Family* (Nashville: Thomas Nelson Publishers, 1992), p. 58.

6. Mrs. Howard Taylor, *John and Betty Stam: A Story of Triumph,* rev. ed. (Chicago: Moody Press, 1982), p. 15.

7. Elliot, *Shaping of a Christian Family,* pp. 205-06.

Chapter 10—A Heart That Prays Faithfully

1. H.D.M. Spence and Joseph S. Exell, eds., *The Pulpit Commentary, Volume 9* (Grand Rapids, MI: Wm. B. Eerdmans Publishing Company, 1978), p. 595.

2. Charles Bridges, *A Modern Study in the Book of Proverbs,* rev. by George F. Santa (Milford, MI: Mott Media, 1978), p. 728.

3. Spence and Exell, eds., *Pulpit Commentary, Volume 9,* p. 607.

4. Stanley High, *Billy Graham* (New York: McGraw Hill, 1956), p. 71.

5. Linda Raney Wright, *Raising Children* (Wheaton, IL: Tyndale House Publishers, Inc., 1975), p. 50.

6. E. Schuyler English, *Ordained of the Lord* (Neptune, NJ: Loizeaux Brothers, 1976), p. 35.

Chapter 11—A Heart Overflowing with Motherly Affection—Part 1

1. Marvin R. Vincent, *Word Studies in the New Testament,* vol. IV (Grand Rapids, MI: Wm. B. Eerdmans Publishing Co., 1973), p. 341.

2. Dwight Spotts, "What Is Child Abuse?" in *Parents & Teenagers,* Jay Kesler, ed. (Wheaton, IL: Victor Books, 1984), p. 426.

3. Curtis Vaughan, ed., *The Old Testament Books of Poetry from 26 Translations* (Grand Rapids, MI: Zondervan Bible Publishers, 1973), p. 399.

4. Gary Smalley, *For Better or for Best* (Grand Rapids, MI: Zondervan Publishing House, 1988), p. 95.

5. Edith Schaeffer, *What Is a Family?* (Old Tappan, NJ: Fleming H. Revell Company, 1975).

Chapter 12—A Heart Overflowing with Motherly Affection—Part 2

1. Julie Nixon Eisenhower, *Special People* (New York: Ballantine Books, 1977), p. 69.

2. Linda Dillow, *Creative Counterpart* (Nashville: Thomas Nelson Publishers, 1977), p. 24.

Chapter 13—A Heart That Makes a House a Home

1. Catherine Marshall, *A Man Called Peter* (New York: McGraw-Hill, 1961), p. 65.

2. James Strong, *Strong's Exhaustive Concordance of the Bible* (Nashville: Abingdon Press, 1973), p. 22.

3. Robert Alden, *Proverbs* (Grand Rapids, MI: Baker Book House, 1983), p. 110.

4. Edith Schaeffer, *What Is a Family?* (Old Tappan, NJ: Fleming H. Revell Company, 1975).

5. Julie Nixon Eisenhower, *Special People* (New York: Ballantine Books, 1977), p. 209.

6. Jim Conway, *Men in Mid-Life Crisis* (Elgin, IL: David C. Cook Publishing Company, 1987), pp. 250-52.

7. Edith Schaeffer, *Tapestry* (Waco, TX: Word Books, 1981), p. 616.

8. Strong, *Strong's Exhaustive Concordance,* p. 34.

9. William J. Peterson, *Martin Luther Had a Wife* (Wheaton, IL: Tyndale House Publishers, Inc., 1983), p. 67.

10. Bonnie McCullough, *Los Angeles Times,* date unknown.

Chapter 14—A Heart That Watches Over the Home

1. Jo Berry, *The Happy Home Handbook* (Old Tappan, NJ: Fleming H. Revell Co., 1976).

2. James Strong, *Strong's Exhaustive Concordance of the Bible* (Nashville: Abingdon Press, 1973), p. 118.

3. H.D.M. Spence and Joseph S. Exell, *Pulpit Commentary, Vol. 8* (Grand Rapids, MI: Wm. B. Eerdmans Publishing Company, 1978), p. 30.

4. Derek Kidner, *Psalms 1–72* (Downers Grove, IL: InterVarsity Press, 1973), p. 58.

5. William Peterson, *Martin Luther Had a Wife* (Wheaton, IL: Tyndale House Publishers, Inc., 1983), p. 81.

Chapter 15—A Heart That Creates Order from Chaos

1. Curtis Vaughan, ed., *The New Testament from 26 Translations* (Grand Rapids, MI: Zondervan Publishing House, 1967), p. 981.

2. James Strong, *Strong's Exhaustive Concordance of the Bible* (Nashville: Abingdon Press, 1973), p. 51.

3. William Peterson, *Martin Luther Had a Wife* (Wheaton, IL: Tyndale House Publishers, Inc., 1983), p. 27.

4. Alan Lakein, *How to Control Your Time and Your Life* (New York: Signet Books, 1974), p. 48.

Chapter 16—A Heart That Weaves a Tapestry of Beauty

1. H.D.M. Spence and Joseph S. Exell, eds., *The Pulpit Commentary, Volume 21* (Grand Rapids, MI: Wm. B. Eerdmans Publishing Company, 1978), p. 36.

2. James Strong, *Strong's Exhaustive Concordance of the Bible* (Nashville: Abingdon Press, 1973), p. 51.

3. Donald Guthrie, *Tyndale New Testament Commentaries, The Pastoral Epistles* (Grand Rapids, MI: Wm. B. Eerdmans Publishing Company, 1976), p. 194.

4. Robert Jamieson, A.R. Fausset, and David Brown, *Commentary on the Whole Bible* (Grand Rapids, MI: Zondervan Publishing House, 1973), p. 1387.

5. Curtis Vaughan, ed., *The New Testament from 26 Translations* (Grand Rapids, MI: Zondervan Publishing House, 1967), p. 1017.

6. Anne Ortlund, *Love Me with Tough Love* (Waco, TX: Word, Incorporated, 1979).

Chapter 17—A Heart Strengthened by Spiritual Growth

1. Ted W. Engstrom, *The Pursuit of Excellence* (Grand Rapids, MI: Zondervan Publishing House, 1982), pp. 30-31.

2. Anne Ortlund, *The Disciplines of the Beautiful Woman* (Waco, TX: Word, Incorporated, 1977), pp. 96, 98.

Chapter 18—A Heart Enriched by Joy in the Lord

1. Check out Moody Correspondence School, 820 North LaSalle Street, Chicago, IL 60610, 1-800-621-7105.

2. Jack and Carole Mayhall, *Marriage Takes More Than Love* (Colorado Springs: NavPress, 1978), p. 157.

3. Betty Frist, *My Neighbors, The Billy Grahams* (Nashville: Broadman Press, 1983), p. 143.

4. Michael LeBoeuf, *Working Smart* (New York: Warner Books, 1979), p. 182.

5. Ted W. Engstrom, *The Pursuit of Excellence* (Grand Rapids, MI: Zondervan Publishing House, 1982), page unknown.

6. LeBoeuf, *Working Smart*, p. 182.

7. Denis Waitley, *Seeds of Greatness* (Old Tappan, NJ: Fleming H. Revell Company, 1983), p. 95.

8. Gigi Tchividjian, *In Search of Serenity* (Portland, OR: Multnomah, 1990).

Chapter 19—A Heart That Shows It Cares

1. Elisabeth Elliot, *Through Gates of Splendor* (Old Tappan, NJ: Fleming H. Revell Company, 1957), page unknown.

2. Anne Ortlund, *The Disciplines of the Beautiful Woman* (Waco, TX: Word, Inc., 1977), p. 35.

3. J. Sidlow Baxter, "Will and Emotions," *Alliance Life Magazine* (formerly Alliance Witness), November 1970. Used by permission.

4. Elizabeth George, *Woman of Excellence* (Christian Development Ministries, P.O. Box 33166, Granada Hills, CA 91394, 1987).

Chapter 20—A Heart That Encourages

1. Charles Caldwell Ryrie, *Balancing the Christian Life* (Chicago: Moody Press, 1969), pp. 96-97.
2. Ibid.
3. C.A. Stoddards, source unknown.

Chapter 21—A Heart That Seeks First Things First

1. Janice Ericson. Used by permission
2. Michael DeBoeuf, *Working Smart* (New York: Warner Books, 1979), pp. 129, 249.
3. *The Amplified Bible* (Grand Rapids, MI: Zondervan Bible Publishers, 1965), p. 302.
4. Pat King, *How Do You Find the Time?* (Edmonds, WA: Aglow Publications, 1975), page unknown.
5. Ibid.

Chapter 22—Following After God's Heart

1. Elizabeth George, *Loving God with All Your Mind* (Eugene, OR: Harvest House Publishers, 1994).
2. Edith Schaeffer, *Common Sense Christian Living* (Nashville: Thomas Nelson Publishers, 1983), p. 196.

Chapter 23—The Legacy of *A Woman After God's Own Heart*

1. Jim George, *A Man After God's Own Heart* (Eugene, OR: Harvest House Publishers, 2002).

Personal Notes

Personal Notes

Personal Notes

Personal Notes

Personal Notes

Personal Notes

Personal Notes

Personal Notes

Personal Notes

About the Author

Elizabeth George is a bestselling author and speaker whose passion is to teach the Bible in a way that changes women's lives. For information about Elizabeth's books or speaking ministry, to sign up for her mailings, or to share how God has used this book in your life, please write to Elizabeth at:

Elizabeth George
PO Box 2879
Belfair, WA 98528

Toll-free fax/phone: 1-800-542-4611
www.ElizabethGeorge.com

$\mathcal{I}$f you've benefited from *A Woman After God's Own Heart®*, you'll want the complementary book

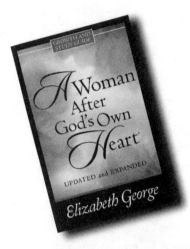

A $\mathcal{W}$oman $\mathcal{A}$fter $\mathcal{G}$od's $\mathcal{O}$wn $\mathcal{H}$eart®

Growth and Study Guide

This guide offers thought-provoking questions, reflective studies, and personal applications that will enrich your life as you study to become a woman after God's own heart.

This growth and study guide is perfect for both personal and group use.

A Woman After God's Own Heart® Growth and Study Guide
is available at your local Christian bookstore
or can be ordered from:

Elizabeth George
PO Box 2879
Belfair, WA 98528
Toll-free fax/phone: 1-800-542-4611
www.ElizabethGeorge.com

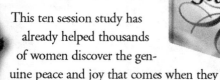

After God's Own Heart

Elizabeth George's *A Woman After God's Own Heart*® showed you how to draw closer to God, to your husband, to your family, and to become more effective in your work and ministry. These other bestselling books by Elizabeth and her husband, Jim, will help you and your family experience God's love and provision in greater measure and enable you to reach out to others with the hope and love of the gospel.

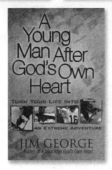 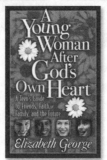

A Woman After God's Own Heart® Study Series

Bible Studies for Busy Women

God wrote the Bible to change hearts and lives. Every study in this series is written with that in mind—and is especially focused on helping Christian women know how God desires for them to live."

—Elizabeth George

Sharing wisdom gleaned from more than 20 years as a women's Bible study teacher, Elizabeth has prepared insightful lessons that can be completed in 15 to 20 minutes per day. Each lesson includes thought-provoking questions, insights, Bible-study tips, instructions for leading a discussion group, and a "heart response" section to make the Bible passage more personal.

Living with Passion and Purpose — LUKE — Elizabeth George — 978-0-7369-0816-0

Becoming a Woman of Beauty & Strength — ESTHER — Elizabeth George — 978-0-7369-0489-6

Putting On a Gentle & Quiet Spirit — I PETER — Elizabeth George — 978-0-7369-0290-8

Discovering the Treasures of a Godly Woman — PROVERBS 31 — Elizabeth George — 978-0-7369-0818-4

Nurturing a Heart of Humility — CHARACTER STUDIES MARY — Elizabeth George — 978-0-7369-0300-4

Walking in God's Promises — CHARACTER STUDIES SARAH — Elizabeth George — 978-0-7369-0301-1

Experiencing God's Peace — PHILIPPIANS — Elizabeth George — 978-0-7369-0289-2

Pursuing Godliness — I TIMOTHY — Elizabeth George — 978-0-7369-0665-4

Cultivating a Life of Character — JUDGES/RUTH — Elizabeth George — 978-0-7369-0498-8

Growing in Wisdom & Faith — JAMES — Elizabeth George — 978-0-7369-0490-2

HARVEST HOUSE PUBLISHERS
EUGENE, OREGON 97402
www.harvesthousepublishers.com

Books by Elizabeth George

- Beautiful in God's Eyes
- Life Management for Busy Women
- Loving God with All Your Mind
- A Mom After God's Own Heart
- Powerful Promises for Every Woman
- The Remarkable Women of the Bible
- Small Changes for a Better Life
- A Wife After God's Own Heart
- A Woman After God's Own Heart®
- A Woman After God's Own Heart® Deluxe Edition
- A Woman's Call to Prayer
- A Woman's High Calling
- A Woman's Walk with God
- A Young Woman After God's Own Heart
- A Young Woman's Call to Prayer
- A Young Woman's Walk with God

Children's Books

- God's Wisdom for Little Girls
- A Little Girl After God's Own Heart

Study Guides

- Beautiful in God's Eyes Growth & Study Guide
- Life Management for Busy Women Growth & Study Guide
- Loving God with All Your Mind Growth & Study Guide
- A Mom After God's Own Heart Growth & Study Guide
- Powerful Promises for Every Woman Growth & Study Guide
- The Remarkable Women of the Bible Growth & Study Guide
- Small Changes for a Better Life Growth & Study Guide
- A Wife After God's Own Heart Growth & Study Guide
- A Woman After God's Own Heart® Growth & Study Guide
- A Woman's Call to Prayer Growth & Study Guide
- A Woman's High Calling Growth & Study Guide
- A Woman's Walk with God Growth & Study Guide

Books by Jim & Elizabeth George

- God Loves His Precious Children
- God's Wisdom for Little Boys

Books by Jim George

- The Bare Bones Bible Handbook
- God's Man of Influence
- A Husband After God's Own Heart
- A Man After God's Own Heart
- The Remarkable Prayers of the Bible
- The Remarkable Prayers of the Bible Growth & Study Guide
- What God Wants to Do for You
- A Young Man After God's Own Heart